Praise for *A Voice in the Wilderness*

"Archbishop Viganò is that rarest of mortal men: one who speaks the truth whatever the cost to his career or his standing with his fellow bishops. To be sure, his writings cast light on some of the darker corners of the institutional Church and on the abuses of some of its officials, but they are also suffused with hope by a prelate whose vibrant Christian faith shines through on every page."—STEVEN W. MOSHER, president of the Population Research Institute

"Angelico Press has done an important service in gathering together in one volume Archbishop Carlo Maria Viganò's stunning August 2018 Memorandum and his subsequent writings, in which he details his personal knowledge of how the Holy See has failed to deal effectively with grave immorality in the Church's hierarchy, particularly in the case of ex-cardinal Theodore McCarrick. Viganò decided in conscience to expose the ways in which clerical expediency, self-interest, and a misplaced desire to avoid public scandal have in fact done grave harm to the Church and her mission. These collected interventions give a clear insight into Viganò's thinking and allow readers to judge for themselves the cogency of his analysis of the causes, and the remedies, of the present crisis in the Church."—FR. GERALD E. MURRAY, pastor of Church of the Holy Family

"In an era of increasing moral darkness, Archbishop Viganò soars as a meteoric light for the Children of Light. Within these pages lies the call to action by the Oracle of Christian Truth. God has not abandoned his flock. Archbishop Viganò leads them out of the desolate desert into the sustaining waters of faith, truth, and hope with the courage and clarity of a modern-day prophet. His bold and steadfast witness elevates the weary, rescues the lost, and leads the disheartened to Christ. This paragon of moral clarity and courage belongs among the pantheon of great Catholic thinkers and saints."—LIZ YORE, founder of Yore Children

"What would we do without Angelico Press! Once again, it presents us with a collection of documents that speak most closely to the needs of the Catholic Church at this exact moment. As we face the imminent prospect of a Conclave, the voice of His Grace Archbishop Viganò makes a decisively synthetic contribution to understanding where we are now, and offers an analytic exploration of the possibilities that lie before God's Church Militant. In these documents, usefully supported by explanatory notes, we behold an Archbishop, a man of the Holy Spirit, gradually discerning from contemporary events what must be offered to thoughtful Catholics. Papa Bergoglio has spoken about the 'God of surprises.' One of the biggest surprises, however, must surely be that a highly intelligent member of the Vatican's diplomatic service should emerge to offer, on the basis of his own careful observations, a critical judgement of the Church's problems and needs as she awaits her next supreme Pastor. Timely and most welcome!"—FR. JOHN HUNWICKE, moderator of "Fr Hunwicke's Mutual Enrichment" blog

"St. Matthew tells us that the crowds were astonished by Christ's words because He taught them 'as one having authority and not as the scribes did.' Tragically, we believing Catholics have come to expect our leaders, from the top on down, to offer us the 'mess of pottage' provided by our pathetic contemporary media scribes, handing us over in the process to be devoured by their wolf-like political, economic, technocratic, and medical allies. I felt the crowd's astonishment anew when reading the words of Archbishop Viganò in this book. For he shows us that there are still true shepherds of the flock who know that their task is that of repeating the Master's unchangeable authoritative teaching in all its fullness, and of driving those who do not do so from the temple precincts. Viva Viganò!"—JOHN RAO, director of the Roman Forum

"I first met Archbishop Viganò in 2013 to present him with a request to the Holy Father to declare Planned Parenthood an enemy of the Catholic Church. Even in that first meeting, though he never said it, he seemed aware that something was amiss and that the pope would not be amenable to such a request. When I saw him again in Rome, just before he published his first testimony regarding Theodore McCarrick, I could tell something weighed heavily on his heart. Since that time, his missives have been a beacon of light and a freshening spring to souls thirsting for the light-infused waters of Truth."—MICHAEL HICHBORN, president of the Lepanto Institute

"Archbishop Viganò's willingness while he was U.S. nuncio to relay messages from us at the Covenants Initiative (a Muslim peace movement) to Pope Francis about the newly-rediscovered Prophetic Covenants was very helpful to our efforts. These Covenants, authored by Muhammad himself, place groups like ISIS under the curse of God and command all Muslims not to attack or rob or damage the buildings of Christians living in peace with Islam, or even to prevent their Christian wives from going to church, but rather to defend the Christians until the end of time. Seeing that ISIS has massacred more Muslims than Christians, this is a sterling example of the 'united front ecumenism' against the common enemies of religion so necessary in our times."—CHARLES UPTON, co-founder of the Covenants Initiative

A Voice in the Wilderness

*Archbishop Carlo Maria Viganò
on the Church, America, and the World*

A Voice
in the Wilderness

Archbishop Carlo Maria Viganò
on the Church, America, and the World

✠

Edited and Introduced by
Brian M. McCall

✠

✟ Angelico Press

First published in the USA
by Angelico Press 2021
© Carlo Maria Viganò 2021
Introductions and notes © Brian M. McCall 2021

For information, address:
Angelico Press
169 Monitor St.
Brooklyn, NY 11222
angelicopress.com
info@angelicopress.com

ISBN 978 1 62138 696 4 pb
ISBN 978 1 62138 697 1 cloth
ISBN 978 1 62138 698 8 ebook

Cover design: Michael Schrauzer

CONTENTS

PART III
A VOICE DECRYING THE DEEP STATE: CHINA, COVID, AND THE GREAT RESET VS. PRESIDENT DONALD J. TRUMP

EPILOGUE

Editor's Note on the Texts

THE various written interventions of Archbishop Carlo Maria Viganò that appear in this volume, dating from August 2018 to January 2021, have been assembled with the permission of the archbishop from published sources of the English translations of his texts. In many instances, I used the text exactly as I received it from Archbishop Viganò for publication with *Catholic Family News* and there may be minor variations between that text and versions published by others. The font, formatting, capitalization, and other incidental features of the texts have been standardized for their inclusion in this collection. All footnotes are my own unless preceded by VN (for Viganò's Note). When the archbishop embedded a hyperlink in his text, the hyperlink was converted to a footnote that begins VN.

Within each section the documents do not appear precisely in chronological order. Often they are rearranged to organize issues in a more coherent manner. Instances in which the archbishop had his own approved English translation prepared do not identify the translator. In cases where another person or organization independently of the archbishop prepared the translation, the translators are identified; in these cases, the archbishop has not necessarily approved the translation.

His Excellency uses a number of foreign-language phrases (mostly Latin, some French, occasionally Italian). Translations of these are given on their first occurrence in the pages of the book, which is sometimes in the midst of the editor's introductions when they cite passages from Viganò.

Finally, it is important for American readers to be aware that it is quite common in Europe, especially among Italian writers, to refer to popes by their last names, as in "Ratzinger and Bergoglio" or "Pope Ratzinger and Pope Bergoglio." No disrespect is intended by it, and certainly not any calling into question of the office held by the named individual.

General Introduction

ST. John the Baptist, the son and heir of a priest of Israel, left the hallowed halls of the Temple to retreat into the wilderness. From his desert seclusion he became a voice crying out in the wilderness. He denounced the hypocrisy of the first deep church that had superimposed itself on the religion of the Old Law. Our Savior told us that the Chief Priests, Scribes, and Pharisees attempted to nullify the law of God and substitute in its place their own man-made customs (cf. Mk 7:13). This attempted nullification essentially defines a deep church. It is the artificial imposition, by those who hold offices, of man-made doctrines and practices that obscure the doctrine and practices established by God. Years before Our Lord pronounced this judgement on those who sat on the seat of Moses but whose lives should not be imitated (Mt 23:2), John the Baptist denounced these agents of the Sanhedrin as a brood of vipers (Mt 12:34). From his desert, John performed this two-part role—to denounce the Sanhedrin that eclipsed the true Jewish religion and to point to the coming of Our Lord to destroy them.

Over two thousand years after the birth of St. John the Baptist, God has sent the new Israel another voice crying in the wilderness. Archbishop Carlo Maria Viganò fled the palaces of Rome into the solitude of a hiding place to decry a new brood of vipers. Beginning in August of 2018, the former Apostolic Nuncio to the United States began issuing public statements denouncing the evil men and ideas that had superimposed themselves over the Church of Christ. His interventions eventually took on the language of apocalyptic times and he placed contemporary events in the context of a biblical struggle that will end only in the Second Coming of Our Lord. Over the past two and a half years, a Vatican diplomat, little known outside of Vatican and political bureaucracies, would become almost a household name for informed Catholics. From the wilderness of his retreat, he would denounce clerical sexual lasciviousness and its

3

cover up, write open letters to the President of the United States, speak by video to tens of thousands of political protesters in Washington, D.C., and engage in a relentless struggle against the new Chief Priests, Scribes, and Pharisees who attempt, once again, to void the Word of God.

This volume collects together the principal public interventions of Archbishop Viganò from August 2018 to January 2021 while providing supporting commentary and explanations. The goal is to make the archbishop's voice crying in the wilderness accessible to a wider audience. The commentary and explanations are designed to make his keen analysis accessible to Catholics and non-Catholics alike. For this reason hundreds of footnotes have been added to the texts to expand upon references or concepts succinctly alluded to by Viganò but which may be unfamiliar to non-Catholics and even to some Catholics who have not been informed previously on some of these topics. The archbishop's interventions have been organized according to three major topics. Part I concerns his denunciation of the clerical sexual scandals that have rocked the Church for decades and that culminated in the laicization of former Cardinal Theodore McCarrick. Intimately familiar with the McCarrick case through his various bureaucratic and diplomatic roles, Viganò reveals the underlying causes of this scandal, which epitomizes a deep cancer that festers in the Church's hierarchy. Part II of the book presents Viganò's developing analysis of the Second Vatican Council and its relationship not only to the sexual scandals but also to the unprecedented pontificate of Francis (formerly Cardinal Jorge Bergoglio). The documents in Part III connect the crisis in the Church to the great political crisis of the early twenty-first century. Here, the archbishop traces the connections among the Great Reset, the COVID pandemic and lockdowns, the tumultuous US presidential election of 2020, the rising power of the Chinese Communist dictatorship, and Francis's Vatican. He identifies a deep state and a deep church that have allied themselves to make war on the Church of Christ and all of humanity. These children of darkness work to enslave the free peoples of earth and the traditions of the Church to a global totalitarian New World Order supported by a pantheistic One World Religion.

Just as St. John the Baptist coupled his denunciation of the brood of vipers of his time with the announcement of the longed-for Messiah, so too Archbishop Viganò both condemns the new brood of vipers and reminds us to pray, to hope, and to trust in God's Providence. The book concludes with an epilogue that contains a powerful spiritual meditation composed by the archbishop as well as a prayer for the resurgence of Christianity in America. Like John the Baptist, this twenty-first-century voice crying in the wilderness offers us a clear path out of the vice grip of the deep state and deep church. As he explains in his interview with Steve Bannon's War Room (contained in Part III), the plan involves three steps: become informed about the true nature of the epochal struggle being waged in Church and State; denounce the evil plans of these enemies; and pray for God's mercy to intervene to rescue us from these evil men. This book is meant to advance those aims.

The Serene Years in Italy

Carlo Maria Viganò was born on January 16, 1941 in Varese, Italy, in northwest Lombardy. He entered the world at the height of the bloody conflict of World War II; he entered the Church under the pontificate of Pope Pius XII, the last pope before the era of Vatican II. His life thus spans the last of the preconciliar popes through the Council until its "most faithful son," Pope Francis. Viganò's early years were shaped by a secular world torn to pieces in the violent conflict that ravaged Europe; yet they were also marked by a Church enjoying strength and vigor. At and after the Second Vatican Council, the Church under Pius XII and his predecessors was characterized— meant by progressives to be an insult—as a fortress. Certainly there were dangerous currents within the Church in the 1940s and 1950s that would emerge into the light of day at the time of the Council, but for ordinary Catholics in the 1940s and 1950s who did not move in the circles of the learned revolutionaries, the Church appeared to be a massive rock with a rich two-millennia history that stood immovable in the face of the whirlwind of the Second World War.

Viganò was born and raised in a Catholic household. The future archbishop was the seventh of nine children that God granted to Adeodato and Sophia Viganò. In a series of interviews with Robert Moynihan, Viganò describes a deep Catholic home life with a strong devotion to Our Lady.[1] His parents gave all their children the middle name Maria and the archbishop can recall the regular recitation of the Rosary as a family, including a touching memory of his father who, returning from a long day of work, would encourage the others not to dose off to sleep during the evening Rosary. The archbishop dated his vocation to the time of his First Holy Communion. He exhibited a deep love for the Mass from an early age. He told Dr. Moynihan: "I was deeply moved by the Mass, and I attended Mass often."[2] This Mass that he loved for his formative years would have been the traditional Latin Mass as canonized by Pope St. Pius V in his bull *Quo Primum* of 1570. Living in and near Milan, he also experienced the traditional Ambrosian rite, one of several distinctive centuries-old Western rites and uses that continued to exist alongside the Roman rite. This contact with the Ambrosian form of Mass would give Viganò a sense of the richness of the Tradition of the Church. As he noted: "Our whole life was imbued with the liturgical life of the Church and with the memory of the Church's history in Milan going back to St. Ambrose."[3]

He received a rigorous education. He spent five years at a Jesuit secondary school, and was sent to a summer camp in the Alps run by a Jesuit priest whom Viganò considered holy.[4] In his later writings (mostly in Part III of this book) he discusses the corruption of the Jesuit order about which he had fond early memories. In these later writings I can discern a sense of regret over what the Jesuits who educated him had become. He attended university before entering the seminary, in fulfillment of a promise made to his father. Before ordination he had completed a Masters degree in theology from the Gregorian University and a doctorate "*in utroque iure*," that is, in civil and canon law, from the Lateran University. I find the doctorate to be a sign of his future apostolate to speak as a bishop to our modern world. As will be seen in the pages of this

---

1. See Robert Moynihan, *Finding Viganò* (Gastonia, NC: TAN Books, 2020), 12–18.
2. Ibid., 18.
3. Ibid., 19.
4. Ibid., 22.

book, Viganò is firmly rooted in both the temporal sphere of geo-politics and the spiritual jurisdiction of the Church. His studies in the law of civil society and the law of the Church prepared him to be a voice decrying the undermining of law on all its levels—divine, natural, and human—by revolutionaries operative in both the deep state and the deep church.

A Priest Forever According to the Order of Melchizedek

Carlo Maria Viganò was ordained a priest on March 24, 1968, for the diocese of Pavia, Italy. I find this date significant. According to the traditional calendar, this day immediately prior to the feast of the Annunciation is the feast of St. Gabriel, the Archangel. In addition to being sent to invite the Blessed Virgin Mary to become the Mother of God, St. Gabriel was also sent to the Jewish priest Zachary to announce the birth of St. John the Baptist. Archbishop Viganò was thus ordained on the feast of a messenger of God who was the first creature to honor Our Lady with the salutation "Hail Mary, full of grace." He was ordained on the Feast of the Archangel who was the herald of the voice that would cry out in the wilderness of first-century Israel. His ordination occurred almost three months prior to the promulgation of the new rite of ordination by Pope Paul VI on June 18, 1968; thus, Viganò was ordained in the traditional rite.[5]

Like most priests around the world, Viganò offered the new Mass created after the Council throughout his time as a priest and bishop.[6] After Viganò went into hiding following the release of his

---

5. Most Catholics know that the Mass was changed after the Council, but relatively few are aware that *every* sacramental rite was built over again nearly from scratch. The rite of priestly ordination had been so heavily modified that doubts began to emerge about its validity. Michael Davies penned an important work, *The Order of Melchisedech: A Defense of the Catholic Priesthood* (originally published in 1979, revised in 1993, and republished in 2020 by Roman Catholic Books), in which he both identified this new rite's manifold defects and defended its sacramental validity.

6. It is true that he would have been using a hybrid missal—part old, part "reformed"—in the short period between his ordination and the implementation of the *Novus Ordo Missae*; but by this time (June 1968), the Mass, especially in its rubrics and accidental features, bore little kinship with the traditional form as found in the *Missale Romanum* of 1962.

7

first Testimony about McCarrick, he learned to offer the traditional Latin Mass of his childhood, and at some point after 2018, he began offering this rite of Mass exclusively.

After a brief two years of parish work and some schooling in Belgium, Viganò was called to the Vatican to begin a diplomatic career. He spent time under Paul VI in diplomatic postings in Iraq and Great Britain. He then spent many years in the Vatican itself working in the Secretariat of State. The archbishop related to Dr. Moynihan another interesting story concerning the Jesuits. Viganò claims that shortly before John Paul I's untimely death,[7] the pope wrote a letter to the head of the Jesuit order, Father Pedro Arrupe. Viganò claims to have held in his own hands this letter as he was entrusted with transmitting it. According to Viganò, the letter inquired about an interview in which Father Vincent O'Keefe, a possible successor to Arrupe, had claimed that in the Church revolutionary change would soon occur. The letter indicated that O'Keefe should either make clear the interview was inaccurate or resign.[8] Once again Viganò's path crossed with the Jesuits, yet this time it seems to forebode the confrontation he would enter into with the first Jesuit pope in history, Pope Francis.

During his long service in the Vatican diplomatic corps, Viganò had a front-row seat to the tumultuous days of the Church's confrontation with Soviet Communism. He worked for the diplomatic arm of Pope John Paul II who supported the Solidarity movement in Poland and who travelled to his home country to challenge the totalitarian grip of the Soviets. Thus, when Archbishop Viganò speaks about the Marxists of our day who menace our world with the heavy involvement of the Chinese Communist Party, he speaks as a collaborator of a pope who lived under Marxist oppression and fought to defend the rights of the Church against this enemy.

---

7. John Paul I reigned for only thirty-three days. The cause of his death has been a source of speculation for decades, with some alleging he was murdered. See, e.g., David Yallop, *In God's Name* (New York: Basic Books, 2007) and John Cornwell, *A Thief in the Night* (New York: Simon & Schuster, 1989).

8. See Moynihan, *Finding Viganò*, 40–41.

General Introduction

The Fullness of the Priesthood: Bishop and Nuncio

After serving the diplomatic arm of the Church from 1973 to 1992, John Paul II personally consecrated Viganò a bishop, assigned to the titular see of Ulpiana. A titular bishop is one who is not appointed to govern an active diocese within the Church. The consecration of a bishop requires the bishop to be the head of a particular diocese, yet the Church has need of consecrated bishops to serve in other capacities such as auxiliaries to diocesan bishops who govern large dioceses and as diplomats and other papal officials. These men are thus consecrated titular bishops assigned to titular dioceses. "Titular bishops are those who have been appointed by the Holy See to a see or diocese which, in former times, had been canonically established and possessed a cathedral church, clergy, and laity, but at present, on account of pagan occupation and government, has neither clergy nor people."[9] These dioceses were in ancient times functioning dioceses, but were either absorbed into other dioceses or conquered by infidels and are no longer part of the Church. As a result, titular bishops were also known as bishops *"in partibus infidelium"* (in the lands of unbelievers). Ulpiana was an ancient Roman city located in the Province of Dardania. Today the location is in the municipality of Lipljan, Serbia. The diocese eventually became defunct after the region was lost from the jurisdiction of the Roman Church. The Titular Diocese of Ulpiana was established in 1933 and Viganò was made its sixth titular bishop upon his consecration in 1992. It also seems symbolic that Viganò was assigned to a titular diocese that was part of the Soviet Eastern Bloc, Serbia, which was at that time part of the Communist nation of Yugoslavia.

The consecration as bishop came with a transfer out of Rome to be the apostolic pro-nuncio for the African nation of Nigeria, where he spent six years serving as nuncio. A nuncio is "an ordinary and permanent representative of the pope, vested with both political and ecclesiastical powers, accredited to the court of a sovereign or

---

9. See P.M.J. Rock, "Auxiliary Bishop," in *The Catholic Encyclopedia*, vol. 2 (New York: Robert Appleton Company, 1907), accessed at www.newadvent.org/cathen/02145b.htm.

assigned to a definite territory with the duty of safeguarding the interests of the Holy See; . . . his mission is general, embracing all the interests of the Holy See" and "includes both diplomatic and ecclesiastical powers."[10] Holding the position of nuncio prepared the archbishop in many ways for his later public interventions. The nuncio works in two spheres. As mentioned, he holds both political and ecclesiastical powers: he is the diplomatic representative of the Holy See to temporal powers, moving in the world of ambassadors and heads of state; yet his powers are also ecclesiastical, as he participates to a degree in the governing of the Church by the Holy Father. The nuncio thus has a bird's-eye view of both the temporal power structure and the internal governance of the Church.

The archbishop was summoned from Nigeria to work once again in Rome, this time as the delegate for pontifical representations in the Vatican Secretariat of State. This is a long title to indicate that he was the chief personnel officer for the Vatican Curia and the diplomatic corps. Serving in this capacity for well over a decade gave Viganò an opportunity to become well-acquainted with personal issues and scandals within the bureaucracy. It was during his tenure in this office, from 1998 into 2009, that he received information about the allegations against (at that time Cardinal) Theodore McCarrick. It is also during this period that the archbishop penned the memos, referenced in his Testimony, that recommended a trial of and restrictions upon McCarrick.

After over a decade in this position, Viganò was appointed by Pope Benedict XVI to be the secretary general of the Vatican City Governorate. In this role, Viganò essentially exercised the temporal authority of the pope as the temporal ruler of the Vatican City State. The archbishop proved himself an able and careful administrator. In his first year in the City State, the $10.5 million deficit he inherited was transformed into a $44 million surplus.[11] After this brief interlude in administration, Viganò was appointed by Benedict XVI

---

10. Johann Peter Kirsch, "Nuncio," *The Catholic Encyclopedia*, vol. 11 (New York: Robert Appleton Company, 1911), accessed at www.newadvent.org/cathen/11160a. htm.

11. See Moynihan, *Finding Viganò*, 45.

apostolic nuncio to the United States of America after the unexpected death of the prior nuncio during lung surgery. There is some suggestion that Viganò was transferred to the US because his work at reforming Vatican finances was getting too close to exposing corruption. As with the McCarrick allegations, Viganò seems to have been an eyewitness to the financial and other corruption within the administration of the Vatican City State.[12]

Whatever the circumstances of his appointment, Viganò threw himself into his new role with the same dedication to duty and love for the Church that characterized his entire career. Upon taking up his post, he indicated he wanted to "know this people, this country, and come to love them."[13] Viganò's six years as nuncio covered the end of the first term of Barack Hussein Obama and his entire second term. He would retire just as Donald J. Trump was surprising the pundits to capture the Republican nomination for president. His service also spanned the final two years of the Benedict papacy and the first three years of the Francis pontificate.

One of his significant duties was to organize Pope Francis's visit to the United States in September 2015. An event occurred during that visit that would reemerge in public fury just after Viganò published his Testimony in 2018. On August 28, 2018, just days after the Testimony appeared, the New York Times published a story that contained an attack on Viganò relating to one of the meetings he arranged during the papal visit to the US. In June of 2015, the US Supreme Court effectively vetoed any state's law that recognized marriage as capable of being contracted solely between a man and a woman. The high court claimed the Constitution required all states to permit people of the same sex to get married even though the Constitution says not a word on the subject. That summer, a county clerk in Kentucky, Kim Davis, was arrested and thrown in prison because she refused to sign marriage licenses (part of her duties as county clerk) for applicants of the same sex. Davis, a Protestant, was thrown into jail by a Catholic judge for refusing to put her name on

---

12. For a discussion of these claims, see Moynihan, 48–52.
13. Quoted in Moynihan, 52.

a document she understood to violate the divine law.[14] Viganò arranged for her to meet Pope Francis privately while they were both in Washington. After the pope returned to Rome, there was a media uproar over the visit and several Vatican spokesmen tried to downplay the meeting, acting as if it were just a fleeting encounter among many people. The August 2018 *New York Times* article quoted Juan Carlos Cruz who claimed the subject of the Davis meeting came up in an audience he had with Pope Francis.[15] According to the *Times*, Cruz claimed that Francis said to him: "I didn't know who that woman [Davis] was, and he [Viganò] snuck her in to say hello to me. . . . I was horrified and I fired that nuncio." This article was clearly an *ad hominem* attack meant to discredit the Testimony. It tried to cast the Testimony as that of a disgruntled diplomat who had been "fired" by Francis for tricking Francis into a meeting with Davis. On August 31, 2018, *LifeSiteNews* published Archbishop Viganò's rebuttal of this attack on his integrity.[16] In this article Viganò made clear that he personally informed Pope Francis and two senior members of his entourage of the identify and case of Kim Davis. He corroborated his claim by publishing a memo that he prepared and gave to the pope's collaborators that plainly stated that Kim Davis was arrested for refusing to sign marriage certificates for people of the same sex. In any event, Archbishop Viganò was not "fired"; he tendered his resignation as required by current Church practice upon reaching the age of 75 and Pope Francis accepted that resignation.

14. For commentary on the Kim Davis affair and what it reveals, see Thaddeus J. Kozinski, *Modernity as Apocalypse* (Brooklyn, NY: Angelico Press, 2019), ch. 14, "When Christians Persecute Their Own," 153–61.

15. Jason Horowitz, "The Man Who Took on Pope Francis: The Story Behind the Viganò Letter," *New York Times*, August 28, 2018.

16. See Diane Montagna, "Viganò reveals what really happened when Pope Francis met privately with Kim Davis," *LifeSiteNews*, August 31, 2018, www.lifesite-news.com/news/exclusive-Viganò-reveals-what-really-happened-when-pope-francis-met-private. See a follow-up story in which Archbishop Viganò insists again on the veracity of his version of the events: Diane Montagna, "Archbishop Viganò responds to Vatican pushback about Pope's meeting with Kim Davis," *LifeSiteNews*, September 4, 2018, www.lifesitenews.com/news/archbishop-Viganò-responds-to-vatican-pushback-about-popes-meeting-with-kim.

General Introduction

Archbishop Viganò departed Washington, D.C. in May of 2016. Yet his name would explode on the public stage two years later when, after spending two years of reflection in his retirement, he issued his Testimony. After its release, Archbishop Viganò departed to an undisclosed location and, according to reports, the mobile phone he had previously used was no longer functional. He chose to remain hidden from the public eye apparently for two reasons: he seemed to think it prudent for his safety to disappear for some time, and he wished to devote himself to studying the crisis in which the Church and the world found themselves. The fruit of these years of reflection would produce his later interventions on the Second Vatican Council and on the American and global political situation.

Two Voices Fifty Years Apart

In composing a brief sketch of the life of Archbishop Viganò, I could not help noting some striking parallels with the life of another archbishop, Marcel Lefebvre (1905–1991)—another voice crying in the wilderness. Like Viganò, Lefebvre was born into a devout European Catholic family. His hardworking and pious parents of a large family produced vocations for the Church from their fruitful marriage. Both archbishops served the pope in a diplomatic capacity, with Archbishop Lefebvre serving as Apostolic Delegate[17] to French-speaking Africa. Both archbishops served in Africa, although Lefebvre did so for a longer period. Both prelates had long and well-respected ecclesiastical careers. They both retired, only to emerge on the international scene as a sign of contradiction to the state of the Church in the wake of the Council. Lefebvre did so by founding in his retirement a priestly order and seminaries to preserve the traditional priesthood and Mass. Viganò emerged as a whistleblower upon corruption and decomposition in the Church and State. Finally, in the process of closely re-reading the texts of Viganò, I found many similarities between them and the writings of

---

17. An apostolic delegate is similar to a nuncio but is not accredited to the civil government in a country. He serves the same administrative function within the Church but does not have the same formal relationship with a nation's civil government. Delegates were most often sent as personal representatives of the pope to mission lands.

Archbishop Lefebvre with which I was already familiar. Obviously, the critiques of Vatican II are similar, but more strikingly, I find in the writings of both prelates a deep love for the priesthood and the Blessed Mother. These spiritual sentiments run powerfully through the words of these two prelates whom I believe will stand out in the history of our times as prophets and shepherds for the confused and disturbed Catholic faithful.

PART I

A VOICE DECRYING SEXUAL DEVIANCE: THE McCARRICK TESTIMONY

Introduction to Part I

OUTSIDE of inner circles in the Church, the name of Archbishop Viganò was little known, yet the document he released in the hot days of August 2018 would propel his name onto the world scene. On August 25, 2018, Edward Pentin, Rome Correspondent for the *National Catholic Register*, and Diane Montagna, then Rome Correspondent for *LifeSiteNews*, published the now famous text of Archbishop Viganò, for which he had chosen the title "Testimony." The full testimony is contained in three documents, the second and third of which were released over the next few months in response to the violent attacks against the archbishop. To entitle each of these interventions "Testimony" is an interesting choice of terminology. First, it has a legal connotation. It is the term used to describe the evidence given by a witness to a crime. Yet it also has another connotation. Before one dies, it is customary to leave a testimony behind. This is called a Last Will and Testament. The document gives the sense of one nearing the end of his life, disposing of the knowledge he has acquired in his years spent serving the Church. He alludes to this connotation when in the Third Testimony he explains his reason for speaking publicly despite the pain it causes him to do so: "I am an old man, one who knows he must soon give an accounting to the Judge for his actions and omissions, one who fears Him who can cast body and soul into hell." He speaks as one preparing for death and who needs to clear his conscience.

Background to the Testimony
Theodore McCarrick had been ordained a bishop and appointed auxiliary bishop in New York in 1977. Throughout the next several decades he was installed in dioceses in New Jersey. In the year 2000, John Paul II appointed him archbishop of Washington, D.C. As would later be learned, at that time the Vatican was in possession of, and Pope John Paul II considered, detailed allegations of abuse and

homosexual behavior. John Paul II eventually reversed his earlier decision not to move McCarrick to Washington. The report released in November 2020 by Francis's Vatican speculates about the reasons for John Paul II's change of mind, but ultimately only John Paul II knows his reasons. A year later, McCarrick was made a cardinal. In May 2006, Pope Benedict accepted McCarrick's resignation as archbishop upon reaching the now customary age of 75. After retirement, McCarrick remained a public figure (both in the secular world and in the Church) and traveled extensively. In September of 2015 when Pope Francis visited Washington, McCarrick concelebrated Mass with the pope at the Basilica of the National Shrine of the Immaculate Conception in Washington.

Almost two years later, news of the serious allegations against McCarrick began to emerge. Pope Francis ordered a preliminary investigation after the Archdiocese of New York informed the Vatican of an allegation of abuse of an altar boy in the 1970s. In June of 2018, the Archdiocese of New York made a public announcement that after receiving "credible and substantiated" allegations, McCarrick was removed from public ministry. Around the same time, the two dioceses in New Jersey in which McCarrick had worked as bishop publicly revealed that they settled two cases brought by men who alleged that molestation occurred while they were adults. In July of the same year, in response to mounting public outrage over the revelations about McCarrick, Pope Francis expelled McCarrick from the College of Cardinals and forbade him from performing any public ministry. These acts were announced as administrative penalties pending the outcome of a promised canonical trial. (In early 2019, Pope Francis decided against a trial and used an administrative procedure to reduce McCarrick to the lay state, commonly known as defrocking a priest.) These events set the stage for the Testimony.

Structure and Key Themes of the Testimony
After opening the first Testimony by invoking the example of the North American Martyrs who gave their lives for the truth, Archbishop Viganò explains his intention in publishing the document. He releases his written testimony of the crimes and scandals he has seen in the Church "[t]o restore the beauty of holiness to the face of

the Bride of Christ, which is terribly disfigured by so many abominable crimes." To restore the Church, it is necessary "to free the Church from the fetid swamp into which she has fallen." This phrase is very striking for its similarity to the rhetoric of President Donald J. Trump, who was elected on the promise, among others, to "drain the swamp" in Washington, D.C. We shall see throughout this text how Archbishop Viganò shares some common vocabulary and expressions with President Trump in his fight against evil in the United States government. The image of the swamp is only the first.

The archbishop then makes clear that a "conspiracy of silence" must be broken. His conscience requires that what he had previously kept secret must be spoken. In so speaking, Viganò is laying the groundwork for the attack that will be made to discredit his Testimony—that he had broken the Pontifical Secret. Vatican officials who work in the Secretariat of State are bound to secrecy in order to protect sensitive confidential information they learn in the course of their work. The Pontifical Secret is an instrumental good that must be oriented to the greater good of protecting the interests of the Church. As Archbishop Viganò came to realize, it ceases to be a good when the Secret is used to harm the Church by protecting those who disfigure her. Notwithstanding Vatican apologists who lashed out at the archbishop for violating the Pontifical Secret, the pope in December 2019 removed the obligation of secrecy from cases involving abuse of minors or vulnerable people. This papal act confirms that the criticism of Archbishop Viganò for breaking the Secret was unfounded. The vociferous criticism of the archbishop for making his Testimony public caused him to release a Second Testimony dated the Feast of St. Michael the Archangel, September 29, 2018, in which he provides a justification for breaking the "Pontifical Secret."

The testimony of all witnesses must be weighed for credibility. One source of credibility is direct access to the facts about which one testifies. A witness is more credible if he can demonstrate he had direct access to know personally that about which he testifies. A second test of credibility is specificity. One who can consistently recount details, down to minute ones, is more believable, since one who invents a story will likely not have invented the non-essential details that would accompany a true experience, or might end up contradicting himself. On each of these accounts, the archbishop is a credible witness. He claims that the events and facts to which he will testify came to his knowledge through his work as a Delegate for Pontifical Representations from 1998 to 2009 and as Apostolic Nuncio to the United States of America, from October 2011 until May 2016. He refers in detail to two memoranda he wrote in December 2006 and April 2008 and describes his detailed conclusions. The presence of contemporaneous written evidence that corroborates testimony is another hallmark of credibility.

The Testimony commits to writing the direct experience that the archbishop had with the case in his position as Delegate in the Secretariat of State and as Nuncio to the United States. He then names many members of the Roman Curia and the US hierarchy whom he either directly knows or has strong reason to believe were aware of the behavior of, or the accusations against, McCarrick. After identifying these officials, many of whom are very prominent names, he turns to his encounter with Pope Francis. This episode, which the Vatican would attempt in 2020 to contradict by calling into doubt its occurrence, is presented with great detail. Viganò provides dates and detailed surrounding circumstances that led to the meeting. He also explains how he was brought into an unexpected conversation with the pope in an informal manner. This is significant because in 2020 the Vatican would base its attack on his account on the fact that there is no record of the meeting, but Viganò had already presented facts in 2018 that explain why no official appointment would appear in the papal calendar.

Viganò did not seek a meeting to report about McCarrick. He remained in Rome because he was troubled by a disturbing brief conversation he had with the pope as he left an audience with all the nuncios. As he filed past the pope, Viganò introduced himself as the US Nuncio and Pope Francis responded in a way that seemed strange to the archbishop: "He immediately assailed me with a tone of reproach, using these words: 'The bishops in the United States must not be ideologized! They must be shepherds!' Of course I was not in a position to ask for explanations about the meaning of his words and the aggressive way in which he had upbraided me." Hoping to clarify what this reproach meant, during the subsequent ad hoc meeting Viganò appears to have been caught off guard when Pope Francis asked what he (Viganò) thought of McCarrick. This is the critical moment when Viganò asserts he informed Pope Francis of two facts: first, that there was a thick file on McCarrick concerning his corruption of many seminarians, and second, that Pope Benedict had imposed restrictions on McCarrick. Viganò concludes that Francis did not ask the question to learn about McCarrick (Viganò claims that it seemed as if Francis already knew the facts he relayed) but to discern if Viganò was an ally of McCarrick.

Much about the strange encounter with the pope became clearer upon Viganò's return to the United States. Viganò's assistant, Monsignor Jean-François Lantheaume, reported a short time later that he met McCarrick in Texas and McCarrick repeated the same sentence to him that the pope had used with Viganò: "The bishops in the United States must not be ideologized! They must be shepherds!" It seems that this encounter prompted Viganò to realize there was a deeper connection between McCarrick and Francis.

It is important to note that the archbishop's emphasis in this Testimony is not upon crimes committed against minors. He does acknowledge the scandal and horror of such acts. Yet the Testimony as a whole is more directed at the underlying cause of those crimes, a "homosexual current" that he identifies as present in the Church and the Vatican. This current seeks to change the Church's clear and perennial condemnation of sodomy. He identifies those members of the hierarchy that he knows to be part of this current and clearly identifies the acceptance and promotion of homosexuality and its lifestyle as the "swamp" in which the Church is mired. Unlike Cardinal Cupich who flatly denies the abuse crisis has anything to do with homosexuality, Viganò points out that "80% of the abuses found were committed against young adults by homosexuals who were in a relationship of authority over their victims." In response to this time of trial for the Church, Viganò not only proposes doing penance in reparation and to beseech divine aid, but demands that the "seriousness of homosexual behavior must be denounced. The homosexual networks present in the Church must be eradicated." He makes this point even more forcefully in the Third Testimony:

This very grave crisis cannot be properly addressed and resolved unless and until we call things by their true names. This is a crisis due to the scourge of homosexuality, in its agents, in its motives, in its resistance to reform. It is no exaggeration to say that homosexuality has become a plague in the clergy, and it can only be eradicated with spiritual weapons. It is an enormous hypocrisy to condemn the abuser, to claim to weep for the victims, and yet to refuse to denounce the root cause of so much sexual abuse: homosexuality.

The archbishop keenly points out the red herring used by some, including Pope Francis, to shift attention away from unnatural sins: they excuse homosexuality as a cause and instead blame "clericalism." To this Viganò retorts: "It is well established that homosexual predators exploit clerical privilege to their advantage. But to claim the crisis itself to be clericalism is pure sophistry. It is to pretend that a means, a new instrument, is in fact the main motive." If there is a fault of clericalism (using honors and privileges of the clerical state to intimidate and oppress others), he makes clear that this method is merely the means to cover up the main sin of homosexuality.

Viganò sees and insists on the strong connection between teaching and praxis. A failure to adhere faithfully to, and proclaim publicly, the Church's unequivocal teaching on homosexuality is a prominent cause of the abuse crisis. Having found this root of the problem, over the next two years the archbishop would dig deeper to find the underlying cause of the conspiracy of silence on this sin. He will eventually find it in the revolution that occurred in the Second Vatican Council, the topic of Part II of this book.

Archbishop Viganò closes his Testimony in a way that many in the media found shocking. He called upon Pope Francis to set a good example for those bishops who enabled and covered for McCarrick by resigning his office. Certainly, it is an extraordinary event to call for the abdication of the Supreme Pontiff. Yet, as Viganò says, it would merely be consistent with Francis's own rhetoric that there should be "zero tolerance" for covering up abuse. After making this jarring claim, Viganò ends his Testimony, as will be his practice throughout his interventions, by reminding us not to lose hope. He reminds us that the Church will emerge from this trial and prevail over her enemies.

The Second and Third Testimonies

The appearance of the Testimony evoked strong reactions. Cardinal Marc Ouellet responded with an open letter to Viganò published by the Vatican Press Office.[1] In the letter he lashes out at Viganò for damaging the Church by his Testimony. Among other attacks, he uses the classic canard employed repeatedly against anyone who attempts to call out the fact that the emperor has no clothes—the loss of "full communion." Anyone who questions misdeeds or mistakes of a pope is "breaking communion." Ouellet writes: "Is not communion with the Successor of Peter the expression of our obedience to Christ?" They imply one must be loyal to Christ by keeping quiet about actions that attack Him.

As described in the Second Testimony, Pope Francis had also attacked the archbishop. In addition to refusing to respond to the allegations of the first Testimony, the Argentine pope blasphemously (in my opinion) compared himself to Our Lord who remained silent at his trial and compares Viganò to the devil. I say this is blasphemous because Our Lord as the Son of God was truly innocent. He wanted to be the meek lamb led to the sacrificial altar on which he would redeem the world. Pope Francis is not Our Lord. He may be a pope but he is still a man capable of sin. Many of his predecessors fell into scandalous sin. Alexander VI lived a scandalous life, keeping mistresses and siring children that he promoted in the Church. Yet Alexander VI did not dare to compare himself to Christ in being accused of such moral failings. It is primarily the attacks of Cardinal Ouellet and Pope Francis that precipitated the Second and Third Testimonies. These further documents are very useful as they provide cogent replies to his accusers and more insight into his state of mind and motivations for releasing the original Testimony.

---

1. The text of the letter may be found here: www.vaticannews.va/en/vatican-city/news/2018-10/letter-ouellet-vigano-mccarrick-sexual-abuse-united-states.html.

23

The Fraudulent "McCarrick Report"

Over two years after the Testimony and its two sequels appeared, the Vatican finally released the long-awaited report that was supposed to explain how McCarrick was able to climb the rungs of the hierarchy and wield so much influence in the Church.[2] Archbishop Viganò released two statements in reply to this report: a short statement declaring it a "fraud," that is, another coverup, and a longer analysis, a comprehensive analysis of the 460-page labyrinth.

The McCarrick Report, although it places some blame at the feet of John Paul II and Benedict XVI, would be better titled "The Viganò Investigation" or "The Report to Shift Suspicion from Francis." The name of Archbishop Viganò appears 306 times in the document. He is named in order to discredit his Testimony and to maintain the story that Francis knew nothing about McCarrick's homosexual lifestyle. The authors of the report try to create doubt around the June 23, 2013 meeting between Viganò and Francis that is at the heart of the Testimony. First, they claim there are no written records of the accusations Viganò claims to have shared with the pope. As is evident from Viganò's description of the event, however, that is because it was a private spur-of-the-moment meeting and an oral conversation. The report further claims that the pope has no recollection of the meeting and that the claims about what were said are in dispute: "Pope Francis did not recollect what Viganò said about McCarrick during these two meetings. However, because McCarrick was a cardinal known personally to him, Pope Francis was certain that he would have remembered had Viganò spoken about McCarrick with any 'force or clarity.'" This a long-winded way of saying the pope is accusing him of lying. As Viganò states in the Third Testimony, "at a second, private meeting, I informed the pope, answering his own question about Theodore McCarrick, then cardinal archbishop emeritus of Washington, a prominent figure of the Church in the US, telling the pope that McCarrick had sexually corrupted his own seminarians and priests. No pope could forget that."

2. A copy of the report may be found here: www.vatican.va/resources/resources _rapporto-card-mccarrick_20201110_en.pdf.

Introduction to Part I

Worse than trying to discredit the Testimony, the Report attempts to blame Viganò for dereliction of duty in not investigating and reporting McCarrick's conduct. This claim is outrageous in light of Viganò's having authored two lengthy memos in the Secretariat of State recommending trial and punishment of McCarrick, and given his Testimony of his repeated conversations with cardinals, and the pope himself, about the danger McCarrick posed. The archbishop's scathing assessment of the Report as a "fraud" seems well founded.

His Grace details many inconsistencies in the report and the process that produced it. The report accepts without question the testimony of witnesses whose credibility strains belief, such as McCarrick allies Bishop Kevin Farrell (former bishop of Dallas, created a cardinal by Pope Francis in 2016) and Cardinal Donald Wuerl, who was forced to resign following public accusations against him. At the same time, the investigation ignores the testimony of some of "Uncle Ted's" key victims, whose testimony appears nowhere in the Report. Viganò notes that typically in ecclesiastical trials, clerics are entitled to a presumption of credibility. Yet that presumption must be dismissed when the cleric has a vested interest in covering up a crime. He highlights the fact that the investigation and report were highly selective in their collection and reporting of evidence. He explains:

> We are also left bewildered by the fact that Msgr. Farrell's testimony in defense of McCarrick has been reported with emphasis—the bishop is even referred to with the title of "Most Excellent"—but that at the same time the testimony of James Grein was completely omitted, just as the choice was prudently made not to take a deposition from the Secretaries of State Sodano and Bertone.

He also notes the irony that whereas the Report attempts to place blame on Viganò (who repeatedly warned the Vatican about McCarrick), it portrays McCarrick's successor and protégé, Donald Wuerl, as unaware and blameless:

> It is therefore very strange that the serious suspicions which weighed on the cardinal [McCarrick] prior to my appointment

[as Nuncio], which are amply documented in the Report, are considered grounds for censure against me—despite my having once again notified the Secretariat of State about them—but not against Wuerl, who even after his resignation as archbishop of Washington retained his posts in the Roman Dicasteries, including the Congregation for Bishops where he retained his voice in the appointment of bishops.

Although the claim of Francis that he "fired that nuncio" is false (Viganò resigned at the customary age), it is true that the pope chose to accept the resignation and to give him no position in the Vatican. Cardinal Wuerl however resigned as bishop of Washington amidst scandals. The pope accepted his resignation but kept Wuerl in his post at a key office in the Vatican from which he could influence the selection of new bishops.

The explanation for these inconsistencies is that the investigators were charged not with uncovering the truth but rather with supporting Pope Francis's dictate that all blame be placed on the deceased John Paul II and on the neutralized-by-abdication Benedict XVI. As Archbishop Viganò asserts: "The only one who in the narrative of the Secretariat of State cannot be touched by any suspicion, by any accusation—even if only indirect—or by any shadow of coverup, should obviously be the Argentine [i.e., Pope Francis]." This attempt to exonerate Francis is the only explanation for the report's embrace of McCarrick's housemate, Farrell, and its calumnious attack on Viganò, even though he outranked Farrell during his time as Apostolic Nuncio to the United States (2011–2016). Viganò notes:

> Nor is it clear for what reason Farrell's words in defense of his friend and housemate are considered valid and credible, while mine are not, even though I am an archbishop and Apostolic Nuncio. The only reason I can identify is that while Farrell's words confirm Bergoglio's thesis, mine refute it and demonstrate that it was not only the bishop of Dallas who was lying.

The archbishop notes the clear double standard in the way John Paul II and Francis are handled:

Introduction to Part I

It is not clear why the drafters of the Report are so casual in judging John Paul II for having put faith in his secretary's words in defense of McCarrick, yet so absolving towards Bergoglio, despite the fact that there was a pile of dossiers concerning "Uncle Ted," whom Bergoglio's predecessor had requested to "keep a low profile."

Viganò argues that these inconsistencies are the work of a biased and interested judge. Ultimately, he accuses Pope Francis of manipulating the investigation to protect McCarrick and his accomplices because Francis owes his election, at least in part, to McCarrick's dirty network. He explains:

If Jorge Mario Bergoglio owes his election to the conspiracy of the so-called Saint Gallen Mafia,[3] which included ultraprogressive cardinals in constant and assiduous relationship with McCarrick; if McCarrick's endorsement of candidate Bergoglio found a hearing among the conclave electors and those who have the power of persuasion in the Vatican . . . if the resignation of Benedict XVI was in some way provoked or favored by interference from the deep church and the deep state, it is logical to suppose that Bergoglio and his collaborators did not have any intention of letting the names of McCarrick's accomplices leak into the Report, nor the names of those who favored him in his ecclesiastical *cursus honorum*,[4] nor above all the names of those who in the face of the possibility of a conviction could in some way take revenge—for example, by revealing the involvement of prominent personalities of the Roman Curia, if not of Bergoglio himself.

---

3. For more information, see the discussion "Exposing the Plots of the Deep Church: Interview with Julia Meloni on the St. Gallen Mafia," posted by *Catholic Family News* on YouTube, November 17, 2020. In brief, the name refers to a group of progressivist bishops who met regularly in St. Gallen, Switzerland to plot a transformation of the Church. They appear to have had ties to McCarrick and to have worked for the election of Pope Francis.

4. The Latin term referring to the ancient Roman "course of honor," that is, the "ladder of offices" through which a Roman senator would pass in his climb to higher and higher posts. It is used here in an ironic sense for ambitious ecclesiastical ladder-climbing.

Viganò's conclusion on the corruption of the Secretariat of State, the organ that was charged by Bergoglio with preparing the report, is chilling: "This point must be denounced loudly: the Report drawn up by the Secretariat of State is an indecent and clumsy attempt to give a semblance of credibility to a gang of perverts and corrupt men in the service of the New World Order."

Archbishop Viganò points out a sinister fact not discussed by the media. The actual sentence imposed on McCarrick was lenient. Yes, he was laicized, but he was not sentenced to prison in the Vatican, which could have been the result of an actual canonical trial. Bergoglio preempted a trial by accomplishing the reduction to the lay state through an administrative process that precluded prison. Rather than being confined to prison where he belongs, McCarrick "resides in a secret locality, where he can continue undisturbed in his paradiplomatic activity on behalf of the deep state and the deep church in the anonymous guise of a layman."

Ultimately, Viganò concludes that the judges in the case of the McCarrick scandal, Bergoglio and his associates, are conflicted due to their extensive ties to the deep state and the Chinese Communist Party. He notes the striking similarities between the methods used in the McCarrick report and the dishonest methods used to promote the totalitarian COVID lockdowns and to perpetrate the election fraud in the United States. Viganò demonstrates how (to use a famous phrase of Pope Francis ironically) "everything is connected."[5]

For the first time publicly, Archbishop Viganò even alludes to possible election fraud in the 2013 papal conclave, an illegal balloting on which Francis was elected. In all of these cases, he notes, "in the kingdom of lies, if reality does not correspond to the narrative, it is reality that must be corrected and censured." The McCarrick Report's attempt to change reality is merely one piece in an elaborate puzzle. He notes:

Vices and corruption find the deep church and deep state united in a cesspool of repugnant crimes, in which the defenseless and

5. Viganò's writings on the alliance of the deep church and the deep state in regard to the 2020 US presidential election, the political manipulation of COVID-19, and the creation of a New World Order are collected in Part III.

children are the victims of exploitation, violence, and harassment committed by characters who at the same time promote abortion, gender ideology, and the sexual freedom of minors, including sex changes.

The most significant difference between this 2020 statement on the McCarrick affair and the original Testimony occurs toward the end when he places this issue in a broader context which he had studied deeply during the intervening two years. He argues that McCarrick's career of crimes and debauchery is a product of two larger phenomena: the Second Vatican Council and an alliance between the deep state and the deep church. Toward the end of his lengthy analysis, the archbishop connects the sham Vatican investigation to his recent condemnations of Vatican II,[6] seeing in the pontificate of the pope who convened the Council (John XXIII) the seeds of the current corruption. He argues that a truly independent investigation would confirm "what many do not yet dare admit, namely, the role played by the deep church, since the election of John XXIII, in creating the theological premises and the ecclesial climate that would allow the Church to be the servant of the New World Order and to replace the pope with the false prophet of the Antichrist."

Here, the archbishop refers to the "intrinsic link between doctrinal deviation and moral deviation." The McCarrick scandal, and the greater scandal of its continued coverup, are a product of doctrinal deviance with its roots in Vatican II. The attempt begun at Vatican II to subvert and overturn the condemnation by divine and natural law of sodomy as intrinsically evil is intimately connected to the crimes of McCarrick and the exoneration of Bergoglio. To further this goal, the report scrupulously avoids any condemnation of McCarrick's unnatural acts with adult men. A recent report by the Pew Institute[7] demonstrates how successful the gay lobby of the deep church has been in changing the beliefs of Catholics. Here is a summary of the percentage of Catholics in each country who sup-

---

6. Contained in Part II of this book.

7. Located at www.pewresearch.org/fact-tank/2020/11/02/how-catholics-around
-the-world-see-same-sex-marriage-homosexuality.

port so-called gay "marriage," a legal act that epitomizes the acceptance of unnatural sin as normal and socially acceptable:

% of Catholics in each country who favor or oppose
allowing gays and lesbians to marry legally

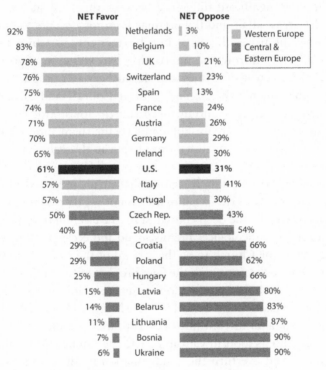

Note: Don't know/refused responses not shown.
Source: Surveys conducted 2015–2017 in European countries and 2019 in the United States.

PEW RESEARCH CENTER

The archbishop notes that, although he as the whistleblower of the gay lobby is scapegoated by the report, the root of McCarrick's perversity (sodomy) is not condemned. "[T]he crimes for which McCarrick was summoned to judgment only concern the abuse of minors, while his unnatural relationships with consenting adults are quietly accepted and tolerated, as if the immoral and sacrilegious acts of a cleric are not to be deplored...." Because for now pedophilia is illegal in most countries, the report must grudgingly admit this scandal while utterly ignoring the root cause of sodomy. Moreover, the continued conspiracy to cover up homosexuality in the clergy and the complicity of Pope Francis in this endeavor is the product of a coordinated effort between the deep church and the deep state. He describes this unholy contract as one between "the deviant part of the hierarchy—the deep church, precisely—and the deviant part of the State, of the world of finance and information."

As with his prior interventions, the archbishop inspires us to hope by reminding us that this, too, shall pass. After condemning the failure of Bergoglio and his accomplices in the gay lobby to bring perpetrators of moral crimes to justice or to compensate their victims, Viganò reminds us of the most important victim of this corruption: the Bride of Christ, disfigured and dishonored by this attempt to remake her into the image of the Communist-directed New World Order. But Viganò reminds us that Christ will not remain, as it were, asleep in the back of the boat (cf. Mt 8:24; Mk 4:38).

> In all of this, however, our adversaries forget that the Church is not a faceless collection of persons without faces who blindly obey mercenaries, but rather a Living Body with a Divine Head: Our Lord Jesus Christ. To think of being able to kill the Spouse of Christ without the Spouse intervening is a delusion that only Satan could believe possible.

The Church remains His Spouse and in the fullness of time He will come to her rescue.

The System that Produced McCarrick Operates in Francis's Vatican

The final document of Part I, a letter entitled "The Faithful Have a Right to Know," is included because it testifies that as of January 2020, one of the two forces that enabled and protected McCarrick is still alive and well in Francis's Vatican. As we have seen, those two forces are (1) a theological shift to tolerate or excuse homosexuality in practice and (2) a corrupt political culture that uses intrigue and graft to control the bureaucracy. This letter highlights two examples of what Viganò calls "shady maneuvers" and the "sordid intrigues of a corrupt court."

The letter opens with a reference to an attempt to discredit a book that appeared in January 2020, coauthored by Pope (Emeritus) Benedict XVI and Cardinal Robert Sarah. The book *From the Depths of Our Hearts* appeared on the eve of the release of the Apostolic Exhortation *Querida Amazonia* (which was dated February 2, 2020). Ever since Paul VI introduced the Synod of Bishops, the practice has been for the synod to adopt a final report that is submitted to the pope. The Holy Father, after considering the report, issues an Apostolic Exhortation adopting (or modifying or amplifying) the themes and positions of the report. The Synod on the Amazon that took place in Rome in October 2019 as well as the text of the final report led to speculation that Pope Francis would relax the Church's discipline requiring the celibacy of priests, at least in the Amazon region. It was hoped by some and feared by others that Francis would authorize the ordination of married men as priests. If this were Francis's plan, the book coauthored by his still-living predecessor was a huge embarrassment, as the book eloquently defended and praised the practice of priestly celibacy.

Querida Amazonia did not deliver the definitive change of discipline (although it did leave the door open for it in the future). It is in this context that, on January 13, 2020, Eva Fernández, the Rome correspondent for a radio station owned by the Spanish Bishops' Conference, claimed that Benedict XVI did not coauthor the book and did not authorize its publication.[8] This claim essentially calls both Cardinal Sarah and the English version's publisher, Ignatius Press, liars for attaching Benedict's name. The Jesuit magazine *America* immediately doubled down and claimed on January 14 that Benedict had demanded the removal of his name from the book.[9] The article cited a statement from the secretary of the Pope Emeritus. Notwithstanding these claims that Benedict denied authoring it and demanded his name be removed, as of February 2021 the book continues to be for sale with the name of Benedict XVI as author

8. See www.catholicnewsagency.com/news/ignatius-press-claim-that-benedict-xvi-did-not-co-author-book-on-celibacy-is-false-70714.

9. See www.americamagazine.org/faith/2020/01/14/benedict-xvi-has-asked-cardinal-sarah-have-his-name-removed-book-priestly-celibacy.

and his picture on the front cover.[10] If the claims of unauthorized publication were true, the publisher would have been legally obligated to remove the book and republish it correctly attributed.

Archbishop Viganò claims that this lie was invented to discredit the book, presumably as its publication embarrassed Francis who was on the verge of attacking the discipline of celibacy. Viganò seems to suggest the vile lies about the authorship originated with Francis. He is cryptic but he refers to the "pope's jailer" whom he labels "Judas." Since his abdication and the election of Francis, Benedict XVI has continued to live in a small part of the Vatican and is rarely seen or heard from.

The next suggestion by Viganò is that this fiasco over the book also served another purpose, namely, to distract from a "devious" appointment that was announced in January. Pope Francis confirmed the appointment of Cardinal Giovanni Battista Re as Dean of the College of Cardinals and Leonardo Sandri as Vice-Dean on January 18 and 24, respectively.[11] The Dean of the College of Cardinals presides at the conclave to elect a pope and represents the Vatican during the period between the death (or abdication) of a pope and the election of his successor. He wields great power in the ability to control the proceedings of the Conclave. Since Cardinal Re is 85, pursuant to modern legislation he will not be able to participate in the Conclave. This means that Cardinal Sandri would in fact wield the power as Vice-Dean (if a Conclave occurred in the next ten years before he reached the age of 85). Archbishop Viganò is very complimentary of Cardinal Re but unveils troubling information about Cardinal Sandri that suggests he is part of the corrupt network that protects profligate clergy like McCarrick.

Viganò finds it difficult to relate what he knows from his work in the Vatican about Sandri, with whom he had been friends. Yet he claims that Sandri was recruited by Cardinal Angelo Sodano, former Secretary of State, to help with the coverup of Marcial Maciel.

10. See, e.g., the Amazon listing at www.amazon.com/Depths-Our-Hearts-Priesthood-Celibacy/dp/1621644146.

11. See www.catholicnewsagency.com/news/cardinal-re-elected-new-dean-of-the-college-of-cardinals-14275.

Father Marcial Maciel Degollado was a Mexican priest who founded the Legion of Christ and the Regnum Christi movement. He was highly respected by the Vatican during the pontificate of John Paul II, especially as a fundraiser. Cardinal Ratzinger began an investigation into allegations of sexual abuse and lasciviousness against Maciel. A year after becoming pope, Benedict administratively removed Maciel from public ministry and sent him to a life of prayer and penance[12]—a remedy similar to the one Viganò claims was imposed by Benedict XVI on Theodore McCarrick. Sodano, Secretary of State under John Paul II, appears to have been a key figure in protecting Maciel, and recruited Sandri as an accomplice. Having removed the nuncio of Mexico City, Bishop Justo Mullor, for refusing to cover for Father Maciel, Sodano—claims Viganò on the basis of firsthand knowledge—sent Sandri to Mexico City because he would cooperate with the coverup. Viganò references a large reception with the Legionaries upon Sandri's elevation to cardinal as evidence of the shady deals. Viganò issued this letter in January of 2020 to warn us that the network of coverup and court intrigue that he denounced in his Testimony is alive and well, as evidenced by these two affairs. He is telling us that nothing has changed since the exposure and seeming departure of McCarrick in the summer of 2018.

12. See for example, www.nytimes.com/2006/05/19/world/europe/19cnd-vatican.html.

1

First Testimony[1]

by
His Excellency Carlo Maria Viganò
Titular Archbishop of Ulpiana
Apostolic Nuncio

IN this tragic moment for the Church in various parts of the world —the United States, Chile, Honduras, Australia, etc.[2]—bishops have a very grave responsibility. I am thinking in particular of the United States of America, where I was sent as Apostolic Nuncio by Pope Benedict XVI on October 19, 2011, the memorial feast of the First North American Martyrs. The bishops of the United States are called, and I with them, to follow the example of these first martyrs who brought the Gospel to the lands of America, to be credible witnesses of the immeasurable love of Christ, the Way, the Truth and the Life.

Bishops and priests, abusing their authority, have committed horrendous crimes to the detriment of the faithful, minors, inno-

---

1. English translation by Diane Montagna, first published in the *National Catholic Register* and shortly thereafter in *LifeSiteNews*: www.lifesitenews.com/news/former-us-nuncio-pope-francis-knew-of-mccarricks-misdeeds-repealed-sanction.

2. The United States was experiencing the explosion of the McCarrick scandal as well as various grand jury reports, including one released in Pennsylvania on August 14, 2018 that collated information about alleged abuse in six of Pennsylvania's eight dioceses. In July of that year, Pope Francis accepted the early resignation (age 57) of Juan José Pineda Fasquelle, auxiliary bishop of Tegucigalpa in Honduras, who was under investigation for abusing seminarians. In May of 2018, every bishop in the country of Chile (31 active and 3 retired) offered their resignation simultaneously in response to allegations of abuse. In August, Cardinal George Pell was on trial for alleged sexual abuse in Australia. Pell's conviction was eventually thrown out by the Australian High Court in 2020.

cent victims, young men eager to offer their lives to the Church, or by their silence have not prevented such crimes from continuing to be perpetrated.

To restore the beauty of holiness to the face of the Bride of Christ, which is terribly disfigured by so many abominable crimes, and if we truly want to free the Church from the fetid swamp into which she has fallen, we must have the courage to tear down the culture of secrecy and publicly confess the truths we have kept hidden. We must tear down the conspiracy of silence with which bishops and priests have protected themselves at the expense of their faithful, a conspiracy of silence that in the eyes of the world risks making the Church look like a sect, a conspiracy of silence not so dissimilar to the one that prevails in the mafia. "Whatever you have said in the dark . . . shall be proclaimed from the housetops" (Lk 12:3).

I had always believed and hoped that the hierarchy of the Church could find within itself the spiritual resources and strength to tell the whole truth, to amend and to renew itself. That is why, even though I had repeatedly been asked to do so, I always avoided making statements to the media, even when it would have been my right to do so, in order to defend myself against the calumnies published about me, even by high-ranking prelates of the Roman Curia. But now that the corruption has reached the very top of the Church's hierarchy, my conscience dictates that I reveal those truths regarding the heartbreaking case of the archbishop emeritus of Washington, D.C., Theodore McCarrick, which I came to know in the course of the duties entrusted to me by St. John Paul II, as Delegate for Pontifical Representations, from 1998 to 2009, and by Pope Benedict XVI, as Apostolic Nuncio to the United States of America, from October 19, 2011 until the end of May 2016.

As Delegate for Pontifical Representations in the Secretariat of State, my responsibilities were not limited to the Apostolic Nunciatures, but also included the staff of the Roman Curia (hires, promotions, informational processes on candidates to the episcopate, etc.) and the examination of delicate cases, including those regarding cardinals and bishops, that were entrusted to the Delegate by the Cardinal Secretary of State or by the Substitute of the Secretariat of State.

To dispel suspicions insinuated in several recent articles, I will immediately say that the Apostolic Nuncios in the United States, Gabriel Montalvo and Pietro Sambi, both prematurely deceased, did not fail to inform the Holy See immediately, as soon as they learned of Archbishop McCarrick's gravely immoral behavior with seminarians and priests. Indeed, according to what Nuncio Pietro Sambi wrote, Father Boniface Ramsey, O.P.'s letter, dated November 22, 2000, was written at the request of the late Nuncio Montalvo. In the letter, Father Ramsey, who had been a professor at the diocesan seminary in Newark from the end of the '80s until 1996, affirms that there was a recurring rumor in the seminary that the archbishop "shared his bed with seminarians," inviting five at a time to spend the weekend with him at his beach house. And he added that he knew a certain number of seminarians, some of whom were later ordained priests for the Archdiocese of Newark, who had been invited to this beach house and had shared a bed with the archbishop.

The office that I held at the time was not informed of any measure taken by the Holy See after those charges were brought by Nuncio Montalvo at the end of 2000, when Cardinal Angelo Sodano[3] was Secretary of State.

Likewise, Nuncio Sambi transmitted to the Cardinal Secretary of State, Tarcisio Bertone,[4] an Indictment Memorandum against McCarrick by the priest Gregory Littleton of the diocese of Charlotte, who was reduced to the lay state for a violation of minors, together with two documents from the same Littleton, in which he recounted his tragic story of sexual abuse by the then-archbishop of Newark and several other priests and seminarians. The Nuncio added that Littleton had already forwarded his Memorandum to

3. Cardinal Angelo Sodano has been implicated in the plot to cover up the full text of the Third Secret of Fatima. See Christopher Ferrara, *The Secret Still Hidden* (Pound Ridge, NY: Good Counsel Publications, 2000).

4. Cardinal Bertone had previously served as second in command to Cardinal Joseph Ratzinger at the Congregation for the Doctrine of the Faith at the time the CDF was tasked to assist the Secretary of State with the release of the alleged complete text of the Third Secret of Fatima. Bertone is also alleged to have been deeply involved in the suppression of the full text of the Third Secret; see Ferrara, *The Secret Still Hidden*.

about twenty people, including civil and ecclesiastical judicial authorities, police and lawyers, in June 2006, and that it was therefore very likely that the news would soon be made public. He therefore called for a prompt intervention by the Holy See.

In writing up a memo[5] on these documents that were entrusted to me, as Delegate for Pontifical Representations, on December 6, 2006, I wrote to my superiors, Cardinal Tarcisio Bertone and the Substitute Leonardo Sandri, that the facts attributed to McCarrick by Littleton were of such gravity and vileness as to provoke bewilderment, a sense of disgust, deep sorrow and bitterness in the reader, and that they constituted the crimes of seducing, requesting depraved acts of seminarians and priests, repeatedly and simultaneously with several people, derision of a young seminarian who tried to resist the archbishop's seductions in the presence of two other priests, absolution of the accomplices in these depraved acts, sacrilegious celebration of the Eucharist with the same priests after committing such acts.

In my memo, which I delivered on that same December 6, 2006 to my direct superior, the Substitute Leonardo Sandri, I proposed the following considerations and course of action to my superiors:

• Given that it seemed a new scandal of particular gravity, as it regarded a cardinal, was going to be added to the many scandals for the Church in the United States,
• and that, since this matter had to do with a cardinal, and according to can. 1405 §1, no. 2, *"ipsius Romani Pontificis dumtaxat ius est iudicandi"*;
• I proposed that an exemplary measure be taken against the cardinal that could have a medicinal function, to prevent future abuses against innocent victims and alleviate the very serious scandal for the faithful, who despite everything continued to love and believe in the Church.

---

5. VN: All the memos, letters, and other documentation mentioned here are available at the Secretariat of State of the Holy See or at the Apostolic Nunciature in Washington, D.C.

First Testimony

I added that it would be salutary if, for once, ecclesiastical authority would intervene before the civil authorities and, if possible, before the scandal had broken out in the press. This could have restored some dignity to a Church so sorely tried and humiliated by so many abominable acts on the part of some pastors. If this were done, the civil authority would no longer have to judge a cardinal, but a pastor with whom the Church had already taken appropriate measures to prevent the cardinal from abusing his authority and continuing to destroy innocent victims.

My memo of December 6, 2006 was kept by my superiors, and was never returned to me with any actual decision by the superiors on this matter.

Subsequently, around April 21–23, 2008, the *Statement for Pope Benedict XVI about the Pattern of the Sexual Abuse Crisis in the United States*, by Richard Sipe, was published on the internet, at richardsipe.com. On April 24, it was passed on by the Prefect of the Congregation for the Doctrine of the Faith, Cardinal William Levada, to the Cardinal Secretary of State Tarcisio Bertone. It was delivered to me one month later, on May 24, 2008.

The following day, I delivered a new memo to the new Substitute, Fernando Filoni, which included my previous one of December 6, 2006. In it, I summarized Richard Sipe's document, which ended with this respectful and heartfelt appeal to Pope Benedict XVI: "I approach Your Holiness with due reverence, but with the same intensity that motivated Peter Damian to lay out before your predecessor, Pope Leo IX, a description of the condition of the clergy during his time. The problems he spoke of are similar and as great now in the United States as they were then in Rome. If Your Holiness requests, I will personally submit to you documentation of that about which I have spoken."

I ended my memo by repeating to my superiors that I thought it was necessary to intervene as soon as possible by removing the cardinal's hat from Cardinal McCarrick and that he should be subjected to the sanctions established by the Code of Canon Law, which also provide for reduction to the lay state.

This second memo of mine was also never returned to the Personnel Office, and I was greatly dismayed at my superiors for the inconceivable absence of any measure against the cardinal, and for the continuing lack of any communication with me since my first memo in December 2006.

But finally I learned with certainty, through Cardinal Giovanni Battista Re, then-Prefect of the Congregation for Bishops, that Richard Sipe's courageous and meritorious Statement had had the desired result. Pope Benedict had imposed on Cardinal McCarrick sanctions similar to those now imposed on him by Pope Francis: the cardinal was to leave the seminary where he was living, he was forbidden to celebrate [Mass] in public, to participate in public meetings, to give lectures, to travel, with the obligation of dedicating himself to a life of prayer and penance.

I do not know when Pope Benedict took these measures against McCarrick, whether in 2009 or 2010, because in the meantime I had been transferred to the Governorate of Vatican City State, just as I do not know who was responsible for this incredible delay. I certainly do not believe it was Pope Benedict, who as cardinal had repeatedly denounced the corruption present in the Church, and in the first months of his pontificate had already taken a firm stand against the admission into seminary of young men with deep homosexual tendencies. I believe it was due to the pope's first collaborator at the time, Cardinal Tarcisio Bertone, who notoriously favored promoting homosexuals into positions of responsibility, and was accustomed to managing the information he thought appropriate to convey to the pope.

In any case, what is *certain* is that Pope Benedict imposed the above canonical sanctions on McCarrick and that they were communicated to him by the Apostolic Nuncio to the United States, Pietro Sambi. Monsignor Jean-François Lantheaume, then first Counselor of the Nunciature in Washington and *ad interim chargé d'affaires* after the unexpected death of Nuncio Sambi in Baltimore, told me when I arrived in Washington—and he is ready to testify to it—about a stormy conversation, lasting over an hour, that Nuncio Sambi had with Cardinal McCarrick whom he had summoned to the Nunciature. Monsignor Lantheaume told me that "the Nuncio's voice could be heard all the way out in the corridor."

Pope Benedict's same dispositions were then also communicated to me by the new Prefect of the Congregation for Bishops, Cardinal Marc Ouellet, in November 2011, in a conversation before my departure for Washington, and were included among the instructions of the same Congregation to the new Nuncio.

In turn, I repeated them to Cardinal McCarrick at my first meeting with him at the Nunciature. The cardinal, muttering in a barely comprehensible way, admitted that he had perhaps made the mistake of sleeping in the same bed with some seminarians at his beach house, but he said this as if it had no importance.

The faithful insistently wonder how it was possible for him to be appointed to Washington, and as cardinal, and they have every right to know who knew, and who covered up his grave misdeeds. It is therefore my duty to reveal what I know about this, beginning with the Roman Curia.

Cardinal ANGELO SODANO was Secretary of State until September 2006: all information was communicated to him. In November 2000, Nunzio Montalvo sent him his report, passing on to him the aforementioned letter from Father Boniface Ramsey in which he denounced the serious abuses committed by McCarrick.

It is known that Sodano tried to cover up the Father Maciel scandal to the end. He even removed the Nuncio in Mexico City, Justo Mullor, who refused to be an accomplice in his scheme to cover Maciel, and in his place appointed Sandri, then-Nuncio to Venezuela, who was willing to collaborate in the coverup. Sodano even went so far as to issue a statement to the Vatican press office in which a falsehood was affirmed, that is, that Pope Benedict had decided that the Maciel case should be considered closed. Benedict reacted, despite Sodano's strenuous defense, and Maciel was found guilty and irrevocably condemned.

Was McCarrick's appointment to Washington and as cardinal the work of Sodano, when John Paul II was already very ill? We are not given to know. However, it is legitimate to think so, but I do not think he was the only one responsible for this. McCarrick frequently went to Rome and made friends everywhere, at all levels of the Curia. If Sodano had protected Maciel, as seems certain, there is no reason why he wouldn't have done so for McCarrick, who according to many had the financial means to influence decisions.

His nomination to Washington was opposed by then-Prefect of the Congregation for Bishops, Cardinal Giovanni Battista Re. At the Nunciature in Washington there is a note, written in his hand, in which Cardinal Re disassociates himself from the appointment and states that McCarrick was 14th on the list for Washington.

Nuncio Sambi's report, with all the attachments, was sent to Cardinal TARCISIO BERTONE, as Secretary of State. My two above-mentioned memos, dated December 6, 2006 and May 25, 2008, were also presumably handed over to him by the Substitute. As already mentioned, the cardinal [Bertone] had no difficulty in insistently presenting for the episcopate candidates known to be active homosexuals—I cite only the well-known case of Vincenzo de Mauro, who was appointed archbishop of Vigevano and later removed because he was undermining his seminarians—and in filtering and manipulating the information he conveyed to Pope Benedict.

Cardinal PIETRO PAROLIN, the current Secretary of State, was also complicit in covering up the misdeeds of McCarrick who had, after the election of Pope Francis, boasted openly of his travels and missions to various continents. In April 2014, the *Washington Times* had a front page report on McCarrick's trip to the Central African Republic, and on behalf of the State Department no less. As Nuncio to Washington, I wrote to Cardinal Parolin asking him if the sanctions imposed on McCarrick by Pope Benedict were still valid. *Ça va sans dire*[6] that my letter never received any reply!

The same can be said for Cardinal WILLIAM LEVADA, former Prefect of the Congregation for the Doctrine of the Faith, for Cardinals MARC OUELLET, Prefect of the Congregation for Bishops, and LORENZO BALDISSERI,[7] former Secretary of the same Congregation for Bishops, and for Archbishop ILSON DE JESUS MONTANARI, current Secretary of the same Congregation. They were all aware by

---

6. French for "it goes without saying."

7. Baldisseri has been a close collaborator with Pope Francis and was appointed Secretary of the Synod of Bishops. In this role he has played a critical part in engineering the various synods Francis has used to advance radical changes in the Church.

reason of their office of the sanctions imposed by Pope Benedict on McCarrick.

Cardinals LEONARDO SANDRI, FERNANDO FILONI and ANGELO BECCIU,[8] as Substitutes of the Secretariat of State, knew in every detail the situation regarding Cardinal McCarrick.

Nor could Cardinals GIOVANNI LAJOLO and DOMINIQUE MAMBERTI have failed to know. As Secretaries for Relations with States, they participated several times a week in collegial meetings with the Secretary of State.

As far as the Roman Curia is concerned, for the moment I will stop here, even if the names of other prelates in the Vatican are well known, even some very close to Pope Francis, such as Cardinal FRANCESCO COCCOPALMERIO and Archbishop VINCENZO PAGLIA,[9] who belong to the homosexual current in favor of subverting Catholic doctrine on homosexuality, a current already denounced in 1986 by Cardinal Joseph Ratzinger, then-Prefect of the Congregation for the Doctrine of the Faith, in the *Letter to the Bishops of the Catholic Church on the Pastoral Care of Homosexual Persons.* Cardinals EDWIN FREDERICK O'BRIEN and RENATO RAFFAELE MARTINO also belong to the same current, albeit with a different ideology. Others belonging to this current even reside at the *Domus Sanctæ Marthæ.*[10]

Now to the United States. Obviously, the first to have been informed of the measures taken by Pope Benedict was McCarrick's successor in the Washington See, Cardinal DONALD WUERL, whose situation is now completely compromised by the recent revelations regarding his behavior as bishop of Pittsburgh.[11]

---

8. Becciu appears to have been forced to resign in September 2020 over the financial scandals involving the Vatican finances and the Vatican Bank.

9. In 2016, Pope Francis completely transformed the Pontifical Academy for Life by rewriting its statutes and essentially dismissing all of its members. Paglia was installed as the new head by Francis to remake the Academy.

10. A hotel built by the Vatican in which cardinals are housed during a conclave. Following his election, Francis refused to move into the papal apartments and set up his residence in this hotel instead.

11. The Pennsylvania Grand Jury report released a week before this Testimony accused Wuerl of protecting and moving around priests in the diocese of Pittsburgh who were accused of abusing minors.

It is absolutely unthinkable that Nuncio Sambi, who was an extremely responsible person, loyal, direct and explicit in his way of being (a true son of Romagna) did not speak to him about it. In any case, I myself brought up the subject with Cardinal Wuerl on several occasions, and I certainly didn't need to go into detail because it was immediately clear to me that he was fully aware of it. I also remember in particular the fact that I had to draw his attention to it, because I realized that in an archdiocesan publication, on the back cover in color, there was an announcement inviting young men who thought they had a vocation to the priesthood to a meeting with Cardinal McCarrick. I immediately phoned Cardinal Wuerl, who expressed his surprise to me, telling me that he knew nothing about that announcement and that he would cancel it. If, as he now continues to state, he knew nothing of the abuses committed by McCarrick and the measures taken by Pope Benedict, how can his answer be explained?

His recent statements that he knew nothing about it, even though, at first, he cunningly referred to compensation for the two victims, are absolutely laughable. The cardinal lies shamelessly and prevails upon his Chancellor, Monsignor Antonicelli, to lie as well.

Cardinal Wuerl also clearly lied on another occasion. Following a morally unacceptable event authorized by the academic authorities of Georgetown University, I brought it to the attention of its President, Dr. John DeGioia, sending him two subsequent letters. Before forwarding them to the addressee, so as to handle things properly, I personally gave a copy of them to the cardinal with an accompanying letter I had written. The cardinal told me that he knew nothing about it. However, he failed to acknowledge receipt of my two letters, contrary to what he customarily did. I subsequently learned that the event at Georgetown had taken place for seven years. But the cardinal knew nothing about it!

Cardinal Wuerl, well aware of the continuous abuses committed by Cardinal McCarrick and the sanctions imposed on him by Pope Benedict, transgressing the pope's order, also allowed him to reside at a seminary in Washington, D.C. In doing so, he put other seminarians at risk.

Bishop PAUL BOOTKOSKI, emeritus of Metuchen, and Archbishop

First Testimony

JOHN MYERS, emeritus of Newark, covered up the abuses committed by McCarrick in their respective dioceses and compensated two of his victims. They cannot deny it and they must be interrogated in order to reveal every circumstance and all responsibility regarding this matter.

Cardinal KEVIN FARRELL, who was recently interviewed by the media, also said that he didn't have the slightest idea about the abuses committed by McCarrick. Given his tenure in Washington, Dallas and now Rome, I think no one can honestly believe him. I don't know if he was ever asked if he knew about Maciel's crimes. If he were to deny this, would anybody believe him given that he occupied positions of responsibility as a member of the Legionaries of Christ?

Regarding Cardinal SEAN O'MALLEY, I would simply say that his latest statements on the McCarrick case are disconcerting and have totally obscured his transparency and credibility.

* * *

My conscience requires me also to reveal facts that I have experienced personally, concerning Pope Francis, that have a dramatic significance, which as bishop, sharing the collegial responsibility of all the bishops for the universal Church, do not allow me to remain silent, and that I state here, ready to reaffirm them under oath by calling on God as my witness.

In the last months of his pontificate, Pope Benedict XVI had convened a meeting of all the apostolic nuncios in Rome, as Paul VI and St. John Paul II had done on several occasions. The date set for the audience with the pope was Friday, June 21, 2013. Pope Francis kept this commitment made by his predecessor. Of course, I also came to Rome from Washington. It was my first meeting with the new pope elected only three months prior, after the resignation of Pope Benedict.

On the morning of Thursday, June 20, 2013, I went to the *Domus Sanctæ Marthæ*, to join my colleagues who were staying there. As soon as I entered the hall, I met Cardinal McCarrick, who was wearing a red-trimmed cassock. I greeted him respectfully as I had always done. He immediately said to me, in a tone somewhere between ambiguous and triumphant: "The pope received me yesterday, tomorrow I am going to China."

At the time I knew nothing of his long friendship with Cardinal Bergoglio and the important part he had played in his recent election, as McCarrick himself would later reveal in a lecture at Villanova University[12] and in an interview with the *National Catholic Reporter*. Nor had I ever thought of the fact that he had participated in the preliminary meetings of the recent conclave, and the role he had been able to have as a cardinal elector in the 2005 conclave. Therefore, I did not immediately grasp the meaning of the cryptic message that McCarrick had communicated to me, but that would become clear to me in the days immediately following.

The next day the audience with Pope Francis took place. After his address, which was partly read and partly delivered off the cuff, the pope wished to greet all the nuncios one by one. In single file, I remember that I was among the last. When it was my turn, I just had time to say to him, "I am the Nuncio to the United States." He immediately assailed me with a tone of reproach, using these words: "The bishops in the United States must not be ideologized! They must be shepherds!" Of course, I was not in a position to ask for explanations about the meaning of his words and the aggressive way in which he had upbraided me. I had in my hand a book in Portuguese that Cardinal O'Malley had sent me for the pope a few days earlier, telling me "so he could go over his Portuguese before going to Rio for World Youth Day." I handed it to him immediately, and so freed myself from that extremely disconcerting and embarrassing situation.

At the end of the audience the pope announced: "Those of you who are still in Rome next Sunday are invited to concelebrate with me at the *Domus Sanctæ Marthæ*." I naturally thought of staying on to clarify as soon as possible what the pope intended to tell me.

On Sunday June 23, before the concelebration with the pope, I

12. This lecture, "Who Is Pope Francis?," was recorded and can be viewed on YouTube at youtu.be/b3iaBLqt8vg.

asked Monsignor Ricca, who as the person in charge of the house helped us put on the vestments, if he could ask the pope if he could receive me sometime in the following week. How could I have returned to Washington without having clarified what the pope wanted of me? At the end of Mass, while the pope was greeting the few lay people present, Monsignor Fabián Pedacchio, his Argentine secretary, came to me and said: "The pope told me to ask if you are free now!" Naturally, I replied that I was at the pope's disposal and that I thanked him for receiving me immediately. The pope took me to the first floor in his apartment and said: "We have 40 minutes before the Angelus."

I began the conversation, asking the pope what he intended to say to me with the words he had addressed to me when I greeted him the previous Friday. And the pope, in a very different, friendly, almost affectionate tone, said to me: "Yes, the bishops in the United States must not be ideologized, they must not be right-wing like the archbishop of Philadelphia (the pope did not give me the name of the archbishop), they must be shepherds; and they must not be left-wing"—and he added, raising both arms—"and when I say left-wing I mean homosexual." Of course, the logic of the correlation between being left-wing and being homosexual escaped me, but I added nothing else.

Immediately after, the pope slyly asked me: "What is Cardinal McCarrick like?" I answered him with complete frankness and, if you like, with great naiveté: "Holy Father, I don't know if you know Cardinal McCarrick, but if you ask the Congregation for Bishops there is a dossier *this thick* about him. He corrupted generations of seminarians and priests and Pope Benedict ordered him to withdraw to a life of prayer and penance." The pope did not make the slightest comment about those very grave words of mine and did not show any expression of surprise on his face, as if he had already known the matter for some time, and he immediately changed the subject. But then, what was the pope's purpose in asking me that question: "What is Cardinal McCarrick like?" He clearly wanted to find out if I was an ally of McCarrick or not.

Back in Washington everything became very clear to me, thanks also to a new event that occurred only a few days after my meeting

47

with Pope Francis. When the new Bishop Mark Seitz took possession of the Diocese of El Paso on July 9, 2013, I sent the first Counselor, Monsignor Jean-François Lantheaume, while I went to Dallas
that same day for an international meeting on Bioethics. When he
got back, Monsignor Lantheaume told me that in El Paso he had
met Cardinal McCarrick who, taking him aside, told him almost the
same words that the pope had said to me in Rome: "the bishops in
the United States must not be ideologized, they must not be right-
wing, they must be shepherds. . . ." I was astounded! It was therefore
clear that the words of reproach that Pope Francis had addressed to
me on June 21, 2013 had been put into his mouth the day before by
Cardinal McCarrick. Also the pope's mention "not like the archbishop of Philadelphia" could be traced to McCarrick, because there
had been a strong disagreement between the two of them about the
admission to Communion of pro-abortion politicians. In his communication to the bishops, McCarrick had manipulated a letter of
then-Cardinal Ratzinger who prohibited giving them Communion.[13] Indeed, I also knew how certain cardinals such as Mahony,
Levada and Wuerl were closely linked to McCarrick; they had
opposed the most recent appointments made by Pope Benedict for
important posts such as Philadelphia, Baltimore, Denver and San
Francisco.

---

13. In the summer of 2004, Cardinal Ratzinger, then Prefect for the Congregation for the Doctrine of the Faith, sent a letter to McCarrick and the President of
the US Bishops' Conference, Wilton Gregory, concerning the Church's discipline
about refusing Communion to politicians who advocate positions contrary to the
Church's teachings. The issue was raised in the context of the presidential candidacy of Democrat John Kerry who, although Catholic, advocated positions contrary to the Church's, including on abortion. In early June, McCarrick summarized
the letter to the US Bishops' Conference in a way that downplayed its clear teaching. When Italian journalist Sandro Magister published the actual text of Ratzinger's letter in July, McCarrick's deceptions became known. For a contemporary
account of how McCarrick mischaracterized the letter, see the *Washington Times*
article: "McCarrick tempered letter on pro-choice politicians," July 7, 2004, www.
washingtontimes.com/news/2004/jul/7/20040707-122623-1092r. A copy of the letter
of Ratzinger can be found on the website of Priests for Life at www.priestsforlife.
org/library/749-worthiness-to-receive-holy-communion.

First Testimony

Not happy with the trap he had set for me on June 23, 2013, when he asked me about McCarrick, only a few months later, in the audience he granted me on October 10, 2013, Pope Francis set a second one for me, this time concerning a second of his protégés, Cardinal Donald Wuerl. He asked me: "What is Cardinal Wuerl like, is he good or bad?" I replied, "Holy Father, I will not tell you if he is good or bad, but I will tell you two facts." They are the ones I have already mentioned above, which concern Wuerl's pastoral carelessness regarding the aberrant deviations at Georgetown University and the invitation by the Archdiocese of Washington to young aspirants to the priesthood to a meeting with McCarrick! Once again, the pope did not show any reaction.

It was also clear that, from the time of Pope Francis's election, McCarrick, now free from all constraints, had felt free to travel continuously, to give lectures and interviews. In a team effort with Cardinal RODRIGUEZ MARADIAGA, he had become the kingmaker for appointments in the Curia and the United States, and the most listened-to advisor in the Vatican for relations with the Obama administration. This is how one explains that, as members of the Congregation for Bishops, the pope replaced Cardinal Burke with Wuerl and immediately appointed Cupich, who was promptly made a cardinal. With these appointments the Nunciature in Washington was now out of the picture in the appointment of bishops. In addition, he appointed the Brazilian Ilson de Jesus Montanari—the great friend of his private Argentine secretary Fabian Pedacchio—as Secretary of the same Congregation for Bishops and Secretary of the College of Cardinals, promoting him in one single leap from a simple official of that department to Archbishop Secretary. Something unprecedented for such an important position!

The appointments of BLASE CUPICH to Chicago and JOSEPH W. TOBIN to Newark were orchestrated by McCarrick, Maradiaga and Wuerl, united by a wicked pact of abuses by the first, and at least of coverup of abuses by the other two. Their names were not among those presented by the Nunciature for Chicago and Newark.

Regarding Cupich, one cannot fail to note his ostentatious arrogance, and the insolence with which he denies the evidence that is now obvious to all: that 80% of the abuse found was committed against young adult males by homosexuals who were in a relationship of authority over their victims.

During the speech he gave when he took possession of the Chicago See, at which I was present as a representative of the pope, Cupich quipped that one certainly should not expect the new archbishop to walk on water. Perhaps it would be enough for him to be able to remain with his feet on the ground and not try to turn reality upside-down, blinded by his pro-gay ideology, as he stated in a recent interview with *America* magazine. Extolling his particular expertise in the matter, having been President of the Committee on Protection of Children and Young People of the USCCB, he asserted that the main problem in the crisis of sexual abuse by clergy is not homosexuality, and that affirming this is only a way of diverting attention from the real problem which is clericalism. In support of this thesis, Cupich "oddly" made reference to the results of research carried out at the height of the sexual abuse of minors crisis in the early 2000s, while he "candidly" ignored that the results of that investigation were totally denied by the subsequent Independent Reports by the John Jay College of Criminal Justice in 2004 and 2011, which concluded that, in cases of sexual abuse, 81% of the victims were male. In fact, Father Hans Zollner, S.J., Vice-Rector of the Pontifical Gregorian University, President of the Centre for Child Protection, and Member of the Pontifical Commission for the Protection of Minors, recently told the newspaper *La Stampa* that "in most cases it is a question of homosexual abuse."

The appointment of McElroy to San Diego was also orchestrated from above, with a cryptic peremptory order to me as Nuncio from Cardinal Parolin: "Reserve the See of San Diego for McElroy." McElroy was also well aware of McCarrick's abuses, as can be seen from a letter sent to him by Richard Sipe on July 28, 2016.

These characters are closely associated with individuals belonging in particular to the deviated wing of the Society of Jesus, unfortunately today a majority, which had already been a cause of serious concern to Paul VI and subsequent pontiffs. We need only consider Father Robert Drinan, S.J., who was elected four times to the House of Representatives, and was a staunch supporter of abortion; or Father Vincent O'Keefe, S.J., one of the principal promoters of *The*

Land O' Lakes Statement of 1967, which seriously compromised the Catholic identity of universities and colleges in the United States.[14] It should be noted that McCarrick, then President of the Catholic University of Puerto Rico, also participated in that inauspicious undertaking which was so harmful to the formation of the consciences of American youth, closely associated as it was with the deviated wing of the Jesuits.

Father James Martin, S.J., acclaimed by the people mentioned above, in particular Cupich, Tobin, Farrell and McElroy, appointed Consultor of the Secretariat for Communications, well-known activist who promotes the LGBT agenda, chosen to corrupt the young people who will soon gather in Dublin for the World Meeting of Families, is nothing but a sad recent example of that deviated wing of the Society of Jesus.

Pope Francis has repeatedly asked for total transparency in the Church and for bishops and faithful to act with *parrhesia*.[15] The faithful throughout the world also demand this of him in an exemplary manner. He must honestly state when he first learned about the crimes committed by McCarrick, who abused his authority with seminarians and priests.

In any case, the pope learned about it from me on June 23, 2013 and continued to cover for him. He did not take into account the sanctions that Pope Benedict had imposed on him and made him his trusted counselor along with Maradiaga. The latter (Maradiaga) is so confident of the pope's protection that he can dismiss as "gossip" the heartfelt appeals of dozens of his seminarians, who found the courage to write to him after one of them tried to commit suicide over homosexual abuse in the seminary. By now the faithful have well understood Maradiaga's strategy: insult the victims to save himself, lie to the bitter end to cover up a chasm of abuses of

14. In the summer of 1967, presidents of Catholic Universities gathered in Land O' Lakes, Wisconsin, and signed a protest claiming that their universities were independent from the Church and essentially could teach things contrary to the Faith, in the name of free academic inquiry. The statement can be read at archives.nd.edu/episodes/visitors/lol/idea.htm.

15. Greek for "bold or candid speech."

power, of mismanagement in the administration of Church property, and of financial disasters even against close friends, as in the case of the Ambassador of Honduras Alejandro Valladares, former Dean of the Diplomatic Corps to the Holy See.

In the case of the former Auxiliary Bishop Juan José Pineda, after the article published in the [Italian] weekly *L'Espresso* last February, Maradiaga stated in the newspaper *Avvenire*: "It was my auxiliary bishop Pineda who asked for the visitation, so as to 'clear' his name after being subjected to much slander." Now, regarding Pineda the only thing that has been made public is that his resignation has simply been accepted, thus making any possible responsibility of his and Maradiaga vanish into nowhere. In the name of the transparency so hailed by the pope, the report that the Visitator, Argentine bishop Alcides Casaretto, delivered more than a year ago only and directly to the pope, must be made public.

Finally, the recent appointment as Substitute of Archbishop EDGAR PEÑA PARRA is also connected with Honduras, that is, with Maradiaga. From 2003 to 2007 Peña Parra worked as Counselor at the Tegucigalpa Nunciature. As Delegate for Pontifical Representations I received worrisome information about him.

In Honduras, a scandal as huge as the one in Chile is about to be repeated. The pope defends his man, Cardinal Rodriguez Maradiaga, to the bitter end, as he had done in Chile with Bishop Juan de la Cruz Barros, whom he himself had appointed bishop of Osorno against the advice of the Chilean bishops. First he insulted the abuse victims. Then, only when he was forced by the media, and a revolt by the Chilean victims and faithful, did he recognize his error and apologize, while stating that he had been misinformed, causing a disastrous situation for the Church in Chile, but continuing to protect the two Chilean Cardinals Errázuriz and Ezzati.

Even in the tragic affair of McCarrick, Pope Francis's behavior was no different. He knew from at least June 23, 2013 that McCarrick was a serial predator. Although he knew that he was a corrupt man, he covered for him to the bitter end; indeed, he made McCarrick's advice his own, which was certainly not inspired by sound intentions and for love of the Church. It was only when he was forced by the report of the abuse of a minor, again on the basis of media attention, that he took action [regarding McCarrick] to save his image in the media.

Now in the United States a chorus of voices is rising especially from the lay faithful, and has recently been joined by several bishops and priests, asking that all those who, by their silence, covered up McCarrick's criminal behavior, or who used him to advance their career or promote their intentions, ambitions and power in the Church, should resign.

But this will not be enough to heal the situation of extremely grave immoral behavior by the clergy: bishops and priests. A time of conversion and penance must be proclaimed. The virtue of chastity must be recovered in the clergy and in seminaries. Corruption in the misuse of the Church's resources and of the offerings of the faithful must be fought against. The seriousness of homosexual behavior must be denounced. The homosexual networks present in the Church must be eradicated, as Janet Smith, Professor of Moral Theology at the Sacred Heart Major Seminary in Detroit, recently wrote. "The problem of clergy abuse," she wrote, "cannot be resolved simply by the resignation of some bishops, and even less so by bureaucratic directives. The deeper problem lies in homosexual networks within the clergy which must be eradicated." These homosexual networks, which are now widespread in many dioceses, seminaries, religious orders, etc., act under the concealment of secrecy and lies with the power of octopus tentacles, and strangle innocent victims and priestly vocations, and are strangling the entire Church.

I implore everyone, especially bishops, to speak up in order to defeat this conspiracy of silence that is so widespread, and to report the cases of abuse they know about to the media and civil authorities.

Let us heed the most powerful message that St. John Paul II left us as an inheritance: "Do not be afraid! Do not be afraid!"

In his 2008 homily on the Feast of the Epiphany, Pope Benedict reminded us that the Father's plan of salvation had been fully revealed and realized in the mystery of Christ's death and resurrection, but it needs to be welcomed in human history, which is always a history of fidelity on God's part and unfortunately also of infidelity on the part of us men. The Church, the depositary of the blessing of the New Covenant, signed in the blood of the Lamb, is holy but made up of sinners, as Saint Ambrose wrote: the Church is *"immaculata ex maculatis,"*[16] she is holy and spotless even though, in her earthly journey, she is made up of men stained with sin.

I want to recall this indefectible truth of the Church's holiness to the many people who have been so deeply scandalized by the abominable and sacrilegious behavior of the former archbishop of Washington, Theodore McCarrick; by the grave, disconcerting and sinful conduct of Pope Francis and by the conspiracy of silence of so many pastors, and who are tempted to abandon the Church, disfigured by so many ignominies. At the Angelus on Sunday, August 12, 2018 Pope Francis said these words: "Everyone is guilty for the good he could have done and did not do.... If we do not oppose evil, we tacitly feed it. We need to intervene where evil is spreading; for evil spreads where daring Christians who oppose evil with good are lacking." If this is rightly to be considered a serious moral responsibility for every believer, how much graver is it for the Church's supreme pastor, who in the case of McCarrick not only did not oppose evil but associated himself in doing evil with someone he knew to be deeply corrupt. He followed the advice of someone he knew well to be a pervert, thus multiplying exponentially with his supreme authority the evil done by McCarrick. And how many other evil pastors is Francis still continuing to prop up in their active destruction of the Church!

Francis is abdicating the mandate which Christ gave to Peter to confirm the brethren. Indeed, by his action he has divided them, led them into error, and encouraged the wolves to continue to tear apart the sheep of Christ's flock.

In this extremely dramatic moment for the universal Church, he must acknowledge his mistakes and, in keeping with the proclaimed principle of zero tolerance, *Pope Francis must be the first to set a good example for cardinals and bishops who covered up McCarrick's abuses and resign along with all of them.*

---

16. Latin for "the spotless out of (emerging from) the spotted." The Church herself remains holy even if she is formed out of sinful members.

First Testimony

Even in dismay and sadness over the enormity of what is happening, let us not lose hope! We well know that the great majority of our pastors live their priestly vocation with fidelity and dedication.

It is in moments of great trial that the Lord's grace is revealed in abundance and makes His limitless mercy available to all; but it is granted only to those who are truly repentant and sincerely propose to amend their lives. This is a favorable time for the Church to confess her sins, to convert, and to do penance.

Let us all pray for the Church and for the pope, let us remember how many times he has asked us to pray for him!

Let us all renew faith in the Church our Mother: "I believe in one, holy, catholic and apostolic Church!"

Christ will never abandon His Church! He generated her in His Blood and continually revives her with His Spirit!

Mary, Mother of the Church, pray for us!

Mary, Virgin and Queen, Mother of the King of glory, pray for us!

Rome, August 22, 2018
Queenship of the Blessed Virgin Mary

2

Second Testimony

Scio Cui credidi [I know whom I have believed]
(2 Tim 1:12)

BEFORE starting my writing, I would first of all like to give thanks and glory to God the Father for every situation and trial that He has prepared and will prepare for me during my life. As a priest and bishop of the holy Church, spouse of Christ, I am called like every baptized person to bear witness to the truth. By the gift of the Spirit who sustains me with joy on the path that I am called to travel, I intend to do so until the end of my days. Our only Lord has addressed also to me the invitation, "Follow me!", and I intend to follow him with the help of his grace until the end of my days.

> "As long as I have life, I will sing to the Lord,
> I will sing praise to my God while I have being.
> May my song be pleasing to him;
> For I rejoice in the Lord."
> (Psalm 103:33–34)

* * *

It has been a month since I offered my testimony, solely for the good of the Church, regarding what occurred at the audience with Pope Francis on June 23, 2013 and regarding certain matters I was given to know in the assignments entrusted to me at the Secretariat of State and in Washington, in relation to those who bear responsibility for covering up the crimes committed by the former archbishop of that capital.

My decision to reveal those grave facts was for me the most painful and serious decision that I have ever made in my life. I made it after long reflection and prayer, during months of profound suffering and anguish, during a crescendo of continual news of terrible events, with thousands of innocent victims destroyed and the vocations and lives of young priests and religious disturbed. The silence of the pastors who could have provided a remedy and prevented new victims became increasingly indefensible, a devastating crime for the Church. Well aware of the enormous consequences that my testimony could have, because what I was about to reveal involved the successor of Peter himself, I nonetheless chose to speak in order to protect the Church, and I declare with a clear conscience before God that my testimony is true. Christ died for the Church, and Peter, *servus servorum Dei*,[1] is the first one called to serve the spouse of Christ.

Certainly, some of the facts that I was to reveal were covered by the pontifical secret that I had promised to observe and that I had faithfully observed from the beginning of my service to the Holy See. But the purpose of any secret, including the pontifical secret, is to protect the Church from her enemies, not to cover up and become complicit in crimes committed by some of her members. I was a witness, not by my choice, of shocking facts and, as the *Catechism of the Catholic Church* states (par. 2491), the seal of secrecy is not binding when very grave harm can be avoided only by divulging the truth. Only the seal of confession could have justified my silence.

Neither the pope, nor any of the cardinals in Rome have denied the facts I asserted in my testimony. "*Qui tacet consentit*"[2] surely applies here, for if they deny my testimony, they have only to say so, and provide documentation to support that denial. How can one avoid concluding that the reason they do not provide the documentation is that they know it confirms my testimony?

The center of my testimony was that since at least June 23, 2013, the pope knew from me how perverse and evil McCarrick was in his intentions and actions, and instead of taking the measures that every good pastor would have taken, the pope made McCarrick one of his principal agents in governing the Church, in regard to the

1. Latin for "servant of the servants of God": first used by Pope St. Gregory the Great in reference to himself as pope.
2. A Latin legal aphorism: "he who remains silent consents" or, as we usually say, "silence signifies consent."

United States, the Curia, and even China, as we are seeing these days with great concern and anxiety for that martyr Church.

Now, the pope's reply to my testimony was: "I will not say a word!"[3] But then, contradicting himself, he has compared his silence to that of Jesus in Nazareth and before Pilate, and compared me to the great accuser, Satan, who sows scandal and division in the Church—though without ever uttering my name. If he had said: "Viganò lied," he would have challenged my credibility while trying to affirm his own. In so doing he would have intensified the demand of the people of God and the world for the documentation needed to determine who has told the truth. Instead, he put in place a subtle slander against me—slander being an offense he has often compared to the gravity of murder. Indeed, he did it repeatedly, in the context of the celebration of the most Holy Sacrament, the Eucharist, where he runs no risk of being challenged by journalists. When he did speak to journalists, he asked them to exercise their professional maturity and draw their own conclusions. But how can journalists discover and know the truth if those directly involved with a matter refuse to answer any questions or to release any documents? The pope's unwillingness to respond to my charges and his deafness to the appeals by the faithful for accountability are hardly consistent with his calls for transparency and bridge building.

Moreover, the pope's coverup of McCarrick was clearly not an isolated mistake. Many more instances have recently been documented in the press, showing that Pope Francis has defended homosexual clergy who committed serious sexual abuses against minors or adults. These include his role in the case of Fr. Julio Grassi in Buenos Aires, his reinstatement of Fr. Mauro Inzoli after Pope Benedict had removed him from ministry (until he went to prison, at which point Pope Francis laicized him), and his halting of

3. According to news reports about the occasion, the pope made the statement in response to questions about Viganò's Testimony. In addition to the statement quoted, Francis also said: "I read the statement this morning, and I must tell you sincerely that, I must say this, to you and all those who are interested: Read the statement carefully and make your own judgment." See, for example, the report of Catholic News Agency: www.catholicnewsagency.com/news/pope-i-will-not-say-a-single-word-on-viganos-allegations-of-coverup-65149.

the investigation of sex abuse allegations against Cardinal Cormac Murphy O'Connor.

In the meantime, a delegation of the USCCB, headed by its president Cardinal DiNardo, went to Rome asking for a Vatican investigation into McCarrick. Cardinal DiNardo and the other prelates should tell the Church in America and in the world: did the pope refuse to carry out a Vatican investigation into McCarrick's crimes and of those responsible for covering them up? The faithful deserve to know.

I would like to make a special appeal to Cardinal Ouellet, because as nuncio I always worked in great harmony with him, and I have always had great esteem and affection towards him. He will remember when, at the end of my mission in Washington, he received me at his apartment in Rome in the evening for a long conversation. At the beginning of Pope Francis's pontificate, he had maintained his dignity, as he had shown with courage when he was archbishop of Québec. Later, however, when his work as prefect of the Congregation for Bishops was being undermined because recommendations for episcopal appointments were being passed directly to Pope Francis by two homosexual "friends" of his dicastery, bypassing the cardinal, he gave up. His long article in *L'Osservatore Romano*, in which he came out in favor of the more controversial aspects of *Amoris Laetitia*, represents his surrender. Your Eminence, before I left for Washington, you were the one who told me of Pope Benedict's sanctions on McCarrick. You have at your complete disposal key documents incriminating McCarrick and many in the curia for their coverups. Your Eminence, I urge you to bear witness to the truth.

* * *

Finally, I wish to encourage you, dear faithful, my brothers and sisters in Christ: never be despondent! Make your own the act of faith and complete confidence in Christ Jesus, our Savior, of Saint Paul in his second Letter to Timothy, *Scio cui credidi*,[4] which I choose as my episcopal motto. This is a time of repentance, of conversion, of

---

4. Latin for "I know Him in whom I have believed."

prayers, of grace, to prepare the Church, the bride of the Lamb, ready to fight and win with Mary the battle against the old dragon.

To commemorate my episcopal ordination on April 26, 1992, conferred on me by St. John Paul II, I chose this image taken from a mosaic of the Basilica of St. Mark in Venice. It represents the miracle of the calming of the storm. I was struck by the fact that in the boat of Peter, tossed by the water, the figure of Jesus is portrayed twice. Jesus is sound asleep in the bow, while Peter tries to wake him up: "Master, do you not care that we are about to die?" Meanwhile the apostles, terrified, look each in a different direction and do not realize that Jesus is standing behind them, blessing them and assuredly in command of the boat: "He awoke and rebuked the wind and said to the sea, 'Quiet! Be still,' . . . then he said to them, 'Why are you afraid? Do you still have no faith?'" (Mk 4:38–40).

The scene is very timely in portraying the tremendous storm the Church is passing through in this moment, but with a substantial difference: the successor of Peter not only fails to see the Lord in full control of the boat, it seems he does not even intend to awaken Jesus asleep in the bow.

Has Christ perhaps become invisible to his vicar? Is he perhaps being tempted to try to act as a substitute of our only Master and Lord?

The Lord is in full control of the boat!

May Christ, the Truth, always be the light on our way!

September 29th, 2018
Feast of St. Michael, Archangel

3

Third Testimony:
McCarrick and Ouellet

October 19, 2018

TO bear witness to corruption in the hierarchy of the Catholic Church was a painful decision for me, and remains so.

But I am an old man, one who knows he must soon give an accounting to the Judge for his actions and omissions, one who fears Him who can cast body and soul into hell.

A Judge, even in his infinite mercy, will render to every person salvation or damnation according to what he has deserved.

Anticipating the dreadful question from that Judge—"How could you, who had knowledge of the truth, keep silent in the midst of falsehood and depravity?"—what answer could I give?

I testified fully aware that my testimony would bring alarm and dismay to many eminent persons: churchmen, fellow bishops, colleagues with whom I had worked and prayed.

I knew many would feel wounded and betrayed.

I expected that some would in their turn assail me and my motives.

Most painful of all, I knew that many of the innocent faithful would be confused and disconcerted by the spectacle of a bishop's charging colleagues and superiors with malfeasance, sexual sin, and grave neglect of duty.

Yet I believe that my continued silence would put many souls at risk, and would certainly damn my own.

Having reported multiple times to my superiors, and even to the pope, the aberrant behavior of Theodore McCarrick, I could have publicly denounced earlier the truths of which I was aware.

If I have some responsibility in this delay, I repent for that.

Third Testimony: McCarrick and Ouellet

This delay was due to the gravity of the decision I was going to take, and to the long travail of my conscience.

I have been accused of creating confusion and division in the Church through my testimony.

To those who believe such confusion and division were negligible prior to August 2018, perhaps such a claim is plausible.

Most impartial observers, however, will have been aware of a longstanding excess of both, as is inevitable when the successor of Peter is negligent in exercising his principal mission, which is to confirm the brothers in the faith and in sound moral doctrine.

When he then exacerbates the crisis by contradictory or perplexing statements about these doctrines, the confusion is worsened.

Therefore I spoke.

For it is the conspiracy of silence that has wrought and continues to wreak great harm in the Church—harm to so many innocent souls, to young priestly vocations, to the faithful at large.

With regard to my decision, which I have taken in conscience before God, I willingly accept every fraternal correction, advice, recommendation, and invitation to progress in my life of faith and love for Christ, the Church and the pope.

Let me restate the key points of my testimony.

• In November 2000 the US nuncio Archbishop (Gabriel) Montalvo informed the Holy See of Cardinal McCarrick's homosexual behavior with seminarians and priests.

• In December 2006 the new US nuncio, Archbishop Pietro Sambi, informed the Holy See of Cardinal McCarrick's homosexual behavior with yet another priest.

• In December of 2006 I myself wrote a memo to the Secretary of State Cardinal (Tarcisio) Bertone, and personally delivered it to the Substitute for General Affairs, Archbishop Leonardo Sandri, calling for the pope to bring extraordinary disciplinary measures against McCarrick to forestall future crimes and scandal. This memo received no response.

• In April 2008 an open letter to Pope Benedict by Richard Sipe was relayed by the Prefect of the CDF, Cardinal (William) Levada, to the Secretary of State, Cardinal Bertone, containing further accusations of McCarrick's sleeping with seminarians and priests.

I received this a month later, and in May 2008 I myself delivered a second memo to the then Substitute for General Affairs, Archbishop Fernando Filoni, reporting the claims against McCarrick and calling for sanctions against him. This second memo also received no response.

• In 2009 or 2010 I learned from Cardinal (Giovanni Battista) Re, prefect of the Congregation for Bishops, that Pope Benedict had ordered McCarrick to cease public ministry and begin a life of prayer and penance. The nuncio Sambi communicated the pope's orders to McCarrick in a voice heard down the corridor of the nunciature.

• In November 2011 Cardinal (Marc) Ouellet, the new Prefect of Bishops, repeated to me, the new nuncio to the US, the pope's restrictions on McCarrick, and I myself communicated them to McCarrick face-to-face.

• On June 21, 2013, toward the end of an official assembly of nuncios at the Vatican, Pope Francis spoke cryptic words to me criticizing the US episcopacy.

• On June 23, 2013, I met Pope Francis face-to-face in his apartment to ask for clarification, and the pope asked me, "*Il cardinale McCarrick, com'è?*" [Cardinal McCarrick—what do you make of him?]—which I can only interpret as a feigning of curiosity in order to discover whether or not I was an ally of McCarrick. I told him that McCarrick had sexually corrupted generations of priests and seminarians, and had been ordered by Pope Benedict to confine himself to a life of prayer and penance.

• Instead, McCarrick continued to enjoy the special regard of Pope Francis and was given new responsibilities and missions by him.

• McCarrick was part of a network of bishops promoting homosexuality who exploiting their favor with Pope Francis manipulated episcopal appointments so as to protect themselves from justice and to strengthen the homosexual network in the hierarchy and in the Church at large.

• Pope Francis himself has either colluded in this corruption, or, knowing what he does, is gravely negligent in failing to oppose it and uproot it.

Third Testimony: McCarrick and Ouellet

I invoked God as my witness to the truth of my claims, and none has been shown false.

Cardinal Ouellet has written to rebuke me for my temerity in breaking silence and leveling such grave accusations against my brothers and superiors, but in truth his remonstrance confirms me in my decision and, even more, serves to vindicate my claims, severally and as a whole.

• Cardinal Ouellet concedes that he spoke with me about McCarrick's situation prior to my leaving for Washington to begin my post as nuncio.

• Cardinal Ouellet concedes that he communicated to me in writing the conditions and restrictions imposed on McCarrick by Pope Benedict.

• Cardinal Ouellet concedes that these restrictions forbade McCarrick to travel or to make public appearances.

• Cardinal Ouellet concedes that the Congregation for Bishops, in writing, first through the nuncio Sambi and then once again through me, required McCarrick to lead a life of prayer and penance.

What does Cardinal Ouellet dispute?

• Cardinal Ouellet disputes the possibility that Pope Francis could have taken in important information about McCarrick on a day when he met scores of nuncios and gave each only a few moments of conversation. But this was not my testimony. My testimony is that at a second, private meeting, I informed the pope, answering his own question about Theodore McCarrick, then cardinal archbishop emeritus of Washington, prominent figure of the Church in the US, telling the pope that McCarrick had sexually corrupted his own seminarians and priests. No pope could forget that.

• Cardinal Ouellet disputes the existence in his archives of letters signed by Pope Benedict or Pope Francis regarding sanctions on McCarrick. But this was not my testimony. My testimony was that he has in his archives key documents—irrespective of provenance—incriminating McCarrick and documenting the measures taken in his regard, and other proofs on the coverup regarding his situation. And I confirm this again.

• Cardinal Ouellet disputes the existence in the files of his predecessor, Cardinal Re, of "audience memos" imposing on McCarrick the restrictions already mentioned. But this was not my testimony. My testimony is that there are other documents: for instance, a note from Card. Re not *ex-Audientia SS.mi*, or signed by the Secretary of State or by the Substitute.

• Cardinal Ouellet disputes that it is false to present the measures taken against McCarrick as "sanctions" decreed by Pope Benedict and canceled by Pope Francis. True. They were not technically "sanctions" but provisions, "conditions and restrictions." To quibble whether they were sanctions or provisions or something else is pure legalism. From a pastoral point of view they are exactly the same thing.

In brief, Cardinal Ouellet concedes the important claims that I did and do make, and disputes claims I don't make and never made.

There is one point on which I must absolutely refute what Cardinal Ouellet wrote. The cardinal states that the Holy See was only aware of "rumors," which were not enough to justify disciplinary measures against McCarrick.

I affirm to the contrary that the Holy See was aware of a variety of concrete facts, and is in possession of documentary proof, and that the responsible persons nevertheless chose not to intervene or were prevented from doing so.

Compensation by the Archdiocese of Newark and the Diocese of Metuchen to the victims of McCarrick's sexual abuse, the letters of Fr. Ramsey, of the nuncios Montalvo in 2000 and Sambi in 2006, of Dr. Sipe in 2008, my two notes to the superiors of the Secretariat of State which described in detail the concrete allegations against McCarrick; are all these just rumors?

They are official correspondence, not gossip from the sacristy.

The crimes reported were very serious, including those of attempting to give sacramental absolution to accomplices in perverse acts, with subsequent sacrilegious celebration of Mass.

These documents specify the identity of the perpetrators and their protectors, and the chronological sequence of the facts.

They are kept in the appropriate archives; no extraordinary investigation is needed to recover them.

Third Testimony: McCarrick and Ouellet

In the public remonstrances directed at me I have noted two omissions, two dramatic silences.

The first silence regards the plight of the victims.

The second regards the underlying reason why there are so many victims, namely, the corrupting influence of homosexuality in the priesthood and in the hierarchy.

As to the first, it is dismaying that, amid all the scandals and indignation, so little thought should be given to those damaged by the sexual predations of those commissioned as ministers of the gospel. This is not a matter of settling scores or sulking over the vicissitudes of ecclesiastical careers. It is not a matter of politics. It is not a matter of how church historians may evaluate this or that papacy. This is about souls. Many souls have been and are even now imperiled of their eternal salvation.

As to the second silence, this very grave crisis cannot be properly addressed and resolved unless and until we call things by their true names. This is a crisis due to the scourge of homosexuality, in its agents, in its motives, in its resistance to reform. It is no exaggeration to say that homosexuality has become a plague in the clergy, and it can only be eradicated with spiritual weapons. It is an enormous hypocrisy to condemn the abuser, to claim to weep for the victims, and yet to refuse to denounce the root cause of so much sexual abuse: homosexuality. It is hypocrisy to refuse to acknowledge that this scourge is due to a serious crisis in the spiritual life of the clergy and to fail to take the steps necessary to remedy it.

Unquestionably there exist philandering clergy, and unquestionably they too damage their own souls, the souls of those whom they corrupt, and the Church at large. But these violations of priestly celibacy are usually confined to the individuals immediately involved.

Philandering clergy usually do not recruit other philanderers, nor work to promote them, nor cover up their misdeeds—whereas the evidence for homosexual collusion, with its deep roots that are so difficult to eradicate, is overwhelming.

It is well established that homosexual predators exploit clerical privilege to their advantage.

But to claim the crisis itself to be clericalism is pure sophistry.

It is to pretend that a means, a new instrument, is in fact the main motive.

Denouncing homosexual corruption and the moral cowardice that allows it to flourish does not meet with congratulation in our times, not even in the highest spheres of the Church.

I am not surprised that in calling attention to these plagues I am charged with disloyalty to the Holy Father and with fomenting an open and scandalous rebellion. Yet rebellion would entail urging others to topple the papacy.

I am urging no such thing.

I pray every day for Pope Francis—more than I have ever done for the other popes. I am asking, indeed earnestly begging, the Holy Father to face up to the commitments he himself made in assuming his office as successor of Peter.

He took upon himself the mission of confirming his brothers and guiding all souls in following Christ, in the spiritual combat, along the way of the cross.

Let him admit his errors, repent, show his willingness to follow the mandate given to Peter and, once converted, let him confirm his brothers (Lk 22:32).

In closing, I wish to repeat my appeal to my brother bishops and priests who know that my statements are true and who can so testify, or who have access to documents that can put the matter beyond doubt.

You too are faced with a choice.

You can choose to withdraw from the battle, to prop up the conspiracy of silence and avert your eyes from the spreading of corruption.

You can make excuses, compromises and justifications that put off the day of reckoning.

You can console yourselves with the falsehood and the delusion that it will be easier to tell the truth tomorrow, and then the following day, and so on.

On the other hand, you can choose to speak.

You can trust Him who told us, "the truth will set you free."

I do not say it will be easy to decide between silence and speaking.

I urge you to consider which choice—on your deathbed, and then before the just Judge—you will not regret having made.

4

The First Reaction
to the McCarrick Report

TODAY[1] the official Report of the Holy See regarding the McCarrick case has been made public. Before I express myself on its merit, I will take time to analyze its content.

However, I cannot fail to note the surreal operation of mystification regarding who are the ones responsible for covering up the scandals of the deposed American cardinal, and at the same time I cannot help expressing my indignation in seeing the same accusations of coverup being made against me, when in fact I repeatedly denounced the inaction of the Holy See in the face of the gravity of the accusations concerning McCarrick's conduct.

An unprejudiced commentator would note the more than suspicious timing of the report's publication, as well as the attempt to throw discredit upon me, accused of disobedience and negligence by those who have every interest in delegitimizing the one who brought to light an unparalleled network of corruption and immorality. The effrontery and fraudulent character shown on this occasion would seem to require, at this point, that we call this suggestive reconstruction of the facts "The Viganò Report," sparing the reader the unpleasant surprise of seeing reality adulterated once again. But this would have required intellectual honesty, even before love for justice and the truth.

Unlike many characters involved in this story, I do not have any reason to fear that the truth will contradict my denunciations, nor am I in any way blackmailable. Anyone who launches unfounded accusations with the sole purpose of distracting the attention of

1. November 10, 2020.

public opinion will have the bitter surprise of finding that the operation conducted against me will not have any effect, other than giving further proof of the corruption and bad faith of those who for too long have been silent, made denials, and turned their gaze elsewhere, who today must be held accountable. The Vatican fiction continues.

5

The Second Reaction
to the McCarrick Report

Between the Lines of the Report of
the Secretariat of State on Theodore McCarrick

THE McCarrick Report published by the Secretariat of State on November 10, 2020, has been the object of numerous comments. Some point out its shortcomings, while others praise it as a proof of Bergoglio's transparency and the groundlessness of my accusations. I would like to focus on some aspects that deserve to be further explored, which do not concern me personally. The purpose of these reflections is thus not to adduce further evidence concerning the falsity of arguments raised against me, but rather to highlight the inconsistencies of the report and the conflict of interest that exists between the one who judges and the one being judged, which in my opinion is such as to invalidate the investigation, the trial, and the sentence.

The Disinterestedness of the Judging Body

First of all, I must say that, in contrast with a normal civil or penal trial, in ecclesiastical investigations there is a sort of implicit right to credibility in testimonies given by clerics. This seems to have allowed even testimonies of prelates who could find themselves in a position of complicity with regard to McCarrick to be considered as evidence, even though they would have had no interest in revealing the truth, since doing so would have harmed themselves and their own image. In short, to borrow an image from Carlo Collodi, it is hard to imagine that the Cat (Kevin Farrell)[1] could credibly exoner-

---

1. Before Cardinal Farrell was appointed prefect of the Dicastery for the Laity, Family, and Life, he served as bishop of Dallas. He was a protégé of McCarrick and

ate the Fox (Theodore McCarrick); yet this is what has happened, just as it was possible to deceive John Paul II about the advisability of appointing McCarrick as cardinal archbishop of Washington, or Benedict XVI about the gravity of the accusations that weighed on the cardinal.

By now it is understood that this right to credibility, when applied to the Argentine, has risen to the level of a dogma, perhaps the only dogma that cannot be questioned in the "church of mercy,"[2] especially when alternative interpretations of reality—which mortals prosaically call lies—are formulated precisely by him.

We are also left bewildered by the fact that Msgr. Farrell's testimony in defense of McCarrick has been reported with emphasis— the bishop is even referred to with the title of "Most Excellent"—but that at the same time the testimony of James Grein was completely omitted, just as the choice was prudently made not to take a deposition from the Secretaries of State Sodano and Bertone. Nor is it clear for what reason Farrell's words in defense of his friend and housemate are considered valid and credible, while mine are not, even though I am an archbishop and Apostolic Nuncio. The only reason I can identify is that while Farrell's words confirm Bergoglio's thesis, mine refute it and demonstrate that it was not only the bishop of Dallas who was lying.

It should also be remembered that Cardinal Wuerl, McCarrick's successor on the chair of Washington, resigned on October 12, 2018, due to pressure from public opinion after his repeated denials of having been aware of the depraved conduct of his brother bishop. Yet in 2004 Wuerl had to handle the complaint made by Robert Ciolek, a former priest of the Diocese of Metuchen, against McCarrick, sending it to the then-Apostolic Nuncio Msgr. Gabriel Montalvo. In 2009, it was Wuerl who ordered McCarrick's transfer from Redemptoris Mater Seminary to Saint Thomas the Apostle Parish in Washington, and in 2010 it was Wuerl himself, along with the Presi-

_____

lived in the same residence with him during the time that some of the cases of abuse are alleged to have occurred. He was made a cardinal by Francis in 2016.

2. Here Archbishop Viganò refers to a theme of this pontificate. Francis declared 2016 a "Jubilee Year of Mercy": see www.im.va/content/gdm/en.html.

dent of the Bishops' Conference, Cardinal Francis George, who advised the Secretariat of State against sending a congratulatory message to McCarrick on the occasion of his 80th birthday. The Report also cites the correspondence between Nuncio Sambi and Wuerl concerning the danger of scandal surrounding McCarrick's person; the same may be said for the correspondence of Cardinal Re, the Prefect of the Congregation for Bishops, which confirms that Wuerl "constantly favored McCarrick even when he was not living in the seminary." It is therefore very strange that the serious suspicions which weighed on the cardinal prior to my appointment [as Nuncio], which are amply documented in the Report, are considered grounds for censure against me—despite my having once again notified the Secretariat of State about them—but not against Wuerl, who even after his resignation as archbishop of Washington retained his posts in the Roman Dicasteries, including the Congregation for Bishops where he retained his voice in the appointment of bishops.

It is not clear why the drafters of the Report are so casual in judging John Paul II for having put faith in his secretary's words in defense of McCarrick, yet so absolving towards Bergoglio, despite the fact that there was a pile of dossiers concerning "Uncle Ted," whom Bergoglio's predecessor had requested to "keep a low profile."

I believe the time has come to clarify once and for all the position of the judging body—*rectius*:[3] of *this* judging body—with respect to the accused.

According to the law, a judge must be impartial, and in order to be such he must not have any interest or connection with the one being judged. In reality, this impartiality fails in one of the most sensational canonical processes in the history of the Church, in which the scandals and crimes alleged against the accused are of such gravity that they merited his deposition from being a cardinal and his reduction to the lay state.

The Absence of a True Condemnation

It is necessary to emphasize the extreme mildness of the sentence inflicted on the offender, indeed one could even say its absence,

---

3. Latin: "more correctly."

since the one accused was only deprived of the clerical state with an administrative procedure from the tribunal of the Congregation for the Doctrine of the Faith, ratified as *res iudicata*[4] by Bergoglio. And yet it would have been possible to give him a prison sentence, as was done for the counselor at the Nunciature in Washington who in 2018 was sentenced to five years in prison in the Vatican for the possession and dissemination of child pornography.

In truth, dismissal from the clerical state reveals the essence of that *clericalism*—so deplored in words—which considers the lay state almost as a punishment in itself, while it ought to be the premise for the imposition of a penal sanction. Among other things, the lack of imprisonment or at least house arrest permits McCarrick to have a total freedom of movement and action that keeps his situation unchanged. He is therefore in a position to commit new crimes and to continue to carry out his criminal activities in both the ecclesial and political spheres.

Finally, it should be remembered that the canonical process does not eliminate the criminal cases against the former cardinal which have been introduced in American courts, which strangely languish in the utmost secrecy, further demonstrating McCarrick's political power and media influence not only in the Vatican but also in the United States.

Conflicts of Interest and Omissions

It is difficult to look at the "judge" of this case without considering the fact that he may find himself in a position of having a debt of gratitude towards the accused and his accomplices: that is, that he has a clear conflict of interest.

If Jorge Mario Bergoglio owes his election to the conspiracy of the so-called Saint Gallen Mafia, which included ultraprogressive cardinals in constant and assiduous relationship with McCarrick; if McCarrick's endorsement of candidate Bergoglio found a hearing among the conclave electors and those who have the power of persuasion in the Vatican, for example the famous "Italian gentleman"

---

4. Latin: "a matter (already) judged." As a legal term it means the matter has been legally decided and cannot be tried or reevaluated by a court.

whom the American cardinal referred to in a 2013 conference at Villanova University;[5] if the resignation of Benedict XVI was in some way provoked or favored by interference from the deep church and the deep state,[6] it is logical to suppose that Bergoglio and his collaborators did not have any intention of letting the names of McCarrick's accomplices leak into the Report, nor the names of those who favored him in his ecclesiastical *cursus honorum*, nor above all the names of those who in the face of the possibility of a conviction could in some way take revenge—for example, by revealing the involvement of prominent personalities of the Roman Curia, if not of Bergoglio himself.

In blatant contradiction of the claimed pretense of transparency, the Report took great care not to reveal the acts of the administrative process. It is therefore possible to ask if McCarrick's defense may have agreed to the sentencing of his client in exchange for a ridiculously small sentence that in fact leaves the offender who committed such serious crimes in total freedom, while preventing the victims from challenging the "judge" and demanding fair compensation. Certainly, the anomaly is obvious, even to those who are not experts in the law.

The Shared Interests of the Deep Church and the Deep State[7]
In this network of complicity and blackmail, it is also possible to highlight ties of both the "judge" and the accused with politics, in particular with the American Democratic Party, with Communist China, and more generally with the globalist movements and parties. The fact that in 2004 McCarrick, who was then archbishop of Washington, worked strenuously to prevent the dissemination of the letter of the then-Prefect of the Congregation for the Doctrine of

5. The Villanova lecture can be watched here: youtu.be/b3iaBLqt8vg.

6. Reports have surfaced that the US deep state intelligence agencies were spying on the Vatican before the conclave that elected Francis. See, for example, "US Spied on Vatican before Conclave—Report," *The Local IT,* October 30, 2013, www.thelocal.it/20131030/us-spied-on-vatican-ahead-of-conclave-report.

7. In this section Viganò touches on the theme of his writings collected in Part III. The deep state and the deep church seem to work in a coordinated manner toward the same evil ends.

the Faith, Joseph Cardinal Ratzinger, to the bishops of the United States with regard to the ban on administering Holy Communion to politicians who support abortion, undoubtedly represents an assist to self-styled Catholic Democratic politicians, beginning with John Kerry[8] all the way up to Joe Biden. The latter, a convinced supporter of abortion, merited the almost unanimous support of the hierarchy, thus being able to count on the votes of an electorate that would otherwise have been destined for Trump. Strange coincidences, to be honest: on the one hand the deep state struck at the Church and Benedict XVI with the intention of electing a representative of the deep church as pope; on the other hand the deep church struck at the State and Trump with the intention of electing a representative of the deep state as President. Let the reader judge whether the plans of the conspirators have achieved their intended purpose.

This collusion with the global Left is the necessary corollary of a much larger project, in which the fifth columns of dissolution that have penetrated into the heart of the Church actively collaborate with the deep state following a single script under a single direction: the actors in this *pièce* [play] have different parts, but they follow the same plot on the same stage.

Analogies with the Pandemic and the Electoral Fraud

On closer inspection, both the pandemic and the electoral fraud in the United States have disturbing similarities to the McCarrick case and to what is happening in the Church. Those who have to decide whether to confine the entire population at home or to obligate it to be vaccinated make use of unreliable detection tools, precisely because by means of these they succeed in falsifying the data, with the complicity of the mainstream media. It matters little whether the virus has a mortality rate similar to that of a seasonal flu or if the number of deceased is similar to that of preceding years: someone has decided that there simply *is* a pandemic and that the world economy must be demolished in order to create the premise for the

---

8. The letter sent by Cardinal Ratzinger was in response to the candidacy of John Kerry, a pro-abortion Catholic candidate for president.

Great Reset.[9] Rational arguments, scientific evaluations, and the experience of serious scientists engaged in the care of patients are all worth nothing in the face of the script that has been imposed on the actors. The same holds true for the elections in the United States: in the face of the evidence of fraud—which is acquiring the contours of a true and proper *coup d'état* carried out by criminal minds—the media insist on presenting Joe Biden as the victor, and world leaders—including the Holy See[10]—are in a hurry to acknowledge his victory, to discredit his Republican adversaries, and to present Trump as a lonely bully who is about to be abandoned by his family and even by the First Lady. It matters little that there are dozens and dozens of videos on the internet showing the irregularities committed during the counting of the votes, or that there are hundreds of testimonies of fraud: the Democrats, the media, and the entire cast repeat that Biden is President-Elect and that Trump should step aside. Because, in the kingdom of lies, if reality does not correspond to the narrative, it is reality that must be corrected and censured. Thus, millions of people in the streets to protest against the lockdown or against electoral fraud simply do not exist, because of the simple fact that the mainstream media does not show them on television and censors them on the internet, and that whatever it denounces as fake news must acritically[11] be considered as such.

The Enslavement of Part of the Hierarchy
It is therefore not surprising that the United States Conference of

---

9. The Great Reset is a plan of the World Economic Forum to destroy the current economic and political system and replace it with a completely new system. Their motto is to "build back better." See Part III for further analysis.

10. According to many reports, Pope Francis called Biden to congratulate him on November 12, 2020. See, e.g., Amanda Macias, "Biden speaks with Pope Francis, the latest world leader to acknowledge the new president-elect," *CNBC*, November 12, 2020, www.cnbc.com/2020/11/12/joe-biden-speaks-with-pope-francis.html. The US Conference of Catholic Bishops also acknowledged and congratulated Biden. See, e.g., "US Catholic bishops congratulate Biden as president-elect," *Catholic News Agency*, November 7, 2020, www.catholicnewsagency.com/news/us-catholic-bishops-congratulate-biden-as-president-elect-44702.

11. By this Viganò means that the media expects its lies to be accepted as true, without critical thought.

Catholic Bishops, followed like clockwork by Vatican News and an affectionate phone call from Bergoglio to Biden, made haste to give proof of its fidelity to the system: these ecclesiastics are intrinsically involved and must scrupulously stick to the part that has been given to them. They did the same, on the global level, by supporting COVID restrictions with the closure of the churches, ordering the suspension of the celebration of Masses and even inviting the faithful to obey the civil authorities. The archbishop of Washington allowed himself to criticize the official visit of the First Couple to the Shrine of Saint John Paul II[12] and expressed himself, along with other bishops and clerics, in support of BLM:[13] such self-sacrifice for the cause merited him the cardinal's red hat during these very days. And it is no coincidence that adherence to the globalist agenda comes from people who are fully compromised in supporting the LGBTQ movements, beginning with Cupich, Tobin, Wuerl, McElroy, and Stowe. The deafening silence of the Holy See and the world episcopate in the face of ethical problems posed by the soon-to-be-distributed vaccines, which contain cells from aborted human fetuses, is quite significant. God forbid that the speculation of the pharmaceutical companies on the pandemic also sees the deep church as the recipient of generous "donations"—as has already happened with the Agreement between China and the Vatican.[14]

Vices and corruption find the deep church and deep state united in a cesspool of repugnant crimes, in which the defenseless and

---

12. On June 1, 2020, President Trump paid a visit to this Catholic shrine. The archbishop of Washington criticized the visit and the Knights of Columbus who administer the shrine. See "'I find it baffling and reprehensible': Catholic archbishop of Washington slams Trump's visit to John Paul II shrine," *Washington Post*, June 2, 2020, www.washingtonpost.com/religion/2020/06/02/trump-catholic-shrine-church-bible-protesters.

13. Black Lives Matter is a Marxist-inspired organization that supports positions contrary to Catholic truth, such as gay "marriage" and the destruction of the nuclear family. See "Can Catholics support 'Black Lives Matter'?," *CNA*, June 17, 2020, www.catholicnewsagency.com/news/can-catholics-support-black-lives-matter-92926.

14. In other documents contained in Part III, Archbishop Viganò claims that the Vatican has received extensive sums of money from China in payment for the agreement reached with the Chinese Communist Party in 2018. There is docu-

children are the victims of exploitation, violence, and harassment committed by characters who at the same time promote abortion, gender ideology, and the sexual freedom of minors, including sex changes.

Illegal immigration as well—which is supported in order to destabilize nations and cancel their identities—finds support from both the Left as well as the church of Bergoglio, despite the fact that it is directly connected with the trafficking of minors, the increase of criminality and the destruction of the social fabric. Indeed, it is supported for precisely this reason, just as there has been a desire to encourage the political crisis in the US elections, the economic crisis through the criminal manipulation of the pandemic, and possibly also religious warfare via the Islamic attacks and profanations of churches throughout Europe.

The Need for an Overview

It is also very disconcerting that, in this perfectly coherent framework, there are many prelates—if not almost all of them—who limit themselves to analyzing the events that affect the Catholic Church almost as if they existed only in the ecclesial sphere, as if they did not have any relation with the political and social events that are unfolding on the global level. There are bishops who formulate some timid stances in the face of Bergoglio's words in support of the legalization of civil unions, or over the inconsistencies and falsifications that emerge in the McCarrick Report; but none of them, even if animated by good intentions, dares to denounce the evidence of the facts, namely the existence of a *pactum sceleris*[15] between the deviant part of the hierarchy—the deep church, precisely—and the deviant part of the State, of the world of finance and information. Yet it is so evident that it has been the object of analysis by numerous, mostly secular, intellectuals.

---

mented evidence of acknowledged "donations": see, e.g., "Vatican thanks Chinese groups for donations to combat coronavirus," *CNA*, April 9, 2020, www.catholic-newsagency.com/news/vatican-thanks-chinese-groups-for-donations-to-combat-c oronavirus-23469.

15. Latin for "an agreement or contract to commit crimes."

The Loss of Credibility

This point must be denounced loudly: the Report drawn up by the Secretariat of State is an indecent and clumsy attempt to give a semblance of credibility to a gang of perverted and corrupt men in the service of the New World Order. The surreal thing is that this operation of impudent mystification has been carried out, not by the accused, but by those who ought to judge him, and along with him they paradoxically ought to judge themselves, their brothers, their friends, and those to whom they guaranteed impunity, promotions, and careers.

The credibility of the writers of the Report may be demonstrated from its mild condemnation of a prelate organic to the system, whom Bergoglio himself sent as an interlocutor of the Holy See with the Chinese communist dictatorship, and who at the same time carried out official assignments on behalf of the US State Department, frequenting the Clintons, Obamas, Bidens, and the Democrats. This credibility may also be confirmed by the fact that a corrupt homosexual, a molester of young men and children, a corrupter of clergy and seminarians, was simply deprived of the dignity of cardinal and of the clerical state without any prison sentence and without excommunicating him for the delicts with which he stained himself, including the crime of *sollicitatio ad turpia*[16] in Confession, one of the most hateful crimes that a priest can commit. In this "process," as summary as it was omissory, the spiritual dimension of guilt was completely absent: the guilty party was not subjected to excommunication, which is an eminently medicinal sanction ordered towards eternal salvation, nor was he exhorted to do penance, to make public amends and reparation.

An Independent Commission

When the Nuremberg trials were held after World War II against the crimes of Nazism, the court was presided over by a Russian judge who was charged with judging the invasion of Poland that Ger-

---

16. Latin for "solicitation to commit a grave sin against the sixth commandment (obscene sin)." Viganò is alluding to the allegation that McCarrick offered to absolve those he solicited to engage in unnatural acts with him.

many, as we know, had undertaken precisely with Russia. It seems to me that there is not much difference between this and what we see happening today in the attempt to lay responsibility for the McCarrick case on John Paul II, Benedict XVI, and the undersigned. The only one who in the narrative of the Secretariat of State cannot be touched by any suspicion, by any accusation—even if only indirect—or by any shadow of coverup, should obviously be the Argentine.

It would seem appropriate for an independent commission to be constituted—as was already hoped for by the US Bishops' Conference in November 2018 and as was then firmly blocked by the Congregation for Bishops at the order of Bergoglio—that would investigate this case without external influences and without hiding decisive evidence. However, I doubt that the improbable hopes of the US Bishops' Conference will be heard, since among those being raised to cardinal in the upcoming consistory is the archbishop of Washington,[17] the executor of Santa Marta's orders, who joins the most faithful servants Cupich and Tobin.

If light would truly be shed on the entire affair, the whole house of cards constructed in these years would collapse, and the complicity of members of the hierarchy at the highest levels would also emerge, as well as their ties with the American Democrats and the global Left. In short, there would be confirmed what many do not yet dare admit, namely, the role played by the deep church, since the election of John XXIII, in creating the theological premises and the ecclesial climate that would allow the Church to be the servant of the New World Order and to replace the pope with the false prophet of the Antichrist. If this has not yet completely happened, we must give thanks only to Providence.

Intellectual Honesty

I imagine that the moderates—as silent today in the face of COVID as they are in deploring the electoral fraud or the farce of the McCarrick Report—are horrified at the mere mention of calling into ques-

17. Wilton Gregory, archbishop of Washington, D.C., who as noted earlier attacked President Trump for visiting the John Paul II shrine.

tion the Second Vatican Council. The Democrats too are horrified to hear criticism of the laws thanks to which the United States has come to see the will of the voters subverted. The self-styled health experts are horrified to see their claims contested which contrast with the scientific truth and with the epidemiological evidence. The supporters of the reception of illegal immigrants are horrified when they are shown the rate of murder, rape, violence and robbery committed by those same illegal immigrants. The supporters of the gay lobby are horrified when the criminal offenses of a predatory nature committed by clerics are shown to involve a very high percentage of homosexuals. In this general tearing of garments, I would like to recall that it would be enough to have a little intellectual honesty and a little critical judgment to look the evidence in the face, even if it is painful.

The Link between Heresy and Sodomy

This intrinsic link between doctrinal deviation and moral deviation emerged clearly on the occasion of the head-on clash with those covering up the McCarrick case: the people involved are almost always the same, with the same vices against faith and morals. They defend, cover for, and promote each other, because they are part of a true and proper "lobby," understood as a group holding power that is capable of influencing the activity of the legislator and the decisions of the government or the other administrative organs to their own advantage.

In the ecclesiastical field, this lobby works to cancel the moral condemnation of sodomy, and it does so first of all for its own advantage, since it is primarily composed of sodomites. It adapts to the political agenda in legitimizing the demands of the LGBTQ movements, promoted by politicians who are no less given over to vice. And the role played by the Catholic Church in recent decades is also evident—or better said, by its morally and doctrinally deviant part—in opening the Overton window[18] on homosexuality, in such a way that the sin against nature that the Church has always con-

18. This expression refers to the range of policies deemed acceptable by the so-called mainstream at any given time. It is named for James P. Overton, who popularized the idea that policies must be conceived or publicized within this spectrum.

demned was somehow disavowed from the evidence of the increasingly emergent scandals. If forty years ago it was horrifying to learn about a priest molesting a little boy, for some years now the news has been informing us of the raid of the Vatican Gendarmerie in the apartment of the secretary of Cardinal Coccopalmerio in the palace of the Holy Office, where a party was being held by clergy with drugs and prostitutes. From here it will be a relatively small step to legitimizing pedophilia, as certain politicians would like: the premises made by the theorization of the alleged "sexual rights" of minors, the imposition of sexual education in primary schools at the recommendation of the United Nations, and the attempts to pass legislation in Parliaments to lower the age of consent are all heading in the same direction. Some naive person—assuming that it is still possible to speak of naivety—will say that the Church will never be able to say that she is in favor of the corruption of children, because this would contradict the uninterrupted Catholic Magisterium. I limit myself to recalling what was said only a few years ago with regard to so-called homosexual "matrimony"—or about the ordination of women, ecclesiastical celibacy, or the abolition of the death penalty—and that which *vice versa* is affirmed with impunity today, to the world's applause.

The McCarrick "Line"

What should be noted in the Report is not so much what it contains as what it is silent about and what it hides under a mountain of documents and testimonies, no matter how horrifying they may be. Many journalists and many ecclesiastics were aware of the scandalous life of the "man with the red hat," but nevertheless considered him Machiavellianly useful to the interests of the Democratic Party expression of the deep state and the progressive Catholic expression of the deep church. As the *Washingtonian* wrote in 2004: "With a controversial Catholic in the presidential race [John Kerry], the cardinal is seen by many as the Vatican's man in Washington—and he may play a big role in the selection of the next pope."[19] A role

19. VN: www.getreligion.org/getreligion/2020/11/12/new-podcast-was-there-more-than-one-team-ted-that-helped-keep-mccarrick-in-power.

McCarrick proudly claimed in the address he gave on October 11, 2013, at Villanova University, and that today, with Cardinal Farrell raised by Bergoglio's appointment to Camerlengo of the Holy Roman Church, could be realized once again. Given the relationships of loyalty that are consolidated between the members of the "lavender mafia," it is at least reasonable to think that McCarrick is still able to intervene in the election of the pope, not only thanks to his network of friends and accomplices, some of whom are cardinals electors, but also by playing an active role in the procedures of the conclave and its preparation.

Would we be surprised if, after noting the electoral fraud in the presidential election in the United States, "someone" would even try to manipulate the election of the Supreme Pontiff? Let us not forget that, as has already been noted by several parties, on the fourth vote of the second day of the last conclave an irregularity emerged in the counting of the ballots, which was remedied by a new vote, in derogation from the provisions of the Apostolic Constitution *Universi Dominici Gregis* promulgated by John Paul II in 1996.[20]

It is however significant that, while on the one hand McCarrick is now ousted from his functions and resides in a secret locality (where he can continue undisturbed in his paradiplomatic activity on behalf of the deep state and the deep church in the anonymous guise of a layman), on the other hand all those who have made a career in the Church thanks to McCarrick are still in their places and have even been promoted: all people whom he favored because of a common lifestyle and common intentions; all blackmailable and blackmailers because of the secrets which they have come to know thanks to their position; all of them ready to pull out names and circumstances and dates if anyone dares to touch them. Some could still be forced to obey Mr. McCarrick, if he can keep them under blackmail or bribe them with the huge money at his disposal, even now that he is no longer a prince of the Church.

---

20. According to the rules that govern the functioning of the conclave, balloting may occur only four times in a day. The reports to which the archbishop refer claim that in the 2013 Conclave a fifth ballot was taken contrary to the rules, after the fourth ballot was found to have some irregularity.

The Second Reaction to the McCarrick Report

The "line" which this cardinal began is today capable—as we see—of interfering and working in the life of the Church and society, with the advantage of having discharged the sins of the entire "lavender mafia" onto a convenient scapegoat and to be able to appear today as if it is a stranger to allegations of abuse. But it is enough to walk through the gates of the Porta Angelica to come across unpresentable characters, some of whom have been called to the Vatican to save them from investigations that were pending on them abroad; others are even regulars at Santa Marta or perform managerial duties there, consolidating the network of connivances and complicities under the indulgent eyes of the Prince. On the other hand, the emphasis on Bergoglio's moralizing role smashes against the crude reality that nothing has ever really changed behind the high Leonine Wall, given the protection enjoyed by, among others, Peña Parra and Zanchetta.

The Failure to Condemn Sodomy

Some commentators have rightly highlighted a disheartening fact: the crimes for which McCarrick was summoned to judgment only concern the abuse of minors, while his unnatural relationships with consenting adults are quietly accepted and tolerated, as if the immoral and sacrilegious acts of a cleric are not to be deplored, but rather only his imprudence in not having known how to keep them within the secrecy of the home. This too will have to be accounted for by those responsible, above all in consideration of Bergoglio's increasingly clear will to apply a laxist pastoral approach—according to the tested method of *Amoris Lætitia*—in derogation of the moral condemnation of sodomy.

The Guilty and the Victims of the Scandals

The paradoxical thing that emerges from the scandals of the clergy is that the latest concern of Bergoglio's magic circle is to give justice to the victims, not only by compensating them (which, moreover, is not done by the perpetrators but by the dioceses, using the goods donated by the faithful) but also by punishing those responsible in an exemplary way. There ought to be punishment not only for delicts recognized as penal crimes by the laws of the State, but also for moral delicts, by which adults have been led into grave sin by sacred ministers. Who will heal the wounds of the soul, the stains on the purity of so many youths, including also seminarians and priests? By contrast, it appears that those who have been discovered and exposed to public execration consider themselves to be true victims: they feel they have been hindered in their interests, their trafficking, and their intrigues. Meanwhile, those who have denounced scandals, who ask for justice and truth, are considered guilty,[21] beginning with priests who are transferred or deprived of the care of souls because they have dared to inform their bishop of the perversions of one of their brothers.

The Holy Church is the Victim of the Crimes of Her Ministers

But there is another completely innocent victim of these scandals: the Holy Church. The image of the Spouse of Christ has been tarnished, humiliated and discredited, because those who committed these crimes acted by exploiting the trust placed in the dress which they wear, using their own role as priest or prelate to ensnare and corrupt souls. The ones responsible for this discrediting of the Church include also those in the Vatican, in dioceses, in convents, in Catholic schools and in religious organizations—we think, for example, of the Boy Scouts—who did not eradicate this scourge in the bud but even hid it and denied it. By now it is evident that this invasion of homosexuals and perverts was planned and intended: it was not a fortuitous event that occurred only due to the omission of controls, but rather a precise plan of systematic infiltration of the Church in order to demolish it from within. And those to whom the Lord has entrusted the governance of His Spouse will have to answer to Him for this.

In all of this, however, our adversaries forget that the Church is not a faceless collection of persons without faces who blindly obey mercenaries, but rather a Living Body with a Divine Head: Our Lord Jesus Christ. To think of being able to kill the Spouse of Christ without the Spouse intervening is a delusion that only Satan could

21. VN: www.churchmilitant.com/news/article/exclusive-interview-fr-mark-white.

believe possible. Indeed, he will come to realize that precisely in crucifying her, in covering her with spit and lashes of the whip just as the Savior was crucified two thousand years ago, he is signing his own definitive defeat. *O mors, ero mors tua: morsus tuus ero, inferne* [O death, I will be your death: Hell, I shall be your sting] (cf. Hos 13:14).

November 21, 2020
Presentation of the Most Blessed Virgin Mary

6

The Faithful
Have a Right to Know[1]

January 31, 2020

WE have just been through one of the most disgraceful episodes in which we have seen the prince of lies at work to discredit the book of Pope Benedict XVI and Cardinal Robert Sarah by covering them with vile insults and vulgar insinuations, and the pope's jailer, as a Judas, now also acting as a hitman. And once again we find ourselves dealing with another masterpiece of deception: the confirmation by the pope of the elections of the new Dean and Vice-Dean of the College of Cardinals by the Cardinal-Bishops. This has gone almost unnoticed and yet conceals a devious strategy. It should be borne in mind, in fact, that in June 2018 Pope Francis increased the number of Cardinal-Bishops, which had remained unchanged for centuries, promoting four new ones in one fell swoop. In this way, he secured a majority in favor of him, as he has always done with the creation of new members of the College of Cardinals.

To Cardinal Giovanni Battista Re, appointed Dean of the College at the age of 86 and therefore excluded from the next conclave, I wish an even longer life than that of his father. But his appointment is a cover for that other more effective appointment—of Cardinal Sandri—which has been prepared ad hoc to pilot the next conclave *secundum Franciscum*, that is, according to an updated and augmented edition of the St. Gallen Mafia.

I have a longstanding friendship with Cardinal Sandri that dates back to the time shared in the Pontifical Ecclesiastical Academy,

1. The English translation by Diane Montagna first appeared at https://inside-thevatican.com/news/newsflash/letter-4-2020-vigano-on-next-conclave.

then during eleven years in the same office as secretaries to three Substitutes of the Secretariat of State, and seven years of collaboration once he was appointed Substitute for General Affairs in the Secretariat of State, having returned after just six months from his mission as Nuncio to Mexico.

Amicus Plato sed magis amica veritas [I am a friend of Plato, but more a friend of truth]. This maxim, attributed to Aristotle, used also by Plato towards Socrates and later by Cicero, is explained by St. Thomas Aquinas in *Sententia libri Ethicorum*, book 1, lectio 6, nn. 4–5 as follows:

> That truth should be preferred to friends he proves in this way. He is the greater friend for whom we ought to have greater consideration. Although we should have friendship for both truth and our fellow man, we ought rather to love truth because we should love our fellow man especially on account of truth and virtue. . . . Now truth is a most excellent friend of the sort to whom the homage of honor is due. Besides, truth is a divine thing, for it is found first and chiefly in God. He concludes, therefore, that it is virtuous to honor truth above friends.[2]

Which is why what I am about to write concerning Cardinal Leonardo Sandri is inspired solely by the friendship that has bound me to him for almost fifty years, for the good of his soul, for the love of the Truth who is Christ Himself, and for the Church, His Bride, whom we served together.

In the first audience that Francis granted me after the one on June 23, 2013, that I have already mentioned (in my first testimony), in which he asked me about Cardinal McCarrick, he asked me a similar question: "What is Cardinal Sandri like?" Caught by surprise

---

2. "Quod autem oporteat veritatem praeferre amicis, ostendit hac ratione. Quia ei qui est magis amicus, magis est deferendum. Cum autem amicitiam habeamus ad ambo, scilicet ad veritatem et ad hominem, magis debemus veritatem amare quam hominem, quia hominem praecipue debemus amare propter veritatem et propter virtutem... Veritas autem est amicus superexcellens cui debetur reverentia honoris; est etiam veritas quiddam divinum, in Deo enim primo et principaliter invenitur. Et ideo concludit, quod sanctum est praehonorare veritatem hominibus amicis."

by the question about a dear friend of mine, and feeling put on the spot, I did not answer. Then Francis, joining his hands in a characteristically Italian gesture, waved them back and forth—as if to say that Sandri "knows how to get by"—and he looked me in the eyes seeking my consent to his suggestion. So I told him in confidence: "Holy Father, I don't know if you are aware that Nuncio Justo Mullor, President of the Pontifical Ecclesiastical Academy, was removed from the Apostolic Nunciature in Mexico because he opposed the directives coming from the Secretariat of State to cover up the very serious accusations against Marcial Maciel." This is what I told the pope, so that he would take it into account and eventually remedy the injustice that Archbishop Mullor had suffered for not compromising himself, for remaining faithful to the truth, and for love of the Church. I reaffirm this truth here, so as to honor this faithful servant of the Holy See, on whose tomb, in the cathedral of Almeria, Spain, I celebrated a Holy Mass of suffrage.

I already wrote in my first testimony that the person chiefly responsible for covering up the misdeeds committed by Maciel was then-Secretary of State Cardinal Angelo Sodano, whose recent acceptance to resign as Dean of the College of Cardinals was linked to his involvement in the Maciel affair. He, in addition to protecting Maciel, is certainly no stranger to McCarrick's promotions...

Meanwhile, Cardinal Francis Arinze deserves to be recognized for having opposed, within the Congregation for the Doctrine of the Faith, Sodano's attempt to cover up the Maciel case.

Unfortunately for him, Sandri also allowed himself to be involved by Sodano in this operation to cover up Maciel's horrible misdeeds. To replace Archbishop Mullor in Mexico City, it was necessary to appoint a person of unfailing loyalty to Sodano. Sandri had already given proof of this as Assessor for the section of General Affairs in the Secretariat of State. Serving at the time as Nuncio in Venezuela for just a little over two years, he was transferred to Mexico.

I was a direct witness to these shady maneuvers (which those in charge would describe as normal personnel transfers) through a conversation they had on January 25, 2000, the feast of the Conversion of St Paul, while we were on our way to the Basilica that bears his name, for the closing of the Week of Prayer for Christian Unity.

The Faithful Have a Right to Know

The chain linking the dates of these transfers is very significant: on January 19, 2000, Archbishop Giorgio Zur, who had been President of the Pontifical Ecclesiastical Academy (PAE) for only one year, was transferred to Moscow; on February 11, 2000, Archbishop Justo Mullor, who at this point had been in Mexico for just two and a half years, was appointed President of the PAE; on March 1, 2000, Archbishop Sandri was transferred to Mexico after spending only two and a half years in Venezuela. Just six months later, on September 16, 2000, Sandri was promoted to Substitute of the Secretariat of State, i.e., Sodano's right-hand man.

The Legionaries of Christ did not fail to show their gratitude to Sandri. On the occasion of a lunch held in the atrium of the Paul VI Hall to honor the cardinals, including Sandri, who were created at the November 24, 2007 consistory, I was bewildered when Sandri told me in advance what he was about to tell Pope Benedict as he made his entrance: "Holy Father, you will excuse me if I don't stay for lunch, but I am expected by five hundred of my guests at the Legionaries of Christ."

Francis, after having repeatedly and obsessively referred to an unspecified "clericalism" as the cause of sexual abuse, in order to avoid denouncing the scourge of homosexuality, is now flaunting the most unscrupulous clericalism (an accusation he levels at others): he promotes Sandri to Cardinal-Priest in May 2018 and a month later to Cardinal-Bishop, so that he might confirm him as Vice-Dean of the College of Cardinals, a candidate prepared by Francis to preside at the next Conclave.

The faithful have a right to know these sordid intrigues of a corrupt court. In the Heart of the Church we seem to glimpse the approaching shadow of Satan's synagogue (Rev 2:9).

PART II

A VOICE DECRYING THE REVOLUTION IN TIARA AND COPE: VATICAN II

Introduction to Part II

IN his response to the sham report on McCarrick, Archbishop Viganò noted that a root cause of the toleration of the evil of sodomy among clerics lay in the attempt to change theology that began in the Second Vatican Council. During the two years between the Testimony and the McCarrick report, Archbishop Viganò spent much time tracing the roots of the homosexual scandals in the Church. The conclusion he reached is that those roots were sown in the Second Vatican Council and its implementation. As he will explain, this conclusion involved a significant conversion of thought for the archbishop. He spent his entire ecclesiastical career primarily serving two popes, John Paul II and Benedict XVI, who held up the Council as a watershed and irreversible moment in the Church's life, a lens through which everything has to be seen. In his discussion of the Council, Viganò must admit that he was wrong for many decades about the attempt to save the Council, an admission that is difficult for anyone to make, especially publicly.

To introduce the topic of Vatican II is a vast challenge that would take a book in and of itself. In fact, many books have been written on the subject, the most comprehensive of which is Professor Roberto de Mattei's *The Second Vatican Council—An Unwritten Story*.[1]

Background to the Council

Where to begin a discussion of the Second Vatican Council is a difficult question to answer. In this context I can only sketch the historical context briefly. Since the outbreak of the French Revolution (1789), the Church has been engaged in a struggle against a revolu-

---

1. Fitzwilliam, NH: Loreto Publications, 2012. De Mattei's work is a comprehensive history of the Council as historical event. A work that analyzes the Council and its implementation as intellectual history (or the history of ideas) is Romano Amerio, *Iota Unum: A Study of Changes in the Catholic Church in the Twentieth Century*, 2nd ed. (Kansas City, MO: Sarto House, 1996).

tion that operates under many names: Liberalism, Secularism, Naturalism, etc. In the initial phase of the Revolution, the enemies of the Church attempted to destroy her from without by persecution. Priests and faithful Catholics were executed and imprisoned for refusing to renounce their faith. Over the course of the nineteenth century, the nature of the conflict began to change. In lieu of, and in some cases in addition to, persecution from without, the forces of the Revolution attempted to change the Church from within. The so-called Liberal Catholics strove to temper or moderate the teachings of the Church to make them more acceptable to the post-Revolutionary era. The popes of the nineteenth century were staunchly antirevolutionary. Several high water marks of this resistance to revolutionary ideas appear in *Quanta Cura* and the *Syllabus of Errors* of Pius IX and the encyclicals *Diuturnum Illud, Immortale Dei,* and *Libertas Præstantissimum* of Leo XIII.

Playing its own role in the Revolution to change the Church was the activity of Freemasonry. This worldwide secret society emerged officially in 1717 and played a significant role in fomenting the French Revolution. The Church repeatedly condemned Freemasonry and forbade Catholics to have anything to do with it on pain of excommunication.[2] Unlike the persecutions of the French Revolution, Freemasonry sought to infiltrate the Church so as to remake the Church in Freemasonry's image over the course of time. An internal document containing plans to infiltrate the Church, *The Permanent Instruction of the Alta Vendita,* fell into the hands of the popes.[3] Pius IX and Leo XIII ordered its publication to warn the Church against this evil organization's endeavors. What is striking

---

2. Pope Clement XII was the first to condemn Freemasonry and prohibit Catholic participation in the bull *In Eminenti* (1738). This condemnation was confirmed and repeated by Benedict XIV (1751), Pius VII (1821), Leo XII (1825), Pius VIII (1829), Gregory XVI (1832), and Pius IX (1846, 1849, 1864, 1865, 1869, 1873). See Peter A. Kwasniewski, "Freemasonry and Catholicism: Implacable Enemies," *The Remnant* online, July 22, 2020.

3. See John Vennari, *The Permanent Instruction of the Alta Vendita* (Rockford, IL: TAN Books and Publishing, 1999), which contains extensive excerpts from the document as well as an introduction and explanation. The *Permanent Instruction* is

Introduction to Part II

about the plan unveiled in *The Permanent Instruction* is that it does not propose attempting to initiate the princes of the Church into the secret sect. Rather, the idea was to plant certain seeds in the Church so that churchmen would unwittingly begin to adopt the ideas of Freemasonry. The *Alta Vendita* explains:

> You wish to establish the reign of the elect upon the throne of the prostitute of Babylon? Let the clergy march under your banner in the belief always that they march under the banner of the Apostolic Keys. . . . Lay your nets like Simon Barjona. Lay them in the depths of sacristies, seminaries, and convents. . . . You will bring yourselves as friends around the Apostolic Chair. You will have fished up a Revolution in Tiara and Cope,[4] marching with Cross and banner.

Rather than attacking the Church directly as in 1789, the plan was to put their false ideas into circulation surreptitiously. The text advises Freemasons to appear as devout Catholics, go to Confession, and live apparently in accord with Catholic morality. But this façade is to be a mask whereby they can slowly corrupt the minds of the next generations until they can elect a pope imbued with their philosophy. The *Alta Vendita* states:

> That reputation [of being a good Catholic] will open the way for our doctrines to pass to the bosoms of the young clergy, and go even to the depths of convents. In a few years the young clergy will have, by the force of events, invaded all the functions. They will govern, administer, and judge. They will form the council of the Sovereign. They will be called upon to choose the Pontiff

also contained as an appendix in Taylor R. Marshall's *Infiltration: The Plot to Destroy the Church from Within* (Manchester, NH: Sophia Institute Press, 2019). For further discussion of Freemasonry, see Bishop Athanasius Schneider, *Christus Vincit: Christ's Triumph Over the Darkness of the Age* (Brooklyn, NY: Angelico Press, 2019), 51–69, 71, 73, 98, 131, 134, 165, 191, 195–97, 215, 297.

4. The phrase "tiara and cope" refers to the triple crown worn by popes until Paul VI cast it aside and the cape worn by all priests, including the pope, during certain liturgical functions. The phrase means the revolution in the Church will be led not by a Freemason but by a pope and will be a revolution in teaching and governing (the tiara) and liturgy (cope).

who will reign; and that Pontiff, like the greater part of his contemporaries, will be necessarily imbued with the Italian and humanitarian principles which we are about to put in circulation.

This plan appeared to have achieved success already by the time of the reign of Pope St. Pius X. The first pope to be canonized since the sixteenth century unmasked these purveyors of error within the Church and took decisive action to crush their influence. This revolutionary set of ideas that had wormed its way into the Church he labeled Modernism. In his landmark encyclical *Pascendi Dominici Gregis*,[5] he defined Modernism as "the synthesis of all heresies" because (even as the *Alta Vendita* had predicted) it comprises errors that undermine every aspect of religion (philosophy, theology, scripture, liturgy, etc.). To expose and root out the Modernists, he prescribed vast disciplinary measures that included a requirement that all clergy, pastors, confessors, preachers, religious superiors, and professors in philosophical-theological seminaries swear an oath against Modernism.[6] Yet Pius X, often referred to as "the Hammer of Modernists," did not vanquish this enemy but only drove it for a time underground. Some clerics and scholars kept the errors alive in dark corners and hushed tones. During the reign of Pope Pius XII they reemerged in what is sometimes called the Neo-Modernist movement.[7] By 1950, Neo-Modernist infiltration had grown to such an extent that it once again provoked papal condemnation in the form of Pope Pius XII's encyclical *Humani Generis*. Yet the disciplinary measures employed after Pius X were less rigorous and the Neo-Modernists often continued to circulate their poisonous doctrines in private manuscripts and secret meetings.[8]

---

5. Promulgated September 8, 1907; available at www.vatican.va/content/pius-x/en/encyclicals/documents/hf_p-x_enc_19070908_pascendi-dominici-gregis.html.

6. The text is available at www.papalencyclicals.net/pius10/p10moath.htm; interestingly, although this oath was taken by countless thousands of clergy for decades, the text seems to be found nowhere on the Vatican website.

7. See De Mattei, *The Second Vatican Council*, 4–9 and 50–54.

8. For an excellent history of Modernist ideas and invasion of the Church, see Father Dominic Bormaud, *One Hundred Years of Modernism: A Genealogy of the Principles of the Second Vatican Council* (Kansas City, MO: Angelus Press, 2006).

Introduction to Part II

The Storm Breaks

Upon the death of Pius XII, John XXIII ascended the throne and began planning for a Council to achieve what he called *aggiornamento*, literally "updating" or even "todaying," which was broadly interpreted as an opening up to or reconciliation with the modern world. Notwithstanding that top Vatican prelates warned against calling a Council which could be dangerous in view of the recrudescence of Neo-Modernism, John XXIII dismissed what he called the "prophets of doom." He opened the Second Vatican Council in October of 1962 but would not live to see its end, dying after the first of four sessions. Most of the gathering's work was completed under his successor Paul VI, who closed the Council in December of 1965. The Council produced sixteen documents. Collectively they cover a vast range of topics including the sacred liturgy, the nature of the Church, divine revelation, missionary work, religious life, the lay apostolate, ecumenism, and relations with non-Christians. Here I will introduce briefly only those documents that are referenced in Archbishop Viganò's writings.

Dignitatis Humanæ is a declaration dealing with religious freedom. It claimed that by virtue of "human dignity," a concept never clearly defined, all people have a right to practice publicly whatever religion they choose without restrictions by the state, within due limits (another phrase never defined). The Church for centuries had always claimed *libertas ecclesiæ*, the freedom of the Church, to fulfill her divine commission. She had also taught that nobody has a natural right to practice a false religion, although under many circumstances the government should tolerate false religions for prudential reasons. In spite of differences in interpretation, *Dignitatis Humanæ* has been widely seen as marking an epochal shift away from Constantinian confessional Christendom towards modern democratic pluralism and humanism.

Nostra Ætate is a document that discusses non-Christian religions, especially Islam and post-Christian Judaism. Historically the Church had clearly taught that the Church is the exclusive means of salvation and that all other religions were, as religious systems, false and incapable of obtaining eternal redemption for their adherents. This document appeared to soften that stand and treat these other religions as containing salvific truth, albeit incomplete.

Lumen Gentium is a document that deals with the nature of the Church and covers a wide variety of topics. Much of this document can be understood in an orthodox sense. Yet it contains one of the most controversial statements of the Council. Traditionally the Church had taught that the Catholic Church *is* the Church of Christ, that is, that there was no distinction between the two terms. *Lumen Gentium* claimed that the Church of Christ *subsists in* the Catholic Church.[9] This wording is understood by many to open up the possibility that the Church of Christ may have concrete existence (subsist) in other places or groups outside of the Catholic Church. At least it opens up the possibility of the Church of Christ not being identical to the Catholic Church.

Finally, the first document approved by the Council was *Sacrosanctum Concilium*, which was on the Sacred Liturgy. This text called for the revision of all the liturgical books (Mass, sacraments, Divine Office, blessings, etc.) according to the principles articulated in the document. Even before the Council ended, the pope appointed a commission to undertake this task. This body of experts and prelates, the *Consilium ad exsequendam Constitutionem liturgicam «Sacrosanctum Concilium»* (usually abbreviated to *Consilium*), radically revised all the liturgical rites of the Church.[10] The version of Mass they created that was eventually adopted virtually everywhere in the world is called the "new Mass" or the *Novus Ordo* (Latin for "new order [of Mass]"), or the Mass of Paul VI. By contrast, the Mass that existed at the time of the Council is called variously the Latin Mass, the traditional Mass, the Tridentine Mass (referring to the Council of Trent), the ancient Mass, the Gregorian Mass (referring to Pope St. Gregory the Great who gave the final

---

9. See *Lumen Gentium* 8. The difference in Latin is between *est* and *subsistit in*.

10. In the biography *Annibale Bugnini, Reformer of the Liturgy* (Brooklyn, NY: Angelico Press, 2018), Yves Chiron provides a useful overview of the entire liturgical reform, from the 1940s through the 1970s.

shape to its definitive element, the Roman Canon), or the *Vetus Ordo* ("old order").[11] Debates raged throughout the Church for decades as to whether Paul VI had mandated that all priests must use his new missal or whether the traditional Mass was still permitted. Almost everywhere the *Novus Ordo* was adopted *de facto* as the only form of Mass. In 2007, Pope Benedict XVI resolved aspects of this debate in his Motu Proprio[12] *Summorum Pontificum* by declaring that a priest is "permitted to celebrate the Sacrifice of the Mass following the typical edition of the Roman Missal, which was promulgated by Blessed John XXIII in 1962 [a way of referring to the traditional Mass] and never abrogated."[13] For most Catholics, the new Mass with its new language and dramatic changes has been the main point of contact with the Second Vatican Council.

The Council can be understood as a grand battle between the Modernists/Neo-Modernists and those faithful to the long line of popes who opposed them. Throughout his participation in meetings of the preparatory commissions in the years leading up to the Council, Archbishop Marcel Lefebvre witnessed these forces battle for control of its agenda.[14] Cardinal Óscar Andrés Rodríguez Maradiaga, close collaborator with Pope Francis, claims that the impor-

11. The best one-volume treatment may be found in Michael Fiedrowicz, *The Traditional Mass: History, Form, and Theology of the Classical Roman Rite* (Brooklyn, NY: Angelico Press, 2020). The familiar expression "Latin Mass" can be a bit confusing because technically the *Novus Ordo* Mass was composed and approved in Latin and is capable of being said in Latin (see canon 928 of the 1983 *Code*: "The eucharistic celebration is to be carried out in the Latin language or in another language provided that the liturgical texts have been legitimately approved"). However, the Vatican permitted—indeed, encouraged and enforced—the translation of the *Novus Ordo* into ordinary or vernacular languages, and almost immediately those translations were the only form of the new Mass that could be found. Although to this day in some isolated places one can find a new Mass said in Latin, the overwhelming majority of new Masses are said in a vernacular language.

12. Latin for "by his own action." This phrase designates a form of document issued by the direct act of the pope and not through a part of the Roman Curia or a bureaucratic congregation.

13. *Summorum Pontificum* 1, www.vatican.va/content/benedict-xvi/en/motu_p roprio/documents/hf_ben-xvi_motu-proprio_20070707_summorum-pontificum. html.

14. See Bernard Tissier de Mallerais, *The Biography of Archbishop Marcel Lefebvre* (Kansas City, MO: Angelus Press, 2004).

tance of Vatican II is that it ended the Church's condemnation of Modernism: "The Second Vatican Council . . . meant an end to the hostilities between the Church and modernism, which was condemned in the First Vatican Council. . . . The Vatican II Council officially acknowledged that things had changed, and captured the need for such a change in its Documents. . . ."[15] He is not alone. Cardinal Joseph Ratzinger expressed almost the same conclusion when he characterized the Pastoral Constitution on the Church in the Modern World as a "countersyllabus" to Pius IX's *Syllabus of Errors* that condemned the revolutionary ideas. Ratzinger explains:

> If it is desirable to offer a diagnosis of the text [*Gaudium et Spes*] as a whole, we might say that (in conjunction with the texts on religious liberty [*Dignitatis Humanae*] and world religions [*Nostra Ætate*]) it is a revision of the Syllabus of Pius IX, a kind of countersyllabus. Harnack, as we know, interpreted the *Syllabus* of Pius IX as nothing less than a declaration of war against his generation. This is correct insofar as the *Syllabus* established a line of demarcation against the determining forces of the nineteenth century: against the scientific and political world view of liberalism. In the struggle against modernism this twofold delimitation was ratified and strengthened. Since then many things have changed. . . . As a result, the one-sidedness of the position adopted by the Church under Pius IX and Pius X in response to the situation created by the new phase of history inaugurated by the French Revolution was to a large extent corrected *via facti* [in the practical sphere], especially in Central Europe, but there was still no statement of the relationship that would exist between the Church and the world that had come into existence after 1789. In fact, an attitude that was largely prerevolutionary continued to exist in countries with strong Catholic majorities. . . . Only a careful investigation of the different ways in which acceptance of the new era was accomplished in various parts of the Church

15. Cardinal Óscar Andrés Rodríguez Maradiaga, "The Importance of the New Evangelization," University of Dallas Ministry Conference, delivered October 25, 2013, available at http://whispersintheloggia.blogspot.com/2013/10/the-councils-unfinished-business.html.

102

could unravel the complicated network of causes that formed the background of the "Pastoral Constitution" [*Gaudium et Spes*], and only thus can the dramatic history of its influence be brought to light. Let us be content to say that the text serves as a counter-syllabus and, as such, represents, on the part of the Church, an attempt at an official reconciliation with the new era inaugurated in 1789.[16]

Cardinal Leo Joseph Suenens of Belgium called Vatican II the "French Revolution in the Church"[17] and Dominican priest Yves Congar stated that "the Church has peacefully undergone its October Revolution."[18] During the final session of the Council, Congar wrote in his diary: "Little by little we are escaping from [the era] of Pius IX and Pius XII. . . . The page is being turned over on Augustinianism and on the Middle Ages."[19] We could multiply examples drawn from both Vatican II's supporters and critics. All agree that it brought into the Church the very ideas that Liberals had sought to inject, which are the same as or similar to the ideas that the Freemasons had plotted to usher in through a revolution in Tiara and Cope.

The Second Vatican Council presents many historical anomalies when compared to councils that preceded it. Councils were previously called in response to specific challenges to Catholic dogma or discipline. The First Council of Nicaea was called in response to Arianism. The Council of Trent was called in response to Protestantism. Once convened, councils would of course address a variety of matters involving the life of the Church, but their main work focused on defining the truth of the Faith and definitively condemning specific heresies against it. By the admission of its architects, the Second Vatican Council was not called to do any such thing (although it could have been called to respond to Commu-

16. Joseph Cardinal Ratzinger, *Principles of Catholic Theology: Building Stones for a Fundamental Theology* (San Francisco: Ignatius Press, 1987), 381–82.

17. Quoted in Paul L. Kramer, *The Devil's Final Battle* (n.p.: The Missionary Association, 2002), 64–65.

18. *Le Concile au jour le jour deuxième session* (Paris: Cerf, 1964), 115.

19. See de Mattei, *Second Vatican Council*, 484.

nism).[20] In opening the Council, Pope John XXIII stated that its mission was not to condemn errors. Having acknowledged that the Church in the past condemned errors, he stated: "Nowadays, however, the Spouse of Christ prefers to make use of the medicine of mercy rather than that of severity."[21] Pope John announced this would be a new kind of Council, not doctrinal but pastoral. This mantra would linger for decades as a justification for why the Council could say unusual things that appeared in conflict with prior councils—after all, its purpose was different. Pope John explained:

> The salient point of this Council is not, therefore, a discussion of one article or another of the fundamental doctrine of the Church which has repeatedly been taught by the Fathers and by ancient and modern theologians, and which is presumed to be well known and familiar to all. For this a Council was not necessary. . . . The substance of the ancient doctrine of the deposit of faith is one thing, and the way in which it is presented is another. And it is the latter that must be taken into great consideration, with patience if necessary, everything being measured in the forms and proportions of a magisterium which is predominantly pastoral in character.[22]

The final phrase remains to this day a mystery; one could argue it is oxymoronic. It says that the conciliar magisterium must be "predominantly pastoral." Magisterium, however, refers to formal and definitive teaching, while pastoral refers to care for the life of the Church's members. Magisterium involves defining, distinguishing, explaining, and anathematizing; the canons of prior councils provide crystal-clear examples. Pastoral activities include preaching retreats, giving spiritual direction, marriage preparation, visiting the sick and the homebound. The two terms refer to two distinct

20. In fact, several hundred Council fathers formally requested the condemnation of Communism, but their request was "lost in a drawer" by the powerful clerics who controlled the proceedings. See de Mattei, 469–81.

21. John XXIII, *Opening Speech to the Council*, October 11, 1962, https://vatican2 voice.org/91docs/opening_speech.htm.

22. Ibid.

spheres of human operation, the intellectual and the active. To be effective, teaching must be clear, coherent, and precise. Yet pastoral work is more flexible in its operation. When to give spiritual direction or what to say to a scrupulous soul are not matters suited to a precise definition. How then can a magisterium be primarily pastoral? This question lacks a satisfactory answer to this day.

This new type of council consequently poses a problem for the whole Church that reads its acts.[23] In prior councils, it was easy to identify precisely what beliefs members of the Church were bound to hold according to the council in question. Its acts would include statements formulated in the negative: the councils would make clear what errors could *not* be held by Catholics. The propositions that were condemned could be identified by the phrase "Anyone who says thus-and-such, let him be anathema." For example, at Nicaea, the council declared:

> Whosoever shall say that there was a time when the Son of God was not, or that before he was begotten he was not, or that he was made of things that were not, or that he is of a different substance or essence [from the Father], or that he is a creature, or subject to change or conversion—all that so say, the Catholic and Apostolic Church anathematizes them.[24]

Such language clearly distinguishes what propositions must be refused by Catholics from other decisions by and statements of the council. In addition to these anathematized propositions and the prescribed creed, this council issued twenty-five canons that make pastoral decisions such as the date of Easter and the process for appointing bishops. The pastoral is clearly distinguished from the doctrinal (and even so, the pastoral determinations are quite sufficiently clear). Yet Vatican II uses no anathemas. It never clearly defines any propositions that must be believed or rejected. It merely issues lengthy discourses on topics, interspersed with practical policies and recommendations. Due to the confusing nature of the doc-

---

23. See de Mattei, *Second Vatican Council*, x–xi.
24. Council of Nicaea, translated by Henry Percival, available at www.newadvent.org/fathers/3801.htm.

uments, the bishops participating in Vatican II had to ask what authority or weight the documents carried as teaching. The answer they received from the officials of the Council was essentially that they all carried whatever weight the nature of their statements demanded, and that this could be determined by the usual theological tools. This evasive answer provides no sure criterion on which to judge the authority of any statements in the vast expanse of documents.

The processes of conducting the Council were also highly unusual and apparently subject to manipulation. First, the goal of being pastoral rather than dogmatic produced an important phenomenon: politics and diplomacy were placed above truth. This inversion is exemplified by two events. In 1962, a secret meeting occurred in Metz between Cardinal Tisserant and the Orthodox (i.e., not Catholic) archbishop of Yaroslavl. They struck a deal that if the Orthodox Patriarch of Moscow would accept the pope's invitation to come to the Council as an observer, the pope would guarantee the Council would not condemn communism.[25] Secondly, Paul VI reorganized the Roman Curia to place the Secretariat of State (which handles political negotiations) over the Congregation for the Doctrine of the Faith. One thing that being pastoral seems to mean is to subject truth to diplomacy.

During the Council, the political manipulations of the proceedings were evident. It was Pope Pius IX who prepared the First Vatican Council and posed the questions to be decided by the assembly. John XXIII, on the other hand, took a "democratic turn" and sent inquiries to thousands of individuals and communities asking what they wanted the Council to discuss.[26] Prior to the Council, a carefully selected body guided by the Roman Congregations prepared

---

25. See de Mattei, *Second Vatican Council* 149–51. This is the reason the petition to condemn Communism was "lost in a drawer." This matter has been written about extensively: see, e.g., Edward Pentin, "Why Did Vatican II Ignore Communism?," *Catholic World Report*, December 10, 2012; Matthew Cullinan Hoffman, "Vatican II's lost condemnations of communism revealed to public for first time," *LifeSiteNews*, October 25, 2017; Paul Kengor, "Vatican II's Unpublished Condemnations of Communism," *Crisis Magazine*, November 30, 2017.

26. De Mattei, *Second Vatican Council*, 101.

Introduction to Part II

"schemas" or detailed drafts of the documents that would be discussed and revised by the council fathers, who would then vote on the adoption of revised texts. At the very start of Vatican II, however, the assembly took the multi-year work of the commissions and, with one exception, tossed it into the rubbish bin.[27] This radical move to unmoor the council from its preparations and throw open the floor for "new material" was orchestrated by a revolutionary minority well connected to the levers of power. Having discarded the work of the preparatory commissions, the body set about drafting new documents from scratch. Progressives used their power to stack drafting committees. This radical process, which can be likened to the dramatic transformation of the Estates General into the National Assembly at the opening of the French Revolution, means that the texts themselves were prepared in an act of rebellion. The Council's proceedings were dominated not by the bishops, the successors of the Apostles, but by a cadre of *periti*,[28] one of whom was Joseph Ratzinger, who decades later would assume the chair of Peter as Benedict XVI.[29] These experts wielded enormous power over the texts. One of them, Father Chenu, explained:

> Backbiters even say that the experts were the ones who actually conducted the Council. It is not totally wrong. I remember a minute but revealing episode. At the time when the Decree on the laity was to be discussed, I had noticed a paragraph still . . . inspired by a dual vision: the world on the one side, and the Church on the other. I was there with another French expert, and we agreed that it was bad. That paragraph had however already

27. See de Mattei, 210–13 and 237–41; for a more in-depth examination, see Paolo Pasqualucci, *The Parallel Council: The Anomalous Beginning of the Second Vatican Council* (Fort Collins, CO: Gondolin Press, 2018).

28. Theological experts who accompanied and advised the prelates who were the voting members of the Council. The *periti* had no official voice but were allowed to attend the sessions and held many influential private meetings at which they agitated for particular theological views and redrafted documents on behalf of, or to exercise pressure on, the prelates.

29. See Maike Hickson, "New biography describes great influence of Joseph Ratzinger in the revolutionary upheaval of Vatican II," *LifeSiteNews*, December 11, 2020.

been adopted by the commission; it was consequently impossible to change it. We then drafted an additive, a second paragraph which was more or less saying the opposite. The first paragraph was in a way establishing that dualism, and the second one was saying, the action of the Church must go beyond it. Bishops from Western France proposed our new text, and it was adopted.[30]

Chenu also bragged that "a very efficient infiltration was carried out through notes proposed to the various commissions."[31]

Postconciliar Clash: Continuity or Rupture?

As a result of the novelties in procedure and in the documents produced by the Second Vatican Council, the period following its close has been marked by strife and conflict. Two main methods of understanding the Council have been developed. Benedict XVI assigned names to them in his address to the Roman Curia in December of 2005. He referred to each as a hermeneutic, a word which means a method for interpreting something. One, labeled the "hermeneutic of discontinuity or rupture," understands Vatican II as a break with the history of the Church: its documents say something contrary to, or in rupture with, prior teachings of the Church. Two contrary conclusions can be drawn from this hermeneutic. One concludes that this rupture means the documents of Vatican II must be refused as erroneous to the extent they contain such a rupture with what has come before. The opposite conclusion celebrates the rupture: whatever was previously taught or done that is contrary to Vatican II is now to be held as wrong or at very least treated as no longer relevant. In either case, the older understanding must be rejected. The other hermeneutic he called "the hermeneutic of reform," although many refer to it as the "hermeneutic of continuity."[32] Benedict defines this method of interpretation to be

---

30. M.D. Chenu, O.P., *Un theologien en liberté* [A theologian without restraint], interviewed by Jacques Duquesne (Paris: Le Centurion, 1975), 16–17.

31. Chenu, 187–88.

32. Pope Benedict in fact used both expressions: see Peter Kwasniewski, "The Ongoing Saga of 'the Hermeneutic of Continuity,'" *New Liturgical Movement*, November 26, 2013.

"renewal in the continuity of the one subject-Church which the Lord has given to us. She is a subject which increases in time and develops, yet always remaining the same, the one subject of the journeying People of God."[33] Benedict XVI is arguing that the object of belief can change over time as long as the Church remains the same subject proposing those developing beliefs. It seeks revisions of teaching over time through a process that keeps the structure of the Church in place.

Although Benedict XVI, himself an influential participant in the Council, attempted to persuade the Church to reject a hermeneutic of rupture, other key participants in the Council characterized it precisely as a rupture or break with the Church's prior teaching. Cardinal Suenens, a prominent figure in the Council, proclaimed: "One could make an astonishing list of propositions taught yesterday, and the day before, in Rome, as the only acceptable ones, and which were eliminated by the conciliar Fathers."[34] Yves Congar, fellow *peritus* with Ratzinger, claimed:

> The Council has wiped out what I would call the unconditionality of the system. By "system," I mean a coherent set of notions conveyed by the Roman universities, codified by Canon Law, protected by a tight and rather efficient control under Pius XII, with reports, calls to order, control of writings by Roman censorship, etc. The Council just disintegrated it.[35]

Viganò and Vatican II: An Overview

Before presenting the detailed interventions of Archbishop Viganò, I will attempt to synthesize his teaching on this matter. It is important to note that his thinking, or at least his public expression of it, has developed over the two years between his Testimony on McCarrick and his interventions in 2019 and 2020. The development is epitomized by a phrase he used in his September 14, 2020 interview

---

33. Benedict XVI, *Speech to the Roman Curia*, December 22, 2005 available at www.vatican.va/content/benedict-xvi/en/speeches/2005/december/documents/hf_ben_xvi_spe_20051222_roman-curia.html.

34. Interview in *Informations Catholiques Internationales*, May 15, 1969.

35. Yves Congar, O.P., *Une vie pour la vérité* (Paris: La Centurion, 1975), 220.

with Marco Tosatti: "Moral corruption and doctrinal deviation are intrinsically linked." Having denounced the moral corruption epitomized by the McCarrick scandal culminating in the corruption of Francis's Vatican, Viganò seeks to uncover the corresponding doctrinal deviations that emanate from Vatican II.

Toward the end of 2019, Viganò begins to address two aspects of Francis's pontificate: the pope's signing of a troubling document on false religions and the pope's attack on Marian doctrines. In these interventions, the archbishop notes connections to Vatican II but does not explore them in detail. In June of 2020, the archbishop starts addressing the Council and its effects more deeply, and in so doing, explains his proposed solution to the crisis.

The archbishop approaches Vatican II by addressing individual contemporary problems in the Church that he traces back to the Council. In the first text in this section, an article on an Italian blog in November of 2019, the archbishop addresses the document signed by Francis and the Grand Imam of Al-Azhar, Ahmed Al-Tayeb, entitled *A Document on Human Fraternity for World Peace and Living Together*. The *Document* proposes grand plans for ecumenical ventures between the Vatican and the Grand Imam. Shortly after the *Document* was signed, a Higher Commission was established for its implementation. Its first project was to propose the construction of an Abrahamic House, a facility that will comprise a Mosque, a Church, and a Synagogue. What is striking about Viganò's commentary is not that he denounces the scandalous words and actions of Pope Francis, but that he connects the dots directly from Francis to two documents of Vatican II. Viganò explains:

> Pope Bergoglio thus proceeds to further implement the apostasy of Abu Dhabi, the fruit of pantheistic and agnostic neo-modernism that tyrannizes the Roman Church, germinated by the conciliar document *Nostra Ætate*. We are compelled to recognize it: the poisoned fruits of the "conciliar springtime" are before the eyes of anyone who does not allow himself to be blinded by the dominant Lie.

"Germinated" is a key word. He calls what Francis has done "poisoned fruit" that hangs off the Council tree. In a sense, Pope Francis concurs with Viganò. On the plane back to Italy after signing the document, the pope told journalists: "I openly reaffirm this: from the Catholic point of view the *Document* does not move one millimeter away from the Second Vatican Council. It is even cited, several times. The *Document* was crafted in the spirit of the Second Vatican Council."

In the second most significant passage in this article, Viganò claims that the Vatican II documents that were the seeds of this new document (he mentions *Nostra Ætate* and *Dignitatis Humanæ*) represent a "terrible discontinuity" with the prior teaching of the Church, especially in Pius XI's *Mortalium Animos*.[36] He argues that the "lie" of these documents having "thrown to the winds" the prior teaching "must be acknowledged and . . . must be amended as soon as possible." Archbishop Viganò did not explain what he believes can and should be done to "amend" this discontinuity until June of 2020.

In December 2019, the archbishop intervened in a dramatic text denouncing Pope Francis's attacks on the holiness and spotlessness of the Blessed Virgin Mary and her prerogatives. He went so far as to compare the words and actions of Pope Francis to the enmity that God put between the serpent and the Blessed Mother in the second chapter of Genesis. The intervention characterizes the pontificate of Francis as exhibiting a false piety toward Mary (for consumption by the media) and an attack on perennial doctrines about Mary and the prerogatives that flow from her divine Motherhood. One of his most virulent denunciations is the following: "To attack Mary is to venture against Christ himself; to attack the Mother is to rise up against her Son and to rebel against the very mystery of the Most Holy Trinity." This intervention essentially calls into question two changes initiated by the Council. First, in order to appease Protestants, the importance of the Blessed Mother in Catholic theology and life

---

36. This document, promulgated by Pius XI in 1929, forbade Catholics from participating in ecumenical meetings (meetings among different Christian denominations to explore ways of creating unity among them). Pius XI declared that the only form of legitimate ecumenism was the return of dissidents to the Catholic Church.

tended to be downplayed. It is true that Paul VI during the Council did bestow on Mary the title of "Mother of the Church," although the progressives were distressed by his action. Yet many had expected and called for the definitive proclamation of another title that had been believed by the Church for centuries but had never been defined: *Co-Redemptrix*. The title means that the Mother of God participated in a uniquely intimate and efficacious way with her Son's work of Redemption, so much so that she can be referred to as a co-Redeemer *sub et cum eo*, subordinate to Him and with Him. Like the condemnation of Communism, this definition was bypassed so as to avoid upsetting the Protestant observers for whom any unique honor given to the Mother of God is considered idolatrous. While the term "Mother of the Church" can be explained away as a pious metaphor, Co-Redemptrix is a weighty theological concept that identifies a unique privilege of the great Mother of God.

The second problem with Vatican II addressed in this intervention is religious indifferentism, which the archbishop believes was introduced primarily in *Dignitatis Humanæ* and *Nostra Ætate*. He denounces the substitution of the Pachamamas[37] for Our Lady of Guadalupe as a new paganism that has invaded the Church.

With the December 2019 text, Viganò clearly enters a new phase in his public interventions. Up to this point, his discourses have focused primarily on the failures and problems of the Francis pontificate. The McCarrick Testimony focuses on the personal failure of Francis and his collaborators to deal with the McCarrick scandal. It is true that in the article on the Abu Dhabi declaration, Viganò touched on the root of this horror in Vatican II. Yet there is a qualitative difference in the intervention on Mary. He clearly lays blame at the feet of the Council and considers Francis as merely "accelerating" the problems created by the Council. He traces back the scandals and outrages of the first six years of Francis's reign to their proximate source:

For more than six years now we have been poisoned by a false magisterium, a sort of extreme synthesis of all the conciliar mis-

---

37. An Amazonian pagan idol that was installed in Catholic churches and included in ceremonies during the Amazon Synod in October 2019.

conceptions and postconciliar errors that have been relentlessly propagated, without most of us noticing. Yes, because the Second Vatican Council opened not only Pandora's Box but also Overton's Window, and so gradually that we did not realize the upheavals that had been carried out, the real nature of the reforms and their dramatic consequences, nor did we suspect who was really at the helm of that gigantic subversive operation.

For the first time, he denounces in bold and almost shocking language many aspects of the Council and its aftermath:

> Thus, over these last decades, the Mystical Body has been slowly drained of its lifeblood through unstoppable bleeding: the Sacred Deposit of Faith has gradually been squandered, dogmas denatured, worship secularized and gradually profaned, morality sabotaged, the priesthood vilified, the Eucharistic Sacrifice protestantized and transformed into a convivial banquet. . . .

In this intervention, Viganò moves from highlighting the dangers of Francis to the broader dangers "over these last decades," flowing from the Council. This is a significant turn.

Fully Engaging the Council: The Hot Summer of 2020

The first text that fully engages the problem of the Council is an interview that appeared in Portuguese at the website *Dies Iræ* and was published in English at the website of *Inside the Vatican* on April 22, 2020. The interview places the consideration of the Revolution at Vatican II in the context of the apparitions of Fatima. In the summer of 1917, the Blessed Mother appeared to three shepherd children, to whom, in addition to her other instructions, she entrusted three secrets. The first two have been fully revealed. She predicted an end to World War I and the coming of a second world war if men did not stop offending God. She showed the children a vision of hell and stated that many souls would fall into hell because there was nobody to pray and offer sacrifices for them. She predicted that Russia would spread her errors around the world—a clear allusion to the Communism that would conquer Russia in the Bolshevik Revolution a few months after the apparition—and the

Church would be persecuted. Our Lady points to a crisis in the world (the spread of Communism) and in the Church, where persecution would reign. She then entrusted a third secret to the children, which Sister Lucia, one of the visionaries, wrote down, indicating that Our Lady wanted the Holy Father to reveal its contents by 1960 at the latest. The first sentence of the third secret was revealed to be: "In Portugal the dogma of the Faith will be preserved." In 1960, Pope John XXIII read the secret that was kept under lock and key in the Vatican but announced, contrary to Sister Lucia's instructions, which she claimed came from Our Lady herself, that it would not be revealed to the public. In his interview, Viganò points to this decision as a critical moment for the Church. He claims that with the suppression of the text in 1960, "a coverup operation was started, evidently because the content of the message would have revealed the terrible conspiracy against the Church of Christ by its enemies." The archbishop discerns a connection between the unrevealed third secret of Fatima and Vatican II. The pope who was about to convene the Council did not want the full message of the third secret known because, according to Viganò, it exposes the conspiracy against the Church that would infiltrate the Council.

In the year 2000, John Paul II surprised the world by announcing that the text of the third secret would finally be revealed. Under the direction of the Secretary of State, Cardinal Angelo Sodano (whom Viganò identifies as part of the "gay lobby" that covered up the sexual perversions of McCarrick, Maciel, and others), a text of a vision seen by the Fatima visionaries was released, but without the accompanying words of Our Lady. Yet many claimed that the evidence indicated that just as the second secret contained both a vision of hell and words of Our Lady predicting future events, so too this third part contained a vision followed by words of prediction.[38] The suppression of the full text is an attempt to hide Our Lady's predictions about the great spread of Communism around the world and

---

38. For the most comprehensive treatment of this suppression of the words of Our Lady, see Ferrara, *Secret Still Hidden*; cf. Antonio Socci, *The Fourth Secret of Fatima* (Fitzwilliam, NH: Loreto Publications, 2009).

the persecution of the true Church. Fatima is a critical element in the connection Viganò makes between the betrayals of Bergoglio and a Council opened by a pope who suppressed the words of Our Lady and who agreed to suppress the conciliar condemnation of Communism.

Having set the stage by describing this conspiracy to hide the warnings of the third secret, he draws a direct line between Pope Francis's attempts to open the door to the ordination of female deacons and Vatican II. He notes that the Modernists of the early twentieth century dreamed of a church that broke open the male ministerial priesthood. He then goes on to explain that their "delusions . . . subtly reemerged at the Council, with an attempt to insinuate a certain equivalence between the ministerial priesthood deriving from Holy Orders and the common priesthood of the faithful deriving from Baptism." This subtle doctrinal ambiguity blurs the distinctions between the active ministerial priesthood that offers the sacrifice and administers the sacraments and the laity's passive participation in Christ's priesthood, by which they are empowered to receive the sacraments. By collapsing these two distinct concepts, the Council paves the way for married men and for women to invade the ministerial priesthood. Viganò sees this doctrinal ambiguity in the Council as a root of Bergoglio's attempts to accomplish both of these practical goals. Viganò points to another link that will be developed in his writings over the next few months, namely, the way in which the doctrinal errors of the Council are encapsulated and promoted in the new Mass that followed it. He argues that the distortion of distinctions between the clergy's and the laity's participation in Christ's priesthood is reflected in the new Mass: "It is significant that, precisely by playing on this intentional ambiguity, the reformed liturgy also suffered from the doctrinal error of *Lumen Gentium* and ended up reducing the ordained minister to the [status of a] simple president of an assembly of priests [i.e., the baptized]." This nexus between doctrinal errors and liturgical errors will lead Viganò later in the summer of 2020 in his replies to *Catholic Family News* to advise the laity that they have a right and a duty to seek out the traditional liturgy, which contains none of these doctrinal dangers.

In response to the interviewer's question about the Second Vatican Council representing a rupture with the Church's past, Viganò implies he has now moved beyond Benedict XVI's hermeneutic of continuity: "A Church that presents herself as new with respect to the Church of Christ is simply not the Church of Christ!" He will manifestly adopt this position by June 2020. He also seems to anticipate his ecclesiological explanation of the rupture; later he will say the new religion is superimposed over the true Church like an eclipse that blocks the sun. In the interview, he claims: "It seems that also the postconciliar Church, modernist and Masonic, aspires to transform, to overcome the Church of Christ, replacing it with a 'neo-Church,' a deformed and monstrous creature that does not come from God."

A few months later, in his reply at OnePeterFive to a sympathetic article published at the same site by Dr. Peter Kwasniewski, the archbishop makes clear that the hermeneutic of continuity offers no way out of the crisis. The hermeneutic contains within itself a hidden postulate that obscures the issue. It assumes, as an unstated postulate, that the documents of Vatican II are part of the Magisterium in light of which they should be read. Yet, Viganò explains, this is precisely the question that needs to be addressed, but is instead swept under the carpet by the postulate. He also explains in the same reply:

> It isn't possible to change reality to make it correspond to an ideal schema. If the evidence shows that some propositions contained in the Council documents (and similarly, in the acts of Bergoglio's magisterium) are heterodox, and if doctrine teaches us that the acts of the Magisterium do not contain error, the conclusion is not that those propositions are not erroneous, but that they cannot be part of the Magisterium. Period.

In other words, a hermeneutic is a tool for interpreting, not a tool for correcting errors. Its use will fail us if the matter to which it is being applied resists a traditional Catholic interpretation.

Towards the end of the *Dies Irae* interview, the archbishop is asked about how the Church should resolve this crisis of Vatican II. In response, Viganò introduces the proposed solution that he will explicitly adopt in June. In this interview, he merely refers to it as the proposal of some scholars whom he calls more worthy than himself. The proposal takes as an historical precedent the Italian Synod of Pistoia, which, having adopted a list of heterodox propositions, was "let to fall into oblivion."

Archbishop Viganò returns to adopt and develop the idea of letting Vatican II fall into oblivion in a series of letters issued in the summer of 2020. In a June 9, 2020 letter, we find Viganò's proposed solution to the problem of the Council. The letter was written in response to an article of Bishop Athanasius Schneider.[39] In this article Schneider addresses the *Document on Human Fraternity* that had been the subject of Viganò's article in November 2019. Like Viganò, Schneider understands the errors of the *Document* to have their origin in Vatican II. Schneider sees the error of Pope Francis as flowing from a "dangerous ambiguity" in *Dignitatis Humanæ* and concludes, as had Francis, that the *Document* "does not differ substantially" from *Dignitatis Humanæ*. So far Bishop Schneider is in agreement with Archbishop Viganò's position from November 2019. Schneider then proposes a solution: "One may rightly hope and believe that a future pope or Ecumenical Council will correct the erroneous statement made in the Second Vatican Council's Declaration *Dignitatis Humanæ*." Schneider believes that a particular statement in the text can be extracted and corrected to solve the problem. It is to this proposed solution that Viganò responds on June 10.

This first letter on the problem of Vatican II introduces two significant points. First, it introduces a personal confession. In addition to addressing the fact of the Council, the archbishop in great humility confesses his participation in what he is about to expose:

> There comes a moment in our life when, through the disposition
> of Providence, we are faced with a decisive choice for the future
> of the Church and for our eternal salvation. I speak of the choice

39. "Bishop Schneider: There is no divine positive will or natural right to the diversity of religions," *LifeSiteNews*, June 1, 2020, www.lifesitenews.com/opinion/bishop-schneider-how-church-could-correct-erroneous-view-that-god-wills-diversity-of-religions.

between understanding the error into which practically all of us have fallen, almost always without evil intentions, and wanting to continue to look the other way or justify ourselves. We have also committed the error, among others, of considering our interlocutors as people who, despite the difference of their ideas and their faith, were still motivated by good intentions and who would be willing to correct their errors if they could open up to our Faith.

He humbly admits that although he was troubled by some doubts or concerns throughout his life as a priest and bishop, he did not question the Council or its implementation by the popes that followed it. He admits that he let unconditional obedience restrain him from admitting the contradictions before his eyes. He admits it was only the pontificate of Francis that made those contradictions visible.

The second significant development in this document is his polite disagreement with the solution proposed by Bishop Athanasius Schneider. Essentially both bishops agree that there are problems with Vatican II and that there is a connection between those problems and the scandalous words and actions of Pope Francis. Schneider's solution is that a future pope or ecumenical council should correct the specific statements in the Vatican II documents that are erroneous. Schneider seems to suggest such a pope or Council would say "Vatican II taught X but we find that to be erroneous, so we teach not X." Viganò finds this solution inadequate and potentially harmful. He states that Schneider's proposed solution "appears to me to be an argument that, although made with the best of intentions, undermines the Catholic edifice from its foundation." By this he means that if we can go through conciliar documents and reverse statements, it opens up the possibility that other councils and texts can undergo the same process. This would pull all doctrine into doubt.

Rather than seeing the solution in excising and correcting individual statements in the Council documents, Viganò argues that the entire Council (from its documents through all of its implementations and uses) must be jettisoned. Rather than questioning isolated texts, he is concerned with the entire event. For example, he states:

Introduction to Part II

The Council was used to legitimize the most aberrant doctrinal deviations, the most daring liturgical innovations, and the most unscrupulous abuses, all while Authority remained silent. This Council was so exalted that it was presented as the only legitimate reference for Catholics, clergy, and bishops, obscuring and connoting with a sense of contempt the doctrine that the Church had always authoritatively taught, and prohibiting the perennial liturgy that for millennia had nourished the faith of an uninterrupted line of faithful, martyrs, and saints. Among other things, this Council has proven to be the only one that has caused so many interpretative problems and so many contradictions with respect to the preceding Magisterium, while there is not one other council—from the Council of Jerusalem to Vatican I—that does not harmonize perfectly with the entire Magisterium or that needs so much interpretation.

In other words, it is not this or that text which is inconsistent with prior councils, but the Council itself. He explains how the conciliar system has superimposed a new religion onto the Church. He says the innovators at the Council planned it, inserting in the texts "time bombs" that could be detonated later on to revolutionize the Church. The conciliar work was a collaboration of a variety of Church officials, all with differing motives and culpability. He explains:

> This operation of intellectual honesty requires a great humility, first of all in recognizing that for decades we have been led into error, in good faith, by people who, established in authority, have not known how to watch over and guard the flock of Christ: some for the sake of living quietly, some because of having too many commitments, some out of convenience, and finally some in bad faith or even malicious intent.

In contrast to Bishop Schneider's more surgical approach, in this first letter Viganò suggests that the entire Council and postconciliar era is the problem, and that unless it is dealt with *en bloc*, the solution will remain piecemeal and haphazard.

Notwithstanding its breadth, this First Letter did not provide a precise solution to this vast problem. Professor Paolo Pasqualucci wrote to the archbishop asking for clarification. In his request, the Professor expressed his opinion that "if the Council has deviated from the Faith, the pope has the power to invalidate it. Indeed, it is his duty." Viganò adopts this statement of the Professor as his own and then goes on to explain what he means by "invalidate it." Viganò states that "a pope could very well finally quash the entire Council"; in his opinion that is exactly what a pope should do. He states: "it is preferable to let the whole thing drop and be forgotten." "The mere fact that Vatican II is susceptible to correction," explains Archbishop Viganò, "ought to be sufficient to declare its oblivion as soon as its most obvious errors are seen with clarity." Rather than correcting texts, the Council as a whole should be forgotten and presumably the Church should pick up where she left off at the convening of the Council. We can look at two of the metaphors Viganò uses to understand what he means by "letting the whole thing drop and be forgotten." First, he uses the image of a pathology invading a body. To be cured, the body must expel or remove the pathogen. In the first letter on Vatican II, he argues: "If we do not recognize that the roots of these deviations are found in the principles laid down by the Council, it will be impossible to find a cure: if our diagnosis persists, against all the evidence, in excluding the initial pathology, we cannot prescribe a suitable therapy." Secondly, in the response to Phil Lawler he uses the metaphor of a cut thread. The current magisterium has been cut off from the rest of the thread by the Council and we must "rejoin the thread of Tradition there where it was cut off." Both of these metaphors imply more than simply correcting a word or a phrase here or there. They call for a more thorough change.

This bold claim that a pope should invalidate the entire Council and we should just forget about it begs many further questions. Over the next several weeks, Archbishop Viganò both defends the claim from criticism and replies to questions to clarify the implications of his claim.

Neither Schismatic nor Heretic

In his response to the attacks of various critics, including Sandro Magister, Fr. Raymond de Souza, and Fr. Thomas Weinandy, O.F.M. Cap., Viganò takes the opportunity to clarify his position and distinguish it from the distorted versions of it created by his critics. Sandro Magister interprets Viganò's criticism of the hermeneutic of continuity as a personal attack on Benedict XVI and implies that Viganò is schismatic. The archbishop clarifies that his rejection of the "hermeneutic of continuity" as a way out of the crisis of the Council is not a personal attack on Benedict XVI. Magister had also accused Viganò of blaming Benedict XVI and accusing the Pope Emeritus of deceiving Viganò and others. Viganò makes clear that almost everyone has suffered from deception in these confusing times and that he had never accused Benedict XVI of being a willful deceiver. He noted that Benedict XVI's own position concerning the Council had changed over the decades and that the "hermeneutic of continuity" was a revision to Benedict's earlier more progressivist understanding of the Council.

Father Weinandy, in his August 13 attack on Viganò, expressed his "concern" that in Viganò's "radical reading of the Council, the archbishop is spawning his own schism...."[40] Father de Souza goes even further in his *ad hominem* attack by adding, to the labels schismatic and heretic, mentally unstable.[41] In his response to Fathers de Souza and Weinandy, Viganò exposes the hypocrisy and shallowness of his critics, who seem more willing to find fault among those who defend orthodoxy than among those who have been spreading heterodoxy for decades. These critics throw out the labels of schismatic and heretic or "a bit unstable" to silence the archbishop's legitimate questions about what happened at and following Vatican II. Viganò replies that rather than "assuming schisms and heresies where there are none, it would be appropriate and more useful to fight error and division where they have nested and spread for decades." By calling him names, the critics can avoid entering into the substance of the questions he raised: serious questions can sim-

---

40. "A Response to Archbishop Viganò's Letter about Vatican II," *Catholic World Report*, August 13, 2020, www.catholicworldreport.com/2020/08/13/a-response-to-archbishop-viganos-letter-about-vatican-ii.

41. "Is Archbishop Viganò's Rejection of the Second Vatican Council Promoting Schism?," *National Catholic Register*, August 28, 2020, www.ncregister.com/commentaries/is-archbishop-vigano-s-rejection-of-the-second-vatican-council-promoting-schism.

ply be waved aside as the ranting of a schismatic or an unstable person. They dismiss the debate rather than entering into it because the contradictions of their principles would be exposed. Viganò notes in his responses that while it is permitted by these critics to disregard and dismiss previous councils and the perennial Magisterium of 2,000 years, it is not allowed even to suggest that the same might be done with the Second Vatican Council. Thus, according to Viganò, in their "defense of the conciliar totem the only response is the delegitimization of the interlocutor, his ostracization, and the generic accusation of wanting to attack the unity of the Church."

In the documentary film *Francesco*, Viganò sees another attempt by Pope Francis to distract the Church from the legitimate questions raised by a few prelates. Archbishop Viganò accuses Pope Francis, through this flashy film, of attempting to bait the good prelates who seek to defend the Church into taking action against him. He believes that Bergoglio is increasing his outrageous heterodox statements to move other prelates to speak out as Viganò has done, so that they may all be labeled schismatics and driven out of the Church. Viganò argues:

> It appears that Bergoglio is impudently trying to "raise the stakes" in a crescendo of heretical affirmations, in such a way that it will force the healthy part of the Church—which includes bishops, clergy, and faithful—to accuse him of heresy, in order to declare that healthy part of the Church schismatic and "the enemy of the pope."

This dangerous tactic must be met, as Viganò has done, by distinguishing between, on the one hand, legitimate objections to acts that exceed the authority of a council or pope, and, on the other hand, schism, which is defined as a refusal in principle of the exercise of ecclesiastical authority. Viganò was quite clear in the discourses of the summer of 2020 that he is not advocating schism but rather a truly Catholic obedience to the higher authority of the perennial Magisterium. In responding to the attacks of Magister, Weinandy, and De Souza, and the baiting of Francis in his documentary, Viganò makes clear that he has no intention of questioning the legitimate exercise of papal authority and in fact his interventions are required by that respect for the authoritative doctrine of all the preconciliar popes.

Viganò's Approach Distinguished from Schneider's

In these clarifications we see that, notwithstanding the similarities in the critiques of Bishop Schneider and Archbishop Viganò, they differ in a fundamental way in understanding the nature of the problem. Following the two June interventions of Archbishop Viganò, Bishop Athanasius Schneider issued a new statement clarifying his initial position, to which Viganò reacted in his First Letter on Vatican II.[42] In this text, Schneider explained that he believes that most of the Council texts "are in organic continuity with the previous Magisterium."[43] As to the defective texts, Schneider adds:

> Ultimately, the papal magisterium has to clarify in a convincing manner the controversial points of some of the expressions in the Council texts. Until now, this has not always been done in an intellectually honest and convincing way. Were it necessary, a pope or future ecumenical Council would have to add explanations (a kind of "*notæ explicativæ posteriores*") or even amendments and corrections of those controversial expressions, since they were not presented by the Council as an infallible and definitive teaching.[44]

For Schneider, the problem is one of language that needs correction or explanation, after which what remains will be in organic continuity.

In contrast, Viganò's claim, as it emerged in the summer of 2020, is not that some texts or documents suffer from verbal mistakes, from linguistic imprecisions that merely need focusing. Viganò's appraisal of the Council seems to be indebted to Professor Roberto de Mattei's masterful work *The Second Vatican Council—An Unwrit-*

---

42. Athanasius Schneider, "55 YEARS LATER: Bishop Athanasius Schneider's Appraisal of Vatican II," *The Remnant Newspaper*, June 24, 2020, https://remnantnewspaper.com/web/index.php/articles/item/4949-55-years-later-bishopathanasius-schneider-s-appraisal-of-vatican-ii.

43. Ibid.

44. Ibid.

ten Story, in which the author argues that the Council must be understood in both historical and theological contexts. In his treatment of the Council, he claims that the "historical reconstruction of the conciliar *iter* [journey] is indispensable for understanding the meaning and the significance of those documents of the Church that theologians help us to read in their theological dimension."[45] Schneider's position understands the Council as primarily texts that can be dealt with by adding or excising words. For de Mattei, the Council is first and foremost an *event* that includes texts but is not limited to them. In fact, the event as a whole gives meaning to the texts that are a part of it. Such an approach differs significantly from the "hermeneutic of continuity" of Benedict XVI, in which Schneider still seems to find a solution but which, as Viganò realized by June of 2020, had failed to solve the problem of the Council. Unlike De Mattei's approach, Benedict's and Schneider's approach insists upon a major premise that cannot be questioned: the texts of the Council can be read and interpreted in continuity with the other texts of the Church that predate them. This premise is treated as an axiom. The other aspect of this hermeneutic involves dividing the Council from its aftermath. To save the conciliar documents, they must be severed from the historical facts of their aftermath. The texts are not the cause of the errors and deformations that followed, since those were precisely distortions of the texts, according to Benedict XVI. In his final address to the Roman Clergy before his abdication took effect, he distinguished between the "true council" and the "virtual council"[46]—the former existing in the sixteen approved documents of the Council Fathers, and the latter existing in the historical facts surrounding and following those texts in the mode in which they were reported and distorted by the media.[47] It was this understanding of the Council that Viganò, not without some mis-

---

45. De Mattei, *Second Vatican Council*, xviii.

46. Benedict XVI, *Address to the Meeting with Parish Priests and Clergy of Rome*, February 14, 2013, www.vatican.va/content/benedict-xvi/en/speeches/2013/february/documents/hf_ben-xvi_spe_20130214_clero-roma.html.

47. He explains: "There was the Council of the Fathers—the real Council—but there was also the Council of the media. It was almost a Council apart, and the world perceived the Council through the latter, through the media."

givings, had followed throughout his public career. Yet, by June of 2020, he admits that the unquestioned axiom must be turned into a question for investigation. *Are* the texts, when read in the context in which they were written and the context in which they were later implemented by the very same people who wrote them, in continuity with the 2,000-year history of the Church? By the summer of 2020 Viganò realized that, once converted into a question, the flaw in the axiom of the hermeneutic of continuity is easier to grasp. Limiting the Council to the abstractly-considered texts in an attempt to square them with prior texts is artificial and fruitless. The texts are part of, and must be understood in light of, the historical event of the Council, which explains their genesis, their meaning, and their potentiality.

What is the nature of that event, according to Viganò? It is nothing short of a revolution or a *coup* within the Church. As a result, instead of surgically correcting the texts, the Council must be forgotten, because the texts are inextricably connected to a revolution that must be quashed. In his response to Fathers de Souza and Weinandy, he makes clear the reason why forgetting the Council *en masse* is the necessary remedy. The Council is more than its texts. It is a "superdogma" that "prevails over everything else, it annuls everything, cancels everything, but it does not permit itself to suffer the same fate." The entire revolution of the Council is inseparable from its texts and unless this "superdogma" is removed as an obstacle, nothing can be done. In saying this, the archbishop hastens to add that his proposed remedy does not deny that the Council was legitimately convened. Nevertheless, it developed into a council that went so wrong that it must be annulled. He states in the same response:

> It is precisely this that confirms that Vatican II, *although a legitimate Ecumenical Council*—as I have elsewhere affirmed—*is not like the others*, because if this were the case the councils and the Magisterium that preceded it would have had to be held as equally binding (not only in words), preventing the formulation of the errors contained or implied in the texts of Vatican II.

In his clarification sent to Phil Lawler, Viganò explains that he now understands how the Council documents came to contain those erroneous statements that have been developed to their full logical endpoint by Francis: "The Council Fathers were the object of a sensational deception, of a fraud that was cleverly perpetrated by having recourse to the most subtle means." The well-meaning Council Fathers who sought to defend the perennial teaching of the Church "found themselves in the minority in the linguistic groups, excluded from meetings convened at the last moment, pressured into giving their *placet*[48] by making them believe that the Holy Father wanted it." This covert operation to subvert the Council was not only waged in the official meetings of the Council Fathers but also through other instruments and means: "And what the innovators did not succeed in obtaining in the conciliar *Aula*,[49] they achieved in the commissions and committees, thanks also to the activism of theologians and *periti* who were accredited and acclaimed by a powerful media machine." According to Viganò's new understanding, correcting the texts does not correct the *coup* as a whole, which *coup* is the product of a "malicious" attitude on the part of those who manipulated the Council. He explains to Lawler: "There is a vast array of studies and documents that testify to this systematic malicious *mens*[50] of some of the Council Fathers on the one hand, and the naïve optimism or carelessness of other well-intentioned Council Fathers on the other." In his response to Lawler, Viganò carries further his analysis of the malicious state of mind and underhanded tactics that deceived bishops of good will in the postconciliar period. The way out of the conundrum that has become more evident in the Francis pontificate

> lies above all in an act of humility that all of us, beginning with
> the hierarchy and the pope, must carry out: recognizing the infil-

48. Latin for "it pleases": the phrase used to vote in favor of a document. To vote against it one would say "*non placet*," it does not please.
49. Latin for "hall," referring to the space in which the Council Fathers officially met and voted (St. Peter's Basilica).
50. Latin for "mind," in the sense of mentality, frame of mind, outlook, intention.

tration of the enemy into the heart of the Church, the systematic occupation of key posts in the Roman Curia, seminaries, and ecclesiastical schools, the conspiracy of a group of rebels—including, in the front line, the deviated Society of Jesus—which has succeeded in giving the appearance of legitimacy and legality to a subversive and revolutionary act.

He goes on to explain that we must "also recognize the inadequacy of the response of the good, the naivety of many, the fearfulness of others, and the interests of those who have benefited thanks to that conspiracy." An infiltration of conspirators is not destroyed by wordsmithing texts with a fine-tooth comb. The conspiracy must be expelled. To do this, the entire event of the Council must be disaffirmed.

In like manner, in his response to Phil Lawler, the archbishop dismisses the explanation that the "spirit" of Vatican II must be distinguished from the "letter." Some defenders of the Council use this aphorism to argue it is the text in the abstract that matters, not the spirit of the Council, which they claim can be ignored. In reply to such an attempt, the archbishop claims: "when we commonly speak of the spirit of an event, we mean precisely that which constitutes the soul, the *essence* of that event. We can thus affirm that the spirit of the Council is the Council itself, that the errors of the *postconciliar period* were contained *in nuce*[51] in the conciliar Acts...." The texts are imbued with the Council's spirit and cannot be corrected outside of expelling the entire spirit.

Viganò is Not a Sedevacantist

The *ad hominem* attacks against Archbishop Viganò did not relent. In addition to being labeled a schismatic, he was also accused of being a sedevacantist. This term, which comes from a Latin phrase meaning "the seat is empty," has been used to refer to Catholics who do not accept that either Pope Francis or some or all of the popes following Pius XII are or were true popes. They argue for a variety

---

51. Latin for "in the nut" or "in the seed." By this expression he means the postconciliar errors were contained in the Acts of the Council as an oak tree is contained in an acorn.

of reasons that these men were ineligible to become pope or lost the office at some point. Therefore, the seat of St. Peter is or has been vacant, according to Catholics who make these claims. Sedeva-cantism is a theory that offers an easy way out of the Church's present crisis: its proponents can say that the scandalous changes in liturgy, doctrine, and moral life are not a crisis *in the Church*, because they were accomplished not by popes but by antipopes. Through this sleight of hand, the crisis is swept out of view. The more difficult path lies in recognizing the holders of the papal throne as popes but distinguishing their unjust and illegal actions from those that are binding on the Church.

In support of this allegation, many point to Archbishop Viganò's claim that the Church has been infiltrated and his references to Pope Francis by his given name (Jorge Bergoglio). Yet neither of these arguments proves that Viganò thinks Jorge Bergoglio is a pre-tender and an antipope. First, it is a common idiom to refer to popes by their given names as well as by their papal names. Thus, sometimes Pope Pius XII is referred to as Pacelli and Leo X as Med-ici. I personally believe that the archbishop uses the name Bergoglio to remind us that we may and must distinguish between what Fran-cis does as pope for the common good of the Church and what he does in his personal capacity, which, if it be evil or a danger to the faith, we have no obligation to accept. As to the infiltration argu-ment, again it does not mean that Archbishop Viganò has accepted the arguments of sedevacantists. In his clarifications provided to *Catholic Family News*, he explains his understanding of the claim that two churches exist within the Catholic Church—one the true Church and one a usurper—and that both of these entities are headed at present by Jorge Bergoglio and the hierarchical bishops. He delineates the need both to refuse any admixture with the Mod-ernist errors and to remain firmly within the Church by refusing to entertain schism or sedevacantism:

> While it is clear that no admixture is possible with those who propose adulterated doctrines of the conciliar ideological mani-festo, it should be noted that the simple fact of being baptized and of being living members of the Church of Christ does not imply

adherence to the conciliar team; this is true above all for the simple faithful and also for secular and regular clerics who, for various reasons, sincerely consider themselves Catholics and recognize the hierarchy.

His point is clear—we do not need to break with the Church or pope to resist the "conciliar team."

His Grace turns the question back on the Modernists of today, who try to claim that the defenders of Tradition, such as Viganò, have broken "full" communion with the Church. With respect to churchmen who "embrace the heterodox doctrines that have spread over these decades, with the awareness that these represent a rupture with the preceding Magisterium," he reassures the faithful that "it is licit to doubt their real adherence to the Catholic Church, in which however they hold official roles that confer authority on them. It is an illicitly exercised authority, if its purpose is to force the faithful to accept the revolution imposed since the Council." This statement draws the proper distinction between holding an office and misusing that office. We can speak to the problem of officeholders (even of the papacy) misusing their offices without claiming their offices are vacant. In a clear refutation of sedevacantist claims, he urges the faithful: "Let us not give in to the temptation to abandon—albeit with justified indignation—the Catholic Church, on the pretext that it has been invaded by heretics and fornicators: it is they who must be expelled from the sacred enclosure, in a work of purification and penance. . . ."

In explaining how members of what he calls the "conciliar sect" can remain in hierarchical offices, His Excellency explains that he accepts the theory of Bishop Bernard Tissier de Mallerais that there are two entities coexisting in the Church.[52] The Church of

---

52. A study by Bishop Tissier de Mallerais was first published in French in the tri-monthly review of the Dominicans of Avrille, *Le Sel de la Terre* 85 (Summer 2013). The purpose of the study was to dispute the claim of Father Jean-Michel Gleize that there is no conciliar church in the sense of an organized society. The dispute centers on the question of both whether there is a real entity called the conciliar church and whether Archbishop Lefebvre believed there to be such an entity. Bishop Tissier answers yes to both questions. He concludes that the conciliar

Christ coexists at least materially with the "strange extravagant Church . . . like wheat with the tare, in the Roman Curia, in dioceses, in parishes." We must acknowledge this sad state but we "cannot judge our pastors for their intentions, nor suppose that all of them are corrupt in faith and morals."

In his speech at the Catholic Identify Conference in October of 2020, Viganò again affirms the important distinction between the Church being infested with enemies and the Church of Christ having failed or having broken into two separate churches. He explains in that address: "Obviously, there are not two Churches, something that would be impossible, blasphemous, and heretical. Nor has the one true Church of Christ today failed in her mission, perverting herself into a sect." Rather, the one true Church is occupied and has suffered the superimposition of what he calls in this speech the "deep church." In his interview with Scott Kesterson, he explains that this occupying body "began to operate during Vatican II in the 1960s." He explains that once the conciliar revolution was established, it "permitted members of the 'deep church' to enter into Vatican Dicasteries, pontifical universities, seminaries, convents, monasteries, and dioceses—that is, right where they could do the most damage." Due to their organization and cunning, the deep church operatives had, he says, "a capacity for capillary infiltration, often due to the naivety of certain prelates or thanks to the complicity of others." As a result, today "the 'deep church' is in possession of practically the entire hierarchical structure of the Catholic Church, especially the highest levels."

---

church "is an association of high-ranking Catholic churchmen inspired by liberal and modernist thinkers, who want, according to the goals of the one-worlders, to bring to fruition a new type of church, with many Catholic priests and faithful won over by this ideal. It is not a pure association of victims. Formally considered, the conciliar church is a sect which occupies the Catholic Church." He goes on to explain that "the conciliar church is not materially separate from the Catholic Church. It does not exist independently from the Catholic Church. There is a distinction certainly between them, a formal one, without an absolute material distinction. The hierarchy of the conciliar church coincides almost exactly with the hierarchy of the Catholic Church, the members of the conciliar church are all members at least materially of the Catholic Church."

He urges the same response as that which Archbishop Marcel Lefebvre urged many decades ago, the path that sedevacantists disapprovingly label "Recognize and Resist." Just as we must avoid the perverted "obeisance of the court" and its blind adherence to novelties, so we must avoid the rejection of authority advocated by sedevacantism. He explains: "We must not rebel, but oppose; we must not be pleased with the errors of our pastors, but pray for them and admonish them respectfully; we must not question their authority but the way in which they use it."

Right and Duty to Avoid New Mass Parishes

In his detailed reply to the questions posed by *Catholic Family News*, Archbishop Viganò demonstrates that he is a true shepherd who cares for the confused and abandoned sheep of our time. He provides clear and practical answers for the increasing number of Catholics whose eyes are being opened to the conciliar revolution. In his prior interventions, Archbishop Viganò accurately diagnosed the cause of the current crisis and identified the ultimate cure for it—the casting aside of the conciliar texts. His Grace offers advice to members of the Church Militant for how they can inoculate themselves against the deadly errors of the conciliar and postconciliar period and live the Faith heroically until that ultimate cure is administered by a future holy pope.

Do Catholics have the right to separate themselves from their geographical parish if it does not offer the sacraments according to the traditional rites and a sound Catholic education? He unambiguously affirms that

> faithful laity have the right and the duty to find priests, communities, and institutes that are faithful to the perennial Magisterium. And may they know how to accompany the laudable celebration of the liturgy in the ancient rite with adherence to sound doctrine and morals, without any subsidence on the front of the Council.

Importantly, Archbishop Viganò declares this avoidance of new Mass parishes not only a right but also a duty. It is not just permissible to avoid the Novus Ordo if one happens to prefer the Latin Mass; for those who understand what is at stake, there is an obligation to avoid the one and assist at the other. He also notes that the faithful need not simply a place where they can attend the traditional Mass but a place that offers the ancient rite together with sound doctrine not based on the faulty theology of the Council. His Grace underscores the inherent connection between the Mass and doctrine by a term he uses several times to refer to the traditional Mass. He calls it simply "the Catholic rite." He eschews the ambiguous and inaccurate term "extraordinary form of the Roman rite," invented by Benedict XVI. He explains that priests should offer the Catholic rite not merely "to preserve the extraordinary form of the rite, but to testify to adherence to the *depositum fidei*[53] that finds perfect correspondence only in the ancient rite." The adverb "only" is noteworthy. The old Mass is not merely one of two equal forms, old and new; it is the only one that perfectly corresponds to the Deposit of Faith.

His Grace acknowledges the more complex situation of clerics. On one hand, clerics have less agility than the laity in seeking a place in the Church to remain Catholic because they must be subject to their ecclesiastical superiors. At the same time, they have greater freedom, as they can at any time legitimately "celebrate the Mass and administer the sacraments in the Tridentine rite and ... preach in conformity with sound doctrine." (Again, note the connection between liturgy and doctrine.) His Grace makes clear that clerics must avoid both the mistake of abandoning the visible Church to set up their own church as well as the opposite error of simply conforming to the new Mass and novel doctrine to avoid internal persecution. Clerics must remain in the Church and remain faithful to the Catholic rite and the true doctrine, even at the cost of persecution, which he acknowledges they will indeed suffer, as did the few faithful clerics in the period of the Arian heresy. He underlines that priests must celebrate only "the Tridentine Mass and preach sound doctrine," and maintains that truth cannot be fully preached if a priest never dares to call out the Council's errors. He acknowledges that fulfilling these three duties (offering only the Catholic rite, preaching the truth, and exposing conciliar

---

53. Latin for "deposit of the faith."

errors) may result in the priest being thrown out of his parish. He reminds such persecuted priests: "No one can ever prevent you from renewing the Holy Sacrifice, even if it is on a makeshift altar in a cellar or an attic. . . ." Priests must be willing to suffer such persecution for the sake of the Church. He urges faithful priests not to fear being called false names: "Let's stop fearing that the fault of the schism lies with those who denounce it, and not, instead, with those who carry it out: the ones who are schismatics and heretics are those who wound and crucify the Mystical Body of Christ, not those who defend it by denouncing the executioners!"

As for the laity, His Grace makes clear (as noted earlier) that they have a right and duty to receive the traditional sacraments and true doctrine. They must seek out ministers who will provide for these basic needs and avoid ministers "contaminated by present errors." He emphasizes that the laity must do more than avail themselves of good priests for their own spiritual benefit; they also have the "sacred task" to "comfort good priests and good bishops" and "give them hospitality, help them, console them in their trials." Just as he puts his finger so accurately on the conciliar errors, His Grace also diagnoses a danger in traditionalist communities that must be avoided, namely, the sowing of division. He calls on the laity to build communities "in which murmuring and division do not predominate, but rather fraternal charity in the bond of faith." There is a temptation simply to look out for oneself that runs the risk of reducing priests to instruments for obtaining the traditional sacraments. Those who fall into this temptation fail in their duty to support and comfort the clergy within a united Catholic community.

What about Archbishop Lefebvre and the Society He Founded?

In the letter to Kokx, Archbishop Viganò reveals his thoughts on the Society of Saint Pius X (SSPX) and its founder, Archbishop Marcel Lefebvre. He believes the SSPX "deserves recognition for not having allowed the flame of Tradition to be extinguished." He considers them to be "a healthy thorn in the side" of the Modernist hierarchy and credits them for shining a light on "the contradictions and errors of the conciliar sect." He appears to condone the consecration by Lefebvre of four bishops without a written papal mandate in

1988 when he observes that these consecrations made it possible for the Society "to protect herself from the furious attack of the innovators."[54] His Grace refers to the punishments inflicted upon the archbishop and his Society—the attempted excommunications, for example—as having been not acts of justice but acts of "persecution." He believes that Archbishop Lefebvre's critique of the Council is "more relevant than ever." Rather than considering Lefebvre a "schismatic" or "excommunicate," Archbishop Viganò calls him "an exemplary confessor of the Faith." In his subsequent response to Father Weinandy, Viganò seems to be referring to Lefebvre in his claim that he did not initiate this debate: "I do not claim myself to have the merit of having initiated this dispute: other eminent prelates and high-profile intellectuals before me have highlighted critical issues that need a solution; others have shown the causal relationship between Vatican II and the present apostasy." Clearly, he must be referring not only to other Catholic authors but, with the reference to "eminent prelates," to the Apostolic Delegate, Archbishop Lefebvre, as well. In his same response to Weinandy he

54. Archbishop Lefebvre maintained at the time and until his death that the consecrations were justified due to the state of necessity the conciliar crisis in the Church had provoked. He argued they were necessary to keep the traditional priesthood and liturgy alive after his death, which he believed to be near at hand. The Vatican claimed at the time that Lefebvre and the four bishops he consecrated excommunicated themselves by participating in the consecration. Although it is true that Lefebvre did not have a specific written mandate to perform the consecration, he maintained that the Vatican had agreed to permit a consecration in May of 1988 but was then engaging in delay tactics until Lefebvre would die. In 2009, Pope Benedict XVI lifted the alleged excommunication of the four consecrated bishops. Given that this decree was issued without the four bishops having been asked to repent of their participation, it seems that Benedict was signaling that they may never have been legally excommunicated. As Lefebvre had died in 1991, he is not mentioned in this decree. Archbishop Viganò is careful to write in the past tense in his praise for the Society and Lefebvre. He has not expressed an opinion on whether the current superiors of the Society of St. Pius X should accept some form of canonical regularization or legal arrangement with the current Vatican. Pope Francis has made it clear that whatever the legal status of the bishops and priests of the Society of St. Pius X may be, they can validly and legally give the sacrament of confession and, under certain conditions, validly and licitly witness marriages. For decades, the Vatican has acknowledged that the laity are permitted to attend Masses offered by the Society of St. Pius X and contribute to the monetary collection.

Introduction to Part II

asserts that the legal sanctions inflicted upon Lefebvre were not justice but "persecuting the good"; similarly, in his speech to the Catholic Identify Conference Viganò again confirms his positive judgement of the "far-sightedness" of Archbishop Lefebvre in resisting the deep church that eclipsed the Church following the Council.

Connecting the Dots: Francis as a Fruit of the Council

The final five documents in this part focus on Viganò's assessment of the pontificate of Francis, beyond his revelations of Francis closing his eyes to clerical sexual abuse. In these documents, he focuses on the moral and theological errors that have proliferated under Francis and that originate in the Council.

Two texts discuss Francis's encyclical *Fratelli Tutti*. This encyclical, released in October 2020, in many ways serves as a synthesis of all of Francis's prior writings, a manifesto for uniting the Church with the New World Order sought by the globalists. The papal text provides the theological rationale for the absorption of the Pachamama into St. Peter's Basilica. Its contents shocked many Catholics; Viganò, for his part, finds nothing surprising, once the revolution at Vatican II is understood.

As we saw earlier, one of the movers and shakers at Vatican II, Cardinal Suenens, called Vatican II the French Revolution in the Church. The slogan of the French Revolution was "Liberty, Equality, Fraternity," by which the revolutionaries meant the false and liberal understanding of these concepts. They advocated license to follow one's opinions and passions in contrast to the true moral liberty of knowing God's truth and obeying His law. They advocated a false equality that destroys our individuality and ordered liberty. Finally, they boasted a false fraternity, based on utopian lies rather than on our common brotherhood that derives from our adoption by God as his children in Christ. Pope Francis adopts this revolutionary motto in *Fratelli Tutti* (n.103). In his comments on the encyclical, Archbishop Viganò makes clear that Francis's embrace of the Revolution is a product of Vatican II. The silence of both the encyclical and the US bishops in election season about the great evil of abortion was foreshadowed in the Council's silence about atheistic Communism. The uncrowning of Christ the King and the relativization of religion in *Dignitatis Humanæ* and *Nostra Ætate* produced the secularist, naturalist false fraternity of Francis.

Viganò persuasively argues that the problem in 2020 is not Pope Francis. He agrees with the pope's own assessment of himself as standing in perfect continuity with Vatican II. In commenting upon the encyclical *Fratelli Tutti*, the archbishop observes that "the reference [in a quotation from the encyclical of Francis] to the conciliar document *Nostra Ætate* is the confirmation of the ideological link of the Bergoglian heretical thought with the premises earlier set by Vatican II." There is no difficulty in proving the continuity of Francis's heretical statements with Vatican II. What cannot be shown to be in continuity is Vatican II/Francis with the preconciliar Church.

In his commentary on the documentary *Francesco*, Viganò synthesizes all of the rotten fruits that the Council has produced on the tree of Bergoglio: the Abu Dhabi Statement, *Amoris Lætitia*'s distortion of the Church's teaching on the sacraments, the changing of the *Catechism* to reverse traditional teaching on the death penalty, the pope's advocating for people living the sins of an LGBT lifestyle to be able to have families and be recognized by civil union laws. Throughout the prior interventions, he has argued that all of these effects have their roots in Vatican II. This revolutionary process has produced what he calls the church of Bergoglio, a new Sanhedrin. The reference is significant to understanding how Viganò is able to accept that Francis can hold the papal office in the true Catholic Church and at the same time can act contrary to the good of the Church. The Sanhedrin was the court of Jewish elders that was the supreme religious body in Israel at the time of Our Lord's public life. It is the court that tried Our Lord and unjustly sentenced him to death. Members of the Sanhedrin held the highest offices in the Jewish religion (cf. Mt 23:2) and were supposed to use their authority to support the mission of the Messiah. Contrary to their duty, they used their legitimate authority illegitimately to condemn the Messiah to death. Thus, they were enemies of the chosen people yet truly occupying seats of authority. They used that power to destroy (to the extent they could) God's chosen nation. This is precisely what Viganò argues Bergoglio has done to the Catholic Church. In the short text, "The 'church' of Bergoglio: The New Sanhedrin," he

Introduction to Part II

catalogues all the ways in which the new Sanhedrin has repeated the unfaithfulness of the old one. In this list he returns to the subject of one of his first interventions that went beyond the abuse crisis—the December 19, 2019 letter in defense of Mary against Francis. He adds to the offenses of the conciliar Church its refusal to honor Our Lady's request that the pope together with all of the bishops of the world consecrate Russia to the Immaculate Heart of Mary. Archbishop Viganò joins the voices of those true sons of Our Lady who have claimed for decades that the consecration was never made according to the instructions of Our Lady of Fatima.[55] In this text on the Sanhedrin of Francis, he clearly avers that the request of Our Lady of Fatima for this specific consecration "remains unheeded to this day, despite the disasters which the world would have to face if it did not heed the requests of the Most Holy Virgin." He repeats this claim when he says: "despite the recognition of the supernatural origin of the apparitions and the evidence of the calamities which afflict mankind, the hierarchy refuses to obey the Blessed Mother." Among those calamities are the spreading everywhere of the "militant atheism of Communism" and the persecution of the Church "by ruthless and cruel enemies, while she is also infested by corrupt clerics given over to vice." In this text, all the strands are drawn together: the consecration of Russia, Vatican II, Communist persecution, the McCarrick sexual scandal, and the rupture with Catholic doctrine.

The final document in this part is Archbishop Viganò's address to the Catholic Identity Conference in October 2020. It is an excellent bridge between this part and the third part of the present collection. In this address, he reaffirms and synthesizes his assessment of Vatican II and its causal link to the pontificate of Francis:

> The Council's first error consists mainly in the lack of a transcendent perspective—the result of a spiritual crisis that was already latent—and in the attempt to establish paradise on earth, with a

---

55. See, for example, Abbé Pierre Caillon, "Fatima May 13, 1982—What Actually Happened? Was Russia Consecrated to the Immaculate Heart of Mary?," https://fatima.org/about/consecration-of-russia/was-russia-consecrated-to-the-immaculate-heart.

sterile human horizon. In line with this approach, *Fratelli Tutti* sees the fulfillment of an earthly utopia and social redemption in human brotherhood, *pax œcumenica* between religions, and welcoming migrants.

Viganò traces many of the problems in the Church in the twenty-first century to specific aspects of Vatican II. For example:

— the democratization of the Church began with *Lumen Gentium* and today it is realized in the Bergoglian synodal path;
— the "freedom of the children of God" theorized by Vatican II has been established regardless of the moral duties of individuals who, according to the conciliar fairytales, are all saved regardless of their inner dispositions and the state of their soul;
— the obfuscating of perennial moral references has led to the revised doctrine on capital punishment; and, with *Amoris Lætitia*, the admission of public adulterers to the sacraments, cracking the sacramental edifice;
— the religious freedom theorized in *Dignitatis Humanæ* is today brought to its logical and extreme consequences with the Declaration of Abu Dhabi and the latest Encyclical *Fratelli Tutti*, rendering the saving mission of the Church and the Incarnation itself obsolete. . . .

Throughout 2020, Viganò had several times repudiated Benedict XVI's hermeneutic of continuity which he once supported as a way to deal with the Council. In the Catholic Identity Conference speech, he repudiates another failed attempt: "conservative Catholicism." The archbishop fully embraces the traditionalists when he makes clear that the so-called conservatives in the Church end up carrying water for the revolutionaries. He explains:

We know that, in addition to the progressive wing of the Council and the traditional Catholic wing, there is a part of the Episcopate, the clergy, and the people that attempts to keep equal distance from what it considers two extremes. I am talking about the so-called "conservatives," that is, a centrist part of the ecclesial body that ends up "carrying water" for the revolutionaries

138

because, while rejecting their excesses, it shares the same principles. The error of the "conservatives" lies in giving a negative connotation to traditionalism and in placing it on the opposite side of progressivism. Their *aurea mediocritas*[56] consists in arbitrarily placing themselves not between two vices, but between virtue and vice. They are the ones who criticize the excesses of the Pachamama or of the most extreme of Bergoglio's statements, but who do not tolerate the Council's being questioned, let alone the intrinsic link between the conciliar cancer and the current metastasis.

Having forgotten who she was at Vatican II, the Church on earth is experiencing a deep crisis of faith, having traded her divine stature for an illusory treaty with the humanists and secularist enemies of the Church. This subjugating of the Church to the world has been an essential element in the plan to build a New World Order of secular and atheistic globalism. Vatican II is thus a watershed moment for both the deep church *and* the deep state.

There are two critical passages of the Catholic Identity Conference in which the archbishop synthesizes the essence of the crisis in the liturgy. He had already told us in the summer of 2020 that the traditional Latin Mass must be restored in place of the new Mass and that the laity had a duty to seek out the ancient rite. The reason is not because the traditional Mass is more solemn or aesthetically pleasing (although it generally is). He explained that the crisis of the Council is ontological—a crisis about the very nature of the Church, her identity, her *being*. Along the same lines, he argues that the new Mass inverts the proper relationship between the individual and the community. It destroys that which the liturgy is meant to nourish—personal and individual sanctity—and it relativizes for each individual that which is meant to be uniform for the community of the Church. He explains:

Allow me to conclude this examination of the links between the Council and the present crisis by emphasizing a reversal that I consider extremely important and significant. I am referring to

56. The golden mean; the *via media* or middle way.

the relationship of the individual layman and community of the faithful with God. While in the Church of Christ the relationship of the soul with the Lord is eminently personal even when it is conveyed by the sacred minister in the liturgical action, in the *conciliar* church the community and the group relationship prevails. Think of their insistence in wanting to make the baptism of a child, or the wedding of a married couple, "an act of the community"; or the impossibility of receiving holy Communion individually outside of Mass, and of the common practice of approaching Communion during Mass even without the necessary conditions. All of this is sanctioned on the basis of a protestantized concept of participation in the Eucharistic banquet, from which no guest is excluded. Under this understanding of community, the person loses his individuality, losing himself in the anonymous community of the celebration.

In the second paragraph, Viganò explains how the proper relationship between individual and community is dismantled from the other side:

So too, the relationship of the social body with God disappears in a personalism that eliminates the role of mediation of both the Church and the State. Individualization in the moral field enters into this as well, where the rights and preferences of the individual become grounds for the eradication of social morality. This is done in the name of an "inclusiveness" that legitimates every vice and moral aberration. Society—understood as the union of several individuals aimed at the pursuit of a common goal—is divided into a multiplicity of individuals, each of whom has his own purpose. This is the result of an ideological upheaval that deserves to be analyzed in depth, because of its implications both in the ecclesial and civil spheres. It is evident, however, that the first step of this revolution is to be found in the conciliar *mens*, beginning with the indoctrination of the Christian people constituted by the reformed liturgy, in which the individual merges into the assembly by depersonalizing himself, and the community devolves into a collection of individuals by losing their identity.

Introduction to Part II

Certainly, there is much more that can be said about the destruction of the liturgy, but these two paragraphs succinctly encapsulate the essence of the problem.

Finally, in this address he returns to his call to consign the Council to oblivion. Asseverating that all the mental and verbal gymnastics to save the Council are fruitless, he pleads:

> Therefore, let us put aside, once and for all, the vain distinctions concerning the presumed goodness of the Council, the betrayal of the will of the Synod Fathers, the *letter* and *spirit* of Vatican II, the magisterial weight (or lack thereof) of its acts, and the *hermeneutic of continuity* versus that *of rupture*. The anti-church has used the label "Ecumenical Council" to give authority and legal force to its revolutionary agenda, just as Bergoglio calls his political manifesto of allegiance to the New World Order an "encyclical letter." The cunning of the enemy has isolated the healthy part of the Church, torn between having to recognize the subversive nature of the Council documents, thus having to exclude them from the Magisterial corpus, and having to deny reality by declaring them apodictically orthodox in order to safeguard the infallibility of the Magisterium. . . . The only way to win this battle is to go back to doing what the Church has always done, and to stop doing what the anti-church asks of us today—that which the true Church has always condemned.

If someone is going to read only a single text of Archbishop Viganò, this address to the Catholic Identity Conference, which synthesizes his theological insight and pastoral message, should be it.

Remain Hopeful

Like Archbishop Lefebvre before him, Archbishop Viganò combines a clear-sighted diagnosis of the conciliar disease with a true Catholic peace of soul that trusts firmly in God. After taking note that clerics and laity alike are beginning to see the conciliar nightmare for what it is, he looks forward in his reply to *Catholic Family News* to a necessary "awakening" that is "almost a resurrection." Just as "no son tolerates his mother being outraged by the servants, or his father being tyrannized by the administrators of his goods," so too the Lord "offers us, in these painful situations, the possibility of being His allies in fighting this holy battle under His banner." Rather than becoming discouraged by unjust persecution, Viganò reminds us of the consoling truth that "the King Who is victorious over error and death permits us to share the honor of triumphal victory and the eternal reward that derives from it, after having endured and suffered with Him." He exhorts us to practice the virtue of fortitude. We must not lose hope. His texts concludes with great confidence that God will rescue us from this crisis: "I am certain, with a certainty that comes to me from faith, that the Lord will not fail to reward our fidelity . . . granting us holy priests, holy bishops, holy cardinals, and above all a holy pope."

7

Thus the World Neo-Religion Will Have Its Temple. With the Pope's Approval[1]

November 20, 2019

IN February 2019, Pope Francis signed a document with the Grand Imam of Al-Azhar, Ahmad Al-Tayyeb, entitled A Document on Human Fraternity for World Peace and Living Together. *This document legitimately condemns using violence to force people to adhere to a certain religious belief. The Church has always condemned using violence to force belief. In fact, professed belief in a creed if compelled by violence is not a product of faith but of fear. Yet this document goes much further beyond this obvious principle. It celebrates the existence of false religions as being willed by God. The troubling passage states: "The pluralism and the diversity of religions, colour, sex, race and language are willed by God in His wisdom, through which He created human beings." It places choices of the will (what religious beliefs to accept) on the same plane as unwilled indelible characteristics such as race or color. It lumps together the essential (true religion) with the accidental.*

"To the Venerable Brothers...who have peace and communion with the Apostolic See in the defense of the truth revealed by Jesus Christ, health and Apostolic Blessing. Perhaps in the past it never happened that the heart of human creatures was taken as today by such a lively desire for fraternity.... One easily understands

---

1. The article, dated November 20, 2019, appeared in Italian on Aldo Maria Valli's blog *Duc in altum*; an English translation was published by *Inside the Vatican*, https://insidethevatican.com/news/newsflash/letter-62-2019-Viganò-on-the-danger-of-syncretism.

143

... how many are those who yearn to see more and more united among themselves the various nations, led to this by this universal feeling of brotherhood." This is how the Supreme Pontiff Pius XI expressed himself at the beginning of his encyclical *Mortalium Animos* in 1928, signed precisely on the day of the Epiphany, when the Church recalls the three wise Magi from the East, leaders of a ceaseless processional caravan guided by a shining star that appeared in the firmament, when on earth the Son of God came in the flesh, the One Savior, center of the cosmos and of history.

Ninety-one years later, last Friday, November 15, 2019—as reported by Vatican News—Pope Bergoglio received the Great Imam Ahmed Al-Tayeb, accompanied by various personalities and representatives of the University of Al-Azhar and the Superior Committee, all animated by the desire to give form and substance to the contents of the Document on Human Brotherhood for World Peace and the Common Cohabitation, agreed upon last August in the wake of the historic Emirate Declaration, signed by the pontiff and by the Imam during the Year of Brotherhood.

About the document mentioned above, His Excellency Mohamed Khalifa Al Mubarak, as the representative of the United Arab Emirates, had previously stated (Vatican News, September 21, 2019) that "in a world where there are so many things that divide, the Emirates are committed to unite. Like a beacon of light, they want to bring light into a dark world, bringing to light this Document, the most important signed in recent times"; as if to say that "the Light from the East" which came to visit us from on high like the sun rising (Lk 1:7–8) is now eclipsed by a new "Bright Lighthouse."

The talks of the Vatican meeting were cordial, with words and expressive gestures of a by now consolidated friendship: we recall that this is the sixth meeting between the pope and the Great Imam. Thus the Latin American warmth has prevailed over the long and rigid "frost" that formerly marked the relations between the Apostolic See and the highest leadership of Sunni Islam. The meeting also offered the opportunity to present the pope with a singular project of which it is possible to get a certain idea through floor plans and 3D models.

Sir David Adjaye OBE is the creator of this architectural project, which will be built in the opulent and extravagant Abu Dhabi. It will be called "The Abrahamic Family House," a sort of New Tent of Universal Brotherhood evoking that other Tent of Hospitality in which the Ancient Patriarch (Abraham) hosted three mysterious Angels (cf. Genesis 18), prefiguration of the Trinitarian God fully revealed to the legitimate Abrahamic posterity, through faith in Jesus Christ. "Abrahamic Family House" is therefore the name of this structure that will house a synagogue, a mosque, and a church—naturally dedicated to the Poverello (St. Francis of Assisi).

Sir David's project envisages that the three different places of worship should be joined together by a single foundation and placed within a garden, evocative of a New Eden, a re-evocation in a gnostic and Masonic key of the paradise of the First Creation. As explained to Pope Bergoglio, this "structure . . . will serve as a place of individual worship, but also for dialogue and interreligious exchange." In fact, a fourth building is also planned, home to the Center for Studies and Research on Human Brotherhood, whose objective, which can be seen from the Abu Dhabi document, will be to "make the three religions known." In this same venue will also take place ceremonies to hand out a Human Brotherhood Prize.

The building of the Abrahamic Family House seems to be a Babelic enterprise, concocted by the enemies of God, of the Catholic Church and of the only true religion capable of saving man and the whole creation from destruction, both now and in eternity, and definitively. The foundations of this "House," destined to give way and collapse, arise where, by the hands of the builders themselves, the One Cornerstone is about to be incredibly removed: Jesus Christ, Savior and Lord, on whom is built the House of God. "Therefore," warns the Apostle Paul, "let everyone be careful how he builds. Indeed, no one can lay a foundation other than the one already found there, which is Jesus Christ" (1 Cor 3:10).

In the garden of Abu Dhabi the temple of the world syncretistic Neo-Religion is about to rise with its anti-Christian dogmas. Not even the most hopeful of the Freemasons would have imagined so much!

Pope Bergoglio thus proceeds to further implement the apostasy of Abu Dhabi, the fruit of pantheistic and agnostic neo-modernism that tyrannizes the Roman Church, germinated by the conciliar document *Nostra Ætate*. We are compelled to recognize it: the poisoned fruits of the "conciliar springtime" are before the eyes of anyone who does not allow himself to be blinded by the dominant lie.

Pius XI had alerted and warned us. But the teachings that preceded Vatican II have been thrown to the winds, as intolerant and obsolete. The comparison between the preconciliar Magisterium and the new teachings of *Nostra Ætate* and *Dignitatis Humanæ*—to mention only those—manifest a terrible discontinuity, which must be acknowledged and which must be amended as soon as possible, *adjuvante Deo* ("with God's help").

Let us listen to the words of the Supreme Pontiff Pius XI, when the popes used to speak the language of truth, chiseled with fire in diamond.

> For which reason conventions, meetings and addresses are frequently arranged by these persons, at which a large number of listeners are present, and at which all without distinction are invited to join in the discussion, both infidels of every kind, and Christians, even those who have unhappily fallen away from Christ or who with obstinacy and pertinacity deny His divine nature and mission. Certainly such attempts can nowise be approved by Catholics, founded as they are on that false opinion which considers all religions to be more or less good and praiseworthy, since they all in different ways manifest and signify that sense which is inborn in us all, and by which we are led to God and to the obedient acknowledgment of His rule. Not only are those who hold this opinion in error and deceived, but also in distorting the idea of true religion they reject it, and little by little turn aside to naturalism and atheism, as it is called; from which it clearly follows that one who supports those who hold these theories and attempt to realize them is altogether abandoning the divinely revealed religion. (*Mortalium Animos*, 2)

The mystical Bride of Christ over the centuries has never been contaminated nor will she ever be contaminated, according to Cyprian's words: "The Bride of Christ cannot be made false to her Spouse: she is incorrupt and modest. She knows but one dwelling, she guards the sanctity of the nuptial chamber chastely and modestly." (*Mortalium Animos*, 10)

Today more than ever ... the Church needs strong and consistent doctrines. In the midst of dissolution ... the compromises become more and more sterile, and each of them takes away a piece of the truth. ... Show yourself, then ... who, in the end, you are, convinced Catholics...! There is a grace linked to the full and complete confession of faith. This confession, the Apostle tells us, is the salvation of those who make it, and experience shows that it is also the salvation of those who understand it. (Dom Prosper Guéranger, *The Christian Meaning of History*)

The Emeritus Pope Benedict XVI recently broke his silence by making public his sorrowful plea for the Church in this hour so troubled in its history:

Even today our faith is threatened by reductive changes to which worldly fashions would like to subject it to take away its greatness. Lord, help us in this time of ours to be and to remain true Catholics—to live and die in the greatness of Your truth and in Your divinity. Give us always courageous bishops who may guide us to unity in faith and with the saints of all times and may show us how to act adequately in the service of reconciliation, to which our episcopate is called in a special way. Lord Jesus Christ, have mercy on us!

8

Letter in Defense
of Mary against Francis[1]

THIS letter dated December 19, 2019, appears to have been prompted by two events. First the Amazon Synod held in Rome in October of that year. As discussed in the letter (and explained in the footnotes) during this synod images of a pagan goddess, the Pachamama, were prominently displayed and even apparently venerated before and during the Synod. The discussions in, and document produced by, the Synod seemed to exalt pagan and pantheistic religious practices of the Amazon region. At times the proceedings conflated the Blessed Mother with the Pachamama.

Secondly during a Mass to observe the Feast of Our Lady of Guadalupe, Francis attacked the centuries-old call of theologians and faithful to definitively declare Mary Co-Redemptrix with Christ. Francis on this occasion called such attempts "foolishness." He insulted any attempt to bestow honors on the Mother of God and suggested she did not want our veneration under these titles: "She never introduced herself as co-redemptrix. No. Disciple . . . meaning that Mary saw herself as a disciple of Jesus."[2] Considering Mary only another disciple of Jesus would be more acceptable to Protestants than a theological term such as Co-Redemptrix. It seems the belittling of this traditional (although not yet infallibly declared) title as "foolishness" called forth an important intervention from Viganò that demonstrates how much his thinking on Vatican II had developed.

1. The English translation by Diane Montagna first appeared at www.lifesitenews.com/news/abp-viganos-defense-of-virgin-mary-in-response-to-pope-francis-full-text.

2. For a report on this sermon, see Inés San Martín, "Pope calls idea of declaring Mary co-redemptrix 'foolishness,'" *Crux*, December 13, 2019, https://cruxnow.com/vatican/2019/12/pope-calls-idea-of-declaring-mary-co-redemptrix-foolishness.

Letter in Defense of Mary against Francis

Thus saith the Lord God that created the heavens, and stretched them out: that established the earth, and the things that spring out of it: that giveth breath to the people upon it, and spirit to them that tread thereon.

I the Lord have called thee in justice, and taken thee by the hand, and preserved thee. And I have given thee for a covenant of the people, for a light of the Gentiles:

That thou mightest open the eyes of the blind, and bring forth the prisoner out of prison, and them that sit in darkness out of the prison house.

I the Lord, this is my name: I will not give my glory to another, nor my praise to graven things.

The things that were first, behold they are come: and new things do I declare: before they spring forth, I will make you hear them.

Sing ye to the Lord a new song, his praise is from the ends of the earth: you that go down to the sea, and all that are therein: ye islands, and ye inhabitants of them.

Let the desert and the cities thereof be exalted: Cedar shall dwell in houses: ye inhabitants of Petra, give praise, they shall cry from the top of the mountains.

They shall give glory to the Lord, and shall declare his praise in the islands.

The Lord shall go forth as a mighty man, as a man of war shall he stir up zeal: he shall shout and cry: he shall prevail against his enemies.

I have always held my peace, I have kept silence, I have been patient, I will speak now as a woman in labour: I will destroy, and swallow up at once.

I will lay waste the mountains and hills, and will make all their grass to wither: and I will turn rivers into islands, and will dry up the standing pools.

And I will lead the blind into the way which they know not: and in the paths which they were ignorant of I will make them walk: I will make darkness light before them, and crooked things straight: these things have I done to them, and have not forsaken them.

149

They are turned back: let them be greatly confounded, that trust in a graven thing, that say to a molten thing: You are our god.

Isaiah 42:5–17

"Is there in the heart of the Virgin Mary anything other than the Name of Our Lord Jesus Christ? We too want to have only one name in our hearts: that of Jesus, like the Most Blessed Virgin."

The tragic story of this failed pontificate advances with a pressing succession of twists and turns. Not a day passes: from the most exalted throne the Supreme Pontiff proceeds to dismantle the See of Peter, using and abusing its supreme authority, not to confess but to deny; not to confirm but to mislead; not to unite but to divide; not to build but to demolish.

Material heresies, formal heresies, idolatry, superficiality of every kind: the Supreme Pontiff Bergoglio never ceases stubbornly to humiliate the highest authority of the Church, "demythologizing" the papacy—as perhaps his illustrious comrade Karl Rahner would say. His action seeks to violate the Sacred Deposit of Faith and to disfigure the Catholic Face of the Bride of Christ by word and action, through duplicity and lies, through those theatrical gestures of his that flaunt spontaneity but are meticulously conceived and planned, and through which he exalts himself in a continuous narcissistic self-celebration, while the figure of the Roman Pontiff is humiliated and the Sweet Christ on earth is obscured.

His action makes use of magisterial improvisation, of that off the cuff and fluid magisterium that is as insidious as quicksand, not only flying at high altitude at the mercy of journalists from all over the world, in those ethereal spaces that can highlight a pathological delirium of illusory omnipotence, but also at the most solemn religious ceremony that ought to incite holy trembling and reverent respect.

On the occasion of the liturgical memorial of the Virgin of Guadalupe, Pope Bergoglio once again gave vent to his evident Marian intolerance, recalling that of the Serpent in the account of the Fall, in that Proto-Gospel which prophesies the radical enmity placed by God between the Woman and the Serpent, and the declared hostility of the latter, who until the consummation of time will seek to undermine the Woman's heel and to triumph over her and her posterity. The Pontiff's intolerance is a manifest aggression against the prerogatives and sublime attributes that make the Immaculate Ever-Virgin Mother of God the feminine complement to the mystery of the Incarnate Word, intimately associated with Him in the economy of Redemption.

After having downgraded her to the "next door neighbor" or a runaway migrant, or a simple lay woman with the defects and crises of any woman marked by sin,[3] or a disciple who obviously has nothing to teach us; after having trivialized and desacralized her, like those feminists who are gaining ground in Germany with their "Mary 2.0" movement which seeks to modernize Our Lady and make her a simulacrum in their image and likeness, Pope Bergoglio has further impugned the August Queen and Immaculate Mother of God, who "became mestiza with humanity . . . and made God mestizo." With a couple of jokes, he struck at the heart of the Marian dogma and the Christological dogma connected to it.

The Marian dogmas are the seal placed on the Catholic truths of our faith, defined at the Councils of Nicaea, Ephesus and Chalcedon; they are the unbreakable bulwark against Christological heresies and against the furious unleashing of the gates of hell. Those who "mestizo" and profane them show that they are on the side of the Enemy. To attack Mary is to venture against Christ himself; to

---

3. Viganò is likely referring to a statement by Pope Francis from December 2013 in which he speculated that Our Lady may have doubted God and even called His promises "lies." The pope is reported as having said in relation to Our Lady at the foot of the Cross: "She was silent, but in her heart, how many things she told the Lord! 'You, that day, this and the other that we read, you had told me that he would be great, you had told me that you would have given him the throne of David, his forefather, that he would have reigned forever, and now I see him *there!*' Our Lady was human! And perhaps she even had the desire to say: 'Lies! I was deceived!' John Paul II would say this, speaking about Our Lady in that moment. But she, with her silence, hid the mystery that she did not understand and with this silence allowed for this mystery to grow and blossom in hope." See, for example, Father Celatus, "Was Mary Tempted to Doubt God?," *The Remnant* online, January 2, 2014, https://remnantnewspaper.com/web/index.php/articles/item/121-was-mary-tempted-to-d oubt-god.

attack the Mother is to rise up against her Son and to rebel against the very mystery of the Most Holy Trinity. The Immaculate *Theotokos*,[4] "terrible as an army with banners" (Canticle 6:10)—*acies ordinata*—will do battle to save the Church and destroy the Enemy's unfettered army that has declared war on her, and with him all the demonic Pachamamas[5] will definitively return to hell.

Pope Bergoglio no longer seems to contain his impatience with the Immaculate, nor can he conceal it under that seeming and ostentatious devotion which is always in the spotlight of the cameras, while he deserts the solemn celebration of the Assumption and the recitation of the Rosary with the faithful, who filled the courtyard of St. Damascene and the upper loggia of St. Peter's Basilica under St. John Paul II and Pope Benedict XVI.

Papa Bergoglio uses the Pachamama to rout the Guadalupana. The enthronement of that Amazonian idol, even at the altar of the confession in St. Peter's Basilica,[6] was nothing less than a declaration of war on the Lady and Patroness of all the Americas, who with her apparition to Juan Diego destroyed the demonic idols and won the indigenous peoples for Christ and the adoration of the "Most True and Only God," through her maternal mediation. And this is not a legend!

---

4. Greek for "God-bearer." This title was infallibly given to Mary at the Council of Ephesus to signify that she was not merely the mother of Jesus (as if he were a mere man) but truly and really the mother of God, because her Son is a divine Person born of her according to His human nature.

5. Pachamama is a pagan deity venerated in many parts of South America, including the Amazon. Statues of this idol were placed in Catholic churches in Rome during the Synod on the Amazon and even venerated in a ceremony in the Vatican Garden on October 4, 2019, attended by Pope Francis. A video recording of the entire ceremony can be viewed at https://youtu.be/H6P39XswlzI; cf. Peter Kwasniewski, "A Theological Review of the Amazon Synod," https://youtu.be/7n64KqYSnMc.

6. During the final Mass of the Synod on the Amazon, a ritual bowl used in the pagan cult of Pachamama was carried with honor into St. Peter's and placed on the papal altar built over the tomb of St. Peter. A video of the ceremony can be viewed at https://youtu.be/T1ud3rCiFog. Since this sacrilege, Pope Francis has not used the papal altar publicly. See Maike Hickson, "A symbolic sign after the Pachamama worship at St. Peter's: Papal Altar unused for months now," *LifeSiteNews*, December 18, 2020.

Letter in Defense of Mary against Francis

A few weeks after the conclusion of the synodal event, which marked the investiture of Pachamama in the heart of Catholicity, we learned that the conciliar disaster of the *Novus Ordo Missæ* is undergoing further modernization, including the introduction of "Dew" in the Eucharistic Canon instead of the mention of the Holy Spirit, the Third Person of the Most Holy Trinity.

This is a further step in the direction of regression towards the naturalization and immanentization of Catholic worship, towards a pantheistic and idolatrous *Novissimus Ordo*.[7] The "Dew," an entity present in the "theological place" of the Amazonian tropics—as we learned from the synodal fathers—becomes the new immanent principle of fertilization of the Earth, which "transubstantiates" it into a pantheistically connected Whole to which men are assimilated and subjugated, to the glory of Pachamama. And here we are plunged back into the darkness of a new globalist and eco-tribal paganism, with its demons and perversions. From this latest liturgical upheaval, divine Revelation decays from fullness to archaism;[8] from the hypostatic identity[9] of the Holy Spirit we slide towards the symbolic and metaphorical evanescence proper to dew, which masonic gnosis[10] has long made its own.

---

7. Latin for the "last order." The word *novissimus* has a connotation that refers to the end of the world, which in Scripture and Catholic writing is sometimes referred to as the *Novissima Dies* or the last day. Here, however, the archbishop is making a play on words: the *Novus Ordo*, "new order," is to become accelerated in its own trajectory until it becomes *novissimus*, "most new."

8. Archaism refers to archaic or ancient times. The acts of Pope Bergoglio are attempting to return to the time before the fullness of revelation in the Gospel, the ancient period when men due to ignorance widely worshiped false gods, with the exception of the chosen people of Israel who alone worshiped the true God.

9. The Greek word *hypostasis*, when used in theology, refers to the distinct Persons within the one divine substance of the Blessed Trinity. The term "hypostatic union" refers to the union of Christ's human nature with the divine nature. Here Viganò is implying that the substitution of the word "dew" in the new Mass (see the Second Eucharistic Prayer: "Make holy, therefore, these gifts, we pray, by sending down your Spirit upon them like the dewfall") for the Holy Ghost is shifting the meaning from the Divine Person in the Blessed Trinity to a pagan concept of the infusion of the divine in nature.

10. *Gnosis* is Greek for "knowledge." Although a neutral term in itself, it often refers (especially in the form of *gnosticism*) to an early heresy in the Church that

But let us return for a moment to the idolatrous statues of rare ugliness, and to Pope Bergoglio's declaration the day after their removal from the church in Traspontina and their drowning in the Tiber.[11] Once again, the pope's words have the scent of a colossal lie: he made us believe that the statuettes were promptly exhumed from the filthy waters thanks to the intervention of the Carabinieri [Italian police]. One wonders why a crew from Vatican News coordinated by Tornielli,[12] and Spadaro of *Civiltà Cattolica*,[13] with reporters and cameramen from the court press, did not come to film the prowess of the divers and capture the rescue of the Pachamamas. It is also unlikely that such a spectacular feat did not capture the attention of a few passers-by, equipped with a mobile phone to film and then launch the scoop on social media. We are tempted to pose the question to the person who made that statement. Certainly, this time too, he would answer us with his eloquent silence.[14]

---

blended words and concepts used in Christian theology with pagan and pantheistic errors, presented as a hidden doctrine. These heretics attached secret meanings to words such as Light, Darkness, and the Word so that they would refer to warring divine or quasi-divine entities. Freemasonry as a secret society is similar to ancient gnosticism, appropriating Christian symbols such as the water of baptism, the tongues of fire of Pentecost, and the Temple of Solomon and imposing pagan meanings upon them.

11. A man who later identified himself as Alexander Tschugguel took the Pachamama statues that had been installed in a place of honor in this Roman church and threw them into the Tiber. The statues were recovered from this main river flowing through Rome and returned to a place of honor in the Vatican. The video he recorded of his actions can be viewed here: https://youtu.be/xoB_gjuZgf8.

12. A famous Italian journalist who became director of communications for Francis's Vatican.

13. Father Antonio Spadaro, S.J., is the head of this Jesuit publication, whose title means "the Catholic City." Founded in the nineteenth century, the journal worked to make the Catholic teachings against Liberalism better known. By the mid-twentieth century and after the Jesuits embraced Liberalism, it had become a mouth-piece for the very Liberalism it was founded to combat.

14. In this passage, Archbishop Viganò seems to express skepticism that the very statues thrown in the Tiber were recovered and that Pope Francis's claim that this was the case is true. The "eloquent silence" seems to refer to the pope's statement that he would remain silent about the Viganò Testimony and not respond to it.

Letter in Defense of Mary against Francis

For more than six years now we have been poisoned by a false magisterium, a sort of extreme synthesis of all the conciliar misconceptions and postconciliar errors that have been relentlessly propagated, without most of us noticing. Yes, because the Second Vatican Council opened not only Pandora's Box[15] but also Overton's Window,[16] and so gradually that we did not realize the upheavals that had been carried out, the real nature of the reforms and their dramatic consequences, nor did we suspect who was really at the helm of that gigantic subversive operation, which the modernist Cardinal Suenens called "the 1789 of the Catholic Church."

Thus, over these last decades, the Mystical Body has been slowly drained of its lifeblood through unstoppable bleeding: the Sacred Deposit of Faith has gradually been squandered, dogmas denatured, worship secularized and gradually profaned, morality sabotaged, the priesthood vilified, the Eucharistic Sacrifice protestantized and transformed into a convivial banquet...

Now the Church is lifeless, covered with metastases and devastated. The people of God are groping, illiterate and robbed of their Faith, in the darkness of chaos and division. In these last decades, the enemies of God have progressively made scorched earth of two thousand years of Tradition. With unprecedented acceleration, thanks to the subversive drive of this pontificate, supported by the powerful Jesuit apparatus, a deadly *coup de grâce* [death blow] is being delivered to the Church.

With Pope Bergoglio—as with all modernists—it is impossible to seek clarity, since the distinctive mark of the modernist heresy is dissimulation. Masters of error and experts in the art of deception, "they strive to make what is ambiguous universally accepted, presenting it from its harmless side which will serve as a passport to introduce the toxic side that was initially kept hidden" (Fr. Matteo

---

15. The phrase refers to the ancient Greek myth in which Pandora opened a box that should have remained sealed and in so doing unleashed chaos and miseries on the world.

16. A phrase referring to the range of policies that are deemed acceptable by the so-called mainstream at any given time. See p. 82, n. 18.

Liberatore, S.J.). And so the lie, obstinately and obsessively repeated, ends up becoming "true" and accepted by the majority.

Also typically modernist is the tactic of affirming what you want to destroy, using vague and imprecise terms, and promoting error without ever formulating it clearly. This is exactly what Pope Bergoglio does, with his dissolving amorphism of the Mysteries of the Faith, with his doctrinal approximation through which he "mestizos" and demolishes the most sacred dogmas, as he did with the Marian dogmas of the Ever-Virgin Mother of God.

The result of this abuse is what we now have before our eyes: a Catholic Church that is no longer Catholic; a container emptied of its authentic content and filled with borrowed goods.

The advent of the Antichrist is inevitable; it is part of the epilogue of the history of Salvation. But we know that it is the prerequisite for the universal triumph of Christ and his glorious Bride. Those of us who have not let ourselves be deceived by these enemies of the Church enfeoffed in the ecclesial Body, must unite and together face off against the Evil One, who is long defeated yet still able to harm and cause the eternal perdition of multitudes of souls, but whose head the Blessed Virgin, our Leader, will definitively crush.

Now it is our turn. Without equivocation, without letting ourselves be driven out of this Church whose legitimate children we are and in which we have the sacred right to feel at home, without the hateful horde of Christ's enemies making us feel marginalized, schismatic and excommunicated.

Now it is our turn! The triumph of the Immaculate Heart of Mary—Coredemptrix and Mediatrix of all graces—passes through her "little ones," who are certainly frail and sinners but are absolutely opposed to the members enlisted in the Enemy's army. "Little ones" consecrated without any limit whatsoever to the Immaculate, in order to be her heel, the most humiliated and despised part, the most hated by hell, but which together with her will crush the head of the infernal Monster.

Saint Louis-Marie Grignion de Montfort asked: "But when will this triumph take place? God knows." Our task is to be vigilant and pray as St. Catherine of Siena ardently recommended: "*Oimè!* That I die and cannot die. Sleep no longer in negligence; use what you can in the present time. Comfort yourselves in Christ Jesus, sweet love. Drown yourselves in the blood of Christ crucified, place yourselves on the cross with Christ crucified, hide yourselves in the wounds of Christ crucified, bathe yourselves in the blood of Christ crucified" (Letter 16).

The Church is shrouded in the darkness of modernism, but the victory belongs to Our Lord and His Bride. We desire to continue to profess the perennial faith of the Church in the face of the roaring evil that besieges her. We desire to keep vigil with her and with Jesus, in this new Gethsemane of the end times; to pray and do penance in reparation for the many offenses caused to them.

December 19, 2019

9

Interview with *Dies Irae* on the Third Secret of Fatima[1]

YOUR Excellency, thank you so much for giving us this interview. The COVID-19 epidemic has, in recent months, affected the lives of millions of people and even caused the deaths of many. In light of this situation, the Church, through the Episcopal Conferences, has decided to close practically all churches and deprive the faithful of access to the sacraments. On March 27, in front of an empty St. Peter's Square, Pope Francis, acting in a manifestly mediatic [i.e., media-conscious] way, presided over a hypothetical prayer for humanity. There were many reactions to the way the pope acted in that moment, one of which tried to associate the solitary presence of Francis with the Message of Fatima, i.e., the third secret. Do you agree?

Allow me first of all to tell you that I am pleased to give this interview for the faithful of Portugal, whom the Blessed Virgin has promised to preserve in the Faith even in these times of great trial. You are a people with a great responsibility, because you may soon find yourself having to guard the sacred fire of Religion while other nations refuse to recognize Christ as their King and Mary Most Holy as their Queen.

The third part of the message that Our Lady entrusted to the shepherd children of Fatima, so that they could deliver it to the Holy Father, remains secret to this day. Our Lady asked for it to be revealed in 1960, but John XXIII had a *communiqué* published on

---

1. This interview first appeared in Portuguese at the website *Dies Irae*; its English translation, by Christopher Hart-Moynihan, was published as "Viganò on the (Unrevealed) Third Secret of Fatima" at *Inside the Vatican*, https://insidethevatican.com/news/newsflash/letter-8-vigano-on-the-unrevealed-third-secret-of-fatima/.

Dies Irae on the Third Secret of Fatima

February 8th of that year in which he stated that the Church "does not wish to take on the responsibility of guaranteeing the truthfulness of the words that the three shepherd children said the Virgin Mary spoke to them." With this distancing [of the Vatican] from the message of the Queen of Heaven, a coverup operation was started, evidently because the content of the message would have revealed the terrible conspiracy against the Church of Christ by its enemies. Until a few decades ago it would have seemed incredible that we would reach the point that even Our Lady could be silenced, but in recent years we have also witnessed attempts to censor the Gospel itself, which is the Word of her divine Son.[2]

In 2000, during the pontificate of John Paul II, Cardinal Sodano presented as the third secret a version of his own that in several elements appeared clearly incomplete. It is not surprising that the new Secretary of State, Cardinal Bertone, sought to draw attention to an event in the past [the assassination attempt on John Paul on May 13, 1981] to cause the people of God to believe that the words of the Virgin [in 1917 when she appeared] had nothing to do with the crisis of the Church [in the decades after 1960] and the marriage of modernists and Freemasonry that was contracted behind the scenes at the Second Vatican Council (1962–1965). Antonio Socci, who has carefully investigated the third secret, unmasked this harmful behavior on the part of Cardinal Bertone.[3] In addition, it was Bertone himself who heavily discredited and censured the *Madonnina delle Lacrime* (Madonna of Tears) of Civitavecchia,[4] whose message perfectly agrees with what she said at Fatima.

Let us not forget Our Lady's unheeded appeal for the pope and all the bishops to consecrate *Russia* to her Immaculate Heart, as a condition for the defeat of Communism and atheistic materialism:

2. An explanation of the events to which the archbishop refers can be found on pp. 113–15.

3. See Socci, *Fourth Secret*.

4. On February 2, 1995, a statuette of Our Lady was reported to have wept and messages from Our Lady were claimed to have warned of scandal and apostasy in the Church. The majority of a diocesan commission that investigated the incident considered the events credibly supernatural. Later, a Vatican commission was established to consider the case, but it never released a conclusion.

consecrate not "the world," not "the nation which You want us to consecrate to You,"[5] but "Russia." Was it so costly to do that?

Evidently so, for those who do not have a supernatural gaze. It was preferred to walk the path of détente with the Soviet regime, inaugurated by Roncalli[6] himself, without understanding that without God no peace is possible.[7] Today, with a President of the Russian Confederation who is certainly a Christian,[8] the Virgin's request could be granted, averting further misfortunes for the Church and the world.

In the middle of Holy Week and after the Pan-Amazonian Synod, the pope decided to establish a commission to discuss and study the female diaconate in the Catholic Church. Do you believe that this is meant to pave the way for the ordination of women or is, in other words, an attempt to tamper with the priesthood established by Our Lord Jesus Christ on Holy Thursday?

It is not possible, and will never be possible, for the Sacred Order to be modified in its essence. The attack on the priesthood has always been at the center of the actions of the heretics and their inspirer, and it is understandable why this is the case: a blow to the priesthood means the destruction of the Holy Mass and the Most Holy Eucharist and the entire sacramental edifice.

---

5. These phrases come from a consecration to Our Lady performed by John Paul II on October 16, 1983. The text never explicitly named Russia.

6. Pope John XXIII, whose baptismal name was Angelo Roncalli.

7. Viganò is referring to the commonly accepted belief that John Paul II, though he had intended to name Russia in the act of consecration, was prevailed upon to leave it out for fear of exacerbating diplomatic difficulties with the Soviet Union. As noted in the introduction to Part II, John XXIII's Vatican, at a meeting in Metz, promised that the Council would not expressly condemn communism in exchange for the presence at the Council of the (schismatic and KGB-controlled) Patriarch of Moscow. This is the "détente" that John Paul II continued to follow by refusing to consecrate Russia.

8. Vladimir Putin has, as President of Russia, publicly shown himself to be a member of the Orthodox Church. Although Viganò recognizes Putin is not Catholic, he argues that, as a Christian who venerates the Holy Theotokos, Putin would likely not oppose the Marian consecration of his country as the Soviets would have done.

Among the sworn enemies of the Sacred Order there were also the modernists, of course, who, from the nineteenth century on, theorized about a Church without priests, or with priests and priestesses. These delusions, which were foreshadowed by some exponents of Modernism in France, subtly reemerged at the Council, with an attempt to insinuate a certain equivalence between the ministerial priesthood deriving from Holy Orders and the common priesthood of the faithful deriving from Baptism.

It is significant that, precisely by playing on this intentional ambiguity, the reformed liturgy also suffered from the doctrinal error of *Lumen Gentium* and ended up reducing the ordained Minister to the [status of a] simple president of an assembly of priests. To the contrary; the priest is an *alter Christus*, not by popular designation, but by ontological configuration to the High Priest, Jesus Christ, whom he must imitate in the holiness of his life and in his absolute dedication represented also by celibacy.

The next step had to necessarily be taken, if not by annulling the priesthood itself, at least by making it ineffective by extending it to women, who cannot be ordained: exactly what happened in the Protestant and Anglican sects, which today also experience the embarrassing situation of having lesbian female bishops in the so-called Church of England. But it is clear that the ecumenical "pretext"—that is, drawing closer to dissident communities by acquiring even their most recent errors—is based on Satan's hatred for the priesthood and would inevitably lead the Church of Christ to ruin.

On the other hand, ecclesiastical celibacy is also the object of the same attack, because it is distinctive of the Catholic Church and constitutes a precious defense of the priesthood that Tradition has jealously guarded through the centuries.

The attempt to introduce a form of ordained female ministry within the Church is not recent, despite repeated statements by the Magisterium. John Paul II also unequivocally defined, and with all the canonical requirements of an infallible *ex cathedra* declaration, that it is absolutely impossible to question the doctrine on this subject. But just as it was possible to fiddle with the *Catechism* to declare the death penalty "not in conformity with the Gospel"— something unheard-of and heretical—so today an attempt is being

161

made to create *ex novo* some form of female diaconate, evidently preparatory to a future introduction of the female priesthood.

The first commission created by Bergoglio years ago gave a negative opinion, confirming what should not even have been the subject of discussion; but if that commission could not obey the wishes of Francis, this does not mean that another commission, whose members, chosen by him, are more "docile" and relaxed in demolishing another pillar of the Catholic Faith, may not do so. I do not doubt that Bergoglio has persuasive methods and that he can exert pressure on the theological commission; but I am equally certain that in the unfortunate event that this consultative body were to give a favorable opinion, it would not necessarily require an official declaration by the pope to see a multiplying of deaconesses in the dioceses of Germany or Holland, with Rome remaining silent. The method is well known, and on the one hand it makes it possible to strike at the priesthood while on the other it gives a convenient alibi to those within the ecclesiastical structure who can always appeal to the fact that "the pope has not allowed anything new." They did likewise by authorizing the Episcopal Conferences to legislate autonomously about Communion in the hand, which, imposed by abuse, has now become universal practice.

It should be said that this will to promote women in the hierarchy betrays the urge [of such movements within the Church] to follow the modern mentality that has taken away the woman's role of mother and wife in order to unhinge the natural family.

Let's keep in mind that this approach to the Church's dogmas confirms an undeniable fact: Bergoglio has adopted the so-called "situation theology," whose theological pillars are accidental facts or subjects: the world, nature, the female figure, young people... This theology does not have God's immutable and eternal truth as its founding center; on the contrary, it starts from the observation of whatever is the current pressing need of these phenomena in order to give answers that are consistent with the expectations of the contemporary world.

Your Excellency, according to historians of recognized merit, the Second Vatican Council represented a rupture of the Church with Tradi-

tion; hence the appearance of currents of thought that want to transform it into a simple humanitarian association that embraces the world and its globalist utopia. How do you see this serious problem?

A Church that presents herself as new with respect to the Church of Christ is simply not the Church of Christ! The Mosaic Religion, that is, the "Church of the ancient law," willed by God to lead His people until the coming of the Messiah, had its fulfillment in the New Covenant, and was definitively revoked on Calvary by the Sacrifice of Christ: from His side was born the Church of the New and Eternal Covenant, which replaces the Synagogue. It seems that also the post-conciliar Church, modernist and Masonic, aspires to transform, to overcome the Church of Christ, replacing it with a "neo-Church," a deformed and monstrous creature that does not come from God.

The purpose of this neo-Church is not to bring the Chosen People to recognize the Messiah, as it is for the Synagogue; it is not to convert and save all people before the second coming of Christ, as it is for the Catholic Church, but to constitute itself as the spiritual arm of the New World Order and an advocate of Universal Religion.

In this sense, the [Second Vatican] Council's revolution first had to demolish the Church's heritage, its millenary Tradition, from which she drew her vitality and authority as the Mystical Body of Christ, then free herself from the exponents of the old hierarchy, and only recently has this revolution begun to offer itself without pretence for what it intends to be.

What you call utopia is actually a dystopia, because it represents the concretization of Freemasonry's plan and the preparation for the advent of the Antichrist.

I am also convinced that the majority of my brethren, and even more so almost all the priests and faithful, are absolutely unaware of this hellish plan, and that recent events have opened many people's eyes. Their faith will allow Our Lord to gather the *pusillus grex* [little flock—cf. Lk 12:32] around the true Shepherd before the final confrontation.

To restore the ancient splendour of the Church, it will be necessary to question many doctrinal aspects of the Council. What points of Vatican II would you question?

I believe that there is no lack of eminent personalities who have expressed, better than me, critical viewpoints of the Council. There are those who believe that it would be less complicated and certainly wiser to follow the practice of the Church and the popes as it applied to the Synod of Pistoia:[9] there was something good in this Synod as well, but the errors it affirmed were considered sufficient to let it fall into oblivion.

Does the present pontificate represent the culmination of a process that opened with the Second Vatican Council, desired in the so-called "Pact of the Catacombs,"[10] or is it still in an intermediate phase?

As is the case with every revolution, the heroes of the first hour often end up falling victim to their own system, as Robespierre did. One who yesterday was judged to be the standard-bearer of the conciliar spirit today appears almost to be a conservative: the examples are before everyone's eyes.

And there are already those who, in the intellectual circles of progressivism (such as the one frequented by a certain Massimo Faggioli, haughty in his first name and ungrammatical in his surname), start spreading here and there some doubts about Bergoglio's real ability to make "courageous choices"—for example, to abolish celibacy, to admit women to the priesthood or to legitimize *communicatio in sacris*[11] with heretics—almost hoping that he would step aside to elect a pope even more obedient to those elites who had in the Catacombs and in the St. Gallen Mafia their most unscrupulous and determined followers.

Your Excellency, we Catholics today often feel isolated from the Church and almost abandoned by our Pastors. What can Your Excellency say

9. A diocesan Synod held in Pistoia, Italy in 1786, later condemned on eighty-five points by Pope Pius VI in the papal bull *Auctorem Fidei* of August 28, 1794.

10. The Pact of the Catacombs is an agreement signed by forty-two bishops of the Catholic Church at a meeting following Mass in the Catacombs of Domitilla near Rome on the evening of November 16, 1965, three weeks before the close of the Second Vatican Council. The bishops pledged to live like the poorest of their parishioners and adopt a lifestyle free of attachment to ordinary possessions.

11. "Communion in sacred things," that is, the Eucharist.

to the hierarchs and the faithful who, despite the confusion and error that are spreading in the Church, try to persevere in this hard battle to maintain the integrity of our Faith?

My words would certainly be inadequate. What I limit myself to doing is repeating the words of Our Lord, the eternal Word of the Father: "Behold, I am with you every day, until the consummation of the ages" (Mt 28:20).

We feel isolated, of course: but didn't the Apostles and all Christians feel this way as well? Did not Our Lord even feel abandoned in Gethsemane? These are the times of trial, perhaps of the final trial; we must drink the bitter cup, and even if it is human to implore the Lord to let it pass from us, we must repeat confidently: "Not my will, but Yours," remembering His comforting words: "In the world you will have tribulations, but have courage, for I have conquered the world!" After the trial, no matter how hard and painful, the eternal prize is prepared for us, which no one can take away from us. The Church will shine again with the glory of her Lord after this terrible and prolonged Easter Triduum.

But if prayer is certainly indispensable, we must also not fail to fight the good fight, making ourselves the witnesses to a courageous militancy under the banner of the Cross of Christ. Let us not find ourselves being pointed out as the handmaiden did with Saint Peter in the high priest's courtyard: "You too were one of his followers," only to then deny Christ. Let us not be intimidated! Let us not allow the gag of tolerance to be placed on those who would proclaim the truth!

Let us ask the Blessed Virgin Mary that our tongue may proclaim with courage the Kingdom of God and His Justice. Let the miracle of Lapa be renewed, when Mary Most Holy gave the word to little Joana, born mute.[12] May she also give voice to us, her children, who for too long have been mute. Our Lady of Fatima, Queen of Victories, *ora pro nobis*.

---

12. In Portugal in the late 900s, nuns fleeing the troops of Almançor, Caliph of Cordoba, hid an image of the Virgin under a boulder, covering a small grotto. Five hundred years later, in 1493, the image was uncovered by a 12-year-old shepherdess named Joana, who found it after squeezing through the narrow crevice. Joana was born mute, but when her mother tried to cast the image into a fire, she recovered her speech (see www.visitportugal.com/en/node/133125).

10

First Letter on Vatican II, Responding to Bishop Schneider[1]

June 9, 2020

I READ with great interest the essay of His Excellency Athanasius Schneider published on *LifeSiteNews* on June 1,[2] subsequently translated into Italian by *Chiesa e post concilio*, entitled "There is no divine positive will or natural right to the diversity of religions." His Excellency's study summarizes, with the clarity that distinguishes the words of those who speak according to Christ, the objections against the presumed legitimacy of the exercise of religious freedom that the Second Vatican Council theorized, contradicting the testimony of Sacred Scripture and the voice of Tradition, as well as the Catholic Magisterium which is the faithful guardian of both.

The merit of His Excellency's essay lies first of all in its grasp of the causal link between the principles enunciated or implied by Vatican II and their logical consequent effect in the doctrinal, moral, liturgical, and disciplinary deviations that have arisen and progressively developed to the present day. The *monstrum* generated in modernist circles could have at first been misleading, but it has grown and strengthened, so that today it shows itself for what it really is in its subversive and rebellious nature. The creature that was conceived at that time is always the same, and it would be naive to think that its perverse nature could change. Attempts to correct

1. Original source for English translation: *Inside the Vatican*, https://insidethe-vatican.com/news/newsflash/letter-11-june-10-2020-the-root-of-the-problem.

2. Bishop Schneider's article, "There is no divine positive will or natural right to the diversity of religions," was published at *LifeSiteNews* on June 1, 2020, www.lifes-itenews.com/opinion/bishop-schneider-how-church-could-correct-erroneous-vie w-that-god-wills-diversity-of-religions.

the conciliar excesses—invoking the hermeneutic of continuity—have proven unsuccessful: *Naturam expellas furca, tamen usque recurret* [Drive nature out with a pitchfork; she will come right back] (Horace, *Epist.* I,10,24). The Abu Dhabi Declaration—and, as Bishop Schneider rightly observes, its first symptoms in the pantheon of Assisi—"was conceived in the spirit of the Second Vatican Council," as Bergoglio proudly confirms.

This "spirit of the Council" is the license of legitimacy that the innovators oppose to their critics, without realizing that it is precisely confessing that legacy that confirms not only the erroneousness of the present declarations but also the heretical matrix that supposedly justifies them. On closer inspection, never in the history of the Church has a Council presented itself as such a historic event that it was different from any other council: there was never talk of a "spirit of the Council of Nicea" or the "spirit of the Council of Ferrara-Florence," even less the "spirit of the Council of Trent," just as we never had a "postconciliar" era after Lateran IV or Vatican I.

The reason is obvious: those councils were all, indiscriminately, the expression in unison of the voice of Holy Mother Church, and for this very reason the voice of Our Lord Jesus Christ. Significantly, those who maintain the novelty of Vatican II also adhere to the heretical doctrine that places the God of the Old Testament in opposition to the God of the New Testament, as if there could be contradiction between the Divine Persons of the Most Holy Trinity. Evidently this opposition, which is almost gnostic or cabalistic,[3] is in function of legitimizing a new subject deliberately different from and opposed to the Catholic Church. Doctrinal errors almost always

---

3. As mentioned in an earlier note, gnosticism was an early Christian heresy that, under the guise of secret knowledge about the invisible world, transformed Christian concepts and words into new meanings that related to a universe of multiple deities. Cabalism, another branch of the occult, refers to an ancient Jewish movement that interprets the Bible in light of secret codes or ciphers that are believed to convey secret knowledge. In contrast to both of these movements, the Church has always maintained that the doctrine of Christ is open and accessible to all, even though inexhaustible in its intelligibility. Some passages of Scripture may be difficult to understand (which is why we need the Church to assist us), but there is no secret knowledge transmitted outside of public Revelation.

betray some sort of Trinitarian heresy, and thus it is by returning to the proclamation of Trinitarian dogma that the doctrines that oppose it can be defeated: *ut in confessione veræ sempiternæque deitatis, et in Personis proprietas, et in essentia unitas, et in majestate adoretur æqualitas*: Professing the true and eternal Divinity, we adore what is proper to each Person, their unity in substance, and their equality in majesty.

Bishop Schneider cites several canons of the Ecumenical Councils that propose, in his opinion, doctrines that today are difficult to accept, such as for example the obligation to distinguish Jews by their clothing, or the ban on Christians serving Muslim or Jewish masters. Among these examples there is also the requirement of the *traditio instrumentorum* declared by the Council of Florence, which was later corrected by Pius XII's Apostolic Constitution *Sacramentum Ordinis*.[4] Bishop Athanasius comments: "One may rightly hope and believe that a future pope or Ecumenical Council will correct the erroneous statement made" by Vatican II. This appears to me to be an argument that, although made with the best of intentions, undermines the Catholic edifice from its foundation. If in fact we admit that there may be Magisterial acts that, due to a changed sensitivity, are susceptible to abrogation, modification, or different interpretation with the passage of time, we inevitably fall under the

---

4. Pope Pius XII determined that the form of the ordination to the priesthood did not include the handing-on of the priest's instruments (*traditio instrumentorum*), the chalice and paten, but consisted solely in the laying-on of hands by the ordaining bishop. The Council of Florence (1431–1449) had taught that the *traditio instrumentorum* was required in addition to the laying-on of hands, although at the same time, the Church had recognized as valid the ordination of Catholic Eastern rites that did not use this ceremony. This produced a debate about what was meant by the Council of Florence and if the *traditio instrumentorum* was required for validity at least in the *Latin* rite. Pius XII clarified that only the laying-on of hands was necessary. To be clear, he did not remove or suppress or consider optional the ceremony of the *traditio instrumentorum*; he merely made clear it was not, strictly speaking, part of the sacramental form that imparts the indelible character of the priesthood. By analogy, the exorcisms in a baptism are extremely important ceremonies, but since they are not part of the form of baptism, they could be omitted in a case of emergency. See Pius XII, *Sacramentum Ordinis*, www.papalencyclicals.net/pius12/p12sacrao.htm.

condemnation of the Decree *Lamentabili*,[5] and we end up offering justification to those who, recently, precisely on the basis of that erroneous assumption, declared that the death penalty "does not conform to the Gospel," and thus amended the *Catechism of the Catholic Church*. And, by the same principle, in a certain way we could maintain that the words of Blessed Pius IX in *Quanta Cura*[6] were in some manner corrected by Vatican II, just as His Excellency hopes could happen for *Dignitatis Humanæ*. Among the examples he presents, none of them is in itself gravely erroneous or heretical: the fact that the Council of Florence declared that the *traditio instrumentorum* was necessary for the validity of Orders did not in any way compromise priestly ministry in the Church, leading her to confer Orders invalidly. Nor does it seem to me that one can affirm that this aspect, however important, led to doctrinal errors on the part of the faithful, something which instead has occurred only with the most recent Council. And when in the course of history various heresies spread, the Church always intervened promptly to condemn them, as happened at the time of the Synod of Pistoia in 1786,[7] which was in some way anticipatory of Vatican II, especially where it abolished Communion outside of Mass, introduced the vernacular tongue, and abolished the prayers of the Canon said *sub-*

---

5. Pope Pius X, *Lamentabili Sane* [Syllabus Condemning the Errors of the Modernists] (1907), www.papalencyclicals.net/pius10/p10lamen.htm. In this document the pope condemns a list of Modernist doctrines, including: "59. Christ did not teach a determined body of doctrine applicable to all times and all men, but rather inaugurated a religious movement adapted or to be adapted to different times and places"; "64. Scientific progress demands that the concepts of Christian doctrine concerning God, creation, revelation, the Person of the Incarnate Word, and Redemption be re-adjusted." Viganò is suggesting that an approach that argues that specific acts or statements of Vatican II should and can be reversed or abrogated due to a new sensibility is condemned by *Lamentabili*.

6. Pius IX, Encyclical *Quanta Cura* (1864), www.papalencyclicals.net/pius09/p9quanta.htm.

7. The Enlightenment-influenced Synod of Pistoia (1786) adopted radical propositions that, as the archbishop notes, are strikingly similar to aspects of Vatican II. By 1794, a papal commission had identified eighty-five propositions of this Synod worthy of condemnation, which Pope Pius VI officially condemned in the bull *Auctorem Fidei*. See John Bertram Peterson, "Synod of Pistoia," *The Catholic Encyclope-*

missa voce;[8] but even more so when it theorized about the basis of episcopal collegiality, reducing the primacy of the pope to a mere ministerial function. Rereading the acts of that Synod leaves us amazed at the literal formulation of the same errors that we find later, in increased form, in the Council presided over by John XXIII and Paul VI. On the other hand, just as the truth comes from God, so error is fed by and feeds on the Adversary, who hates the Church of Christ and her heart: the Holy Mass and the Most Holy Eucharist.

There comes a moment in our life when, through the disposition of Providence, we are faced with a decisive choice for the future of the Church and for our eternal salvation. I speak of the choice between understanding the error into which practically all of us have fallen, almost always without evil intentions, and wanting to continue to look the other way or justify ourselves.

We have also committed the error, among others, of considering our interlocutors as people who, despite the difference of their ideas and their faith, were still motivated by good intentions and who would be willing to correct their errors if they could open up to our Faith. Together with numerous Council Fathers, we thought of ecumenism as a process, an invitation that calls dissidents to the one Church of Christ, idolaters and pagans to the one True God, and the Jewish people to the promised Messiah. But from the moment it was theorized in the conciliar commissions, ecumenism was configured in a way that was in direct opposition to the doctrine previously expressed by the Magisterium.

We have thought that certain excesses were only an exaggeration of those who allowed themselves to be swept up in enthusiasm for novelty; we sincerely believed that seeing John Paul II surrounded by charmers-healers, Buddhist monks, imams, rabbis, Protestant pastors, and other heretics gave proof of the Church's ability to

---

dia, vol. 12 (New York: Robert Appleton Company, 1911), www.newadvent.org/cathen/12116c.htm. For a full-length treatment of the parallels, see Shaun Blanchard, *The Synod of Pistoia and Vatican II: Jansenism and the Struggle for Catholic Reform* (New York: Oxford University Press, 2020).

8. Latin for "quietly or in a low voice."

summon people together in order to ask God for peace,[9] while the authoritative example of this action initiated a deviant succession of pantheons that were more or less official, even to the point of seeing bishops carrying the unclean idol of the Pachamama on their shoulders, sacrilegiously concealed under the pretext of being a representation of sacred motherhood.[10]

But if the image of an infernal divinity was able to enter into Saint Peter's, this is part of a crescendo which the other side foresaw from the beginning. Numerous practicing Catholics, and perhaps also a majority of Catholic clergy, are today convinced that the Catholic Faith is no longer necessary for eternal salvation; they believe that the One and Triune God revealed to our fathers is the same as the god of Mohammed. Already twenty years ago we heard this repeated from pulpits and episcopal *cathedræ*, but recently we hear it being affirmed with emphasis even from the highest Throne.

We know well that, invoking the saying in Scripture *Littera enim occidit, spiritus autem vivificat* [the letter brings death, but the spirit gives life] (2 Cor 3:6), the progressives and modernists astutely knew how to hide equivocal expressions in the conciliar texts, which at the time appeared harmless to most but that today are revealed in their subversive value. It is the method employed in the use of the phrase *subsistit in*: saying a half-truth not so much as not to offend the interlocutor (assuming that is licit to silence the truth of God out of respect for His creature), but with the intention of being able to use the half-error that would be instantly dispelled if the entire truth were proclaimed. Thus "*Ecclesia Christi subsistit in Ecclesia*

---

9. Here the archbishop refers to the World Day of Prayer convened by Pope John Paul II in Assisi on October 27, 1986. The different religions mentioned by the archbishop were all given a place within Catholic churches to conduct their false worship and all prayed together with John Paul II. The pope was placed on the same level as all of these other leaders of false religions. Archbishop Marcel Lefebvre explained that he took this scandalous event as a sign from God that he should consecrate bishops for his Society of St. Pius X so as to preserve the priesthood and integral Catholic doctrine. Similar events were held in Assisi later by John Paul II, Benedict XVI, and Francis.

10. This occurred in a Mass in St. Peter's Basilica during the Amazonian Synod.

Catholica"[11] does not specify the identity of the two, but the subsistence of one in the other and, for consistency, also in other churches: here is the opening to interconfessional celebrations, ecumenical prayers, and the inevitable end of any need for the Church in the order of salvation, in her unicity, and in her missionary nature.

Some may remember that the first ecumenical gatherings were held with the schismatics of the East, and very prudently with other Protestant sects. Apart from Germany, Holland, and Switzerland, in the beginning the countries of Catholic tradition did not welcome mixed celebrations with Protestant pastors and Catholic priests together. I recall that at the time there was talk of removing the penultimate doxology from the *Veni Creator*[12] so as not to offend the Orthodox, who do not accept the *Filioque*.[13] Today we hear the surahs of the Koran recited from the pulpits of our churches,[14] we see an idol of wood adored by religious sisters and brothers,[15] we hear bishops disavow what up until yesterday seemed to us to be the most plausible excuses of so many extremisms. What the world

11. *Lumen Gentium* 8.

12. The penultimate verse of this Latin hymn can be translated as: "Oh, may Thy grace on us bestow / the Father and the Son to know; / and Thee, through endless times confessed, / of both, the eternal Spirit blest."

13. The *Filioque* (Latin for "and the Son") refers to a word added in the sixth century in Spain to the Niceno-Constantinopolitan Creed recited at Mass, and later adopted throughout the West. Its inclusion means that the Holy Ghost proceeds from the Father and the Son as from a single principle. The Eastern Orthodox claim that the Holy Ghost proceeds from the Father only. Since the Council, the Church has encouraged Catholics who use the Eastern forms of the Eucharistic liturgy to omit the *Filioque* because it was never part of the Creed as recited in the East. See "Benedict XVI Honored by Eastern Orthodox Hierarchs," *Catholic World Report*, March 3, 2013, https://www.catholicworldreport.com/2013/03/04/benedict-xvi-honored-by-eastern-orthodox-hierarchs/.

14. It does not seem that the archbishop is referring to a specific event but rather the practice of the past few decades of permitting Islamic groups to use Catholic churches from time to time.

15. The archbishop is referring to the ceremony that occurred in the Vatican Gardens on October 4, 2019 to begin the Amazon Synod. A group of people, including one who appeared to be a Franciscan, knelt around a wooden image of the Pachamama in a circle and bowed down to it. Pope Francis watched this ceremony, which occurred in his presence. He also blessed objects connected with the ceremony.

wants, at the instigation of Masonry and its infernal tentacles, is to create a universal religion that is humanitarian and ecumenical, from which the jealous God whom we adore is banished. And if this is what the world wants, any step in the same direction by the Church is an unfortunate choice which will turn against those who believe that they can jeer at God. The hopes of the Tower of Babel cannot be brought back to life by a globalist plan that has as its goal the cancellation of the Catholic Church, in order to replace it with a confederation of idolaters and heretics united by environmentalism and universal brotherhood. There can be no brotherhood except in Christ, and only in Christ: *qui non est mecum, contra me est* [he who is not with Me is against Me] (Mt 12:30; Lk 11:23).

It is disconcerting that few people are aware of this race towards the abyss, and that few realize the responsibility of the highest levels of the Church in supporting these anti-Christian ideologies, as if the Church's leaders want to guarantee that they have a place and a role on the bandwagon of aligned thought. And it is surprising that people persist in not wanting to investigate the root causes of the present crisis, limiting themselves to deploring the present excesses as if they were not the logical and inevitable consequence of a plan orchestrated decades ago. If the Pachamama could be adored in a church, we owe it to *Dignitatis Humanæ*. If we have a liturgy that is protestantized and at times even paganized, we owe it to the revolutionary action of Msgr. Annibale Bugnini[16] and to the postconciliar

---

16. Archbishop Annibale Bugnini was the secretary of the *Consilium*, the body created by Paul VI to "reform" the entirety of the Roman rite's liturgical books and practice. Bugnini was subsequently accused of being a Freemason, a charge that has grown in plausibility with the detailed information provided by Fr. Charles Murr. See "New Interview with Fr. Charles Murr on Mother Pascalina, Bugnini, Paul VI, and Other Major Figures," *Rorate Caeli*, October 10, 2020; "Fr. Charles Murr on Vatican intrigues surrounding Cardinals Baggio, Benelli, Villot, and Gagnon," *Rorate Caeli*, December 18, 2020; cf. "New historical evidence emerges in support of Bugnini's association with Freemasonry," *Rorate Caeli*, May 6, 2020. Paul VI never addressed this accusation publicly, but shortly after it surfaced, he removed Bugnini from his Vatican positions and sent him off to serve as Papal Nuncio in Tehran, a position for which Bugnini, who had never served in the diplomatic corps, had no particular credentials or aptitude.

reforms. If the Abu Dhabi Declaration was signed, we owe it to *Nostra Ætate*. If we have come to the point of delegating decisions to the Bishops' Conferences—even in grave violation of the Concordat, as happened in Italy—we owe it to collegiality, and to its updated version, synodality. Thanks to synodality, we found ourselves, with *Amoris Lætitia*,[17] having to look for a way to prevent what was obvious to everyone from appearing: that this document, prepared by an impressive organizational machine, intended to legitimize Communion for the divorced and cohabiting, just as *Querida Amazonia* will be used to legitimize women priests (as in the recent case of an "episcopal vicaress" in Freiburg) and the abolition of sacred celibacy. The prelates who sent the *dubia*[18] to Francis, in my opinion, demonstrated the same pious ingenuousness: thinking that Bergoglio, when confronted with the reasonably argued contestation of the error, would understand, correct the heterodox points, and ask for forgiveness.

The Council was used to legitimize the most aberrant doctrinal deviations, the most daring liturgical innovations, and the most unscrupulous abuses, all while Authority remained silent. This Council was so exalted that it was presented as the only legitimate reference for Catholics, clergy, and bishops, obscuring and connoting with a sense of contempt the doctrine that the Church had always authoritatively taught, and prohibiting the perennial liturgy that for millennia had nourished the faith of an uninterrupted line of faithful, martyrs, and saints. Among other things, this Council has proven to be the only one that has caused so many interpreta-

17. Francis's Apostolic Exhortation following the Synod on the Family which, among other things, opened the way for people living in adulterous relationships to receive Holy Communion without relinquishing their union or living together as brother and sister.

18. A *dubium* (plural, *dubia*) is a formal request made to a higher authority for a clarification of a document or teaching that seems problematic. Four cardinals—Carlo Caffarra, Walter Brandmüller, Raymond Burke and Joachim Meisner—hand-delivered *dubia* to Pope Francis that asked for clarification of several problematic passages in *Amoris Laetitia*. When it became clear to them that the pope would not reply, they published their *dubia*. The pope has to this day never answered the *dubia*. A copy of the text can be found here: www.catholicnewsagency.com/news/full-text-of-dubia-cardinals-letter-asking-pope-for-an-audience-15105.

tive problems and so many contradictions with respect to the preceding Magisterium, while there is not one other council—from the Council of Jerusalem to Vatican I—that does not harmonize perfectly with the entire Magisterium or that needs so much interpretation.

I confess it with serenity and without controversy: I was one of the many people who, despite many perplexities and fears which today have proven to be absolutely legitimate, trusted the authority of the hierarchy with unconditional obedience. In reality, I think that many people, including myself, did not initially consider the possibility that there could be a conflict between obedience to an order of the hierarchy and fidelity to the Church herself. What made tangible this unnatural, indeed I would even say perverse, separation between the hierarchy and the Church, between obedience and fidelity, was certainly this most recent pontificate.

In the Room of Tears adjacent to the Sistine Chapel,[19] while Msgr. Guido Marini prepared the white rocchetto, mozzetta, and stole for the first appearance of the "newly elected" pope, Bergoglio exclaimed: "*Sono finite le carnevalate!* [The carnivals are over!]," scornfully refusing the insignia that all the popes up until then had humbly accepted as the distinguishing garb of the Vicar of Christ. But those words contained truth, even if it was spoken involuntarily: on March 13, 2013, the mask fell from the conspirators, who were finally free of the inconvenient presence of Benedict XVI and brazenly proud of having finally succeeded in promoting a cardinal who embodied their ideals, their way of revolutionizing the Church, of making doctrine malleable, morals adaptable, liturgy adulterable, and discipline disposable. And all this was considered, by the protagonists of the conspiracy themselves, the logical consequence and obvious application of Vatican II, which according to them had been weakened by the critiques expressed by Benedict XVI. The greatest affront of that pontificate was the freeing-up of the venera-

---

19. The room in which the cardinal who has been elected changes his garb to that of the pope has been called the Room of Tears because so many newly elected popes shed tears of sorrow and humility at being required to take up the burden of the papacy.

ble Tridentine Liturgy,[20] the legitimacy of which was finally recognized, disproving fifty years of its illegitimate ostracization. It is no accident that Bergoglio's supporters are the same people who saw the Council as the first event of a new church, prior to which there was an old religion with an old liturgy.

It is no accident: what these men affirm with impunity, scandalizing moderates, is what Catholics also believe, namely: that despite all the efforts of the hermeneutic of continuity which shipwrecked miserably at the first confrontation with the reality of the present crisis, it is undeniable that from Vatican II onwards a parallel church was built, superimposed over and diametrically opposed to the true Church of Christ. This parallel church progressively obscured the divine institution founded by Our Lord in order to replace it with a spurious entity, corresponding to the desired universal religion that was first theorized by Masonry. Expressions like new humanism, universal fraternity, dignity of man, are the watchwords of philanthropic humanitarianism which denies the true God, of horizontal solidarity of vague spiritualist inspiration and of ecumenical irenism[21] that the Church unequivocally condemns. *Nam et loquela tua manifestum te facit* [Even your speech gives you away] (Mt 26:73): this very frequent, even obsessive recourse to the same vocabulary of the enemy betrays adherence to the ideology he inspires; while on the other hand the systematic renunciation of the clear, unequivocal and crystalline language of the Church confirms the desire to detach oneself not only from the Catholic form but even from its substance.

What we have for years heard enunciated, vaguely and without clear connotations, from the highest Throne, we then find elaborated in a true and proper manifesto in the supporters of the present pontificate: the democratization of the Church, no longer through the collegiality invented by Vatican II but by the synodal

20. In the motu proprio *Summorum Pontificum* of July 7, 2007, Pope Benedict made clear that every priest had a right to celebrate the traditional Mass and the laity had a right to request and receive it.

21. Irenism is a belief that Christian denominations can be harmonized into one religion by using natural reason to resolve all theological disagreements.

path inaugurated by the Synod on the Family; the demolition of the ministerial priesthood through its weakening with exceptions to ecclesiastical celibacy and the introduction of feminine figures with quasi-sacerdotal duties; the silent passage from ecumenism directed towards separated brethren to a form of panecumenism that reduces the truth of the One Triune God to the level of idolatries and the most infernal superstitions; the acceptance of an interreligious dialogue that presupposes religious relativism and excludes missionary proclamation; the demythologization of the papacy, pursued by Bergoglio as a theme of his pontificate; the progressive legitimization of all that is politically correct: gender theory, sodomy, homosexual marriage, Malthusian doctrines, ecologism, immigrationism… If we do not recognize that the roots of these deviations are found in the principles laid down by the Council, it will be impossible to find a cure: if our diagnosis persists, against all the evidence, in excluding the initial pathology, we cannot prescribe a suitable therapy.

This operation of intellectual honesty requires a great humility, first of all in recognizing that for decades we have been led into error, in good faith, by people who, established in authority, have not known how to watch over and guard the flock of Christ: some for the sake of living quietly, some because of having too many commitments, some out of convenience, and finally some in bad faith or even malicious intent. These last ones who have betrayed the Church must be identified, taken aside, invited to amend and, if they do not repent, must be expelled from the sacred enclosure. This is how a true Shepherd acts, who has the well-being of the sheep at heart and who gives his life for them; we have had and still have far too many mercenaries, for whom the consent of the enemies of Christ is more important than fidelity to his Spouse.

Just as I honestly and serenely obeyed questionable orders sixty years ago, believing that they represented the loving voice of the Church, so today with equal serenity and honesty I recognize that I have been deceived. Being coherent today by persevering in error would represent a wretched choice and would make me an accomplice in this fraud. Claiming a clarity of judgment from the beginning would not be honest: we all knew that the Council would be more or less a revolution, but we could not have imagined that it would prove to be so devastating, even for the work of those who should have prevented it. And if up until Benedict XVI we could still imagine that the *coup d'état* of Vatican II (which Cardinal Suenens called "the 1789 of the Church") had experienced a slowdown, in these last few years even the most ingenuous among us have understood that silence for fear of causing a schism, the effort to repair papal documents in a Catholic sense in order to remedy their intended ambiguity, the appeals and *dubia* made to Francis that remained eloquently unanswered, are all a confirmation of the situation of the most serious apostasy to which the highest levels of the hierarchy are exposed, while the Christian people and the clergy feel hopelessly abandoned and that they are regarded by the bishops almost with annoyance.

The Abu Dhabi Declaration is the ideological manifesto of an idea of peace and cooperation between religions that could have some possibility of being tolerated if it came from pagans who are deprived of the light of faith and the fire of charity. But whoever has the grace of being a Child of God in virtue of Holy Baptism should be horrified at the idea of being able to construct a blasphemous modern version of the Tower of Babel, seeking to bring together the one true Church of Christ, heir to the promises made to the Chosen People, with those who deny the Messiah and with those who consider the very idea of a Triune God to be blasphemous. The love of God knows no measure and does not tolerate compromises, otherwise it simply is not charity, without which it is not possible to remain in Him: *qui manet in caritate, in Deo manet, et Deus in eo* [whoever remains in love remains in God and God in him] (1 Jn 4:16). It matters little whether it is a declaration or a Magisterial document: we know well that the subversive *mens* of the innovators plays games with these sort of quibbles in order to spread error. And we know well that the purpose of these ecumenical and interreligious initiatives is not to convert those who are far from the one Church to Christ, but to divert and corrupt those who still hold the Catholic Faith, leading them to believe that it is desirable to have a great universal religion that brings together the three great Abrahamic religions "in a single house": this is the triumph of the Masonic plan in preparation for the kingdom of the Antichrist! Whether this materializes through a dogmatic Bull, a declaration, or an interview with Scalfari in *La Repubblica* matters little, because Bergoglio's supporters wait for his words as a signal to which they respond with a series of initiatives that have already been prepared and organized for some time. And if Bergoglio does not follow the directions he has received, ranks of theologians and clergy are ready to lament over the "solitude of Pope Francis" as a premise for his resignation (I think for example of Massimo Faggioli in one of his recent essays). On the other hand, it would not be the first time that they use the pope when he goes along with their plans and get rid of him or attack him as soon as he does not.

Last Sunday, the Church celebrated the Most Holy Trinity, and in the Breviary[22] it offers us the recitation of the *Symbolum Athanasianum,*[23] now outlawed by the conciliar liturgy and already reduced to only one occasion after the rubrical reform of 1955. The first words of that now-disappeared *Symbolum* remain inscribed in letters of gold: *Quicumque vult salvus esse, ante omnia opus est ut teneat Catholicam fidem; quam nisi quisque integram inviolatamque servaverit, absque dubio in æternum peribit*—"Whosoever wishes to be saved, before all things it is necessary that he hold the Catholic faith; for unless a person shall have kept this faith whole and inviolate, without doubt he shall eternally perish."

---

22. The breviary is the book that contains the eight daily offices (sometimes called "hours") or sets of prayers, comprised mostly of psalms, that priests and religious are bound to recite every day. Like the new Mass and every other rite, these offices were heavily revised and reduced after the Council. Here the archbishop reveals that he is now praying the preconciliar breviary.

23. One of the great historic creeds of Christianity, this creed shows the strong influence of the theology of St. Athanasius of Alexandria in his lifelong polemic against the heresy of Arianism. Traditionally, it was prayed at Prime on Sundays. In 1911, this was reduced to the Sundays after Epiphany and Pentecost. In 1955, the use was further reduced to a single Sunday a year, namely, Trinity Sunday. In the reformed Liturgy of the Hours, its use was discontinued altogether.

11

Second Letter on Vatican II, Responding to Paolo Pasqualucci

June 14, 2020

DEAR Doctor Guarini,

I have received the observations of Professor Pasqualucci, which you kindly sent to me, and to which I will attempt to respond, as much as possible, in a concise way.

Regarding the possibility of making a correction to the acts of the Second Vatican Council, I think that we can agree: the heretical propositions or those which favor heresy should be condemned, and we can only hope that this will happen as soon as possible.

My objection to Bishop Schneider stems rather from my concern about the possibility that there will be preserved among the official acts of the Church a *hapax* that, beyond ambiguous formulations of discontinuity, was intended and conceived for its subversive value, and which as such has caused many evils. From a legal point of view, the most suitable solution may perhaps be found; but from the pastoral point of view—that is, as regards the Council's usefulness for the edification of the faithful—it is preferable to let the whole thing drop and be forgotten. And if it is true, as Professor Pasqualucci affirms, that the error is not doctrine, it is equally true that a condemnation of heterodox propositions would not remove the shadows that surround the whole undertaking of the Council as a complex whole, and which prejudice the entire corpus of its documents, nor would it remove the consequences that have derived from the Council. It should also be remembered that the event of the Council far surpasses the documents which it produced.

The mere fact that Vatican II is susceptible to correction ought to be sufficient to declare its oblivion as soon as its most obvious errors are seen with clarity. Not by chance does Professor Pasqualucci call it a *"conciliàbolo,"*[1] like the Synod of Pistoia, which merited the condemnation of the entire synod beyond the mere condemnation of the individual errors which it taught. I make my own his statement:

> After having clearly highlighted the procedural subterfuges and the errors against the Faith scattered throughout the documents, a pope could very well finally quash the entire Council, "thereby confirming his brethren in the Faith." This would fall perfectly within his *summa potestas iurisdictionis*[2] over the entire Church, *iure divino.*[3] The Council is not superior to the pope. If the Council has deviated from the Faith, the pope has the power to invalidate it. Indeed, it is his duty.

Allow me to add that, faced with the disastrous situation in which the Church finds herself and the many evils that afflict her, long discourses among "specialists" appear inadequate and inconclusive. There is an urgent need to restore the Bride of Christ to her two-thousand-year Tradition and to recover the treasures that have been plundered and scattered, thus permitting the disoriented flock to be fully nourished by them.

Every discussion, amidst legitimate differences of opinion, must not have as its goal any compromise with the distortions of the truth, but rather that the truth will fully triumph. Virtue is the right mean between two vices, like a peak between two valleys: this ought to be our goal.

It seems to me that from this fruitful exchange with my brother, Bishop Athanasius, what emerges is how much both of us have solely at heart the reestablishment of the Catholic Faith as the essential foundation for union in charity. There is no conflict, no opposi-

---

1. A *conciliàbolo* is a furtive and secluded gathering for illicit or mysterious purposes, or an irregular ecclesiastical council called by those without authority or by schismatics.

2. Latin for "the highest power of jurisdiction," meaning the pope's fullness of power to judge for the Church.

3. Latin for "by divine law."

tion: our zeal springs from and grows in the Eucharistic Heart of Our Lord and returns to it so as to be consumed in love for Him.

Allow me, dear Doctor Guarini, to invite your readers to pray assiduously for their Pastors, and in particular for those who are living through the present crisis with travail and suffering and who are striving to fulfill the mandate they have received from their divine Master. In a moment in which we are all under attack, besieged on every side, it is necessary more than ever to come together with faith and humility underneath the mantle of her who commands us: love for the Queen of Victories who unites her children is the most evident proof that there cannot be and must not be divisions between us, which are the distinctive mark of the Enemy.

My blessing goes to you and to your readers,
✠ Carlo Maria Viganò, Archbishop

12

Clarifying His Position:
Questions from Phil Lawler[1]

FIRST, what are you saying about Vatican II? That things have gone downhill fast since then is certainly true. But if the whole Council is a problem, how did that happen? How do we reconcile that with what we believe about the inerrancy of the magisterium? How were all the Council Fathers deceived? Even if only some parts of the Council (e.g., Nostra Aetate, Dignitatis Humanae) *are problematical, we still face the same questions. Many of us have been saying for years that the "spirit of Vatican II" is in error. Are you now saying that this phony liberal "spirit" does accurately reflect the work of the Council?*

I do not think that it is necessary to demonstrate that the Council represents a problem: the simple fact that we are raising this question about Vatican II and not about Trent or Vatican I seems to me to confirm a fact that is obvious and recognized by everyone. In reality, even those who defend the Council with swords drawn find themselves doing so apart from all the other previous ecumenical councils, of which not even one was ever said to be a *"pastoral council."* And note that they call it *"the Council"* *par excellence*, as if it was the one and only council in the entire history of the Church, or at least considering it as an *unicum,*[2] whether because of the formulation of its doctrine or for the authority of its magisterium. It is a council that, differently from all those that preceded it, called itself a *pastoral council*, declaring that it did not want to propose any new doctrine, but which in fact created a distinction between before and

1. Published by Catholic Culture in June 2020, www.catholicculture.org/culture /library/view.cfm?recnum=12379.
2. Latin for "sole or unique"; something singular or unparalleled.

after, between a dogmatic council and a pastoral council, between unequivocal canons and empty talk, between *anathema sit* and winking at the world.

In this sense, I believe that the problem of the infallibility of the Magisterium (the inerrancy you mention is properly a quality of Sacred Scripture)[3] does not even arise, because the Legislator, that is, the Roman Pontiff around whom the Council was convened, solemnly and clearly affirmed that he did not want to use the doctrinal authority which he could have exercised if he wanted. I would like to make the observation that nothing is more pastoral than what is proposed as dogmatic, because the exercise of the *munus docendi*[4] in its highest form coincides with the order that the Lord gave to Peter to feed his sheep and lambs. And yet this opposition between *dogmatic* and *pastoral* was made precisely by the one who, in his discourse opening the Council, sought to give a severe meaning to dogma and a softer, more conciliatory meaning to pastoral care. We also find the same setting in the interventions of Bergoglio, where he identifies *"pastoralità"* [pastoralism] as a soft version of rigid Catholic teaching in matters of faith and morals, in the name of "discernment." It is painful to recognize that the practice of having recourse to an equivocal lexicon, using Catholic terms understood in an improper way, invaded the Church starting with Vatican II,

---

3. Archbishop Viganò's correction of Lawler here is highly significant. As he notes, inerrancy (free from error) is an attribute of Sacred Scripture alone. It means the texts of the Bible contain absolutely no errors. The teaching of the Church, or Magisterium, is not inerrant. Individual acts of teaching can be erroneous. The quality of the Magisterium that Viganò suggests Lawler really means is *infallibility*, which means that, under certain conditions (ordinary or extraordinary), some specific teachings of the Magisterium are known to be free from error and will not fail. The difference is that every word of Scripture is necessarily free from error because it has God as its primary author, but not every word of the Magisterium is free from error. Only those statements that belong to the ordinary universal Magisterium or to the extraordinary Magisterium (e.g., definitions of *de fide* dogmas and their accompanying anathemas) are free from error or all possibility of correction. According to Viganò, the problematic statements of Vatican II do not meet the standard for infallibility.

4. Latin for "the gift/office of teaching." The three *munera* (gifts/offices) of the Church are teaching, sanctifying, and governing.

which is the first and most emblematic example of so-called *circiterism*, the equivocating and intentionally imprecise use of language. This happened because the *Aggiornamento*,[5] a term in itself ideologically promoted by the Council as an absolute, held dialogue with the world to be its priority above all else.

There is another equivocation that must be clarified. If on the one hand John XXIII and Paul VI declared that they did not want to commit the Council to the definition of new doctrines and wanted it to limit itself to being only pastoral, on the other hand it is true that externally—mediatically or in the media, we would say today—the emphasis given to its acts was enormous. This emphasis served to convey the idea of a *presumed* doctrinal authority, of an *implicit* magisterial infallibility, even though these were clearly excluded right from the beginning. If this emphasis occurred, it was in order to allow the more or less heterodox instances to be perceived as authoritative and thus to be accepted by the clergy and the faithful. But this would be enough to discredit those authors of a similar deception, who still cry out today if anyone touches *Nostra Ætate*,[6] while they are silent even if someone denies the divinity of Our Lord or the perpetual virginity of Mary Most Holy. Let us recall that Catholics do not worship a Council, neither Vatican II nor Trent, but rather the Most Holy Trinity, the One True God; they do not venerate a conciliar declaration or a post-synodal exhortation, but rather the truth that these acts of the Magisterium convey.

You ask me: "How were all the Council fathers deceived?" I reply by drawing on my experience of those years and the words of my brothers with whom I engaged in discussion at that time. No one could have imagined that right in the heart of the ecclesial body there were hostile forces so powerful and organized that they could succeed in rejecting the perfectly orthodox preparatory schemas that had been prepared by cardinals and prelates with a reliable fidelity to the Church, replacing them with a bundle of cleverly dis-

---

5. Italian for "updating" or "bringing up to date," which often took on the sense of modernization and adaptation to modernity.

6. The Declaration on the Relation of the Church to Non-Christian Religions of the Second Vatican Council.

guised errors behind long-winded and deliberately equivocal speeches. No one could have believed that, right under the vaults of the Vatican Basilica, the estates-general could be convoked that would decree the abdication of the Catholic Church and the inauguration of the Revolution. (As I have already mentioned in a previous article, Cardinal Suenens called Vatican II "the 1789 of the Church.") The Council Fathers were the object of a sensational deception, of a fraud that was cleverly perpetrated by having recourse to the most subtle means: they found themselves in the minority in the linguistic groups, excluded from meetings convened at the last moment, pressured into giving their *placet* by making them believe that the Holy Father wanted it. And what the innovators did not succeed in obtaining in the conciliar Aula, they achieved in the commissions and committees, thanks also to the activism of theologians and *periti* who were accredited and acclaimed by a powerful media machine. There is a vast array of studies and documents that testify to this systematic malicious *mens* of some of the Council Fathers on the one hand, and the naïve optimism or carelessness of other well-intentioned Council Fathers on the other. The activity of the *Cœtus Internationalis Patrum*[7] could do little or nothing, when the violations of the rules by the progressives were ratified at the Sacred Table itself [by the pope].

Those who have maintained that the "spirit of the Council" represented a heterodox or erroneous interpretation of Vatican II engaged in an unnecessary and harmful operation, even if they were driven to do so in good faith. It is understandable that a cardinal or bishop would want to defend the honor of the Church and desire that she would not be discredited before the faithful and the world, and so it was thought that what the progressives attributed to the Council was in reality an undue misrepresentation, an arbitrary forcing. But if at the time it could be difficult to think that a reli-

---

7. Latin for "international group of [Council] Fathers." This group of a few hundred prelates was organized during the Council to oppose the agenda of the progressives. Archbishop Marcel Lefebvre was a key figure in the group, which organized the request—unceremoniously suppressed—to condemn Communism. See Bernard Tissier de Mallerais, *The Biography of Marcel Lefebvre*, 289–312.

gious liberty condemned by Pius XI (*Mortalium Animos*[8]) could be affirmed by *Dignitatis Humanæ*,[9] or that the Roman Pontiff could see his authority usurped by a phantom episcopal college, today we understand that what was cleverly concealed in Vatican II is today affirmed *ore rotundo*[10] in papal documents, precisely in the name of the coherent application of the Council.

On the other hand, when we commonly speak of the "spirit" of an event, we mean precisely that which constitutes the soul, the *essence* of that event. We can thus affirm that the spirit of the Council is the Council itself, that the errors of the postconciliar period were contained *in nuce* in the conciliar Acts, just as it is rightly said that the *Novus Ordo* is the Mass of the Council, even if in the presence of the Council Fathers the Mass was celebrated that the progressives significantly call "preconciliar." And again: if Vatican II truly did not represent a point of rupture, what is the reason for speaking of a *preconciliar* Church and a *postconciliar* church, as if these were two different entities, defined in their essence by the Council itself? And if the Council was truly in line with the uninterrupted infallible Magisterium of the Church, why is it the only council that poses grave and serious problems of interpretation, demonstrating its ontological heterogeneity with respect to other councils?

Second, what is the solution? Bishop Schneider proposes that a future Pontiff must repudiate errors; Archbishop Viganò finds that inadequate. But then how can the errors be corrected, in a way that maintains the authority of the teaching magisterium?

The solution, in my opinion, lies above all in an act of humility that all of us, beginning with the hierarchy and the pope, must carry out: recognizing the infiltration of the enemy into the heart of the Church, the systematic occupation of key posts in the Roman Curia, seminaries, and ecclesiastical schools, the conspiracy of a group of

---

8. Encyclical of Pope Pius XI (1929) condemning any ecumenism other than the return of the dissidents to the Catholic Church.

9. Declaration on Religious Liberty of the Second Vatican Council.

10. Latin for "with an open mouth," i.e., directly, without subterfuge.

rebels—including, in the front line, the deviated Society of Jesus—which has succeeded in giving the appearance of legitimacy and legality to a subversive and revolutionary act. We should also recognize the inadequacy of the response of the good, the naivety of many, the fearfulness of others, and the interests of those who have benefited thanks to that conspiracy. After his triple denial of Christ in the courtyard of the high priest, Peter *"flevit amare,"* he wept bitterly (Lk 22:62). Tradition tells us that the Prince of the Apostles had two furrows on his cheeks for the rest of his days, as a result of the tears which he copiously shed, repenting of his betrayal. It will be for one of his Successors, the Vicar of Christ, in the fullness of his apostolic power, to rejoin the thread of Tradition there where it was cut off. This will not be a defeat but an act of truth, humility, and courage. The authority and infallibility of the Successor of the Prince of the Apostles will emerge intact and reconfirmed. In fact, they were not deliberately called into question at Vatican II, but ironically they would be on a future day in which a Pontiff would correct the errors that that Council permitted, playing jests with the equivocation of an authority it officially denied having but that the faithful were surreptitiously allowed to understand that it *did* have by the entire hierarchy, beginning right with the popes of the Council.

I wish to recall that for some people what is expressed above may sound excessive, because it would seem to call into question the authority of the Church and of the Roman Pontiffs. And yet, no scruple impeded the violation of Saint Pius V's Bull *Quo Primum Tempore*,[11] abolishing the entire Roman liturgy from one day to the next, the venerable millenary treasure of the doctrine and spirituality of the traditional Mass, the immense patrimony of Gregorian chant and sacred music, the beauty of the rites and sacred vestments, disfiguring architectural harmony even in the most distinguished basilicas, removing balustrades, monumental altars, and tabernacles: everything was sacrificed on the conciliar renewal's

---

11. This bull of Pius V (1570) promulgated the Roman rite of Mass as restored and emended after the Council of Trent and guaranteed to every Latin rite priest the right to offer that form of Mass until the end of the world.

altar of *coram populo*,[12] with the aggravating circumstance of having done it only because that liturgy was admirably Catholic and irreconcilable with the spirit of Vatican II.

The Church is a divine institution, and everything in her ought to start with God and return to Him. What is at stake is not the prestige of a ruling class, nor the image of a company or a party: what we are dealing with here is the glory of the Majesty of God, of not nullifying the Passion of Our Lord on the Cross, of the sufferings of His Most Holy Mother, of the blood of the Martyrs, of the testimony of the Saints, of the eternal salvation of souls. If out of pride or unfortunate obstinacy we do not know how to recognize the error and deception into which we have fallen, we will have to give an account to God, who is as merciful with his people when they repent as he is implacable in justice when they follow Lucifer in his *non serviam*.

Dearest Doctor Lawler, to you and to your readers, I cordially send my greetings and the blessing of Our Lord, through the intercession of His and our Most Holy Mother.

✠ Carlo Maria Viganò

---

12. Latin for "in the presence of the people." The archbishop is referring to two principles of the new Mass: that the Mass should be said facing the people, and that the presence of people at Mass is somehow necessary for a Mass to be integrally complete (i.e., so-called "private Masses" in which a priest offers the sacrifice without anyone else present are considered by this concept to be defective). This second principle explains why some priests who use only the new missal stopped saying Mass altogether during the closure of churches on the pretext of the COVID-19 virus. Without the ability of people to be present, they considered there to be no reason to celebrate the Mass.

13

Third Letter on Vatican II: Responding to the Attacks of Sandro Magister[1]

July 3, 2020

DEAR Mr. Magister,

Permit me to reply to your article "Archbishop Viganò on the Brink of Schism," published at *Settimo Cielo* on June 29.[2]

I am aware that having dared to express an opinion strongly critical of the Council is sufficient to awaken the inquisitorial spirit that in other cases is the object of execration by right-thinking people. Nonetheless, in a respectful dispute between ecclesiastics and competent laity, it does not seem to me to be inappropriate to raise problems that remain unresolved to date, the foremost of which is the crisis that has afflicted the Church since Vatican II and has now reached the point of devastation.

There are those who speak of the misrepresentation of the Council; others who speak of the need to return to reading it in continuity with the Tradition; others of the opportunity to correct any errors contained in it, or to interpret the equivocal points in a Catholic sense. On the opposing side, there is no lack of those who consider Vatican II as a blueprint from which to proceed in the revolution: the changing and transformation of the Church into an entirely new and modern entity, in step with the times. This is part

---

1. The letter first appeared at the blog of Marco Tosatti on July 6, 2020, www.marcotosatti.com/2020/07/06/vigano-a-magister-sul-vaticano-ii-italiano-and -english.

2. See http://magister.blogautore.espresso.repubblica.it/2020/06/29/archbishop -vigano-on-the-brink-of-schism-the-unheeded-lesson-of-benedict-xvi.

of the normal dynamics of a "dialogue" that is all too often invoked but rarely practiced: those who thus far have expressed dissent about what I have said have never entered into the merit of the argument, limiting themselves to saddling me with epithets that have already been merited by my far more illustrious and venerable brothers in the episcopate. It is curious that, both in the doctrinal as well as the political arena, the progressives claim for themselves a primacy, a state of election, that apodictically places the adversary in a position of ontological inferiority, unworthy of attention or response and simplistically liquidatable as Lefebvrian[3] on the ecclesial front or fascist on the socio-political front. But their lack of arguments does not legitimize them to dictate the rules, nor to decide who has the right to speak, especially when reason, even prior to faith, has demonstrated where the deception is, who the author is, and what the purpose is.

At first it appeared to me that the content of your article was to be considered more an understandable tribute to the Prince, who can be found in the frescoed salons of the Third Loggia or in the stylish offices of the Editor; and yet in reading what you attribute to me I discovered an inaccuracy—let's call it that—that I hope is the result of a misunderstanding. I therefore ask you to grant me space to reply at *Settimo Cielo*.

You state that I have supposedly blamed Benedict XVI "for having 'deceived' the whole Church in that he would have it be believed that the Second Vatican Council was immune to heresies and moreover should be interpreted in perfect continuity with true perennial doctrine." I do not think that I have ever written such a thing about the Holy Father; on the contrary: I said, and I reaffirm, that we were all—or almost all—deceived by those who used the Council as a "container" equipped with its own implicit authority and the authoritativeness of the Fathers who took part in it, while distorting its purpose. And those who fell into this deception did so

---

3. That is, one who follows Archbishop Lefebvre. In Europe "Lefebvrian" or "Lefebvrist" is commonly used in a derogatory way to refer to a Catholic who objects to postconciliar novelties, much as calling someone a "fascist" puts an end to serious political discussion.

because, loving the Church and the papacy, they could not imagine that in the heart of Vatican II a minority of very organized conspirators could use a Council to demolish the Church from within; and that in doing so they could count on the silence and inaction of Authority, if not on its complicity. These are historical facts, of which I permit myself to give a personal interpretation, but one which I think others may share.

I permit myself also to remind you, as if there was any need, that the positions of moderate critical rereading of the Council in a traditional sense by Benedict XVI are part of a laudable recent past, while in the formidable seventies the position of then-theologian Joseph Ratzinger was quite different. Authoritative studies stand alongside the same admissions of the Professor of Tübingen[4] confirming the partial repentances of the Emeritus. Nor do I see a "reckless indictment launched by Viganò against Benedict XVI for his 'failed attempts to correct conciliar excesses by invoking the hermeneutic of continuity,'" since this is an opinion widely shared not only in conservative circles but also and above all among progressives. And it should be said that what the innovators succeeded in obtaining by means of deception, cunning and blackmail was the result of a vision that we have found later applied in the maximum degree in the Bergoglian "magisterium" of *Amoris Lætitia.* The malicious intention is admitted by Ratzinger himself: "The impression grew steadily that nothing was now stable in the Church, that everything was open to revision. More and more the Council appeared to be like a great Church parliament that could change everything and reshape everything according to its own desires."[5] But even more so by the words of the Dominican Edward Schillebeeckx: "We express it diplomatically [now], but after the Council we will draw the implicit conclusions."[6]

4. In 1966, Joseph Ratzinger was appointed to a chair in dogmatic theology at the University of Tübingen.

5. VN. See J. Ratzinger, *Milestones,* trans. Erasmo Leiva-Merikakis (San Francisco: Ignatius Press, 1997), 132.

6. VN. *De Bazuin,* n. 16, 1965. [Examination of the original publication, *De Bazuin* vol. 48, n. 16, of January 23, 1965, indicates that Schillebeeckx did not express this view as his own, but rather quoted it disapprovingly as from the mouth

Third Letter on Vatican II, to Sandro Magister

We have confirmed that the intentional ambiguity in the texts had the purpose of keeping opposing and irreconcilable visions together, in the name of an evaluation of utility and to the detriment of revealed truth. A truth that, when it is integrally proclaimed, cannot fail to be divisive, just as Our Lord is divisive: "Do you think that I have come to bring peace on earth? No, I tell you, but rather division" (Lk 12:51).

I do not find anything reprehensible in suggesting that we should forget Vatican II: its proponents knew how to confidently exercise this *damnatio memoriæ*[7] not just with a Council but with everything, even to the point of affirming that their council was the first of the new church, and that beginning with their council the old religion and the old Mass was finished. You will say to me that these are the positions of extremists, and that virtue stands in the middle, that is, among those who consider that Vatican II is only the latest of an uninterrupted series of events in which the Holy Spirit speaks through the mouth of the one and only infallible Magisterium. If so, it should be explained why the conciliar church was given a new liturgy and a new calendar, and consequently a new doctrine—*nova lex orandi, nova lex credendi*[8]—distancing itself from its own past with disdain.

The mere idea of setting the Council aside causes scandal even in those, like you, who recognize the crisis of recent years, but who persist in not wanting to recognize the causal link between Vatican II and its logical and inevitable effects. You write: "Attention: not the Council interpreted badly, but the Council as such and en bloc."

of an unnamed "theologian from the doctrinal committee" during the Council's second session. All the same, his report suggests that at least some influential members of the groups that prepared and revised documents followed such a strategy.—Ed.]

7. Latin for "the condemnation of memory," meaning the exclusion or removal of someone or something from official records.

8. Latin for "a new law of prayer, a new law of belief": a twist on the phrase *lex orandi, lex credendi*, the law of prayer is the law of belief, meaning that how and what we pray shows and inculcates how and what we believe. Viganò's point is that a new way of praying the Mass and other rites was necessary because the Council initiated a new way of believing; in turn, the new prayer forms the faithful in its novel image.

I ask you then: what would be the correct interpretation of the Council? The one you give or the one given—while they wrote the decrees and declarations—by its very industrious architects? Or perhaps that of the German episcopate? Or that of the theologians who teach in the pontifical universities and that we see published in the most popular Catholic periodicals in the world? Or that of Joseph Ratzinger? Or that of Bishop Schneider? Or that of Bergoglio? This would be enough to understand how much damage has been caused by the deliberate adoption of a language that was so murky that it legitimized opposing and contrary interpretations, on the basis of which the famous conciliar springtime then occurred. This is why I do not hesitate to say that that assembly should be forgotten "as such and en bloc," and I claim the right to say it without thereby making myself guilty of the delict[9] of schism for having attacked the unity of the Church. The unity of the Church is inseparably in charity and in truth, and where error reigns or even only worms its way in, there cannot be charity.

The fairytale of the hermeneutic—even though an authoritative one because of its Author—nevertheless remains an attempt to want to give the dignity of a Council to a true and proper ambush against the Church, so as not to discredit along with it the popes who wanted, imposed, and reproposed that Council. So much so that those same popes, one after the other, rise to the honors of the altar for having been "popes of the Council."[10]

Allow me to quote from the article that Doctor Maria Guarini published on June 29 at *Chiesa e post concilio* in reaction to your piece at *Settimo Cielo*, entitled: "Archbishop Viganò is not on the brink of schism: many sins are coming to a head." She writes:

---

9. A delict is a word meaning a crime under canon law.

10. Viganò is referring to the fact that the Vatican has now purportedly canonized (i.e., declared to be of heroic virtue and therefore worthy of veneration and imitation) John XXIII, Paul VI, and John Paul II, who are all of the deceased popes since the Council with the exception of John Paul I, who reigned for only thirty-three days. Viganò here implies they were canonized in an attempt to legitimize the Council.

Third Letter on Vatican II, to Sandro Magister

And it is precisely from here that is born and for this reason that there risks continuing—without results (thus far, except for the debate triggered by Archbishop Viganò)—the dialogue between deaf people, because the interlocutors use different reality grids: Vatican II, changing the language, has also changed the parameters of approach to reality. And so it happens that we talk about the same thing which, however, is given entirely different meanings. Among other things, the principal characteristic of the present hierarchy is the use of incontestable affirmations, without ever bothering to demonstrate them or with flawed and sophistic demonstrations. But they do not even have need of demonstrations, because the new approach and the new language have subverted everything from the beginning. And the unproven nature of the anomalous "pastorality" without any defined theological principles is precisely what takes away the raw material of the dispute. It is the advance of a shapeless, ever-changing, dissolving fluid in place of the clear, unequivocal, definitive truthful construct: the incandescent perennial firmness of dogma against the sewage and shifting sands of the transient neo-magisterium.

I continue to hope that the tone of your article was not dictated by the simple fact that I have dared to reopen the debate about that Council that many—too many—in the ecclesial structure consider as an *unicum* in the history of the Church, almost an untouchable idol.

You may be certain that, unlike many bishops, such as those of the German Synodal Path,[11] who have already gone far beyond the brink of schism—promoting and brazenly attempting to impose aberrant ideologies and practices on the universal Church—I have no desire to separate myself from Mother Church, for the exaltation of which I daily renew the offering of my life.

---

11. The German Synodal Path is a series of conferences and meetings begun in December 2019. The central body is the Synodal Assembly, which is comprised of an equal number of clerical and lay members. The Synodal Path has been considering radical changes to the Church such as abolishing priestly celibacy, ordaining women, and changing the moral teachings on marriage and sexuality.

Deus refugium nostrum et virtus, populum ad Te clamantem propitius respice; et intercedente Gloriosa et Immaculata Virgine Dei Genitrice Maria, cum Beato Ioseph, ejus Sponso, ac Beatis Apostolis Tuis, Petro et Paulo, et omnibus Sanctis, quas pro conversione peccatorum, pro libertate et exaltatione Sanctæ Matris Ecclesiæ, preces effundimus, misericors et benignus exaudi.[12]

Receive, dear Sandro, my blessing and greeting, with best wishes for every good thing, in Christ Jesus.

✠ Carlo Maria Viganò, Archbishop

---

12. Translation: "O God, our refuge and our strength, look graciously upon the people who cry to Thee, and through the intercession of the glorious and immaculate ever-Virgin Mary, Mother of God, with blessed Joseph her spouse, Thy blessed apostles Peter and Paul, and all the Saints, in Thy goodness and mercy hear the prayers we pour forth for the conversion of sinners and for the freedom and exaltation of Holy Mother Church." This is among the Latin prayers Pope Leo XIII ordered to be said, beginning in 1885, after all low Masses (i.e., Masses said rather than sung by the priest) for the intention of the temporal sovereignty of the Holy See, which had been overthrown by the unification of Italy. After the Vatican City State was recognized by the Lateran Treaty with Italy in 1929, Pope Pius XI commuted the intention to the restoration, to the people of Russia, of tranquility and freedom to profess the Catholic faith. Pope Paul VI suppressed these prayers in 1965, although most priests who celebrate the traditional Latin Mass still lead the recitation of them after low Mass.

14

Fourth Letter on Vatican II, Responding to Stephen Kokx[1]

September 1, 2020

DEAR Mr. Kokx,

I read with lively interest your article "Questions for Viganò: His Excellency is Right about Vatican II, But What Does He Think Catholic Should Do Now?," which was published by *Catholic Family News* on August 22. I am happy to respond to your questions, which address matters that are very important for the faithful.

You ask: "What would 'separating' from the conciliar Church look like in Archbishop Viganò's opinion?" I respond to you with another question: "What does it mean to separate from the Catholic Church according to the supporters of the Council?" While it is clear that no admixture is possible with those who propose adulterated doctrines of the conciliar ideological manifesto, it should be noted that the simple fact of being baptized and of being living members of the Church of Christ does not imply adherence to the conciliar team; this is true above all for the simple faithful and also for secular and regular clerics who, for various reasons, sincerely consider themselves Catholics and recognize the hierarchy.

Instead, what needs to be clarified is the position of those who, declaring themselves Catholic, embrace the heterodox doctrines that have spread over these decades, with the awareness that these

---

1. This letter was sent to *Catholic Family News* in response to questions Stephen Kokx respectfully posed in an article published in the same outlet: "Questions for Viganò: His Excellency is Right about Vatican II, But What Does He Think Catholics Should Do Now?," https://catholicfamilynews.com/blog/2020/08/22/questions-for-Viganò-abp-vigano-is-right-about-vatican-ii-but-what-does-he-think-catholics-should-do-now.

represent a rupture with the preceding Magisterium. In this case it is licit to doubt their real adherence to the Catholic Church, in which however they hold official roles that confer authority on them. It is an illicitly exercised authority, if its purpose is to force the faithful to accept the revolution imposed since the Council.

Once this point has been clarified, it is evident that it is not the traditional faithful—that is, true Catholics, in the words of Saint Pius X—that must abandon the Church in which they have the full right to remain and from which it would be unfortunate to separate; but rather the Modernists who usurp the Catholic name, precisely because it is only the *bureaucratic* element that permits them not to be considered on a par with any heretical sect. This claim of theirs serves in fact to prevent them from ending up among the hundreds of heretical movements that over the course of the centuries have believed that they could reform the Church at their own pleasure, placing their pride ahead of humbly guarding the teaching of Our Lord. But just as it is not possible to claim citizenship in a homeland in which one does not know its language, law, faith and tradition, so it is impossible that those who do not share the faith, morals, liturgy, and discipline of the Catholic Church can arrogate to themselves the right to remain within her and even to ascend the levels of the hierarchy.

Therefore let us not give in to the temptation to abandon—albeit with justified indignation—the Catholic Church, on the pretext that it has been invaded by heretics and fornicators: it is they who must be expelled from the sacred enclosure, in a work of purification and penance that must begin with each one of us.

It is also evident that there are widespread cases in which the faithful encounter serious problems in frequenting their parish church, just as there are ever fewer churches where the Holy Mass is celebrated in the Catholic rite. The horrors that have been rampant for decades in many of our parishes and shrines make it impossible even to assist at a "Eucharist" without being disturbed and putting one's faith at risk, just as it is very difficult to ensure a Catholic education, sacraments being worthily celebrated, and solid spiritual guidance for oneself and one's children. In these cases faithful laity have the right and the duty to find priests, communities, and institutes that are faithful to the perennial Magisterium. And may they know how to accompany the laudable celebration of the liturgy in the ancient rite with adherence to sound doctrine and morals, without any subsidence on the front of the Council.

The situation is certainly more complex for clerics, who depend hierarchically on their bishop or religious superior, but who at the same time have the right to remain Catholic and be able to celebrate according to the Catholic rite. On the one hand laity have more freedom of movement in choosing the community to which they turn for Mass, the sacraments, and religious instruction, but less autonomy because of the fact that they still have to depend on a priest; on the other hand, clerics have less freedom of movement, since they are incardinated in a diocese or order and are subject to ecclesiastical authority, but they have more autonomy because of the fact that they can legitimately decide to celebrate the Mass and administer the sacraments in the Tridentine rite and to preach in conformity with sound doctrine. The Motu Proprio *Summorum Pontificum* reaffirmed that faithful and priests have the inalienable right—which cannot be denied—to avail themselves of the liturgy that more perfectly expresses their Catholic Faith. But this right must be used today not only and not so much to preserve the extraordinary form[2] of the rite, but to testify to adherence to the *depositum fidei* that finds perfect correspondence only in the ancient rite.

I daily receive heartfelt letters from priests and religious who are marginalized or transferred or ostracized because of their fidelity to the Church: the temptation to find an *ubi consistam* [a place to stand firm] far from the clamor of the innovators is strong, but we ought to take an example from the persecutions that many saints have undergone, including Saint Athanasius,[3] who offers us a model

2. Benedict XVI invented this term to refer to the Traditional Mass.

3. Saint Athanasius was a bishop in the fourth century when the vast majority of prelates adhered to or were tolerant of the heresy of Arianism that claimed Jesus was not of the same divine substance as God the Father. Athanasius was persecuted for his faithfulness and even driven out of his diocese. He wrote in a letter: "It is a fact that they have the premises—but you have the apostolic Faith. They can occupy our churches, but they are outside the true Faith. You remain outside the places of worship, but the Faith dwells within you."

of how to behave in the face of widespread heresy and persecuting fury. As my venerable brother Bishop Athanasius Schneider has many times recalled, the Arianism that afflicted the Church at the time of the Holy Doctor of Alexandria in Egypt was so widespread among the bishops that it leaves one almost to believe that Catholic orthodoxy had completely disappeared. But it was thanks to the fidelity and heroic testimony of the few bishops who remained faithful that the Church knew how to get back up again. Without this testimony, Arianism would not have been defeated; without our testimony today, Modernism and the globalist apostasy of this pontificate will not be defeated.

It is therefore not a question of working from within the Church or outside it: the winemakers are called to work in the Lord's Vineyard, and it is there that they must remain even at the cost of their lives; the pastors are called to pastor the Lord's flock, to keep the ravenous wolves at bay and to drive away the mercenaries who are not concerned with the salvation of the sheep and lambs.

This hidden and often silent work has been carried out by the Society of Saint Pius X, which deserves recognition for not having allowed the flame of Tradition to be extinguished at a moment in which celebrating the ancient Mass was considered subversive and a reason for excommunication. Its priests have been a healthy thorn in the side for a hierarchy that has seen in them an unacceptable point of comparison for the faithful, a constant reproach for the betrayal committed against the people of God, an inadmissible alternative to the new conciliar path. And if their fidelity made disobedience to the pope inevitable with the episcopal consecrations,[4] thanks to them the Society was able to protect herself from the furious attack of the innovators and by its very existence it allowed the possibility of the liberalization of the ancient rite, which until then was prohibited. Its presence also allowed the contradictions and errors of the conciliar sect to emerge, always winking at heretics and idolaters but implacably rigid and intolerant towards Catholic truth.

I consider Archbishop Lefebvre an exemplary confessor of the Faith, and I think that by now it is obvious that his denunciation of

---

4. The consecration of four bishops by Lefebvre on June 30, 1988. See p. 134, n. 54.

the Council and the modernist apostasy is more relevant than ever. It should not be forgotten that the persecution to which Archbishop Lefebvre was subjected by the Holy See and the world episcopate served above all as a deterrent for Catholics who were refractory toward the conciliar revolution.

I also agree with the observation of His Excellency Bishop Bernard Tissier de Mallerais[5] about the co-presence of two entities in Rome: the Church of Christ has been occupied and eclipsed by the modernist conciliar structure, which has established itself in the same hierarchy and uses the authority of its ministers to prevail over the Spouse of Christ and our Mother.

The Church of Christ—which not only *subsists in* the Catholic Church, but *is exclusively* the Catholic Church—is only obscured and eclipsed by a strange extravagant Church established in Rome, according to the vision of Blessed Anne Catherine Emmerich.[6] It coexists, like wheat with the tare, in the Roman Curia, in dioceses, in parishes. We cannot judge our pastors for their intentions, nor suppose that all of them are corrupt in faith and morals; on the contrary, we can hope that many of them, hitherto intimidated and silent, will understand, as confusion and apostasy continue to spread, the deception to which they have been subjected and will finally shake off their slumber. There are many laity who are raising their voice; others will necessarily follow, together with good priests, certainly present in every diocese. This awakening of the Church militant—I would dare to call it almost a resurrection—is necessary, urgent and inevitable: no son tolerates his mother being outraged by the servants, or his father being tyrannized by the administrators of his goods. The Lord offers us, in these painful situations, the possibility of being His allies in fighting this holy battle under His banner: the King Who is victorious over error and death permits us to share the honor of triumphal victory and the eternal reward that derives from it, after having endured and suffered with Him.

But in order to deserve the immortal glory of Heaven, we are

5. See p.129, n.52.

6. An Augustinian Canoness Regular who lived between 1774 and 1824 and was a mystic, visionary, and stigmatist.

called to rediscover—in an emasculated age devoid of values such as honor, faithfulness to one's word, and heroism—a fundamental aspect of the faith of every baptized person: the Christian life is a *militia*, and with the sacrament of Confirmation we are called to be soldiers of Christ, under whose insignia we must fight. Of course, in most cases it is essentially a spiritual battle, but over the course of history we have seen how often, faced with the violation of the sovereign rights of God and the liberty of the Church, it was also necessary to take up arms: we are taught this by the strenuous resistance to repel the Islamic invasions in Lepanto[7] and on the outskirts of Vienna,[8] the persecution of the Cristeros in Mexico,[9] of the Catholics in Spain,[10] and even today by the cruel war against Christians throughout the world. Never as today can we understand the theological hatred coming from the enemies of God, inspired by Satan. The attack on everything that recalls the Cross of Christ—on virtue, on the Good and the Beautiful, on purity—must spur us to get up, in a leap of pride, in order to claim our right not only not to be persecuted by our external enemies but also and above all to have strong and courageous pastors, holy and God-fearing, who will do exactly what their predecessors have done for centuries: preach the

7. A great naval battle fought in 1571 at Lepanto during which the forces organized by the Holy Father defeated the Muslim aggressors and averted a likely invasion of Europe. Pope St. Pius V instituted the feast of "Our Lady of Victory" on the date of the victory, October 7, in recognition of Mary's intercession due to the widespread recitation of the Rosary that the pope requested prior to the battle. In 1573, Pope Gregory XIII changed the title of the feast to "Our Lady of the Rosary" and moved it to the first Sunday of October; Pius X in 1913 moved it back to October 7.

8. This refers to the siege of Vienna in 1683 by a Muslim army that was ultimately defeated, again preventing an invasion of Europe.

9. The citizen army of the Cristeros bravely fought the atheist and anticlerical Marxist revolutionaries in Mexico in the 1920s, defending the Catholic Faith and the clergy. Their motto was *¡Viva Christo Rey!* (Long live Christ the King). Eventually the Vatican backed a deal between the exiled Mexican bishops and the government, which resulted in the Cristeros voluntarily laying down their arms. The revolutionaries, having reneged on their side of the deal, rounded up many of the Cristeros and executed them.

10. Catholics, especially priests and religious, were persecuted and martyred in the thousands during the Spanish Civil War fought in the 1930s.

Gospel of Christ, convert individuals and nations, and expand the Kingdom of the living and true God throughout the world.

We are all called to make an act of fortitude—a forgotten cardinal virtue, which not by chance in Greek recalls virile strength, ἀνδρεία—in knowing how to resist the Modernists: a resistance that is rooted in charity and truth, which are attributes of God.

If you celebrate only the Tridentine Mass and preach sound doctrine without ever mentioning the Council, what can they ever do to you? Throw you out of your churches, perhaps, and then what? No one can ever prevent you from renewing the Holy Sacrifice, even if it is on a makeshift altar in a cellar or an attic, as the refractory priests did during the French Revolution,[11] or as happens still today in China. And if they try to distance you, resist: canon law serves to guarantee the government of the Church in the pursuit of its primary purposes, not to demolish it. Let's stop fearing that the fault of the schism lies with those who denounce it, and not, instead, with those who carry it out: the ones who are schismatics and heretics are those who wound and crucify the Mystical Body of Christ, not those who defend it by denouncing the executioners!

The laity can expect their ministers to behave as such, preferring those who prove that they are not contaminated by present errors. If a Mass becomes an occasion of torture for the faithful, if they are forced to assist at sacrileges or to support heresies and ramblings unworthy of the House of the Lord, it is a thousand times preferable to go to a church where the priest celebrates the Holy Sacrifice worthily, in the rite given to us by Tradition, with preaching in conformity with sound doctrine. When parish priests and bishops realize that the Christian people demand the Bread of Faith, and not the stones and scorpions of the neo-church, they will lay aside their fears and comply with the legitimate requests of the faithful. The others, true mercenaries, will show themselves for what they are and will be able to gather around them only those who share their errors and perversions. They will be extinguished by themselves: the

---

11. Refractory priests were those who refused the civil oath of the revolutionary government that subjected the Church to the control of the state; as a result, these clergy had to go into hiding and offer Mass in secret.

Lord dries up the swamp and makes the land on which brambles grow arid; he extinguishes vocations in corrupt seminaries and in convents rebellious to the Rule.

The lay faithful today have a sacred task: to comfort good priests and good bishops, gathering like sheep around their shepherds. Give them hospitality, help them, console them in their trials. Create a community in which murmuring and division do not predominate, but rather fraternal charity in the bond of faith. And since in the order established by God—κόσμος[12]—subjects owe obedience to authority and cannot do otherwise than resist it when it abuses its power, no fault will be attributed to them for the infidelity of their leaders, on whom rests the very serious responsibility for the way in which they exercise the vicarious power which has been given to them. We must not rebel, but oppose; we must not be pleased with the errors of our pastors, but pray for them and admonish them respectfully; we must not question their authority but the way in which they use it.

I am certain, with a certainty that comes to me from faith, that the Lord will not fail to reward our fidelity, after having punished us for the faults of the men of the Church, granting us holy priests, holy bishops, holy cardinals, and above all a holy pope. But these saints will arise from our families, from our communities, from our churches: families, communities, and churches in which the grace of God must be cultivated with constant prayer, with the frequenting of Holy Mass and the sacraments, with the offering of sacrifices and penances that the Communion of Saints permits us to offer to the Divine Majesty in order to expiate our sins and those of our brethren, including those who exercise authority. The laity have a fundamental role in this, guarding the Faith within their families, in such a way that our young people who are educated in love and in the fear of God may one day be responsible fathers and mothers, but also worthy ministers of the Lord, His heralds in the male and female religious orders, and His apostles in civil society.

The cure for rebellion is obedience. The cure for heresy is faithfulness to the teaching of Tradition. The cure for schism is filial

12. Greek for the cosmos or universe, the entire system of creation.

devotion for the Sacred Pastors. The cure for apostasy is love for God and His Most Holy Mother. The cure for vice is the humble practice of virtue. The cure for the corruption of morals is to live constantly in the presence of God. But obedience cannot be perverted into stolid servility; respect for authority cannot be perverted into the obeisance of the court. And let's not forget that if it is the duty of the laity to obey their Pastors, it is even a more grave duty of the Pastors to obey God, *usque ad effusionem sanguinis* [even to the shedding of blood].

✠ Carlo Maria Viganò, Archbishop
September 1, 2020

15

Instead of "Assuming Schisms" Where There Are None, Better to Fight Long-lasting Errors

A FEW days ago, shortly after another article of a similar tone was published by Fr. Thomas Weinandy,[1] Fr. Raymond J. De Souza wrote a commentary titled, "Is Archbishop Viganò's Rejection of the Second Vatican Council Promoting Schism?"[2] The writer's thought is immediately expressed in the subtitle: "In his latest 'testimony,' the former nuncio holds a position contrary to the Catholic faith on the authority of ecumenical councils."

I can understand that in many ways my interventions can provoke no little annoyance with the supporters of Vatican II, and that questioning their idol is reason enough to merit the most severe canonical sanctions, after shouting against schism. Their annoyance is combined with a certain spite in seeing that—despite my choice not to appear in public—my interventions are arousing interest and are fueling a healthy debate about the Council and more generally about the crisis of the ecclesiastical hierarchy. I do not claim myself to have the merit of having initiated this dispute: other eminent prelates and high-profile intellectuals before me have highlighted critical issues that need a solution; others have shown the causal relationship between Vatican II and the present apostasy. Faced with these numerous and well-argued critiques, no one has ever proposed valid responses or shared solutions. On the contrary, in

---

1. VN: The article may be found at www.catholicworldreport.com/2020/08/13/a-response-to-archbishop-viganos-letter-about-vatican-ii.

2. VN: The article may be found at www.ncregister.com/commentaries/is-archbishop-vigano-s-rejection-of-the-second-vatican-council-promoting-schism.

defense of the conciliar totem the only response is the delegitimization of the interlocutor, his ostracization, and the generic accusation of wanting to attack the unity of the Church. And this last
accusation is all the more grotesque when we see how obviously
canonically cross-eyed the accusers are: they unleash the *malleus
hæreticorum* [hammer of heretics] against those who defend Catholic orthodoxy, while they bow down in reverence to ecclesiastics,
religious-S.J.s,[3] and theologians who daily attack the integrity of the
depositum fidei. The painful sufferings of so many prelates, among
whom Archbishop Marcel Lefebvre undoubtedly stands out, confirm that even in the absence of specific accusations there are those
who succeed in using the canonical norm as the tool of persecuting
the good, and at the same time are careful not to use it with real
schismatics and heretics.

How can we forget in this regard those theologians who had been
suspended from teaching, removed from seminaries, or hit by cen-
sures from the Holy Office, and who, precisely because of their "merits," deserved to be called to the Council as consultors and experts?
Those rebels of liberation theology who were admonished under the
pontificate of John Paul II and rehabilitated by Bergoglio must also
be included; not to mention the protagonists of the Amazon Synod
and the bishops of the Synodal Path, promoters of a heretical and
schismatic German national church; without omitting the bishops
of the Patriotic Chinese sect, recognized by the agreement between
the Vatican and the communist dictatorship of Beijing.[4]

Father de Souza and Father Weinandy, without entering into the
merits of the arguments I have presented, which both of them dis-

---

3. An abbreviation for Society of Jesus, the Jesuits.
4. This topic will be addressed more directly in the texts in Part III. The Chinese
Patriotic Association is a schismatic sect created by the Chinese Communist Party
to function as a counterchurch to the true (often called underground) Catholic
Church in China. The Communist Party appoints and controls the bishops and
clergy of the sect and they refuse several teachings of the Church. In 2018, the Vatican in a secret agreement (i.e., the content of it has remained unpublished) recognized and accepted the Chinese Patriotic Association clergy and conceded to the
Communist Party in China the right to appoint new bishops who would be rubber-
stamped by Pope Francis.

dainfully describe as intrinsically schismatic, ought to have the fairness to read my interventions *before* censuring my thoughts. In them they would find mention of the painful labor that led me to understand only in the last few years that I have been misled by those in authority whom I never could have imagined would have been able to betray those who placed their trust in them. I do not think that I am the only one who has understood this deception and denounced it: laity, clerics, and prelates have found themselves in the painful situation of having to recognize a fraud that was cunningly hatched, a fraud that consisted, in my opinion, of having resorted to a Council to give apparent authority to the initiatives of the innovators and obtaining obedience from the clergy and the people of God. And this obedience was demanded by the pastors, allowing no exception, in order to demolish the Church of Christ from within.

I have written and declared many times that it is precisely in virtue of this falsification that the faithful, respectful to the authority of the hierarchy, did not dare to disobey *en masse* the imposition of heterodox doctrines and protestantized rites. Among other things, this revolution was not accomplished all at once, but according to a process by stages, in which the novelties introduced *ad experimentum*[5] were later made a universal norm, with ever tighter turns of the screw. And I have likewise reiterated several times that if the errors and equivocal points of Vatican II had been formulated by a group of German or Dutch bishops, without giving them the mantle of authoritativeness of an ecumenical council, they would probably

---

5. In Church law something permitted *ad experimentum* is authorized on a trial basis for a period of time. Viganò is referring to many uses of this device to permit deviations from Church practice in isolated exceptions that eventually grow to swallow up the rule from which they are an exception. The reception of Holy Communion in the hand is an example: after priests in Holland were found to be illicitly distributing the Sacrament in this way, Paul VI, while reaffirming the traditional practice of receiving on the tongue while kneeling, allowed the episcopal conference to regulate the contrary practice where it already existed, as an experimental exception. Within a decade, the practice had spread to become nearly universal, including in countries where it had never existed.

have merited the condemnation of the Holy Office,[6] and their writings would have ended up on the Index.[7] Perhaps it was precisely for this reason that those who upset the preparatory schemas of the Council took care, during the reign of Paul VI, to weaken the Supreme Congregation and abolish the *Index Librorum Prohibitorum* [Index of Forbidden Books], on which in other times their own writings would have appeared.

De Souza and Weinandy apparently believe that it is not possible to change one's opinion, and that it is preferable to remain in error rather than retrace one's steps. Yet this attitude is very strange: multitudes of cardinals and bishops, priests and clerics, monks and nuns, theologians and moralists, laity and Catholic intellectuals all felt compelled, in the name of obedience to the hierarchy, to renounce the Tridentine Mass and to see it replaced with a rite copied from Cranmer's *Book of Common Prayer*;[8] to throw away treasures of doctrine, morality, spirituality, and an inestimable artistic and cultural patrimony, obscuring 2,000 years of Magisterium in the name of a Council, which moreover intended to be pastoral and not dogmatic. They heard it said that the conciliar church was finally open to the world, stripped of hateful post-Tridentine triumphalism, medieval dogmatic encrustations, liturgical trappings, the sexophobic morality of Saint Alphonsus, the notionism of the Cate-

---

6. The Holy Office is the former name of what is now called the Congregation for the Doctrine of the Faith (CDF). Before the radical changes to the Curia by Paul VI, it was the highest organization in the Roman Curia, the one to which all other departments or congregations reported. Paul VI demoted the Holy Office (in addition to changing its name) and made all parts of the Curia report to the Secretariat of State. Thus, rather than all activities of the Vatican answering to the doctrinal authority, they now answer to the political/diplomatic authority.

7. The *Index Librorum Prohibitorum* was a list of writings proscribed as dangerous to the faith due to their errors. The Index was abolished by Paul VI.

8. This book contains the rewritten form of worship that was substituted for the Holy Sacrifice of the Mass in England under King Edward VI in 1549. As the archbishop notes, following the groundbreaking work of Michael Davies, the *Novus Ordo* Mass of Paul VI is very similar to Cranmer's work. In fact, comparing the various texts, one might reach an even more distressing conclusion: Cranmer's work retains more of the Roman tradition than Paul VI's missal does.

chism of Saint Pius X, and the clericalism of the Pacellian Curia.[9] We were asked to renounce everything, in the name of Vatican II. Now, after more than half a century, we see that nothing was saved of what little apparently still seemed to remain in force!

Yet, if repudiating the *preconciliar* Catholic Church by embracing the *conciliar renewal* was hailed as a gesture of great maturity, a *prophetic sign*, a way of *keeping step with the times* and ultimately something inevitable and incontestable, today repudiating a failed experiment that led the Church to collapse is considered a sign of incoherence or of insubordination, according to the adage "*No going back*" of the innovators. At that time the *revolution* was said to be salutary and necessary, but today the restoration is called harmful and a harbinger of divisions. Back then we were told we could and should deny the glorious past of the Church in the name of *aggiornamento* [updating]; today questioning a few decades of deviation is considered schismatic. And what is even more grotesque is that the defenders of the Council are simultaneously so flexible with those who deny the preconciliar Magisterium, while stigmatizing with the Jesuitical and infamous qualification of *rigid* those who, out of consistency with that same Magisterium, cannot accept ecumenism and interreligious dialogue (which resulted in Assisi and Abu Dhabi), the new ecclesiology and the liturgical reform stirred by Vatican II.

All this, of course, has no philosophical nor even a theological foundation: the superdogma of Vatican II prevails over everything else, it annuls everything, cancels everything, but it does not permit itself to suffer the same fate. It is precisely this that confirms that Vatican II, *although a legitimate Ecumenical Council*—as I have elsewhere affirmed—*is not like the others*, because if this were the case, the councils and the Magisterium that preceded it would have had to be held as equally binding (not only in words), preventing the formulation of the errors contained or implied in the texts of Vatican II. *Civitas divisa contra se* [a city divided against itself].

De Souza and Weinandy do not want to admit that the stratagem adopted by the innovators was very cunning: in order to gain

---

9. A reference to Pope Pius XII, whose civil name was Eugenio Pacelli.

approval for the *revolution* by those who thought that they were dealing with a Catholic Council like Vatican I, the innovators, in an apparent respect for the norms, declared that it was only a *pastoral Council*, not a dogmatic Council. This allowed the Council Fathers to believe that the critical points would in some way be settled, the equivocal points would be clarified, certain reforms would be reconsidered in a more moderate sense. And while the enemies had organized everything, down to the tiniest details, at least twenty years prior to the convocation of the Council, there were those who naively believed that God would prevent the *coup* of the Modernists, as if the Holy Spirit could act against the subversive will of the innovators. A naiveté into which I myself fell together with the majority of my brothers and prelates, who were formed and raised with the conviction that Pastors—and the Supreme Pontiff first and foremost—were owed an unconditional obedience. Thus good Catholics, because of their distorted concept of absolute obedience, obeyed their Pastors unconditionally; they were led to disobey Christ, precisely by those who had made quite clear what their goals were. Even in this case it is evident that assent to the conciliar magisterium did not prevent dissent from the perennial Magisterium of the Church—it actually required such dissent as a logical and inevitable consequence.

After more than fifty years, we still do not want to take note of an uncontestable fact, and that is that there was an intent to use a subversive method that up until then had been adopted in the political and civil sphere, applying it *sine glossa*[10] to the religious and ecclesial sphere. This method, typical of those who have, to say the least, a materialistic vision of the world, found the Conciliar Fathers who *truly* believed in the action of the Paraclete unprepared, while the enemies knew how to falsify the votes in the conciliar commissions, weaken the opposition, obtain exceptions to established procedures, and present a norm as apparently harmless in order to later draw a disruptive and opposite effect from it. And the fact that *that*

---

10. Latin for "without gloss." He means that a civil and political technique was applied to the Church without adapting it to the unique requirements of the Church.

Council took place in the Vatican Basilica, with the Fathers in miter and cope or in choral dress, and John XXIII in tiara and mantle, was perfectly consistent with the orchestration of a scenography especially designed to deceive the participants and indeed reassure them that, in the end, the Holy Spirit would remedy even the messes of *subsistit in*[11] or the blunders on religious freedom.

In this regard, I would like to quote an article that has appeared in the last few days at *Settimo Cielo* entitled, "Historicizing Vatican Council II. Here's How the World of Those Years Influenced the Church."[12] Sandro Magister informs us of a study by Professor Roberto Perici on the Council, which I recommend reading in its entirely but that can be summarized in these two quotes:

> The dispute that is inflaming the Church, on how to judge Vatican II, must not be only theological. Because first of all the historical context of that event must be analyzed, all the more so for a Council that in setting its agenda declared it wanted to "open up to the world."
>
> I know well that the Church—as Paul VI reiterated in *Ecclesiam Suam*—is in the world, but is not of the world: it has values, behaviors, procedures that are specific to it and that cannot be judged and framed with totally historical-political, worldly criteria. On the other hand—it must be added—neither is it a separate body. In the 1960s—and the conciliar documents are full of references to this effect—the world was moving toward what we now call "globalization," it was already strongly influenced by the new mass media, unprecedented ideas and attitudes were spreading very quickly, and forms of generational mimicry were emerging. It is unthinkable that an event of the breadth and relevance of the Council should have been taking place in the enclosure of St. Peter's Basilica without measuring itself against what was happening.

---

11. The claim in *Lumen Gentium* 8 that the Church of Christ subsists in (rather than *is*) the Catholic Church.

12. VN: The link may be found at http://magister.blogautore.espresso.repubblica.it/2020/08/31/historicizing-vatican-council-ii-here%E2%80%99s-how-the-world-of-those-years-influenced-the-church.

Better to Fight Long-lasting Errors

In my opinion this is an interesting interpretative key to Vatican II, which confirms the influence of "democratic" thought at the Council. The great alibi of the Council was to present itself as a collegial and almost plebiscitary decision to introduce otherwise unacceptable changes. It was not in fact the specific content of the Acts nor their future significance in light of the *spirit of the Council* that cleared up heterodox doctrines that were already weaving their way through the ecclesial circles of northern Europe, but the *charism of democracy*, made almost unconsciously by the entire world episcopate, in the name of an ideological subjection that at the time saw many exponents of the hierarchy as almost subordinate to the mentality of the age. The idol of parliamentarianism that arose from the French Revolution—which showed itself to be so effective in subverting the social order—must have represented for some prelates an inevitable stage in the modernization of the Church, to be accepted in exchange for a sort of tolerance on the part of the contemporary world for what was still old and *outmoded* in what it persisted in proposing. This was a very serious mistake! This sense of inferiority on the part of the hierarchy, this feeling of backwardness and inadequacy to the demands of progress and ideologies, betrays a very deficient supernatural vision, and an even more deficient exercise of the theological virtues: it is the Church that ought to attract the world to itself and convert it and not *vice versa*! The world must be converted to Christ and the Gospel, without Our Lord having to be presented as a revolutionary *à la* Che Guevara and the Church as a philanthropic organization more attentive to ecology than to the eternal salvation of souls.

De Souza affirms, contrary to what I have written, that I called Vatican II a "devil council." I would like to know where he found these words of mine reported. I assume that this expression is due to his erroneous and presumptuous translation of the term "*conciliàbolo*," according to its Latin etymology, which does not correspond to the current meaning in the Italian language. From this erroneous translation he infers that I have "a position contrary to the Catholic faith on the authority of ecumenical councils." If he had taken the time to read my statements on this topic, he would have understood that precisely because I have the greatest veneration for the authority of the Ecumenical Councils and for the entire Magisterium in general, I am not able to reconcile the most clear and orthodox teachings of all of the councils up until Vatican I with the equivocal and at times even heterodox teachings of Vatican II. But I don't seem to be the only one. Father Weinandy himself fails to reconcile the role of Vicar of Christ with Jorge Mario Bergoglio, who is simultaneously both the holder and the demolisher of the papacy. But for De Souza and Weinandy, against all logic, one may criticize the Vicar of Christ but not the Council, or rather *that* Council and *only that one*. In fact, I have never encountered such solicitude in reiterating the canons of Vatican I when certain theologians speak of a "*resizing of the papacy*" or of a "*synodal path*"; nor have I ever found so many defenders of the authority of the Council of Trent when the very essence of the Catholic priesthood is denied.

De Souza thinks that, with my letter to Father Weinandy, I looked for an ally in him. Even if that was the case, I do not think that there would be anything wrong in that, as long as this alliance would have for its purpose the defense of truth in the bond of charity. But in reality, my intention was what I stated from the beginning, namely, to make a comparison possible from which we reach a greater understanding of the present crisis and its causes, in such a way that the Authority of the Church can pronounce on it in its time. I have never allowed myself to impose a definitive solution, nor to resolve questions that go beyond my role as archbishop and are instead matters that are the direct competence of the Apostolic See. Thus, what Father De Souza says is not true, and even less that which Father Weinandy incomprehensibly attributes to me, that I find myself in the "*unforgivable sin against the Holy Spirit*." I could perhaps believe their good faith if they both applied the same severity of judgment to their common adversaries and to themselves, something that unfortunately does not seem to me will happen.

Father De Souza asks: "Schism. Heresy. Devil's work. Unforgivable sin. How is it that such words are now being applied to Archbishop Viganò by respected and careful voices?" I think that the answer is obvious by now: a taboo has been broken, and a discussion about Vatican II, that up until now had remained confined to very restricted areas of the ecclesial body, has now begun on a large scale. And what most disturbs the supporters of the Council is the observation that this dispute is not about *if* the Council is open to criticism, but about *what to do* to remedy the errors and equivocal passages found in it. And this is an established fact, on which no work of delegitimization can now be undertaken: Magister also writes this at *Settimo Cielo*, referring to the "dispute that is inflaming the Church over how to judge Vatican II" and to the "controversies that periodically reopen in the various 'Catholic' media about the meaning of Vatican II and the link that exists between that Council and the present situation of the Church." Making people believe that the Council is free from criticism is a falsification of reality, regardless of the intentions of those who criticize its ambiguity or heterodoxy.

Father De Souza further claims that Professor John Paul Meenan, on *LifeSiteNews*,[13] supposedly demonstrated "the weaknesses in Archbishop Viganò's argument and his theological mistakes." I leave to Professor Meenan the burden of refuting my interventions on the basis of what I affirm, and not on what I do not say but that is deliberately misrepresented. Here, too, how much indulgence is shown to the Acts of the Council, and how much implacable severity to those who point out the gaps, to the point of insinuating the suspicion of Donatism.[14]

As for the famous *hermeneutic of continuity*, it seems to me that it is clear that this is and remains an attempt—perhaps inspired by a somewhat Kantian[15] vision of the affairs of the Church—to reconcile a *precouncil* and a *postcouncil* as had never before been neces-

13. VN: The link may be found at www.lifesitenews.com/opinion/catholic-prof-abp-vigano-is-right-in-calling-for-reform-but-church-cannot-simply-repudi ate-vatican-ii.

14. Donatism was a fourth-century heresy whose adherents believed that sacraments could be validly administered only by the holy, and that Catholics who fell away during persecution could not be forgiven and readmitted to their place in the Church.

15. The German Enlightenment philosopher Immanuel Kant attempted, unsuccessfully, to reconcile modern liberal philosophy (especially skepticism) and traditional Lutheran morality.

sary. The hermeneutic of continuity obviously is valid and to be followed within Catholic discourse: in theological language it is called the *analogia fidei* [analogy of faith] and it is one of the cornerstones to which the student of the sacred sciences must adhere. But applying this criterion to a *hapax*[16] that, precisely based on its ambiguity, succeeded in saying or implying what it should have openly condemned does not make sense, because it presupposes as a postulate that there is a real coherence between the Magisterium of the Church and the "magisterium" contrary to it which is taught by the Pontifical Academies and Universities, by the episcopal and seminary chairs and preached from the pulpits. But while it is ontologically necessary that all truth be consistent with itself, at the same time it is not possible to fail in the principle of non-contradiction, according to which two mutually exclusive propositions cannot both be true. Thus, there can be no "hermeneutic of continuity" in supporting the necessity of the Catholic Church for eternal salvation and at the same time what the Abu Dhabi declaration affirms, which is in continuity with the conciliar teaching. It is thus not true that I reject the hermeneutic in itself, but only when it cannot be applied to a clearly heterogeneous context. But if this observation of mine turns out to be unfounded, and if they want to demonstrate the gaps in it, I will be quite happy to repudiate them myself.

At the end of his article, Fr. De Souza asks provocatively: "Priest, curialist, diplomat, nuncio, administrator, reformer, whistleblower. Is it possible that, at the end of it all, heretic and schismatic would be added to that list?" I do not intend to respond to the insulting and gravely offensive expressions of Fr. Raymond. I limit myself to asking him: To how many progressive cardinals and bishops would it be superfluous to ask the same question, already knowing that the

16. An abbreviation for *hapax legomenon*, a Greek phrase referring to a word that appears only once in a text or author's corpus or the written record of a language. The archbishop is arguing that an approach that seeks to interpret Vatican II in a way that makes it in continuity with prior teaching is not possible because Vatican II is a unique word (a *hapax*) in the corpus of the ecumenical councils and, as such, not consistent with the others.

answer is sadly positive? Perhaps, before assuming schisms and heresies where there are none, it would be appropriate and more useful to fight error and division where they have nested and spread for decades.

Sancte Pie X, ora pro nobis![17]

3 September 2020
Saint Pius X, Pope and Confessor

---

17. St. Pius X pray for us. September 3 is the feast of St. Pius X in the traditional calendar.

16

Fifth Letter on Vatican II, Responding to Michael Matt

DEAR Michael,

I saw the catechism on the Council[1] published by Word on Fire,[2] and in response to your request[3] I am sending you a brief reflection. I won't go into the details of the FAQs, which seem to me more suited to an instruction manual on how to use a tool or manage a call centre. I will focus instead on the introductory passage from Benedict XVI: "To defend the true tradition of the Church today means to defend the Council. [...] We must remain faithful to the today of the Church, not the yesterday or tomorrow. And this today of the Church is the documents of Vatican II, without reservations that amputate them and without arbitrariness that distorts them."

The Holy Father states apodictically that "to defend the true tradition of the Church today means to defend the Council" and that "we must remain faithful to the today of the Church." These two propositions, which complement one another, find no support in the Tradition, since the Church's present is always indissolubly linked to her past.

The Church is comprised of three dimensions: one triumphant in Heaven, one militant on earth and one suffering in Purgatory. These three dimensions of the same Church are closely linked, and

---

1. VN: The text may be found at www.wordonfire.org/vatican-ii-faq.

2. Word on Fire is a digital media non-profit founded by Bishop Robert Barron, auxiliary bishop of the archdiocese of Los Angeles. Apparently in response to the criticisms of Vatican II released by Archbishop Viganò, this website published a "catechism on Vatican II."

3. VN: See https://remnantnewspaper.com/web/index.php/articles/item/5024-archbishop-vigano-on-vatican-ii-bishop-barron-s-word-on-fire.

Fifth Letter on Vatican II, to Michael Matt

it is clear that the triumphant and the purgative dimensions exist in a metahistorical or metatemporal metaphysical reality, whereas only the militant Church has a today, a contingency given by the passage of time; it is clear that nothing can change her essence, her mission and above all her doctrine. Therefore, there is no Church only of *today*, in which yesterday is now irremediably past and *tomorrow* has not yet happened: what Christ taught yesterday, we repeat today and His Vicars will profess tomorrow; what the Martyrs witnessed to yesterday, we guard today and our children will confess tomorrow.

Then there is another proposition that "we must remain faithful to the today of the Church, not the yesterday or tomorrow," which significantly was adopted by the proponents of Vatican II precisely in order to erase the past, affirm the conciliar revolution in the today of that time, and prepare the crisis of that tomorrow in which we now find ourselves. And the innovators who wanted *that* Council carried it out precisely with "the reservations that amputated" the uninterrupted Magisterium of the Church and "the arbitrariness that distorted it"—paraphrasing Ratzinger's words.

I do not see why what the innovators accomplished with Vatican II yesterday, to the detriment of Tradition, cannot apply to them today: those who, in the name of being pastoral, did not hesitate to demolish the doctrinal, moral, liturgical, spiritual and disciplinary edifice of the *old religion*—as they call it—in the name of the Council, today would dare to claim for their daring innovations that obsequious submission and that deference that they did not want to apply to two thousand years of infallible Magisterium. And we are to show unconditional support not for Tradition, but for the only event that has contradicted and adulterated that Tradition? It seems to me that this line of reasoning, if only from a purely logical point of view, doesn't have much credibility, and limits itself to reaffirming that self-referentiality of the conciliar church, in rupture with the uninterrupted teaching of the Supreme Pontiffs who preceded it.

Moreover, it seems to me that Benedict XVI's quotation is also in contradiction with that hermeneutic of continuity, according to which the Council should be accepted not as a rupture with the

Church's past, but precisely in continuity with it: but if there is no Church of yesterday, to what does the continuity of the supposed conciliar hermeneutic refer? Another philosophical pun that, unfortunately, has shown signs of failure since the time it was formulated, and that today is denied from the highest Throne.

We can observe with "amazement" the commitment of the zealots of Vatican II in defending their council, to the point of composing no less than a sort of *catechism of the Council*. If they had taken the trouble to reaffirm, with equal commitment, the immutable doctrine of the Church when it was denied or silenced, precisely in the name of conciliar renewal, today there would be less widespread ignorance of the Faith and less confusion. But unfortunately, defending Vatican II is more important than defending the perennial *depositum fidei*.

17

Is Vatican II "Untouchable"?[1]

DR. Peter Kwasniewski's recent commentary, titled "Why Viganò's Critique of the Council Must Be Taken Seriously," impressed me greatly. It appeared at *OnePeterFive* on June 29, and is one of the articles on which I have been meaning to comment: I do so now, with gratitude to the author and publisher for the opportunity they have given me. First, it seems to me that I can agree with practically all of what Kwasniewski has written: his analysis of the facts is extremely clear and polished and reflects my thoughts exactly. What I am particularly pleased about is that "ever since Archbishop Viganò's June 9 letter and his subsequent writing on the subject, people have been discussing what it might mean to 'annul' the Second Vatican Council."

I find it interesting that we are beginning to question a taboo that, for almost sixty years, has prevented any theological, sociological and historical criticism of the Council. This is particularly interesting given that Vatican II is regarded as untouchable, but this does not apply—according to its supporters—to any other magisterial document or to Sacred Scripture. We have read endless addresses in which the defenders of the Council have defined the Canons of Trent, the *Syllabus of Errors* of Blessed Pius IX, the encyclical *Pascendi* of St. Pius X, *Humanæ Vitæ* of Paul VI, and *Ordinatio Sacerdotalis* of John Paul II as "outdated." The change to the *Catechism of the Catholic Church*, whereby the doctrine on the legitimacy of the death penalty was modified in the name of a "changed understanding" of the Gospel, shows that for the innovators there is no dogma, no immutable principle that can be immune from revision or cancellation: the only exception is Vatican II, which by its nature—*ex se,*

---

1. First published at OnePeterFive, September 21, 2020.

theologians would say—enjoys that charism of infallibility and inerrancy that is denied to the entire *depositum fidei*.

I have already expressed my opinion on the hermeneutic of continuity theorized by Benedict XVI, and constantly taken up by the defenders of Vatican II, who—certainly in good faith—seek to offer a reading of the Council that is harmonious with Tradition. It seems to me that the arguments in favor of the hermeneutical criterion, proposed for the first time in 2005,[2] are limited to a merely theoretical analysis of the problem, obstinately leaving aside the reality of what has been happening before our eyes for decades. This analysis starts from a valid and acceptable postulate, but in this concrete case it presupposes a premise that is not necessarily true.

The postulate is that all the acts of the Magisterium are to be read and interpreted in the light of the entire magisterial corpus, because of the *analogia fidei*[3] [analogy of faith], which is somehow also expressed in the hermeneutic of continuity. Yet this postulate assumes that the text we are going to analyze is a specific act of the Magisterium, with its degree of authority clearly expressed in the canonical forms envisaged. And this is precisely where the deception lies, this is where the trap is set. For the innovators maliciously managed to put the label "Sacrosanct Ecumenical Council" on their ideological manifesto, just as, at a local level, the Jansenists who maneuvered the Synod of Pistoia had managed to cloak with authority their heretical theses, which were later condemned by Pius VI.[4]

---

2. See www.vatican.va/content/benedict-xvi/it/speeches/2005/december/documents/hf_ben_xvi_spe_20051222_roman-curia.html.

3. *Catechism of the Catholic Church*, n. 114: "By 'analogy of faith' we mean the coherence of the truths of faith among themselves and within the whole plan of Revelation."

4. It is interesting to note that, of the eighty-five synodal theses condemned by the Bull *Auctorem Fidei*, only seven were branded simply heretical, while the others were defined as schismatic; erroneous; subversive of the ecclesiastical hierarchy; false; reckless; temerarious; capricious; insulting the Church and its authority; leading to contempt for the sacraments and the practices of Holy Church; offensive to the piety of the faithful; disturbing the order of the various churches, the ecclesiastical ministry, and the peace of souls; in contrast to the Tridentine decrees; offensive to the veneration due to the Mother of God; offensive to the rights of the General Councils.

Is Vatican II "Untouchable"?

On the one hand, Catholics look at the *form* of the Council and consider its acts to be an expression of the Magisterium. Consequently, they seek to read its *substance*, which is clearly ambiguous or even erroneous, in keeping with the analogy of faith, out of that love and veneration that all Catholics have towards Holy Mother Church. They cannot comprehend that the Pastors have been so naïve as to impose on them an adulteration of the Faith, but at the same time they understand the rupture with Tradition and try to explain this contradiction.

The modernist, on the other hand, looks at the *substance* of the revolutionary message he means to convey, and in order to endow it with an authoritativeness that it does not and should not have, he "magisterializes" it through the *form* of the Council, by having it published in the form of official acts. He knows well that he is forcing it, but he uses the authority of the Church—which under normal conditions he despises and rejects—to make it practically impossible to condemn those errors, which have been ratified by no less than the majority of the Synod Fathers. The instrumental use of authority for purposes opposed to those that legitimize it is a cunning ploy: on the one hand, it guarantees a sort of immunity, a "canonical shield" for doctrines that are heterodox or close to heresy; on the other hand, it allows sanctions to be imposed on those who denounce these deviations, by virtue of a formal respect for canonical norms. In the civil sphere, this way of proceeding is typical of dictatorships. If this has also happened within the Church, it is because the accomplices of this *coup d'état* have no supernatural sense, they fear neither God nor eternal damnation, and consider themselves partisans of progress invested with a prophetic role that legitimizes them in all their wickedness, just as Communism's mass exterminations are carried out by party officials convinced of promoting the cause of the proletariat.

In the first case, the analysis of the Council documents in the light of Tradition clashes with the observation that they have been formulated in such a way as to make clear the subversive intent of their drafters. This inevitably leads to the impossibility of interpreting them in a Catholic sense, without weakening the whole doctrinal *corpus*. In the second case, the awareness that doctrinal novelty

223

was being slipped into the acts of the Council made it necessary to formulate them in a deliberately ambiguous manner, precisely because it was only in making people believe that they were consistent with the Church's perennial Magisterium that they could be adopted by the authoritative assembly that had to "clear" and circulate them.

It ought to be highlighted that the mere fact of having to look for a hermeneutical criterion to interpret the Council's acts demonstrates the difference between Vatican II and any other Ecumenical Council, whose canons do not give rise to any sort of misunderstanding. An unclear passage from Sacred Scripture or from the Holy Fathers can be the object of a hermeneutic, but certainly not an act of the Magisterium, whose task is precisely to dispel any lack of clarity. Yet both conservatives and progressives find themselves unwittingly in agreement in recognizing a kind of dichotomy between what a council is and what *that* council—i.e., Vatican II— is; between the doctrine of all councils and the doctrine set forth or implied in *that* council.

Archbishop Guido Pozzo, in a recent commentary in which he quotes Benedict XVI, rightly states that "a Council is such only if it remains in the furrow of Tradition and it must be read in the light of the whole Tradition."[5] But this statement, which is irreproachable from a theological point of view, does not necessarily lead us to consider Vatican II as Catholic, but rather to ask ourselves whether it, by not remaining in the furrow of Tradition and not being able to be read in the light of the whole Tradition, without upsetting the *mens* that wanted it, can actually be defined as such. This question certainly cannot be met with an impartial answer in those who proudly profess to be its supporters, defenders and creators. And I am obviously not talking about the rightful defense of the Catholic Magisterium, but only of Vatican II as the "first council" of a "new church" claiming to take the place of the Catholic Church, which is hastily dismissed as *preconciliar.*

5. See "Concilio Vaticano II / Rinnovamento e continuità. Un contributo di monsignor Pozzo," www.aldomariavalli.it/2020/09/10/concilio-vaticano-ii-rinnova mento-e-continuita-un-contributo-di-monsignor-pozzo.

Is Vatican II "Untouchable"?

There is also another aspect that, in my view, should not be over-looked; namely, that the hermeneutical criterion—seen in the context of a serious and scientific criticism of a text—cannot disregard the concept that the text means to express. Indeed, it is not possible to impose a Catholic interpretation on a proposition that, in itself, is manifestly heretical or close to heresy, simply because it is included in a text that has been declared magisterial. *Lumen Gentium*'s proposition: "But the plan of salvation also includes those who acknowledge the Creator. In the first place amongst these there are the Muslims, who, professing to hold the faith of Abraham, along with us adore the one and merciful God, who on the last day will judge mankind" (*LG*, 16) cannot be interpreted in a Catholic way—firstly, because the god of Mohammed is not one and triune, and secondly because Islam condemns as blasphemous the Incarnation of the Second Person of the Most Holy Trinity in Our Lord Jesus Christ, true God and true Man. To affirm that "the plan of salvation also includes those who acknowledge the Creator" and that "in the first place amongst these there are the Muslims" blatantly contradicts Catholic doctrine, which professes that the Catholic Church is the one and only ark of salvation. The salvation eventually attained by heretics, and by pagans even more so, always and only comes from the inexhaustible treasure of Our Lord's Redemption, which is safeguarded by the Church; whereas belonging to any other religion is an impediment to the pursuit of eternal beatitude. Those who are saved, are saved because of at least an implicit desire to belong to the Church, and *despite* their adherence to a false religion—never by virtue of it. For what good it contains does not belong to it, but has been usurped; while the error it contains is what makes it intrinsically false, since the admixture of errors and truth more easily deceives its followers.

It isn't possible to change reality to make it correspond to an ideal schema. If the evidence shows that some propositions contained in the Council documents (and similarly, in the acts of Bergoglio's magisterium) are heterodox, and if doctrine teaches us that the acts of the Magisterium do not contain error, the conclusion is not that those propositions are not erroneous, but that *they cannot be part* of the Magisterium. Period.

Hermeneutics serve to *clarify* the meaning of a phrase that is obscure or that appears to contradict doctrine, not to *correct* it substantially *ex post*. This way of proceeding would not provide a simple key to reading the Magisterial texts, but would constitute a corrective intervention, and therefore the admission that, in that specific proposition of that specific Magisterial document, an error has been stated which must be corrected. And one would need to explain not only why that error was not avoided from the beginning, but also whether the Synod Fathers who approved that error, and the pope who promulgated it, intended to use their apostolic authority to ratify a heresy, or whether they would rather avail themselves of the implicit authority deriving from their role as Pastors to endorse it, without calling the Paraclete into question.

Archbishop Pozzo admits: "The reason why the Council has been received with difficulty therefore lies in the fact that there has been a struggle between two hermeneutics or interpretations of the Council, which indeed have coexisted in opposition to one another." But with these words, he confirms that the Catholic choice to adopt the hermeneutic of continuity goes hand in hand with the novel choice to resort to the hermeneutic of rupture, in an arbitrariness that demonstrates the prevailing confusion and—what is even more serious—the imbalance of the forces at play, in favor of one or the other thesis. "The hermeneutic of discontinuity risks ending in a rupture between the preconciliar and postconciliar Church and presupposes that the texts of the Council as such are not the true expression of the Council, but the result of a compromise," Archbishop Pozzo writes. But this is exactly the reality, and denying it does not resolve the problem in the slightest but rather exacerbates it, by refusing to acknowledge the existence of cancer even when it has very clearly reached its metastasis.

Archbishop Pozzo's affirmation that the concept of religious freedom expressed in *Dignitatis Humanæ* does not contradict Pius IX's *Syllabus of Errors*[6] demonstrates that the Council document is in

---

6. Pozzo's words: "At the same time, however, Vatican II in *Dignitatis Humanae* reconfirms that the only true religion exists in the Catholic and apostolic Church, to which the Lord Jesus entrusts the mission of communicating it to all men (*DH*,

itself deliberately ambiguous. If its drafters had wished to avoid such ambiguity, it would have been sufficient to reference the propositions of the *Syllabus* in a footnote; but this would never have been accepted by the progressives, who were able to slip in a doctrinal change precisely on the basis of the absence of references to the earlier Magisterium. And it doesn't seem that the interventions of the postconciliar popes—and their own participation, even *in sacris*, in non-Catholic or even pagan ceremonies—have ever, or in any way, corrected the error propagated in line with the heterodox interpretation of *Dignitatis Humanæ*. Upon closer examination, the same method was adopted in the drafting of *Amoris Lætitia*, in which the Church's discipline in matters of adultery and concubinage was formulated in such a way that it could *theoretically* be interpreted in a Catholic sense, while *in fact* it was accepted in the one and obvious heretical sense they wanted to disseminate. So much so, that the interpretive key that Bergoglio and his exegetes wanted to use, on the issue of Communion for divorcees, has become the authentic interpretation in the *Acta Apostolicæ Sedis*.[7]

The aim of Vatican II's public defenders has turned out to be the struggle of Sisyphus: as soon as they succeed, by a thousand efforts and a thousand distinctions, in formulating a seemingly reasonable solution that doesn't directly touch their little idol, immediately their words are repudiated by opposing statements from a progressive theologian, a German prelate, or Francis himself. And so, the conciliar boulder rolls back down the hill again, where gravity attracts it to its natural resting place.

It is obvious that, for a Catholic, a Council is *ipso facto* of such authority and importance that he spontaneously accepts its teachings with filial devotion. But it is equally obvious that the authority of a Council, of the Fathers who approve its decrees, and of the popes who promulgate them, does not make the acceptance of documents that are in blatant contradiction with the Magisterium, or at

n.1), and thereby denies relativism and religious indifferentism, also condemned by the *Syllabus* of Pius IX."

7. See *Defending the Faith against Present Heresies*, ed. John Lamont and Claudio Pierantoni (Waterloo, ON: Arouca Press, 2021), 215–33.

least weaken it, any less problematic. And if this problem continues to persist after sixty years revealing a perfect consistency with the deliberate will of the innovators who prepared its documents and influenced its proponents, we must ask ourselves what is the *obex*, the insurmountable obstacle, that forces us, against all reasonableness, to forcibly consider Catholic what is not, in the name of a criterion that applies only and exclusively to what is certainly Catholic?

One needs to keep clearly in mind that the *analogia fidei* applies precisely to the truths of Faith, and not to error, since the harmonious unity of the truth in all its articulations cannot seek coherence with what is opposed to it. If a conciliar text formulates a heretical concept, or one close to heresy, there is no hermeneutical criterion that can make it orthodox simply because that text belongs to the Acts of a Council. We all know what deceptions and skillful maneuvers have been put in place by ultraprogressive consultors and theologians, with the complicity of the modernist wing of the Council Fathers. And we also know with what complicity John XXIII and Paul VI approved these *coups de main* [surprise attacks] in violation of the norms which they themselves approved.

The central vice therefore lies in having fraudulently led the Council Fathers to approve ambiguous texts—which they considered *Catholic enough* to deserve the *placet*—and then using that same ambiguity to get them to say exactly what the innovators wanted. Those texts cannot today be changed in their substance to make them orthodox or clearer: they must simply be rejected— according to the forms that the supreme Authority of the Church shall judge appropriate in due course—since they are vitiated by a malicious intention. And it will also have to be determined whether an anomalous and disastrous event such as Vatican II can still merit the title of Ecumenical Council, once its heterogeneity compared to previous councils is universally recognized. A heterogeneity so evident that it requires the use of a hermeneutic, something that no other Council has ever needed.

It should be noted that this mechanism, inaugurated by Vatican II, has seen a recrudescence, an acceleration, indeed an unprecedented upsurge with Bergoglio, who deliberately resorts to imprecise expressions, cunningly formulated without precise theological language, with the same intention of dismantling, piece by piece, what remains of doctrine, in the name of applying the Council. It's true that, in Bergoglio, heresy and heterogeneity with respect to the Magisterium are blatant and almost shameless; but it is equally true that the Abu Dhabi Declaration would not have been conceivable without the premise of *Lumen Gentium*.

Rightly, Dr. Peter Kwasniewski states: "It is the mixture, the jumble, of great, good, indifferent, bad, generic, ambiguous, problematic, erroneous, all of it at enormous length, that makes Vatican II uniquely deserving of repudiation." The voice of the Church, which is the voice of Christ, is instead crystal clear and unambiguous, and cannot mislead those who rely on its authority! "This is why the last council is absolutely irrecoverable. If the project of modernization has resulted in a massive loss of Catholic identity, even of basic doctrinal competence and morals, the way forward is to pay one's last respects to the great symbol of that project and see it buried."

I wish to conclude by reiterating a fact which, in my view, is very indicative: if the same commitment that Pastors have exerted for decades in defending Vatican II and the "conciliar church" had been used to reaffirm and defend the entirety of Catholic doctrine, or even only to promote knowledge of the *Catechism* of St. Pius X among the faithful, the situation of the ecclesial world would be radically different. But it is also true that faithful formed in fidelity to doctrine would have reacted with pitchforks to the adulterations of the innovators and their protectors. Perhaps the ignorance of God's people was intended, precisely so that Catholics would be unaware of the fraud and betrayal perpetrated against them, just as the ideological prejudice that weighs on the Tridentine rite serves only to prevent it from being compared with the aberrations of the reformed ceremonies.

The cancellation of the past and of Tradition, the denial of roots, the delegitimization of dissent, the abuse of authority and the apparent respect for rules: are not these the recurring elements of all dictatorships?

September 21, 2020
St. Matthew, Apostle and Evangelist

18

Comments on Francis's Encyclical *Fratelli Tutti*[1]

LifeSiteNews presented to Archbishop Viganò several quotations from the encyclical *Fratelli Tutti* of Pope Francis dated October 3, 2020.[2] They asked Archbishop Viganò to comment upon each quotation. In each case the quotation from the encyclical is followed by the archbishop's observations.

274. *From our faith experience and from the wisdom accumulated over centuries, but also from lessons learned from our many weaknesses and failures, we, the believers of the different religions, know that our witness to God benefits our societies.*

The proposition "we, the believers of the different religions, know that our witness to God benefits our societies" is deliberately equivocal: "making God present" means nothing in the strict sense (God is present in Himself). In a broad sense, if one intends "to make God present through the presence of one or more religions" as opposed to the "departure from religious values" referred to in point 275, as the text seems to suggest, the proposition is erroneous and heretical, because it puts on the same level the divine Revelation of the living and true God with the "prostitutions," as the Sacred Scripture calls false religions. To argue that the presence of false reli-

1. These comments were first published by *LifeSiteNews* under the title "Abp. Viganò on Pope's new *Fratelli Tutti* document: Brotherhood against God is 'blasphemous,'" www.lifesitenews.com/blogs/abp-vigano-on-popes-new-fratelli-tutti-document-brotherhood-against-god-is-blasphemous.

2. For the text, see www.vatican.va/content/francesco/en/encyclicals/documents/papa-francesco_20201003_enciclica-fratelli-tutti.html.

gions "benefits our societies" is equally heretical, because it not only offends the Majesty of God, but also legitimizes the action of dissidents, attributing merit rather than responsibility for the damnation of souls and for the wars of religion waged against the Church of Christ by heretics, Muslims and idolaters. This passage is also offensive because it surreptitiously implies that this "good for our societies" has been generically acquired "also by learning from many of our weaknesses and failures," while in reality the "weaknesses and failures" are attributable to sects and only indirectly and *per accidens* to the people of the Church.

Finally, I would like to point out that religious indifferentism, implicitly promoted in the text *Fratelli Tutti*, which defines as "a good for our societies" the presence of any religion—instead of "the liberty and exaltation of Holy Mother Church"[3]—denies in fact the sovereign rights of Jesus Christ, King and Lord of individuals, of the societies and of nations.

Pius XI, in his immortal Encyclical *Quas Primas*,[4] proclaims: "What wonder, then, that he whom St. John calls the 'prince of the kings of the earth' appears in the Apostle's vision of the future as he who 'hath on his garment and on his thigh written "King of kings and Lord of lords!"' It is Christ whom the Father 'hath appointed heir of all things'; 'for he must reign until at the end of the world he hath put all his enemies under the feet of God and the Father.'" And since the enemies of God cannot be our friends, the brotherhood of the peoples against God is not only ontologically impossible, but theologically blasphemous.

277. *The Church esteems the ways in which God works in other religions, and "rejects nothing of what is true and holy in these religions. She has a high regard for their manner of life and conduct, their precepts and doctrines which . . . often reflect a ray of that truth which enlightens all men and women"* (*Decl.* Nostra Aetate, 2).

---

3. This is a quotation from the Leonine Prayers after Low Mass.

4. VN: The text may be found at www.vatican.va/content/pius-xi/en/encyclicals/documents/hf_p-xi_enc_11121925_quas-primas.html.

The reference to the conciliar document *Nostra Ætate* is the confirmation of the ideological link of the Bergoglian heretical thought with the premises earlier set by Vatican II. In false religions there is nothing true and holy *ex se*,[5] since any elements of truth that they can preserve are in any case usurped, and used to conceal the error and make it more harmful. No respect can be accorded to false religions, whose precepts and doctrines must be excluded and rejected in their entirety. If then among these elements of truth and holiness Bergoglio wants to include for example the concept of one God who should bring Catholics closer to those who profess a monotheistic religion, it should be clarified that there is a substantial and unavoidable difference between the true God One and Triune and the merciful god of Islam.

277. *Others drink from other sources. For us the wellspring of human dignity and fraternity is in the Gospel of Jesus Christ.*

The only source from which it is possible to drink is Our Lord Jesus Christ, through the one Church that He has established for the salvation of souls. Those who try to quench their thirst from other sources do not quench their thirst and almost certainly poison themselves. It is also disputable that the heterodox concept of human dignity and brotherhood of which *Fratelli Tutti* speaks can be found in the Gospel, which indeed clearly contradicts this horizontal, immanentist and indifferentist vision theorized by Bergoglio. Finally, the specification "for us" is misleading, because it relativizes the objectivity of the Gospel message to a personal way of seeing or experiencing things, and consequently deprives it of its authority, which arises from the divine and supernatural origin of Sacred Scripture.

279. *[…] One fundamental human right must not be forgotten in the journey towards fraternity and peace. It is religious freedom for believers of all religions.*

---

5. Latin for "out of itself." This means that there is nothing good and holy that is attributable to the false religion itself. To paraphrase St. Augustine, anything true or good in a false religion is only stolen from the Catholic Church.

Religious freedom for believers of all religions is not a human right, but an abuse devoid of any theological foundation, and, even before that, it is neither philosophical nor logical. This concept of religious freedom—which replaces the freedom of the one Religion, the "freedom of the Catholic Religion to exercise its mission," and the "freedom of the faithful to adhere to the Catholic Church without impediment from the State" with the license to adhere to any creed, regardless of its credibility and *credenda* (what we have to believe)—is heretical and irreconcilable with the immutable doctrine of the Church. The human being has no right to error: freedom from coercion magisterially explained by Leo XIII in the Encyclical *Libertas Præstantissimum* does not eliminate the moral obligation to freely adhere only to the good, since upon the freedom of this act depends its morality, that is, one's capacity to deserve a reward or a punishment. The State can tolerate error in certain situations, but it can never legitimately place error on the same level as truth, nor consider all religions to be equivalent or irrelevant: religious indifferentism is condemned by the Magisterium, just as is religious relativism. The Church has the mission of converting souls to the true Faith, snatching them from the darkness of error and vice. Theorizing an alleged right to error and its diffusion is also an offense to God and a betrayal of the vicarious authority of the Sacred Pastors, which they must exercise for the purpose for which it was established, and not to spread error and discredit the Church of Christ. It is unbelievable that the Vicar of Christ (I forgot: Bergoglio has renounced this title!) can recognize any right to false religions, since the Church is the Lamb's Bride, and it would be blasphemous to just think that Our Lord could have more brides.

281. [...] *"God does not see with his eyes, God sees with his heart. And God's love is the same for everyone, regardless of religion. Even if they are atheists, his love is the same. When the last day comes, and there is sufficient light to see things as they really are, we are going to find ourselves quite surprised"* (*from the film* Pope Francis: A Man of His Word, *by Wim Wenders* [2018]).

The use of striking expressions lacking in clarity of meaning is one of the ways that innovators use to insinuate errors without formulating them clearly. The proposition "God does not look with his eyes, God looks with his heart" can be at best a moving expression, but devoid of any doctrinal value. On the contrary, it leads us to believe that in God knowledge and love are dissociated, that God's love is blind and that, consequently, the orientation of our own actions has no value in His eyes.

The proposition "God's love is the same for every person, of whatever religion" is gravely equivocal and deceptive, more insidious than a blatant heresy. It leads us to believe that man's free response and adherence to God's love is irrelevant to his eternal destiny.

In the natural order, God creates every person with an act of gratuitous love: God's love is extended to all his creatures. But every human person is created with a view to filial adoption and eternal glory. God grants each person the supernatural graces necessary so that each one can know Him, love Him, serve Him, obey His law inscribed in the heart, and thus come to embrace the Faith.

In the supernatural order, God's love for a person is proportional to his state of grace, that is to the extent to which this soul corresponds to the gift of God through faith and works, deserving the eternal reward. In the plans of Providence, love for the sinner—including the heretic, the pagan and the atheist—can consist in granting of greater graces touching his heart and leading him to repentance and adherence to the true Faith.

"When the last day arrives and there will be sufficient light on earth to be able to see things as they are, we will have several surprises": this proposition suggests that what the Church teaches can somehow be disproved on the day of the Last Judgment. Among those who will have "several surprises" there will actually be those who believe they can adulterate the Faith and the moral order with the ravings of the Modernists and the adherence to the perverse ideologies of the century, and it will be seen that what the Church has always preached, which the anti-church obstinately denies, corresponds exactly to what Our Lord taught the Apostles.

October 6, 2020

19

Fratelli Tutti and Silent US Bishops: Interview with John-Henry Westen[1]

WHAT is your opinion on Fratelli Tutti, particularly its silence regarding abortion, especially in light of what the encyclical defines as the "biggest concerns" for politicians?

Fratelli Tutti, in speaking about the concerns which should motivate the actions of politicians, mentions the "phenomenon of social and economic exclusion, with its baneful consequences: human trafficking, the marketing of human organs and tissues, the sexual exploitation of boys and girls, slave labor, including prostitution, the drug and weapons trade, terrorism and international organized crime."[2] These are all plagues that need to be denounced, but which I believe are already recognized as such by many people. The focal point, which is much more important from the moral aspect, but not mentioned in the Encyclical, is abortion, which is tragically claimed today as a right.[3]

This deafening silence concerning the most odious crime in the eyes of God—because it is committed upon an innocent and de-

1. Originally published by *LifeSiteNews*, www.lifesitenews.com/images/pdfs/JH_Westen_Interview_with_Vigano_Oct_2020.pdf.

2. VN: Speech at the United Nations Organization, New York, September 25, 2015, *AAS* 107 (2015), 1039. Cited in the encyclical *Fratelli Tutti*, 188.

3. VN: The only indirect mention of abortion is n. 24 of the Encyclical, in which violence that "forces [women] to abort" is denounced, but without condemning the killing of the unborn itself. The reference to the unborn child in *Fratelli Tutti* n.18 is very weak and does not explicitly mention the term "abortion." Spending just three words on the most abominable crime that involves millions of deaths every year in the world does not change the evidence that the encyclical is literally

fenseless child depriving it of life—betrays the twisted vision of this ideological manifesto that is in the service of the New World Order. Its slanted vision lies in psychologically prostrated submission to the requests of mainstream thought, while looking at the teachings of the Gospel with the myopic and embarrassed view of those who consider it unthinkable and outdated.

The spiritual and transcendent dimension is completely ignored, as are natural and Catholic morality. But what *brotherhood* could ever exist between people, if killing an innocent child is considered irrelevant? How can one condemn social exclusion while remaining silent on the most criminal of social exclusions, that of a child who has a right to live, to grow, to be loved and to love, adore, and serve God and attain eternal life? What is the point of addressing arms trafficking, if one can be joined in brotherhood with one who dismembers a child in the womb of its mother, one who sucks the child's brains out the instant before birth? How can one place *brotherhood* ahead of the horror of those who poison the sick or the elderly, who are denied any chance of participating in Our Lord's Passion through suffering? What respect for nature can be invoked, when the gender of a person, written into our chromosomes, can be changed, or when a sterile union of two men or two women could be considered a family? Does not the destructive fury of "mother earth" apply to those who, by altering the wonderful work of the Creator, assume the right to modify the DNA of plants, animals, and human beings?

Fratelli Tutti is an encyclical that not only lacks faith, but also hope and charity. The voice of the Divine Shepherd and Physician of souls does not echo in its language, but rather the rapacious wolf's growl or the mercenary's deafening silence (Jn 10:10). There

---

obsessed with human solidarity in support of a globalist agenda. Besides, in the contest of the US election campaign (concomitant with the publication of the papal document), an explicit condemnation of abortion would openly contradict the Democratic candidate, who is strongly in favor of abortion. I would add that the references to children seems more aimed at the Islamic families, in particular of those of the immigrants, who, according to Bergoglio, represent the demographic future of Europe.

is no breath of love either for God or for man, because in order to truly desire the good of modern man it is necessary to wake him out of his hypnotic spell of do-goodery, ecologism, pacifism, ecumenism, and globalism. In order to want the good of sinful and rebellious man, it is necessary to make him understand that by distancing himself from his Creator and Lord he will end up being a slave of Satan and of himself. No sense of brotherhood with other damned souls can remedy enmity towards God. It will not be the world nor philanthropists who will judge him, but Our Lord Himself, who died on the Cross to save him.

I believe that this very sad *Fratelli Tutti* represents, in a certain way, the emptiness of a withered heart, of a blind man deprived of supernatural sight, who gropingly thinks he can give an answer that he himself first ignores. I recognize that it is a sad and grave statement, but I think that more than asking ourselves about the orthodoxy of this document, we should ask ourselves what is the state of a soul incapable of feeling any surge of charity, of allowing himself to be touched by a divine ray shining into that gloomy grayness represented by his utopian, transient dream, closed to the grace of God.

The Introit[4] of this Sunday's Mass sounds a warning for us: *Salus populi ego sum, dicit Dominus: de quacumque tribulatione clamaverint ad me, exaudiam eos: et ero illorum Dominus in perpetuum. Attendite, popule meus, legem meam: inclinate aurem vestram in verba oris mei.*[5] The Lord is the salvation of His people, who shall be heard in tribulation as long as they listen to His law. Our Lord tells us in no uncertain terms: "Without Me you can do nothing" (Jn 15:8). The utopia of the Tower of Babel, no matter how it may update itself and appear under the guise of the United Nations or the New World Order, is destined to collapse stone upon stone,

---

4. The Introit is a short quotation from the psalms read by the priest after having said the preparatory prayers at the foot of the altar; in a High Mass, it is also sung by the schola during the preparatory prayers.

5. VN: "I am the salvation of the people, says the Lord: Should they cry to me in any distress, I will hear them, and I will be their Lord forever. Hear my law, O my people: incline your ear to the words of my mouth," Introit, Nineteenth Sunday after Pentecost.

because it is not founded on the Cornerstone who is Christ. "Behold they are one people, and they have all one language; and this is only the beginning of what they will do; and nothing that they propose to do will be impossible for them. Come, let us go down, and there confuse their language, that they may not understand one another's speech" (Gen 11:4–7).

The globalist and ecumenical pacifism of *Fratelli Tutti* envisions an earthly paradise that lays its foundations on refusing to recognize the Kingship of Christ over societies and the entire world; on being silent about the scandal of the Cross, considered as "divisive" rather than the only hope of salvation for humanity; on forgetting that the social injustices and the evil present in the world are consequences of sin, and that only by conforming to the will of God can we hope to foster peace and harmony among men. Human beings can be truly brothers only in Christ, by recognizing together the Fatherhood of God.

The Encyclical lacks hope, understood as the theological virtue infused by God into the soul by which we desire the Kingdom of Heaven and eternal life, placing our trust in Christ's promises and relying not on our strength, but on the help of the grace of the Holy Spirit.[6] Hoping that a horizontal brotherhood can guarantee peace and justice has nothing supernatural about it, because it does not look to the Kingdom of Heaven, it is not based on the promises of Christ, and it does not consider divine grace necessary, placing its trust in man who is corrupted by original sin and therefore inclined to evil. Anyone who feeds such false hopes—for example by stating that "there is no need to believe in God to go to heaven"[7]—does not perform an act of charity. On the contrary: this encourages the wicked on the path of sin and perdition, making themselves complicit in their damnation and their despair. It contradicts the very words of the Savior: "I said to you, that you shall die in your sins. For if you believe not that I am He, you shall die in your sin" (Jn 8:24).

6. VN: *Catechism of the Catholic Church*, n.1817.
7. VN: See www.independent.co.uk/news/world/europe/pope-francis-assures-atheists-you-don-thave-believe-god-go-heaven-8810062.html.

I add, with great pain, that lately the answer of the Church in the face of evil, death, sickness, suffering and injustices in the world is lacking, if not completely absent. It is as if the Gospel has nothing to say to modern man, or as if what it has to say is outdated: "I don't want to sell useless recipes, this is the reality."[8] One's blood runs cold when reading these words: "God is unjust? Yes, He was unjust with His Son, by sending Him to the cross."[9] There is no need to refute this statement; it is enough to observe that if we deny that sin is the cause of the suffering and death that afflicts humanity, we inevitably end up placing the responsibility on God, accusing Him of being "unjust" and therefore excluding Him from our very own horizon. From here we understand how the pursuit of human brotherhood is found outlined in the words of the Psalmist: "The kings of the earth rise up, and princes take counsel together, against the Lord and against His Anointed" (Ps 2:2).

Thus the Church—or rather her counterfeit that eclipses her almost entirely—does not offer a Catholic answer anymore to the man who is hopeless and thirsting for truth, but instead advances the scandal of pain and suffering whose root cause is sin, placing the responsibility on God and blaspheming Him as "unjust."

Your Excellency, I imagine that you have seen how pro-life leaders in the United States are begging the bishops to openly declare that abortion is the preeminent question during this presidential election. There have been various bishops who have said the exact opposite and now use the points discussed in the encyclical of Pope Francis in support of their ideas. What advice would give to your brother bishops and to the faithful?

Silence on abortion is a terrible sign of the spiritual and moral deviance in that part of the hierarchy which denies its very own mission because it has denied Christ. And just as in abortion the mother

---

8. VN: "Il Papa: non c'è una risposta alla morte dei bambini," in *Avvenire*, December 15, 2016, www.avvenire.it/papa/pagine/papa-udienza-al-bambino-gesu.
9. VN: Ibid.

kills her own child, whom she should love, protect, and bring forth into this earthly life, so in the present fraud, the Church, willed by God to bring forth souls to eternal life, is found killing them herself spiritually in her own womb, because of the betrayal of her own Ministers. The hatred of the enemies of Christ does not spare even His Most Holy Mother, whose divine Motherhood is hated by Satan, because through her the Second Person of the Blessed Trinity became Man to redeem us. If we are friends of the Blessed Virgin, her enemies are our enemies, according to what has been established by the Lord in the Protoevangelium: "I will put enmity between thee and the Woman, and between your offspring and Hers" (Gen 3:15).

I remind my brother bishops that they were anointed with the Holy Chrism as athletes of the Faith, not as neutral spectators of the struggle between God and the Adversary. I pray that the few courageous Pastors who raise their voices to defend the inviolable and non-negotiable principles which the Lord has established in natural law may be joined by those who today hesitate out of fear, timidity, or a false sense of prudence. *You have the "grace of state" to be heard by your flock, who recognizes in you the voice of the Divine Shepherd* (Jn 10:2–3). Do not be afraid to proclaim the Gospel of Christ, just as the Apostles and the bishops who succeeded them did not fear martyrdom.

I ask the faithful, disoriented by the silence of so many faint-hearted shepherds, to raise their prayers to Heaven, invoking from the Paraclete those graces which only the Holy Spirit can instill in the most hardened and rebellious hearts: *Lava quod est sordidum, riga quod est aridum, sana quod est saucium. Flecte quod est rigidum, fove quod est frigidum, rege quod est devium.*[10] Offer your sacrifices, your penances, and your sufferings in sickness for the Church and for your Pastors.

---

10. These lines are quoted from the Sequence (a poetic hymn sung before the Gospel) for the Mass of Pentecost and its octave. These lines can be translated as "Wash that which is unclean, water that which is dry, heal that which is wounded. Bend that which is rigid, melt that which is chilled, correct that which is crooked."

Interview with John-Henry Westen

I have recently interviewed the wife of the former nominee for the Supreme Court Robert Bork, who spoke about the lack of support from the Church during her husband's outrageous hearings; she even hinted to the fact that the attacks against him were led by the "Catholic" Democratic Senator Ted Kennedy. What is your opinion of the attacks against Judge Barrett,[11] particularly because of her faith?

The hatred of the world, of which Satan is the prince (Jn 12:31), is the most evident disavowal of the utopian dream of *Fratelli Tutti*. There cannot be brotherhood among men, if it excludes the common Fatherhood of the One True God, One and Triune. Those who preach equality and equal rights to the point of giving legitimacy to error and vice become intolerant when they see their own abusive power is at risk—as soon as a Catholic politician, in the name of equal rights, wants to testify to his or her own Faith in legislating and governing. So, in this way the highly touted "brotherhood" is realized only among the children of darkness, necessarily either excluding the children of light or forcing them to deny their own identity. And it is significant that the only requisite of this brotherhood appears to be always founded on the refusal of Christ, while it is considered impossible to have a true and holy brotherhood in the sacred bond of charity, "in justice and holiness that proceeds from truth" (Eph 4:24).

With the unction of Confirmation, a Catholic becomes a soldier of Christ. A soldier who does not fight for his King but allies himself with the enemy is a traitor, a renegade, a deserter. Therefore, let Catholic politicians and those who hold institutional positions bear witness the One who shed His Blood for them. Not only will they receive the necessary graces to carry out their duties in public affairs, but they will also be an example to their brothers and will merit an eternal reward, which is the only thing that really matters.

---

11. President Donald Trump nominated Amy Coney Barrett to be an Associate Justice of the US Supreme Court in September 2020, following the death of Associate Justice Ruth Bader Ginsberg. Many, including Senator Dianne Feinstein, criticized her for being outspoken about her Catholic Faith and particularly for her opposition to the legalization of abortion.

Te nationum præsides honore tollant publico; colant magistri, judices, leges et artes exprimant.[12]

11 October 2020
Divine Motherhood of Mary Most Holy
Nineteenth Sunday after Pentecost

---

12. From the hymn sung at Vespers for the Feast of Christ the King as found in the preconciliar breviary: "The rulers of nations extol You with public honor; governors and judges worship You, the laws and the arts make You known."

20

On Francis's Documentary
Francesco

October 21, 2020

THE Vatican News website[1] has reported the news that today at the Rome Film Festival a documentary film will be screened called *Francesco,* made by director Evgeny Afineevsky. This documentary—according to what has been reported by *Catholic News Agency*[2] and *America* magazine[3]—makes public several pronouncements of Jorge Mario Bergoglio on the topic of homosexuality. Among the various statements, these two are particularly disconcerting: "Homosexuals have a right to be a part of the family. They're children of God and have a right to a family. Nobody should be thrown out, or be made miserable because of it." "What we have to create is a civil union law. That way they are legally covered. I stood up for that." One does not have to be a theologian or a moral expert to know that such statements are totally heterodox and constitute a very serious cause of scandal for the faithful.

But pay careful attention: these words simply constitute the umpteenth provocation by which the "ultraprogressive" part of the hierarchy wants to artfully provoke a schism, as it has already tried to do with the Post-Synodal Exhortation *Amoris Lætitia,* the modification

1. VN: See www.vaticannews.va/it/papa/news/2020-10/papa-francesco-film-documentario-festival-cinema-roma.html.

2. VN: See www.catholicnewsagency.com/news/pope-francis-calls-for-civil-union-law-for-same-sex-couples-in-shift-from-vatican-stance-12462.

3. VN: See www.americamagazine.org/faith/2020/10/21/pope-francis-gay-civil-union-documentary.

243

of doctrine on the death penalty,[4] the Pan-Amazon Synod and the filthy Pachamama, and the Abu Dhabi Declaration which has now been reaffirmed and aggravated by the Encyclical *Fratelli Tutti*.

It appears that Bergoglio is impudently trying to "raise the stakes" in a crescendo of heretical affirmations, in such a way that it will force the healthy part of the Church—which includes bishops, clergy, and faithful—to accuse him of heresy, in order to declare that healthy part of the Church schismatic and "the enemy of the pope."

Jorge Mario Bergoglio is trying to force some cardinals and bishops to separate themselves from communion with him, obtaining as a result not his own deposition for heresy but rather the expulsion of Catholics who want to remain faithful to the perennial Magisterium of the Church. This trap would have the purpose—in the presumed intentions of Bergoglio and his "magic circle"—of consolidating his own power within a church that would only nominally be "Catholic" but in reality would be heretical and schismatic.

This deception draws on the support of the globalist élite, the mainstream media and the LGBT lobby, to which many clergy, bishops, and cardinals are no strangers. Furthermore, let us not forget that in many nations there are laws in force which criminally punish anyone who considers sodomy reprehensible and sinful or who does not approve of the legitimization of homosexual "matrimony"—even if they do so on the basis of their Creed. A pronouncement by the bishops against Bergoglio on a question like homosexuality could potentially lead civil authority to prosecute them criminally, with the approval of the Vatican.

Bergoglio would thus have on his side not only the deep church represented by rebels like Father James Martin, S.J., and those who

---

4. In August 2018, Pope Francis ordered the revision of n. 2267 of the *Catechism of the Catholic Church*. This newly revised section claims that in light of "a new understanding," the Church revokes her prior teaching that the state under proper circumstances can legitimately impose the death penalty. In lieu of this perennial teaching, the section now claims: "the Church teaches, in the light of the Gospel, that 'the death penalty is inadmissible because it is an attack on the inviolability and dignity of the person.'" The only source for this purported teaching of the Church is a 2017 speech by Pope Francis himself.

promote the German "Synodal Path," but also the deep state. It is not surprising that in the documentary there is also an endorsement of the Democratic candidate in the upcoming American presidential election, along with a disconcerting condemnation of the policy of the Trump Administration, which is accused of separating families that want to enter the United States illegally, while the reality is that the President is confronting human trafficking and the trafficking of minors.

Thus, while conservative American bishops are forbidden from intervening in the political debate in support of President Trump, the Vatican allows itself to casually interfere in the elections in favor of his Democratic adversary, in union with the censorship by social and news media of the very serious accusations against the Biden family.

As Catholics, we are called to side with those who defend life, the natural family, and national sovereignty. We thought that we had the Vicar of Christ at our side. We painfully acknowledge that, in this epochal clash, he who ought to be guiding the Barque of Peter has chosen to side with the Enemy, in order to sink it. Recalling the courage of the Holy Pontiffs in defending the integrity of the Faith and promoting the salvation of souls, one can only observe: *Quantum mutatus ab illis!*[5]

---

5. VN: "How changed from what they once were!" (cf. Virgil's *Aeneid*: "*Quantum mutatus ab illo!*").

21

The "church" of Bergoglio:
The New Sanhedrin

December 1, 2020

THE rich man who feasted in the Gospel parable (Lk 16:19–31), after being condemned to hell for not having helped the poor man Lazarus, asks Abraham to warn his five brothers about the torments to which he is subjected, in order to prevent them from falling into the same sin. Abraham answers him: "If they do not listen to Moses and the Prophets, neither will they be persuaded if someone should rise from the dead" (Lk 16:31).

Over the course of history, Our Lady has intervened as a loving Mother to warn us of the punishments that weigh upon the world because of its sins, in order to invite mankind to conversion and penance, and to fill her children with innumerable graces. Wherever the Word of God seems to be forgotten, there the voice of Mary Most Holy is heard, now to announce a particular devotion, now to ask for sacrifices and prayers to escape pestilences and scourges. In Quito, La Salette, Lourdes, Fatima, Rome, Akita, Civitavecchia, and in a thousand other places, the Mediatrix of all graces has admonished us, recalling humanity, misled into rebellion against the Divine Law, to true repentance and the recitation of the Holy Rosary. Although the various times and circumstances of her apparitions change, she who deigns to show herself to us poor mortals is always the same, ever merciful, ever our Advocate.

At Fatima the Lady who appeared to the shepherd children asked the pope, in union with all the bishops, to consecrate Russia to her Immaculate Heart: this appeal remains unheeded to this day, despite the disasters which the world would have to face if it did not heed the requests of the Most Holy Virgin. The militant atheism of

The "church" of Bergoglio: The New Sanhedrin

Communism has spread everywhere, and the Church is persecuted by ruthless and cruel enemies, while she is also infested by corrupt clerics given over to vice. And yet, despite the recognition of the supernatural origin of the apparitions and the evidence of the calamities which afflict mankind, the hierarchy refuses to obey the Blessed Mother. "If they do not listen to Moses and the Prophets, neither will they be persuaded if someone should rise from the dead," Abraham says to the rich man in the parable. Is it possible that they do not even know how to listen to the voice of the Mother of God, who is also our Mother? What oppresses their hearts, what obscures their minds to such an extent that they are deaf and blind, while the world sinks into the abyss and so many souls are damned?

In obedience to the universal Lordship of Christ the King, we also accept venerating Mary Most Holy as our Queen. And when we address our Father with the words, "Thy will be done," we know that this will coincides perfectly with the will of our Mother, the model of obedience and humility who merited to be chosen from the beginning of time to generate the King of Kings in her virginal womb. Every desire of the Mother of God is an order for us: it does not even need to be thought of as a command, because our response and our desire is—and must be—to please her and give her proof of our fidelity. And this is eminently true for the sacred ministers, who in the sacrament of Holy Orders bear upon themselves the priestly anointing of the High Priest Jesus Christ: in each priest, Mary Most Holy sees her Son, who mystically renews his own sacrifice upon the altar through their hands.

It causes pain therefore—a hollow and tearing pain—to see the indifference of so many consecrated souls and of so many bishops—too many—towards the Blessed Virgin Mary. It pains and tears the heart to hear Bergoglio himself speak with such a total lack of respect for Our Lady, and to learn that after he drastically reduced the papal liturgical celebrations for last Easter, he has now sought to take advantage of COVID to cancel part of the liturgical celebrations for Holy Christmas and to cancel the tradition by which each year on December 8 the pope goes to Piazza di Spagna in Rome to venerate the monument of the Immaculate Virgin that was erected there in 1857. Thus another piece of Rome is thrown away, another pound of flesh that the cynical merchant claims from the life of the Roman people as proof of their fidelity to the health dictatorship.

The Church of Catholics, the Church that loves those who honor themselves with the name of Christian, is the Church that does not retreat before civil authority, thereby making herself an accomplice and courtesan of it, but rather the Church that endures persecution with courage and a supernatural gaze, knowing that it is better to die amidst the most atrocious torments than to offend the Most Blessed Virgin and her Divine Son. She is the Church that does not remain silent when the tyrant defies the Majesty of God, afflicts her subjects, and betrays justice and the authority that legitimizes it. She is the Church that does not yield in the face of blackmail nor allow herself to be seduced by power or money. She is the Church that ascends Calvary, as the Mystical Body of Christ, in order to complete in her own members the sufferings of the Redeemer and to rise again triumphantly with Him. She is the Church who assists the weak and the oppressed with mercy and charity, while she stands fearless and terrible in the face of the arrogant and the proud. When the pope of this Church used to speak, the flock of Christ heard the consoling voice of the Shepherd, in a long series of popes who were unanimous and in agreement in the profession of the one Faith.

Conversely, the so-called "church" of Bergoglio does not hesitate to close churches, arrogating to itself the wicked right to deny God public worship and to deprive the faithful of the grace of the sacraments through a wretched connivance with civil power. This "church" humiliates the Most Holy Trinity, lowering it to the level of idols and demons with sacrilegious rituals of a neo-pagan religion. It snatches the crown and scepter away from Christ the King in the name of Masonic globalism; it offends the Co-Redemptrix and Mediatrix in order not to annoy the heretics, her enemies. It betrays the duty of preaching the Gospel in the name of dialogue and tolerance. It silences and adulterates Sacred Scripture and the Commandments of God in order to please the spirit of the world.

It tampers with the sublime and inviolable words of the prayer which the Lord Himself taught us.[1] It profanes the holiness of the priesthood, cancelling the spirit of penance and mortification in clergy and religious and abandoning them to the seductions of the devil. It denies two thousand years of history, despising the glories of Christianity and the wise intervention of Divine Providence in earthly affairs. It zealously follows fashions and ideologies rather than molding souls to follow Christ. It makes itself a slave of the Prince of this world in order to preserve its prestige and power. It preaches the blasphemous cult of man[2] and refuses the sovereign rights of God. And when Bergoglio speaks, the faithful are almost always scandalized and disoriented, because his words are the exact opposite of what they expect to hear from the Vicar of Christ. He asks for obedience to his own authority even as he uses it to destroy the papacy and the Church, contradicting all of his predecessors, none excluded.

We have the promise of Mary Most Holy: "In the end, my Immaculate Heart will triumph." Let us bow before that heart, which beats with the most pure charity, so that the flame of that holy love may reflect on each one of us, so that the flame which burns in it may illuminate our minds and make them capable of grasping the signs of the times. And if our Shepherds are silent out of fear or complicity, the multitude of lay people and good souls

1. Viganò is referring to the fact that Pope Francis ordered the translation of the Lord's prayer to be changed so that "*et ne nos inducas in tentationem*" is no longer translated as "lead us not into temptation" but is rendered rather as "let us not fall into temptation."

2. An allusion to the closing speech of Paul VI to the Second Vatican Council on December 7, 1965, in which he said: "The religion of the God who became man has met the religion (for such it is) of man who makes himself God. And what happened? Was there a clash, a battle, a condemnation? There could have been, but there was none. . . . We call upon those who term themselves modern humanists, and who have renounced the transcendent value of the highest realities, to give the council credit at least for one quality and to recognize our own new type of humanism: we, too, in fact, we more than any others, honor mankind" (www.vatican.va/content/paul-vi/en/speeches/1965/documents/hf_p-vi_spe_19651207_epilogo-concilio.html). The last phrase—in Latin, "*hominis sumus cultores*," uses *cultor* in the sense explained by the Roman orator Cicero: "*Cultor* means one who loves and cares for, instructs, helps" ("*Cultor dicitur qui amat et curat, instituit, opem fert*": *De Officiis* 1.30.109).

249

have the opportunity to compensate for their betrayal and expiate their sins, invoking the mercy of God who "has come to the help of his servant, Israel, remembering his mercy" (Lk 1:54).

Today the high priests of this modern Sanhedrin outrage Our Lord and His Most Holy Mother, complacent servants of the globalist élite who want to establish the kingdom of Satan; tomorrow they will retreat before the victory of the *Virgo Potens* [powerful Virgin], who will restore the Holy Church and will give peace and harmony to society, thanks to the prayers and sacrifices of so many of her humble and unknown children.

May this be our vow for the upcoming Feast of the Immaculate Conception, with which to honor Our Lady and Queen.

22

How the Revolution of Vatican II Serves the New World Order[1]

October 24, 2020

1. WE Live in Extraordinary Times

As each of us has probably understood, we find ourselves in an historic moment in time; events of the past, which once seemed disconnected, prove now to be unequivocally connected, both in the principles that inspire them and in the goals they seek to achieve. A fair and objective look at the current situation cannot help but grasp the perfect coherence between the evolution of the global political framework and the role that the Catholic Church has assumed in the establishment of the New World Order. To be more precise, one should speak about the role of that apparent majority in the Church, which is actually small in number but extremely powerful, and which, for brevity's sake, I will summarize as the deep church.

Obviously, there are not two Churches, something that would be impossible, blasphemous, and heretical. Nor has the one true Church of Christ today failed in her mission, perverting herself into a sect. The Church of Christ has nothing to do with those who, for the past sixty years, have executed a plan to occupy her. The overlap between the Catholic hierarchy and the members of the deep church is not a theological fact, but rather a historical reality that defies the usual categories and, as such, must be analyzed.

We know that the New World Order project consists in the establishment of tyranny by Freemasonry: a project that dates back to the French Revolution, the Age of Enlightenment, the end of the

1. The following is a transcript of Archbishop Viganò's talk from the 2020 Catholic Identity Conference, the video of which can be found on Remnant TV.

251

Catholic monarchies, and the declaration of war on the Church. We can say that the New World Order is the antithesis of Christian society, it would be the realization of the *civitas diaboli* (city of the devil) that is opposed to the *Civitas Dei* (City of God) in the eternal struggle between Light and Darkness, Good and Evil, God and Satan.

In this struggle, Providence has placed the Church of Christ, and in particular the Supreme Pontiff, as *kathèkon*—that is, the one who opposes the manifestation of the mystery of iniquity (2 Thess 2:6–7).[2] And Sacred Scripture warns us that at the manifestation of the Antichrist, this obstacle—the *kathèkon*—will have ceased to exist. It seems quite evident to me that the end times are now approaching before our eyes, since the mystery of iniquity has spread throughout the world with the disappearance of the courageous opposition of the *kathèkon*.

With regard to the incompatibility between the City of God and the City of Satan, the Jesuit advisor to Francis, Antonio Spadaro, sets aside Sacred Scripture and Tradition, making the Bergoglian *embrassons-nous*[3] his own. According to the Director of *La Civiltà Cattolica*, the Encyclical *Fratelli Tutti*

> also remains a message with a strong political value, because—we could say—it overturns the logic of the apocalypse that prevails today. It is the fundamentalist logic that fights against the world, because it believes that it is the opposite of God, that is, an idol, and therefore to be destroyed as soon as possible in order to accelerate the end of time. The abyss of the apocalypse, in fact, before which there are no more brothers: only apostates or mar-

---

2. These verses read: "And now you know what withholdeth, that he may be revealed in his time. For the mystery of iniquity already worketh; only that he who now holdeth, do hold, until he be taken out of the way" (Douai-Rheims translation). This verse has traditionally been understood to mean, as Viganò states, that the Church and especially the pope are the obstacle, the "withholder" who prevents the full manifestation of the mystery of iniquity in the end times. St. Paul tells us the mystery of iniquity is already in the world ("already worketh") but is not fully revealed. This will only come when the Church is eclipsed and the *kathèkon* is removed.

3. French for "Let us embrace."

tyrs running "against" time. [...] We are not militants or apostates, but all brothers.[4]

This strategy of discrediting the interlocutor with the slur of "integralist" is evidently aimed at facilitating the action of the enemy within the Church, seeking to disarm the opposition and discourage dissent. We also find it in the civil sphere, where the democrats and the deep state arrogate to themselves the right to decide whom to grant political legitimacy and whom to condemn without appeal to media ostracism. The method is always the same, because the one inspiring is the same. Just as the falsification of history and of the sources is always the same: if the past disavows the revolutionary narrative, the followers of the Revolution censor the past and replace historical fact with a myth. Even St. Francis is a victim of this adulteration that would have him be the standard-bearer of poverty and pacifism, which are as alien to the spirit of Catholic orthodoxy as they are instrumental to the dominant ideology. Proof of this is the last, fraudulent recourse to the *Poverello*[5] of Assisi in *Fratelli Tutti* to justify dialogue, ecumenism, and the universal brotherhood of the Bergoglian anti-church.

Let us not make the mistake of presenting the current events as "normal," judging what happens with the legal, canonical, and sociological parameters that such normality would presuppose. In extraordinary times—and the present crisis in the Church is indeed extraordinary—events go beyond the ordinary known to our fathers. In extraordinary times, we can hear a pope deceive the faithful; see Princes of the Church accused of crimes that in other times would have aroused horror and been met with severe punishment; witness in our churches liturgical rites that seem to have been invented by Cranmer's perverse mind; see prelates process the unclean idol of the Pachamama into St. Peter's Basilica; and hear the Vicar of Christ apologize to the worshippers of that *simulacrum*[6]

---

4. VN: Padre Antonio Spadaro, S.J., "Fratelli Tutti, la risposta di Francesco alla crisi del nostro tempo," in *Formiche*, October 4, 2020, https://formiche.net/2020/10/enciclica-papa-fratelli-tutti-padre-spadaro.

5. Italian meaning "the poor one."

6. In this context: an image representing a pagan deity or god.

if a Catholic dares to throw it into the Tiber. In these extraordinary times, we hear a conspirator—Cardinal Godfried Danneels—tell us that, since the death of John Paul II, the Mafia of St. Gallen had been plotting to elect one of their own to Peter's Chair, which later turned out to be Jorge Mario Bergoglio. In the face of this disconcerting revelation, we might well be astonished that neither cardinals nor bishops expressed their indignation nor asked that the truth be brought to light.

The coexistence of good and evil, of saints and the damned, in the ecclesial body, has always accompanied the earthly events of the Church, beginning with the betrayal of Judas Iscariot. And it is indeed significant that the anti-church tries to rehabilitate Judas— and with him the worst heresiarchs—as exemplary models, "anti-saints" and "anti-martyrs," and thereby legitimizing themselves in their own heresies, immorality and vices. The coexistence—I was saying—of the good and the wicked, of which the Gospel speaks in the Parable of the Wheat and the Tares, seems to have morphed into the prevalence of the latter over the former. The difference is that vice and deviations once despised are today not only practiced and tolerated more, but even encouraged and praised, while virtue and fidelity to the teaching of Christ are despised, mocked and even condemned.

2. The Eclipse of the True Church

For sixty years, we have witnessed the eclipse of the true Church by an anti-church that has progressively appropriated her name, occupied the Roman Curia and her dicasteries, dioceses and parishes, seminaries and universities, convents and monasteries. The anti-church has usurped her authority, and its ministers wear her sacred garments; it uses her prestige and power to appropriate her treasures, assets, and finances.

Just as happens in nature, this eclipse does not take place all at once; it passes from light to darkness when a celestial body inserts itself between the sun and us. This is a relatively slow but inexorable process, in which the moon of the anti-church follows its orbit until it overlaps the sun, generating a cone of shadow that projects over the earth. We now find ourselves in this doctrinal, moral, liturgical, and disciplinary cone of shadow. It is not yet the total eclipse that we will see at the end of time, under the reign of the Antichrist. But it is a partial eclipse, which lets us see the luminous crown of the sun encircling the black disk of the moon.

The process that led to today's eclipse of the Church began with Modernism, without a doubt. The anti-church followed its orbit despite the solemn condemnations of the Magisterium, which in that phase shone with the splendor of truth. But with the Second Vatican Council, the darkness of this spurious entity came over the Church. Initially it obscured only a small part, but the darkness gradually increased. Whoever then pointed to the sun, deducing that the moon would certainly obscure it, was accused of being a "prophet of doom," with those forms of fanaticism and intemperance that arise from ignorance and prejudice. The case of Archbishop Marcel Lefebvre and a few other prelates confirms, on the one hand, the farsightedness of these shepherds and, on the other hand, the disjointed reaction of their adversaries; who, out of fear of losing power, used all their authority to deny the evidence and kept hidden their own true intentions.

To continue the analogy: we can say that, in the sky of the Faith, an eclipse is a rare and extraordinary phenomenon. But to deny that, during the eclipse, darkness spreads—just because this does not happen under ordinary conditions—is not a sign of faith in the indefectibility of the Church, but rather an obstinate denial of the evidence, or bad faith. The Holy Church, according to Christ's promises, will never be overwhelmed by the gates of hell, but that does not mean that she will not be—or is not already—overshadowed by her infernal forgery, that moon which, not by chance, we see under the feet of the Woman of the Revelation: "A great sign appeared in heaven: a woman clothed with the sun, with the moon under her feet, and on her head a crown of twelve stars" (Rev 12:1).

The moon lies under the feet of the Woman who is above all mutability, above all earthly corruption, above the law of fate and the kingdom of the spirit of this world. And this is because that Woman, who is at once the image of Mary Most Holy and of the Church, is *amicta sole*, clothed with the Sun of Righteousness that is Christ, "exempted from all demonic power as she takes part in the mystery of the immutability of Christ" (Saint Ambrose). She remains unbruised if not in her militant kingdom, certainly in the suffering one in Purgatory and in the triumphant one in Paradise. St. Jerome, commenting on the words of Scripture, reminds us that "the gates of hell are sins and vices, especially the teachings of heretics." We know therefore that even the "synthesis of all heresies" represented by Modernism and its updated conciliar version can never definitively obscure the splendor of the Bride of Christ, but only for the brief period of the eclipse that Providence, in its infinite wisdom, has allowed, to draw from it a greater good.

3. The Abandonment of the Supernatural Dimension

In this talk, I wish especially to deal with the relationship between the revolution of Vatican II and the establishment of the New World Order. The focal element of this analysis consists in highlighting the abandonment on the part of the ecclesiastical hierarchy, even at the top, of the supernatural dimension of the Church and its eschatological role. With the Council, the innovators erased the divine origin of the Church from their theological horizon, creating an entity of human origin similar to a philanthropic organization.

The first consequence of this ontological subversion[7] was the necessary denial of the fact that the Bride of Christ is not, and cannot be, subject to change by those who exercise vicarious authority in the name of the Lord. She is neither the property of the pope nor of the bishops or theologians, and, as such, any attempt at "*aggiornamento*" lowers her to the level of a company that, in order to garner profit, renews its own commercial offer, sells its leftovers stock, and follows the fashion of the moment. The Church, on the other hand, is a supernatural and divine reality: she adapts the way she preaches the Gospel to the nations, but she can never change the content of a single iota (Mt 5:18), nor deny her transcendent momentum by lowering herself to mere social service. On the opposite side, the anti-church proudly lays claims to the right to perform a paradigm shift not only by changing the way doctrine is

---

7. Ontology is the science of being. Thus, an ontological subversion subverts something at the level of being, of what it is.

expounded, but the doctrine itself. This is confirmed by the words of Massimo Faggioli on the new Encyclical *Fratelli Tutti*: "Pope Francis's pontificate is like a standard lifted up before Catholic integralists and those who equate material continuity and tradition: Catholic doctrine does not just develop. Sometimes it really changes: for example on [the] death penalty, [and] war."[8]

Insisting on what the Magisterium teaches is useless. The innovators' brazen claim to have the right to change the Faith stubbornly follows the modernist approach.

The Council's first error consists mainly in the lack of a transcendent perspective—the result of a spiritual crisis that was already latent—and in the attempt to establish paradise on earth, with a sterile human horizon. In line with this approach, *Fratelli Tutti* sees the fulfillment of an earthly utopia and social redemption in human brotherhood, *pax œcumenica* between religions, and welcoming migrants.

4. *The Sense of Inferiority and Inadequacy*

As I have written on other occasions, the revolutionary demands of the *nouvelle théologie*[9] found fertile ground in the Council Fathers because of a serious inferiority complex vis-à-vis the world. There was a time, in the postwar period, when the revolution led by Freemasonry in the civil, political, and cultural spheres breached the Catholic élite, persuading it of its inadequacy in the face of an epochal challenge that is now inescapable. Instead of questioning themselves and their faith, this élite—bishops, theologians, intellectuals—recklessly attributed responsibility for the imminent failure of the Church to her rock-solid hierarchical structure, and to her monolithic doctrinal and moral teaching. Looking at the defeat of the European civilization that the Church had helped to form, the élite thought that the lack of agreement with the world was caused

---

8. VN: Source: https://twitter.com/massimofaggioli/status/1313567320380502018.

9. This term refers to the "new theology" of the Neo-Modernist successors of the early twentieth-century Modernists. It was condemned by Pius XII in his 1950 encyclical *Humani Generis*.

by the intransigence of the papacy and the moral rigidity of priests not wanting to come to terms with the *Zeitgeist*, and "open up."

This ideological approach stems from the false assumption that, between the Church and the contemporary world, there can be an alliance, a consonance of intent, a friendship. Nothing could be further from the truth, since there can be no respite in the struggle between God and Satan, between Light and Darkness. "I will put enmity between thee and the woman, and between thy seed and her seed; it shall bruise thy head, and thou shalt bruise his heel" (Gen 3:15). This is an enmity willed by God Himself, which places Mary Most Holy—and the Church—as eternal enemies of the ancient serpent. The world has its own prince (Jn 12:31), who is the "enemy" (Mt 13:28), a "murderer from the beginning" (Jn 8:44) and a "liar" (Jn 8:44). Courting a pact of non-belligerence with the world means coming to terms with Satan. This overturns and perverts the very essence of the Church, whose mission is to convert as many souls to Christ for the greater glory of God, without ever laying down arms against those who want to attract them to themselves and to damnation.

The Church's sense of inferiority and failure before the world created the "perfect storm" for the revolution to take root in the Council Fathers and by extension in the Christian people, in whom obedience to the hierarchy had been cultivated perhaps more than fidelity to the *depositum fidei*. Let me it be clear: obedience to the Sacred Pastors is certainly praiseworthy if the commands are legitimate. But obedience ceases to be a virtue and, in fact, becomes servility if it is an end in itself and if it contradicts the purpose to which it is ordained, namely faith and morals.

We should add, that this sense of inferiority was introduced into the ecclesial body with displays of great theater, such as the removal of the tiara by Paul VI, the return of the Ottoman flagship banners conquered at Lepanto, the flaunted ecumenical embraces with the schismatic Athenagoras, the requests for forgiveness for the Crusades, the abolition of the Index, the clergy's focus on the poor in place of the alleged triumphalism of Pius XII. The *coup de grâce* of this attitude was codified in the reformed liturgy, which manifests its embarrassment of Catholic dogma by silencing it—and thus denying it indirectly. The ritual change engendered a doctrinal change, which led the faithful to believe that the Mass is a simple fraternal banquet and that the Most Holy Eucharist is merely a symbol of Christ's presence among us.

5. "Idem sentire" of Revolution and Council

The Council Fathers' sense of inadequacy was only increased by the work of the innovators, whose heretical ideas coincided with the demands of the world. A comparative analysis of modern thought confirms the *idem sentire*[10] of the conspirators with every element of the revolutionary ideology:

– the acceptance of the democratic principle as the legitimizing source of power, in place of the divine right of the Catholic monarchy (including the papacy);

– the creation and accumulation of organs of power, in place of personal responsibility and institutional hierarchy;

– the erasure of the historical past, evaluated with today's parameters, which fail to defend tradition and cultural heritage;

– the emphasis on the freedom of individuals and the weakening of the concept of responsibility and duty;

– the continuous evolution of morality and ethics, thus deprived of their immutable nature and of any transcendent reference;

– the presumed secular nature of the State, in place of the rightful submission of the civil order to the Kingship of Jesus Christ and the ontological superiority of the Church's mission over that of the temporal sphere;

– the equality of religions not only before the State, but even as a general concept to which the Church must conform, against the objective and necessary defense of the truth and the condemnation of error;

– the false and blasphemous concept of the dignity of man as connatural to him, based on the denial of original sin and of the need for Redemption as a premise for pleasing God, meriting His grace and attaining eternal beatitude;

10. Having the same sentiment, the same mind.

259

– the undermining of the role of women, and a contempt for the privilege of motherhood;

– the primacy of matter over spirit;

– the fideistic relationship with science,[11] in the face of a ruthless criticism of religion on false scientific grounds.

All these principles, propagated by Freemasonic ideologues and New World Order supporters, coincide with the revolutionary ideas of the Council:

– the democratization of the Church began with *Lumen Gentium* and today it is realized in the Bergoglian synodal path;

– the creation and accumulation of organs of power has been achieved by delegating decision-making roles to episcopal conferences, synods of bishops, commissions, pastoral councils, etc.;

– the Church's past and glorious traditions are judged according to the modern mentality and condemned in order to curry favor with the modern world;

– the "freedom of the children of God" theorized by Vatican II has been established regardless of the moral duties of individuals who, according to the conciliar fairytales, are all saved regardless of their inner dispositions and the state of their soul;

– the obfuscating of perennial moral references has led to the revised doctrine on capital punishment; and, with *Amoris Lætitia*, the admission of public adulterers to the sacraments, cracking the sacramental edifice;

– the adoption of the concept of secularism has led to the abolition of a State religion in Catholic nations. Encouraged by the Holy See and the Episcopate, this has led to a loss of religious identity and the recognition of rights of sects, as well as the approval of norms that violate natural and divine law;

---

11. VN: "Dovremmo evitare di cadere in questi quattro atteggiamenti perversi, che certo non aiutano alla ricerca onesta e al dialogo sincero e produttivo sulla costruzione del futuro del nostro pianeta: negazione, indifferenza, rassegnazione e fiducia in soluzioni inadeguate": cf. www.avvenire.it/papa/pagine/papa-su-clima-basta-negazionismi-su-riscaldamento-globale. The Italian can be translated: "We should avoid falling into these four perverse attitudes, which certainly do not help honest research and sincere and productive dialogue on building the future of our planet: denial, indifference, resignation, and trust in inadequate solutions."

– the religious freedom theorized in *Dignitatis Humanæ* is today brought to its logical and extreme consequences with the Declaration of Abu Dhabi and the latest Encyclical *Fratelli Tutti*, rendering the saving mission of the Church and the Incarnation itself obsolete;

– theories on human dignity in the Catholic sphere have led to confusion about the role of the laity with respect to the ministerial role of the clergy and a weakening of the hierarchical structure of the Church, while the embrace of feminist ideology is a prelude to the admission of women to the Holy Orders;

– an inordinate preoccupation with the temporal needs of the poor, so typical of the left, has transformed the Church into a sort of welfare association, limiting her activity to the mere material sphere, almost to the point of abandoning the spiritual;

– subservience to modern science and technological progress has led the Church to disavow the "Queen of the Science" (Faith), to "demythologize" miracles, to deny the inerrancy of Sacred Scripture, to look at the most sacred Mysteries of our Holy Religion as "myths" or "metaphors," sacrilegiously suggesting that transubstantiation and the Resurrection itself are "magic" (not to be taken literally but rather symbolically), and to describe the sublime Marian dogmas are "*tonterías*" (nonsense).

There is an almost grotesque aspect of this leveling and dumbing down of the hierarchy to comply with mainstream thought. The hierarchy's desire to please its persecutors and serve its enemies always comes too late and is out of sync, giving the impression that the bishops are irremediably outdated, indeed not in step with the times. They lead those who see them so enthusiastically conniving with their own extinction to believe that this demonstration of courtesan submission to the politically correct comes not so much from a true ideological persuasion, but rather from the fear of being swept away, of losing power, and no longer having that prestige that the world still pays them, nonetheless. They do not realize—or do not want to admit—that the prestige and authority whose custodians they are come from the authority and prestige of the Church of Christ, and not from the miserable, pitiful counterfeit of her which they have fashioned.

When this anti-church is fully established in the total eclipse of the Catholic Church, the authority of its leaders will depend on the degree of subjugation to the New World Order, which will not tolerate any divergence from its own creed and will ruthlessly apply that dogmatism, fanaticism, and fundamentalism that many prelates and self-styled intellectuals criticize in those who remain faithful to the Magisterium today. In this way, the deep church may continue to bear the trademark "Catholic Church," but it will be the slave of the New Order thinking, reminiscent of the Jews who, after denying the Kingship of Christ before Pilate, were enslaved to the civil authority of their time: "We have no other king but Caesar" (Jn 19:15). Today's Caesar commands us to close the churches, wear a mask, and suspend the celebrations under the pretext of a pseudo-pandemic. The communist regime persecutes the Chinese Catholics, and the world hears nothing but silence from Rome. Tomorrow a new Titus will sack the Council temple, transporting its remains to some museum, and divine vengeance at the hands of the pagans will have been achieved once again.

6. The Instrumental Role of the Moderate Catholics in the Revolution

Some might say that the Council Fathers and the popes who presided over that assembly did not realize the implications that their approval of the Vatican II documents would have for the future of the Church. If this were the case—i.e., if there had been any subsequent regrets in their hasty approval of heretical texts or texts close to heresy—it is difficult to understand why they were unable to put an immediate stop to abuses, correct errors, clarify misunderstandings and omissions. And above all, it is incomprehensible why the ecclesiastical Authority has been so ruthless against those who defended the Catholic truth, and, at the same time, were so terribly accommodating to rebels and heretics.

In any case, the responsibility for the conciliar crisis must be laid at the feet of the Authority which, even amid a thousand appeals to collegiality and pastoralism, has jealously guarded its prerogatives, exercising them only in one direction, that is, against the *pusillus grex* and never against the enemies of God and of the Church. The

262

very rare exceptions, when a heretic theologian or revolutionary religious has been censored by the Holy Office, only offer tragic confirmation of a rule that has been enforced for decades; not to mention that many of them, in recent times, have been rehabilitated without any abjuration of their errors and even promoted to institutional positions in the Roman Curia or Pontifical Athenaeums.

This is the reality, as it emerges from my analysis. However, we know that, in addition to the progressive wing of the Council and the traditional Catholic wing, there is a part of the Episcopate, the clergy, and the people that attempts to keep equal distance from what it considers two extremes. I am talking about the so-called "conservatives," that is, a centrist part of the ecclesial body that ends up "carrying water" for the revolutionaries because, while rejecting their excesses, it shares the same principles. The error of the "conservatives" lies in giving a negative connotation to traditionalism and in placing it on the opposite side of progressivism. Their *aurea mediocritas* consists in arbitrarily placing themselves not between two vices, but between virtue and vice. They are the ones who criticize the excesses of the Pachamama or of the most extreme of Bergoglio's statements, but who do not tolerate the Council's being questioned, let alone the intrinsic link between the conciliar cancer and the current metastasis. The correlation between political conservatism and religious conservatism consists in adopting the "center," a synthesis between the "right" thesis and the "left" antithesis, according to the Hegelian approach[12] so cherished by moderate supporters of the Council.

In the civil sphere, the deep state has managed political and social dissent by using organizations and movements that are only appar-

---

12. The German philosopher Georg Wilhelm Friedrich Hegel (1770–1831) believed that truth emerges from a dialectic between thesis and antithesis, yielding a synthesis; this, in turn, becomes a new thesis for the process. His philosophy was influential upon Marxism, which sees history as a dialectic process from which communism—or perfect community of goods without state infrastructure—will emerge after the conflict between labor and capital has expended itself. Benedict XVI was in many ways Hegelian, as exemplified in his approach to liturgy: he permitted the traditional Mass because he believed that out of dialectic between the new Mass and the old Mass, "mutually enriching," a synthesis would emerge.

ently opposition, but which are actually instrumental to maintaining power. Similarly, in the ecclesial sphere, the deep church uses the moderate "conservatives" to give an appearance of offering freedom to the faithful. The Motu Proprio *Summorum Pontificum* itself, for example, while granting the celebration in the extraordinary form, demands *saltem impliciter* [at least implicitly] that we accept the Council and recognize the lawfulness of the reformed liturgy. This ploy prevents those who benefit from the Motu Proprio from raising any objection, or they risk the dissolution of the *Ecclesia Dei*[13] communities. And it instills in the Christian people the dangerous idea that a good thing, in order to have legitimacy in the Church and society, must necessarily be accompanied by a bad thing or at least something less good.

However, only a misguided mind would seek to afford equal rights to both good and evil. It matters little if one is personally in favor of good, when he recognizes the legitimacy of those who are in favor of evil. In this sense, the "freedom to choose" abortion theorized by democratic politicians finds its counterbalance in the no less aberrant "religious freedom" theorized by the Council, which today is stubbornly defended by the anti-church. If it is not permissible for a Catholic to support a politician who defends the right to abortion, it is even less permissible to approve a prelate who defends the "freedom" of an individual to endanger his immortal soul by "choosing" to remain in mortal sin. This is not mercy; this is gross dereliction of spiritual duty before God in order to curry the favor and approval of Man.

7. "Open Society" and "Open Religion"

This analysis would hardly be complete without a word on the neo-language so popular in the ecclesiastical sphere. Traditional Catholic vocabulary has been deliberately modified, in order to change

---

13. The Pontifical Commission *Ecclesia Dei* was established by John Paul II in 1988 to facilitate the canonical recognition of groups and priests that broke away from Archbishop Lefebvre after he consecrated four bishops. Pope Benedict XVI made the Prefect of the Congregation for the Doctrine of the Faith the *ex officio* head of the Commission, and Pope Francis suppressed it and ordered the CDF to absorb its duties.

the content it expresses. The same has happened in the liturgy and preaching, where the clarity of the Catholic exposition has been replaced by ambiguity or the implicit denial of dogmatic truth. The examples are endless. This phenomenon also goes back to Vatican II, which sought to develop "Catholic" versions of the slogans of the world. Nevertheless, I would like to emphasize that all those expressions that are borrowed from secularist lexicons are also part of the neo-language. Let us consider Bergoglio's insistence on the "outgoing church," on *openness* as a positive value. Similarly, I quote now from *Fratelli Tutti:* "A living and dynamic people, a people with a future, is one constantly open to a new synthesis through its ability to welcome differences" (160). "The Church is a home with open doors" (276). "We want to be a Church that serves, that leaves home and goes forth from its places of worship, goes forth from its sacristies, in order to accompany life, to sustain hope, to be the sign of unity . . . to build bridges, to break down walls, to sow seeds of reconciliation" (ibid.).

The similarity with the Open Society sought after by Soros' globalist ideology is so striking as to almost constitute an *Open Religion* counterpoint to it. And this Open Religion is perfectly in tune with the intentions of globalism. From the political meetings "for a New Humanism" blessed by the leaders of the Church to the participation of the progressive intelligentsia in green propaganda, it all chases after the mainstream thought, in the sad and grotesque attempt to please the world. The stark contrast with the words of the Apostle is clear: "Am I now trying to win the approval of human beings, or of God? Or am I trying to please people? If I were still trying to please people, I would not be a servant of Christ" (Gal. 1:10).

The Catholic Church lives under the gaze of God; she exists for His glory and for the salvation of souls. The anti-church lives under the gaze of the world, pandering to the blasphemous apotheosis of man and the damnation of souls. During the last session of the Second Vatican Ecumenical Council, before all the Synod Fathers, these astonishing words of Paul VI resounded in the Vatican Basilica:

"The religion of the God who became man has met the religion (for such it is) of man who makes himself God. And what happened? Was there a clash, a battle, a condemnation? There could have been, but there was none. The old story of the Samaritan has been the model of the spirituality of the council. A feeling of boundless sympathy has permeated the whole of it. The attention of our council has been absorbed by the discovery of human needs (and these needs grow in proportion to the greatness which the son of the earth claims for himself). But we call upon those who term themselves modern humanists, and who have renounced the transcendent value of the highest realities, to give the council credit at least for one quality and to recognize our own new type of humanism: we, too, in fact, we more than any others, honor mankind."[14]

This sympathy—in the etymological sense of συμπάθεια, that is, participation in the sentiment of the other—is the figure of the Council and of the new religion (for such it is) of the anti-church. An anti-church born of the unclean union between the Church and the world, between the heavenly Jerusalem and hellish Babylon. Note well: the first time a Pontiff mentioned the "new humanism" was at the final session of Vatican II, and today we find it repeated as a mantra by those who consider it a perfect and coherent expression of the revolutionary *mens* of the Council.[15]

Always in view of this communion of intent between the New World Order and the anti-church, we must remember the *Global Compact on Education*, a project designed by Bergoglio "to generate a change on a planetary scale, so that education is a creator of

---

14. VN: "Religio, id est cultus Dei, qui homo fieri voluit, atque religio—talis enim est aestimanda—id est cultus hominis, qui fieri vult Deus, inter se congressae sunt. Quid tamen accidit? Certamen, proelium, anathema? Id sane haberi potuerat, sed plane non accidit. Vetus illa de bono Samaritano narratio exemplum fuit atque norma, ad quam Concilii nostri spiritualis ratio directa est. Etenim, immensus quidam erga homines amor Concilium penitus pervasit. Perspectae et iterum consideratae hominum necessitates, quae eo molestiores fiunt, quo magis huius terrae filius crescit, totum nostrae huius Synodi studium detinuerunt. Hanc saltem laudem Concilio tribuite, vos, nostra hac aetate cultores humanitatis, qui veritates rerum naturam transcendentes renuitis, iidemque novum nostrum humanitatis studium agnoscite: nam nos etiam, immo nos prae ceteris, hominis sumus cultores." Paul VI, *Allocuzione per l'ultima sessione del Concilio Ecumenico Vaticano II* (December 7, 1965).

15. VN: See https://twitter.com/i/status/1312837860442210304.

brotherhood, peace and justice. An even more urgent need in this time marked by the pandemic."[16] Promoted in collaboration with the United Nations, this "process of formation in the relationship and culture of encounter also finds space and value in the 'common home' with all creatures, since people, just as they are formed to the logic of communion and solidarity, are already working 'to recover serene harmony with creation,' and to configure the world as 'a space of true brotherhood' (*Gaudium et Spes*, 37)."[17] As can be seen, the ideological reference is always and only to Vatican II, because only from that moment on did the anti-church place man in the place of God, the creature in the place of the Creator.

The "new humanism" obviously has an environmental and eco-logical frame into which are grafted both the Encyclical *Laudato Sì* and Green Theology—the "Church with an Amazonian face" of the 2019 Synod of Bishops, with its idolatrous worship of Pachamama (mother earth) in the presence of the Roman Sanhedrin. The Church's attitude during COVID-19 demonstrated, on the one hand, the hierarchy's submission to the *diktats* of the State, in viola-tion of the *libertas ecclesiæ*, which the pope should have firmly defended. It also put on display the denial of any supernatural meaning of the pandemic, replacing the righteous wrath of God offended by the countless sins of humanity and nations with a more disturbing and destructive fury of Nature, offended by the lack of respect for the environment. I would like to emphasize that attributing a personal identity to Nature, almost endowed with intellect and will, is a prelude to her divinization. We have already seen a sacrilegious prelude to this, under the very dome of St. Peter's Basilica.

The bottom line is this: conformity on the part of the anti-church with the dominant ideology of the modern world establishes a real cooperation with powerful representatives of the deep state, starting with those working towards a "sustainable economy" involving

---

16. VN: See www.educationglobalcompact.org.

17. VN: *Congregazione per l'Educazione Cattolica, Lettera Circolare alle scuole, università e istituzioni educative* (September 10, 2020), www.educatio.va/content/dam/cec/Documenti/2020-09/IT-CONGREGATIO-LETTERA-COVID.pdf.

Jorge Mario Bergoglio, Bill Gates,[18] Jeffrey Sachs, John Elkann, Gunter Pauli.[19]

It will be useful to remember that the sustainable economy also has implications for agriculture and the world of work in general. The deep state needs to secure low-cost labor through immigration, which at the same time contributes to the cancellation of the religious, cultural and linguistic identity of the nations involved. The deep church lends an ideological and pseudo-theological basis to this invasion plan, and at the same time guarantees itself a share in the lucrative business of hospitality. We can understand Bergoglio's insistence on the theme of migrants, also reiterated in *Fratelli Tutti*: "A xenophobic mentality of closure and self-restraint is spreading" (39). "Migrations will constitute a founding element of the future of the world" (40). Bergoglio used the expression "founding element," stating that it is not possible to hypothesize a future without migrations.

Allow me a brief word about the political situation in the United States on the eve of the presidential election. *Fratelli Tutti* seems to be a form of Vatican endorsement of the Democratic candidate, in clear opposition to Donald Trump, and come a few days after Francis refused to grant audience to Secretary of State Mike Pompeo in Rome. This confirms which side the children of light are on, and who the children of darkness are.

8. The Ideological Foundations of "Brotherhood"

The theme of brotherhood, an obsession for Bergoglio, finds its first formulation in *Nostra Ætate* and *Dignitatis Humanæ*. The latest Encyclical, *Fratelli Tutti*, is the manifesto of this Masonic vision, in

---

18. Founder of Microsoft. After extensive investigations by the Justice Department into anticompetitive behavior by Gates and Microsoft, Gates diversified his interest away from computers to healthcare. His multi-billion-dollar Gates Foundation promotes vaccinations around the world and is heavily invested in pharmaceutical companies. He is a significant financial supporter of the World Health Organization.

19. VN: See www.lastampa.it/cronaca/2020/10/03/news/green-blue-la-nuova-voce-dell-economia-sostenibile-via-con-il-papa-e-bill-gates-1.39375988 and https://remnantnewspaper.com/web/index.php/articles/item/2990-the-vatican-un-allianc e-architects-of-death-and-doom.

which the cry *Liberté, Égalité, Fraternité!* replaces the Gospel, for the sake of a unity among men that leaves out God. Note that the *Document on Human Fraternity for World Peace and Living Together*[20] signed in Abu Dhabi on February 4, 2019 was proudly defended by Bergoglio with these words:

"From the Catholic point of view the document did not go one millimeter beyond the Second Vatican Council."

Cardinal Miguel Ayuso Guixot, President of the Pontifical Council for Interreligious Dialogue, comments in *La Civiltà Cattolica*:

> With the Council, the embankment gradually cracked and then broke: The river of dialogue has spread with the Council Declarations *Nostra Ætate* on the relationship between the Church and believers of other religions and *Dignitatis Humanæ* on religious freedom, themes and documents that are closely linked to each other, and have allowed St. John Paul II to give life to meetings such as the *World Day of Prayer for Peace* in Assisi on October 27, 1986 and Benedict XVI, twenty-five years later, to make us live in the city of St. Francis the *Day of Reflection, Dialogue and Prayer for Peace and Justice in the World—Pilgrims of Truth, Pilgrims of Peace*. Therefore, the Catholic Church's commitment to interreligious dialogue, which opens the way to peace and fraternity, is part of her original mission and has its roots in the Council event.[21]

Once again, the cancer of Vatican II confirms that it is at the origin of Bergoglian metastasis. The *fil rouge* [common thread] that unites the Council with the cult of the Pachamama also passes through Assisi, as my brother Athanasius Schneider rightly pointed out in his recent speech.[22]

---

20. VN: See www.vatican.va/content/francesco/en/travels/2019/outside/docum ents/papa-francesco_20190204_documento-fratellanza-umana.html.

21. VN: Card. Miguel Ángel Ayuso Guixot, *Il documento sulla Fraternità umana nel solco del Concilio Vaticano II* (February 3, 2020); cf. www.laciviltacattolica.it/ news/il-documento-sulla-fratellanza-umana-nel-solco-del-concilio-vaticano-ii.

22. VN: "Pachamama worship in Rome was 'prepared by Assisi meetings,'" www.cfnews.org.uk/bishop-schneider-pachamama-worship-in-rome-was-prepare d-by-assisi-meetings.

And speaking of the anti-church, Bishop Fulton Sheen describes the Antichrist: "Since his religion will be brotherhood without the paternity of God, he will deceive even the elect."[23] We seem to see the prophecy of the venerable American archbishop coming true before our eyes.

It is no surprise, therefore, that the infamous Grand Lodge of Spain, after having warmly congratulated its paladin raised to the Throne, has once again paid homage to Bergoglio with these words:

> The great principle of this initiatory school has not changed in three centuries: the construction of a universal brotherhood where human beings call themselves brothers to each other beyond their specific beliefs, their ideologies, the color of their skin, their social extraction, their language, their culture or their nationality. This fraternal dream clashed with religious fundamentalism which, in the case of the Catholic Church, led to harsh texts condemning the tolerance of Freemasonry in the nineteenth century. Pope Francis's latest encyclical shows how far the present Catholic Church is from its previous positions. In *Fratelli Tutti*, the pope embraced the Universal Brotherhood, the great principle of modern Freemasonry.[24]

The reaction of the Grande Oriente of Italy is not dissimilar: "These are the principles that Freemasonry has always pursued and guarded for the elevation of Humanity."[25] Austen Ivereigh, the hagiographer of Bergoglio, confirms with satisfaction this interpretation that a Catholic would rightly consider at least disturbing.[26]

I remember that an infiltration of Freemasonry into the Church was planned since the nineteenth century in the masonic documents of the *Alta Vendita*: "You, too, will fish some friends and lead them to the feet of the Apostolic See. You will have preached revolution in Tiara and Cope, proceeded under the cross and banner, a

---

23. VN: Mons. Fulton Sheen, *Discorso radiofonico del 26 Gennaio 1947*, www.tempi.it/fulton-sheen-e-linganno-del-grande-umanitario.
24. VN: Source: www.infocatolica.com/?t=noticia&cod=38792.
25. VN: Source: https://twitter.com/grandeorienteit/status/1312991358886514688.
26. VN: See https://youtu.be/s8v-O_VH1xw.

revolution that will need only a little help to set the quarters of the world on fire."[27]

9. The Subversion of the Individual and Social Relationship with God

Allow me to conclude this examination of the links between the Council and the present crisis by emphasizing a reversal that I consider extremely important and significant. I am referring to the relationship of the individual layman and community of the faithful with God. While in the Church of Christ the relationship of the soul with the Lord is eminently personal even when it is conveyed by the sacred minister in the liturgical action, in the *conciliar* church the community and the group relationship prevails. Think of their insistence in wanting to make the baptism of a child, or the wedding of a married couple, "an act of the community"; or the impossibility of receiving holy Communion individually outside of Mass, and of the common practice of approaching Communion during Mass even without the necessary conditions. All of this is sanctioned on the basis of a protestantized concept of participation in the Eucharistic banquet, from which no guest is excluded. Under this understanding of community, the person loses his individuality, losing himself in the anonymous community of the celebration.

So too, the relationship of the social body with God disappears in a personalism that eliminates the role of mediation of both the Church and the State. Individualization in the moral field enters into this as well, where the rights and preferences of the individual become grounds for the eradication of social morality. This is done in the name of an "inclusiveness" that legitimates every vice and moral aberration. Society—understood as the union of several individuals aimed at the pursuit of a common goal—is divided into a multiplicity of individuals, each of whom has his own purpose.

27. VN: "Vous amènerez des amis autour de la Chaire apostolique. Vous aurez prêché une révolution en tiare et en chape, marchant avec la croix et la bannière, une révolution qui n'aura besoin que d'être un tout petit peu aiguillonnée pour mettre le feu aux quatre coins du monde." Jacques Cretineau-Joly, *L'Église romaine en face de la Révolution* (Paris: Henri Plon, 1859). [Viganò here provides a French version of the English quotation in the text.]

271

This is the result of an ideological upheaval that deserves to be analyzed in depth, because of its implications both in the ecclesial and civil spheres. It is evident, however, that the first step of this revolution is to be found in the conciliar *mens*, beginning with the indoctrination of the Christian people constituted by the reformed liturgy, in which the individual merges into the assembly by depersonalizing himself, and the community devolves into a collection of individuals by losing their identity.

10. Cause and Effect

Philosophy teaches us that to a cause always corresponds a certain effect. We have seen that the actions carried out during Vatican II have had the desired effect, giving concrete form to that anthropological turning point which today has led to the apostasy of the anti-church and the eclipse of the true Church of Christ. We must therefore understand that, if we want to undo the harmful effects we see before us, it is necessary and indispensable to remove the factors that caused them. If this is our goal, it is clear that accepting—or even partially accepting—those revolutionary principles would make our efforts useless and counterproductive. We must therefore be clear about the objectives to be achieved, ordering our action to the goals. But we must all be aware that in this work of restoration no exceptions to the principles are possible, precisely because failure to share them would prevent any chance of success.

Therefore, let us put aside, once and for all, the vain distinctions concerning the presumed goodness of the Council, the betrayal of the will of the Synod Fathers, the *letter* and *spirit* of Vatican II, the magisterial weight (or lack thereof) of its acts, and the *hermeneutic of continuity* versus that *of rupture*. The anti-church has used the label "Ecumenical Council" to give authority and legal force to its revolutionary agenda, just as Bergoglio calls his political manifesto of allegiance to the New World Order an "encyclical letter." The cunning of the enemy has isolated the healthy part of the Church, torn between having to recognize the subversive nature of the Council documents, thus having to exclude them from the Magisterial corpus, and having to deny reality by declaring them apodictically orthodox in order to safeguard the infallibility of the Magisterium.

The *dubia* represented a humiliation for those Princes of the Church, but without untying the doctrinal knots brought to the attention of the Roman Pontiff. Bergoglio does not respond, precisely because he does not want to deny or confirm the implied errors, thus exposing himself to the risk of being declared a heretic and losing the papacy. This is the same method used with the Council, where ambiguity and the use of imprecise terminology prevent the condemnation of the error that has been implied. But the jurist knows very well that, in addition to the blatant violation of the law, one can also commit a crime by circumventing it, using it for evil purposes: *contra legem fit, quod in fraudem legis fit.*[28]

11. Conclusion

The only way to win this battle is to go back to doing what the Church has always done, and to stop doing what the anti-church asks of us today—that which the true Church has always condemned. Let us put Our Lord Jesus Christ, King and High Priest, back at the center of the life of the Church; and before that, at the center of the life of our communities, of our families, of ourselves. Let us restore the crown to Our Lady Mary Most Holy, Queen and Mother of the Church.

Let us return to celebrating the traditional Holy Liturgy worthily, and to praying with the words of the Saints, not with the ramblings of the modernists and heretics. Let us begin again to savor the writings of the Fathers of the Church and the mystics, and to throw into the fire the works imbued with modernism and immanentist sentimentalism. Let us support, with prayer and material help, the many good priests who remain faithful to the true Faith, and withdraw all support from those who have come to terms with the world and its lies.

And above all—I ask you in the name of God!—let us abandon that sense of inferiority that our adversaries have accustomed us to

28. Latin: "What is done to circumvent the law is done against the law." An abbreviated version of the fuller axiom from Justinian's *Digest*: "Contra legem facit qui id facit quod lex prohibet; in fraudem vero qui, salvis verbis legis, sententiam ejus circumvenit" (He who does what the law prohibits acts contrary to law; he who acts in fraud of it, the letter of the law being inviolate, cheats the spirit of it).

accept: in the Lord's war, they do not humiliate us (we certainly deserve every humiliation for our sins). No, they humiliate the Majesty of God and the Bride of the Immaculate Lamb. The truth that we embrace does not come from us, but from God! Letting truth be denied, accepting that it must justify itself before the heresies and errors of the anti-church, is not an act of humility, but of cowardice and pusillanimity.

Let us be inspired by the example of the Holy Maccabees Martyrs, before a new Antiochus who asks us to sacrifice to idols and to abandon the true God. Let us respond with their words, praying to the Lord: "So now, O Sovereign of the heavens, send a good angel to spread terror and trembling before us. By the might of your arm may these blasphemers who come against your holy people be struck down" (2 Mac 15:23).

Let me conclude my talk today with a personal memory. When I was Apostolic Nuncio in Nigeria, I learned about a magnificent popular tradition that came out of the terrible war in Biafra, and which continues to this day. I personally took part in it during a pastoral visit to the Archdiocese of Onitsha, and I was very impressed by it. This tradition—called "Block Rosary Children"—consists in gathering thousands of children (even very young ones) in each village or neighborhood for the recitation of the Holy Rosary to implore peace—each child holding a little piece of wood, like a mini altar, with an image of Our Lady and a small candle on it.

In the days leading up to November 3rd, I invite everyone to join in a Rosary Crusade: a sort of siege of Jericho, not with seven trumpets made of ram's horns sounded by priests, but with the Hail Mary's of the little ones and the innocent to bring down the walls of the deep state and the deep church.

Let us join with little ones in a Block Rosary, imploring the Woman clothed with the Sun that the reign of Our Lady and Mother may be restored, and the eclipse that afflicts us shortened.

And may God bless these holy intentions.

PART III

A VOICE DECRYING THE DEEP STATE: CHINA, BIDEN, COVID, AND THE GREAT RESET VS. PRESIDENT DONALD J. TRUMP

Introduction to Part III
The Deep State and the
Biblical Conflict of Our Time

THERE is an old saying: "As goes the Church, so goes the world." A healthy vibrant Church will coincide with a healthy and calm civil society. When the Church is weak and divided, the secular world will also suffer. Thus, it is not surprising that the archbishop's quest to trace the roots of the current crisis finds a connection between the deep church that began to eclipse the Church at Vatican II and the deep state that is eclipsing free societies.

What exactly is this "deep church" that Viganò claims has superimposed itself on the Church of Christ and has eclipsed the true Church? In his interview with Francesco Boezi, Viganò explains that the term deep church "gives a good idea of what is happening in a parallel way at the political and ecclesial level." The strategy of the deep church "is the same [as the deep state], just as the goals are the same, and, in the final analysis, the *mens* that is behind it." He clarifies that the deep church is "a foreign body that is illegal, subversive, and deprived of any sort of democratic legitimacy that uses the institution in which it is embedded to achieve goals that are diametrically opposed to the goals of the institution itself." In the interview with Scott Kesterson, he explains further that the deep church is related to the deep state as a

> "Vatican branch" which depends on the deep state and closely collaborates with it. Imagine the same people, with the same vices, the same net of intrigue and blackmail, but who instead of wearing suits and ties wear Roman collars and often also pectoral crosses (well hidden inside their pockets) and the rings of episcopal consecration.

They are not merely fellow travelers of each other but share the same vices and techniques.

277

Those who claimed that there was a secret cadre of globalists who sought a Great Reset to overthrow the current political and economic order were once dismissed as delusional conspiracy theorists. Yet in 2020, their dismissed theories became reality. The World Economic Forum explicitly announced its Great Reset, which it claimed was a necessary response to the pretext of COVID-19. The World Economic Forum's own website proclaimed their intention for all the world to read:

> The COVID-19 crisis, and the political, economic and social disruptions it has caused, is fundamentally changing the traditional context for decision-making. . . . As we enter a unique window of opportunity to shape the recovery, this initiative will offer insights to help inform all those determining the future state of global relations, the direction of national economies, the priorities of societies, the nature of business models and the management of a global commons. Drawing from the vision and vast expertise of the leaders engaged across the Forum's communities, the Great Reset initiative has a set of dimensions to build a new social contract that honours the dignity of every human being.[1]

The once-mocked conspiracy had come out of the shadows into the light. The alliance of the deep church and deep state to advance this Great Reset is evident in the common script employed. The World Economic Forum adopted the motto that, in the Great Reset, we must "build back better." A post on the World Economic Forum's website from July 13, 2020 is entitled: "To build back better, we must reinvent capitalism. Here's how."[2] On December 20, 2020, Pope Francis posted the following on his @Pontifex Twitter account: "To help our society to 'build back better,' inclusion of the vulnerable must also entail efforts to promote their active participation."[3] The

---

1. Source: www.weforum.org/great-reset.

2. Source: www.weforum.org/agenda/2020/07/to-build-back-better-we-must-re invent-capitalism-heres-how.

3. Posted December 3, 2020, at 7:31 AM: https://twitter.com/Pontifex/status/1334475219180851202.

Introduction to Part III

Biden/Harris campaign website proclaimed: "Build Back Better: Joe Biden's Jobs and Economic Recovery Plan for Working Families."[4] How is it that a Supreme Pontiff can be speaking from the same script as a radically pro-abortion apostate Catholic politician and a globalist organization that promotes sterilization, contraception, and abortion? The answer is they all work for the same master. In the writings gathered in Part III, Viganò unmasks the Chinese Communist Party (CCP) as the principal power behind Biden and Bergoglio, just as he unmasked the Modernists as the power behind the Vatican II revolution. That intractable enemy of the Church about which Fatima had warned and about which Vatican II was shamefully silent—atheistic Communism—had taken root in the vast land of China and has now entered into an adulterous relationship with the highest authorities in the Church to unite the deep church and deep state. As a Christian, Viganò traces the enemy still further, beyond the CCP, to the ultimate enemy of the human race, the murderer and the liar par excellence (Jn 8:44): the devil himself. In the interventions throughout the summer and fall of 2020, Viganò will cast this conflict in biblical and apocalyptic terms.

He introduces the nature of the conflict in a May 29 letter to a cloistered nun. The globalist New World Order advancing under the banner of COVID-19 that he and others decried in the Appeal to the Church and the World is set in this apocalyptic context:

> With a supernatural gaze, corroborated by Sacred Scripture and various messages of Our Lady, we can understand that in this moment we can now see with greater clarity the real dimension of the epochal clash between Good and Evil, between the sons of Light and the sons of Darkness.

What makes it epochal is that the highest authorities of the Church work not for the children of light but for the sons of darkness. This betrayal by Pope Francis of his mission to confirm the children of light in the Faith has its origins, he tells the cloistered nun, in Vatican II. He connects his developing analysis of the Council and the

---

4. https://joebiden.com/build-back-better.

Great Reset in this letter. Just as Vatican II declared there was no going back to the traditional Church, so too the elites of today claim there is no going back from the Great Reset. Yet Viganò's solution proposed to the sister is precisely that—the world and the Church must return to Tradition in all its aspects.

The alliance of the postconciliar Church with the globalist elites has elevated the conflict to biblical proportions. In his lecture to the Catholic Identity Conference (contained in Part II), Archbishop Viganò reminds us of St. Paul's teaching that God placed the Church, and in particular the Supreme Pontiff, as the *kathèkon* to the manifestation of the mystery of iniquity. The mystery of iniquity is the final appearance of the Antichrist, who will seem to triumph over the Church of Christ but who will be defeated in the end. Only when the *kathèkon* is removed will this mystery of iniquity be able to appear in all its power.[5] Archbishop Viganò explained in the Catholic Identity Conference lecture: "It seems quite evident to me that the end times are now approaching before our eyes, since the mystery of iniquity has spread throughout the world with the disappearance of the courageous opposition of the *kathèkon*." In the interventions in this Part he places the geopolitical crisis of COVID, the Great Reset, and the US Presidential Election in this eschatological context.

Some may be surprised that the reelection of Donald J. Trump is addressed by the archbishop so frequently. What does a twice-divorced, non-Catholic billionaire with a playboy reputation have to do with a biblical conflict? The answer is that God often uses the most unlikely and flawed instruments to manifest his intervention in history. King David was an adulterer and murderer[6] and yet he was the greatest ruler of Israel and the progenitor of the Messiah. Viganò sees in Donald Trump a secular analogy or image of the true *kathèkon*, the Church and, more specifically, the Holy Father. Because he is opposing the instruments of the mystery of iniquity in

---

5. See p. 252, n. 2.

6. See 2 Samuel 11. King David committed adultery with Bathsheba, conceiving a child. He then ordered her husband, Urias, into the front line of battle to have him killed.

the world, the New World Order, this flawed human being who served as the forty-fifth president of the United States is a type of the religious *kathèkon*. Thus, the archbishop tells us in his Second Open Letter to President Donald J. Trump:

> In Sacred Scripture, Saint Paul speaks to us of "the one who opposes" the manifestation of the mystery of iniquity, the *kathèkon* (2 Thess 2:6–7). In the religious sphere, this obstacle to evil is the Church, and in particular the papacy; in the political sphere, it is those who impede the establishment of the New World Order.

This unlikely ally appeared out of nowhere to be an obstacle to the enemy, in the face of the Church's hierarchy and the pope abandoning their role at and following Vatican II.

In the interview with Francesco Boezi, the archbishop explains that, since Bergoglio has already joined the team of the deep state, the final obstacle to total domination by the children of darkness will be removed if Trump fails to secure reelection. On the morning following election day in the US, as a good pastor would do, Viganò writes to all Americans of good will. He urges them not to be discouraged as they awoke to find a landslide election stolen. He reminds them that this was not simply one more political election but a biblical battle against the devil. They should not be surprised by this election fraud. He tells all Americans in this letter: "Do not think that the children of darkness act with honesty, and do not be scandalized if they operate with deception. Do you perhaps believe that Satan's followers are honest, sincere, and loyal?" He inspires hope through prayer, urging all Americans to pray and to get their children to pray for their country.

As with the interventions on Vatican II, Viganò began with an intervention addressing a specific difficulty: the totalitarian measures enacted on the pretext of the COVID-19 virus. The Appeal for the Church and the World was issued early in the long months of government repression.[7] Yet it so clearly warned of all the threats

---

7. This document is included in the present volume although it was not published with Archbishop Viganò's name as author. This Appeal for the Church and

that were to come: the destruction of the economy, the totalitarian repression of individual freedom, and the development of immoral vaccines reliant upon abortion. Most importantly, the Appeal places these contemporary events in a cosmological context. They are part of a great biblical struggle, the war between Our Lord Jesus Christ and his Queen Mother against the Antichrist and his master, the devil. As the Appeal warns, all will be "either with Christ or against Christ."

The Appeal should be read in the context of the interview the archbishop granted to the Portuguese website *Dies Iræ* and that appeared in English translation at *Inside the Vatican* two weeks prior to the Appeal's release. This interview was included in the previous part since its principal subject is Vatican II. Yet the "conspiracy" to suppress the warnings of Our Lady of Fatima contained in the third secret is connected to the conspiracy of the deep state and the deep church that he begins denouncing in May 2020. Fatima is a critical component in the connections that Viganò makes in these interventions among the New World Order, Chinese Communism, and the struggle to remove Donald Trump as an impediment to their plans, with which Bergoglio cooperates.

In his First Open Letter to Donald Trump, Viganò places the US President in this biblical struggle. He identifies Donald Trump as an ally in the confrontation with the two-headed monster. He notes: "as

---

the World was initially signed by four cardinals, eight bishops, three priests, twenty-one journalists, eleven medical doctors, thirteen lawyers, eighteen teachers and professionals, and twelve groups and associations. Cardinal Robert Sarah withdrew his signature after apparent coercion from the court of Bergoglio. The Appeal was a truly pastoral act to warn the Church and the world of the coming totalitarianism that made use of the alleged pandemic of COVID-19 as a pretext for seizing power. Although an appeal by several pastors and even civic leaders, it became clear in time that Archbishop Viganò was the moving force behind the text. As we have seen in Part II, Archbishop Viganò continued to connect the dots that led to Vatican II and unveiled the interdependence of the deep state and the deep church. The revolutionaries who attempted a "great reset" of the Church at Vatican II and those who seek another reset of civil politics and economics are two branches of the same enemy. The phenomenon of the virus from China on the occasion of which an attempt was made to shut down the entire planet unmasked the coordination of the deep state and the deep church.

there is a deep state, there is also a deep church that betrays its duties and forswears its proper commitments before God." Although they each use "different weapons," Viganò and Trump fight together against this unholy alliance. In his Second Open Letter to the President, Viganò identifies the specific principles which demonstrate that Trump, even if not yet a Catholic himself, is fighting on the side of the Church. He identifies Trump's position and actions on the following issues as in harmony with the Church's teaching: "the natural family, respect for human life, love of country, freedom of education and business." He also sees Donald Trump as a force opposed "to this suicide of Western culture and its Christian soul" advocated by the deep state and the deep church. Trump also opposes the denial of the "fundamental rights of citizens and believers . . . in the name of a health emergency that is revealing itself more and more fully as instrumental to the establishment of an inhuman faceless tyranny." In an interview with Francesco Boezi given a few months after the First Open Letter, Viganò lists specific actions of the President that prove he has been fighting on the side of the children of light against the deep state. Viganò explains:

> He has defended the life of the unborn, cutting funding from the abortion multinational, Planned Parenthood, and just in recent days he has issued an executive order that requires immediate care for newborns who are not killed by abortion: up until now they were allowed to die or they were exploited by harvesting their organs and selling them. Trump is fighting pedophilia and pedosatanism. He has not started any new war and he has drastically reduced the existing ones by obtaining peace agreements. He has restored God's right of citizenship, after Obama had even gone so far as to cancel Christmas and impose measures that were repugnant to the religious soul of Americans.

In the same interview a few months after his first Open Letter to Trump, Viganò told Boezi that everything he had said about Donald Trump's relationship to this biblical battle "can form an interpretive key to understanding the events that we are living through." This interpretation of the cosmic scale of events should not lead to despair; rather, it "remains an invitation to have hope." In this way

Viganò reminds us that the interpretive key drawn from the Bible informs us that we need not fear, because the same revelation infallibly assures us that Christ has already won the decisive battle for us. Although we know victory will be Christ's, in his First Open Letter Viganò warns Trump to expect the persecution and ridicule that are always inflicted upon those who fight on the side of the children of light. President Trump graciously accepted the support of the archbishop and sent out the Open Letter in a Tweet to his followers.

The archbishop's support for President Trump was disparaged by the deep state and those connected to it. A Dominican nun, Sister Antonietta Potente, wrote an open letter condemning Viganò's support for Trump, whose policies she castigated as supporting violence and discrimination. Viganò replied in an open letter to her by presenting facts. Trump's opposition to violence is proved most of all by his words and actions to curtail the unspeakable violence of abortion. He also points out that Trump is the only US President in modern history not to start new wars; rather he has ended them. As to discrimination, he points out that fidelity to the truth requires us to discriminate between truth and error, good and evil. He points out that her over-solicitous concern for the weak and the humble seems not to include the victims of abortion. The most powerful lines in Viganò's response demonstrate the way in which the deep church has infiltrated even the religious cloister, where too often the spirit of faith has been superseded by the spirit of the world:

> I fear that your words find too much space for the thinking of the world, rather than a supernatural vision supported by sound doctrine and fed by solid piety. In substance, the absence of an exterior and visible sign of your religious vows appears to me to reveal implicitly your desire to hide your religious identity (perhaps in order not to offend others' sensibilities?), with the risk however of leaving yourself in an interior void that no ideology of this world will be able to fill.

On the Feast of the Assumption, the archbishop replied publicly to a group of Italian mothers who were organizing a public protest against radical changes being made to the education of children in Italian schools. Their concerns encompassed both the subject of the state-mandated education, which was secular and radically leftist, and also the procedures for school in light of COVID-19 (isolation through social distancing and mandated vaccinations from tainted sources). The archbishop's response highlights a common cause between the Great Reset elites and Communism. Both seek to abolish the institution of the family as the indissoluble union of one man and one woman for the procreation and education of children. The deep state will allow the substitution of a mutation of the family to exist so as to deceive the masses that the family still exists, but it will not be the family as ordained by God. The archbishop details all the techniques of the deep state to undermine the family through the corruption of education. He exhorts the Italian mothers to fight to protect their children from a state that is attempting to harm children by mandating immoral vaccines, imposing socially harmful "distancing," and promoting immorality in school curricula. The archbishop explains:

> But there are other disturbing aspects now envisaged, which regard not only the content of instruction but also the method of participation in the lessons: social distancing, the use of masks, and other forms of presumed prevention of contagion in classrooms and school environments cause serious damage to the mental and physical equilibrium of children and young people, compromising their ability to learn and the interpersonal relations between pupils and teachers, and reducing them to automatons that are not only ordered what to think but also how to move and even how to breathe.

In this encouraging letter to Italian mothers, Viganò takes the opportunity to highlight another aspect of the deep state, one that has infected the deep church. He explains: "We should not lose sight of a fundamental element: the pursuit of ideologically perverse goals is invariably accompanied by an interest of an economic nature, like a parallel track." Relying upon an alliance between private profiteering and political ideology, the deep state system's infiltrators work with large private corporate interests to fund their takeover of government and, in exchange, enact policies that increase profits for their private sector partners. One of the examples Viganò cites is the vaccines for the pandemic. He notes that there is no money to be made if the disease runs its course and we develop a natural immunity. There are, however, vast sums to be made from the development and sale of vaccines. COVID-19 is a veritable gold mine for the pharmaceutical industry. He explains that we must simply look at unbridled self-interest to expose the goals of this unholy alliance between profit-seeking corporations and government. The archbishop asks the rhetorical question: "How can we think that the search for cures and therapies is being promoted in a disinterested way if those who finance the search profit disproportionately from the persistence of pathologies?" Viganò warns President Trump of this alliance of profit-seeking corporations and deep state actors in his Second Open Letter to the President. He notes the financial interest in promoting perpetual vaccinations for every new strain of COVID, which will play tidily into the deep state's desire to control people.

Unfortunately, as the archbishop tells Italian mothers, the deep church directed by Pope Francis has joined this unholy alliance and manipulates Catholic teaching to advance these profiteering ideologues. The Pontifical Academy of Life encourages use of vaccines derived from abortion. The Vatican shifts Catholic teaching away from condemning in definitive terms abortion and euthanasia and instead embraces the ideological agenda of the radical environmentalists:

> We remain bewildered, however, as we witness the silence of Rome, which appears to be more concerned with promoting recycling—to the point of writing an encyclical about it—than with the lives of the unborn, the health of the weakest, and the assistance of the terminally ill.

Archbishop Viganò identifies the Jesuits, formally known as the Society of Jesus, as the nexus that unites the deep state, corporate profiteers, and the deep church. So much culpability does he find in the modern Jesuits that he laments their reconstitution by Pius VII in 1814, after they had been suppressed as a religious institute by Pope Clement XIV. Viganò tells us that the Jesuits are the expression of that deplorable "adult Catholicism" that ignores the necessary consistency of Catholics in politics . . . but that holds together the heterogeneous bestiary of progressivism in the name of Malthusian[8] environmentalism, the indiscriminate welcome of immigrants, gender theory, and the religious indifferentism sanctioned by the Abu Dhabi Declaration.

The Jesuits are thus at the heart of transforming the institutions of the Church into spokesmen for the agenda of the enemies of the Church. Viganò explains that the Jesuit promotion of "adult Catholicism" is responsible for politicians like "Joe Biden, Nancy Pelosi, and Andrew Cuomo" becoming proud supporters of "abortion and gender indoctrination . . . [and the] Antifa and Black Lives Matter movements." Viganò claims that there is a "disturbing common thread" that connects Antifa and Black Lives Matter to the Jesuits and radical liberal politicians, namely, large donations from the same sources. As an example, he points to recent reports that the Jesuits in America "received grants of nearly two million dollars (over four years) from George Soros," who financially backs these other radical politicians and groups. This financial thread runs through the Jesuits all the way up to Bergoglio's Vatican apparatus. Viganò tells us that the 2018 secret agreement between the Holy See and the Chinese Communist regime "has been financed by large annual donations from Beijing to the Vatican coffers that are in a disastrous state." These vast sums of money to the Jesuits and the Vatican have resulted in the American Catholic Church coming out "in favor of the Democratic candidate and more generally in favor of the entire apparatus that has been consolidating in recent decades within the public administration." Viganò warns us in his article on the Jesuits:

> The deep state, Trump's sworn enemy, is joined by a deep church that spares no criticisms and accusations against the incumbent President while winking indecorously with Biden and BLM,

8. Thomas Malthus (1766–1834) advanced a hypothesis that the world's population was growing too rapidly to sustain itself and that we needed to actively manage a decline in population. His hypothesis, long since exploded, has been a driving force behind support for contraception, abortion, and euthanasia.

slavishly following the narration imposed by the mainstream. It matters little that Trump is openly pro-life and defends the non-negotiable principles that the Democrats have renounced—the important thing is to transform the Catholic Church into the spiritual arm of the New World Order, so as to have an *imprimatur* from the highest moral authority in the world.

At the heart of this capitulation to the deep state is the decades-long work of the Jesuits, who have violated their oath to defend the papacy. Instead, the Jesuits have paved the way for a deal whereby the Vatican endorses the ideology of the radical Left in exchange for money and the "honor" of becoming the spiritual arm of the New World Order.

In his September 14 interview with Marco Tosatti, Viganò extends his analysis of the formation of the deep state and deep church alliance beyond the Jesuits to the Second Vatican Council and its aftermath. The two causes are interrelated. The Jesuits prepared the Council in many ways by fostering Modernism. They also advanced its revolution through their embedded position within institutions of Catholic education. They educated generations of young people who later became the politicians who have betrayed their faith, such as Joe Biden, and the Catholic electorate that would support them. He explains:

> What I wish to emphasize is the close connection between the rebellion of the ultraprogressive clergy—with the Jesuits in the lead—and the education of generations of Catholics, who were formed according to the modernist ideology, flowing into the Council, which served as a premise not only for the '68 revolution in the political sphere, but also for the doctrinal and moral revolution in the ecclesial sphere. Without Vatican II, we would not have had the student revolution that radically changed life in the Western world, the vision of the family, the role of women, and the very concept of authority.

In this way "the deep state and deep church have clearly acted in concert, with the aim of scientifically destabilizing both the civil and ecclesiastical order."

Introduction to Part III

This extensive coordination between the deep state and the deep church has intersected in the vortex of Communist China. Viganò informs us that the Chinese Communists have emerged as the taskmasters of the deep state/deep church alliance epitomized by Joe Biden and Pope Francis. Viganò explains in the Tosatti interview: "The Chinese communist dictatorship is courted by both the deep state and the deep church: Joe Biden is as subservient to the economic and political interests of Beijing as Jorge Mario Bergoglio." The capitulation of the Vatican to the Chinese was also connected to the preparation by the Jesuits. Viganò recognizes the significance of "the active support carried out by the Jesuits, since the time when McCarrick went to China to prepare the famous agreement that would later be ratified by the Vatican under the Bergoglio pontificate."

In the interview with Scott Kesterson, Viganò reinforces his argument that the deep state acts in coordination with the deep church. They use the same techniques of blackmail and moral corruption. They pursue the same ends. He goes so far as to call the deep church the "Vatican branch" of the deep state. In this interview, he emphasizes that the coordination is rooted in a common leader of the two deep entities, who is none other than the enemy of the human race, Satan. He explains to Kesterson that this is the one he means when he refers to the "invisible enemy" in other texts. The invisible enemy is the devil, the true "power behind the throne" of the deep state and the deep church. It is interesting that following the First Open Letter to Donald Trump, President Trump repeatedly used this expression, the "Invisible Enemy." Sometimes it seemed that by this term the President meant the COVID virus or the Chinese Communists, but it is possible he attaches to it the same meaning as the archbishop.

As an antidote to this alliance among Communist China, the deep state (the Biden Democratic Party) and the deep church (Francis's Vatican), Viganò begins to introduce the reign of Christ the King. In the Tosatti interview, he identifies the rejection in the world today of the obligation of all people and nations to acknowledge Christ's reign, privately *and* publicly, as the heart of the doctrinal corruption engineered by the Jesuits and Vatican II.

Having warned the world about the great hoax of the COVID-19 "pandemic" that has been used by the deep state to advance its goals, Viganò draws our attention to the same technique in the US election. In his letter on Biden, COVID, and the USCCB, he identifies the central role played by the mainstream media in propagating the narrative that COVID requires the loss of liberty and that Joe Biden is the duly and legitimately elected president. In both cases, the media constructs a "grotesque castle of falsehoods to which the majority of the population conforms with resignation." By relentlessly pushing these narratives, the media acts as the fifth column of the Chinese Communist-backed deep state. Rather than proclaiming reality in contrast to the media fiction, the United States Conference of Catholic Bishops becomes the mouthpiece of that media, embracing and extending COVID restrictions and congratulating and celebrating Biden. Viganò notes that for the media and their sycophant allies in the USCCB, "reality no longer matters: it is absolutely irrelevant when it stands between the conceived plan and its realization. COVID and Biden are two holograms, two artificial creations, ready to be adapted time and time again to contingent needs or respectively replaced when necessary with COVID-21 and Kamala Harris." The deep church joins in the fiction of covering up election fraud because it has itself engaged in fraud to advance its takeover of the Catholic Church. Viganò compares the US 2020 presidential election to the 2013 conclave that elected Jorge Mario Bergoglio—an election he describes as "also not free from the shadow of fraud within the Conclave and . . . equally desired by the deep state, as we know clearly from the emails of John Podesta and the ties of Theodore McCarrick and his colleagues with the Democrats and with Biden himself," a set of collaborators he labels "a very nice little group of cronies, no doubt about it." In this comparison he alludes to the rumors that the ballot that elected Jorge Bergoglio was tainted with election irregularities that violated the number of ballots permitted to be taken in one day.

Viganò reminds us not to despair in the face of fraud and deception. He reminds us that truth exists in itself even if the masses are deceived by the fiction of the media. After light is shone on their tower of lies, the truth will remain.

This Part III concludes with three documents that tie together all

Introduction to Part III

of the themes of this part (the Great Reset, the COVID pretext, and the US presidential election fraud). The Meditation on the Great Reset places the current situation in a longer historical context of revolutions. Viganò explains: "The French Revolution wiped out the Western aristocracy. The Industrial Revolution obliterated the peasants and spread the proletarianization which led to the disaster of Socialism and Communism. The Revolution of '68 demolished the family and the school." He then explains the goal of the current revolution:

> This Great Reset, desired by the globalist elite, represents the final revolution with which to create a shapeless and anonymous mass of slaves connected to the internet, confined to the house, threatened by an endless series of pandemics designed by those who already have the miraculous vaccine ready.

In the intervention which the archbishop entitles "Den of Thieves," he underscores the conclusion that the deep church and deep state are fused into a single army under the direction of the great enemy of mankind:

> I believe it is now understood beyond all reasonable doubt that the leaders of the present Catholic hierarchy have placed themselves at the service of the globalist oligarchy and Freemasonry: the idolatrous cult of the Pachamama in the Vatican Basilica is now joined by a sacrilegious Nativity scene, whose symbology appears to allude to ancient Egyptian rites as well as aliens. Only a naive person or an accomplice can deny that in this whole chain of events there is a very clear ideological coherence and a lucid diabolical mind.

Finally, in his New Year's Day interview with Steve Bannon, Viganò reminds us that behind the deep state and the deep church is the Chinese Communist Party, which is exploiting every opportunity that Joe Biden, COVID, and Bergoglio present to increase its totalitarian grasp on power. It exploits all of these to increase China's economic power and to destroy religion, and in particular the Catholic Church, in China. Bergoglio and Biden are twin pawns of the Chinese Communists.

291

Archbishop Viganò nevertheless reminds us, once again, to have hope. We must not despair, for despair strengthens the enemy, who conquers one soul at a time. All is not lost. There is a path out of the grip of the deep state and the deep church. He provides a three-point plan of escape:

1) First of all, becoming aware of what globalism's plan is, and to what extent it is instrumental to the establishment of the kingdom of the Antichrist, since it shares its principles, means, and ends;

2) secondly, firmly denouncing this infernal plan and asking the Shepherds of the Church—and also the laity—to defend her, breaking their complicit silence: God will demand of them an account for their desertion;

3) finally, it is necessary to pray, asking the Lord to grant each one of us the strength to resist—*resistite fortes in fide*, Saint Peter warns us (1 Pet 5:9)—against the ideological tyranny that is daily imposed on us not only by the media but also by the cardinals and bishops who are under Bergoglio's thumb.

The plan to bring down the deep church and the deep state is simple: be aware, denounce the infernal plan, and pray. The third of these three is the ultimate weapon that eludes deep state and deep church actors who place their hope not in Our Blessed Lady and Our Sovereign Lord but in their own finite and fallible powers. They will be defeated and the reign of Christ the King will be established anew.

23

Appeal for the Church and the World[1]

To Catholics and all people of good will
Veritas liberabit vos [The truth shall make you free]
(Jn 8:32)

IN this time of great crisis, we Pastors of the Catholic Church, by virtue of our mandate, consider it our sacred duty to make an Appeal to our Brothers in the Episcopate, to the Clergy, to Religious, to the holy People of God and to all men and women of good will. This Appeal has also been undersigned by intellectuals, doctors, lawyers, journalists and professionals who agree with its content, and may be undersigned by those who wish to make it their own.

The facts have shown that, under the pretext of the COVID-19 epidemic, the inalienable rights of citizens have in many cases been violated and their fundamental freedoms, including the exercise of freedom of worship, expression and movement, have been disproportionately and unjustifiably restricted. Public health must not, and cannot, become an alibi for infringing on the rights of millions of people around the world, let alone depriving the civil authority of its duty to act wisely for the common good. This is particularly true as growing doubts emerge from several quarters about the actual contagiousness, danger and resistance of the virus. Many authoritative voices in the world of science and medicine confirm that the media's alarmism about COVID-19 appears to be absolutely unjustified.

1. This Appeal with its accompanying petition was originally published on http://veritasliberabitvos.info/sign-the-appeal, but the entire site seems to have vanished. This text is taken from the reproduction of the appeal by *LifeSiteNews* at www.lifesitenews.com/news/four-cardinals-join-global-appeal-decrying-crackdown-on-basic-freedoms-over-coronavirus.

We have reason to believe, on the basis of official data on the incidence of the epidemic as related to the number of deaths, that there are powers interested in creating panic among the world's population with the sole aim of permanently imposing unacceptable forms of restriction on freedoms, of controlling people and of tracking their movements. The imposition of these illiberal measures is a disturbing prelude to the realization of a world government beyond all control.

We also believe that in some situations the containment measures that were adopted, including the closure of shops and businesses, have precipitated a crisis that has brought down entire sectors of the economy. This encourages interference by foreign powers and has serious social and political repercussions. Those with governmental responsibility must stop these forms of social engineering, by taking measures to protect their citizens whom they represent, and in whose interests they have a serious obligation to act. Likewise, let them help the family, the cell of society, by not unreasonably penalizing the weak and elderly, forcing them into a painful separation from their loved ones. The criminalization of personal and social relationships must likewise be judged as an unacceptable part of the plan of those who advocate isolating individuals in order to better manipulate and control them.

We ask the scientific community to be vigilant, so that cures for COVID-19 are offered in honesty for the common good. Every effort must be made to ensure that shady business interests do not influence the choices made by government leaders and international bodies. It is unreasonable to penalize those remedies that have proved to be effective, and are often inexpensive, just because one wishes to give priority to treatments or vaccines that are not as good, but which guarantee pharmaceutical companies far greater profits, and exacerbate public health expenditures. Let us also remember, as Pastors, that for Catholics it is morally unacceptable to develop or use vaccines derived from material from aborted fetuses.

We also ask government leaders to ensure that forms of control over people, whether through tracking systems or any other form of location-finding, are rigorously avoided. The fight against COVID-19, however serious, must not be the pretext for supporting the hidden intentions of supranational bodies that have very strong commercial and political interests in this plan. In particular, citizens must be given the opportunity to refuse these restrictions on personal freedom, without any penalty whatsoever being imposed on those who do not wish to use vaccines, contact tracking or any other similar tool. Let us also consider the blatant contradiction of those who pursue policies of drastic population control and at the same time present themselves as the savior of humanity, without any political or social legitimacy. Finally, the political responsibility of those who represent the people can in no way be left to "experts" who can indeed claim a kind of immunity from prosecution, which is disturbing to say the least.

We strongly urge those in the media to commit themselves to providing accurate information and not penalizing dissent by resorting to forms of censorship, as is happening widely on social media, in the press and on television. Providing accurate information requires that room be given to voices that are not aligned with a single way of thinking. This allows citizens to consciously assess the facts, without being heavily influenced by partisan interventions. A democratic and honest debate is the best antidote to the risk of imposing subtle forms of dictatorship, presumably worse than those our society has seen rise and fall in the recent past.

Finally, as Pastors responsible for the flock of Christ, let us remember that the Church firmly asserts her autonomy to govern, worship, and teach. This autonomy and freedom are an innate right that Our Lord Jesus Christ has given her for the pursuit of her proper ends. For this reason, as Pastors we firmly assert the right to decide autonomously on the celebration of Mass and the sacraments, just as we claim absolute autonomy in matters falling within our immediate jurisdiction, such as liturgical norms and ways of administering Communion and the sacraments. The State has no right to interfere, for any reason whatsoever, in the sovereignty of the Church. Ecclesiastical authorities have never refused to collaborate with the State, but such collaboration does not authorize civil authorities to impose any sort of ban or restriction on public worship or the exercise of priestly ministry. *The rights of God and of the faithful are the supreme law of the Church,* which she neither intends to, nor can, abdicate. We ask that restrictions on the celebration of public ceremonies be removed.

We should like to invite all people of good will not to shirk their duty to cooperate for the common good, each according to his or her own state and possibilities and in a spirit of fraternal charity. The Church desires such cooperation, but this cannot disregard either a respect for natural law or a guarantee of individual freedoms. The civil duties to which citizens are bound imply the State's recognition of their rights.

We are all called to assess the current situation in a way consistent with the teaching of the Gospel. This means taking a stand: either with Christ or against Christ. Let us not be intimidated or frightened by those who would have us believe that we are a minority: Good is much more widespread and powerful than the world would have us believe. We are fighting against an invisible enemy that seeks to divide citizens, to separate children from their parents, grandchildren from their grandparents, the faithful from their pastors, students from teachers, and customers from vendors. Let us not allow centuries of Christian civilization to be erased under the pretext of a virus, and an odious technological tyranny to be established, in which nameless and faceless people can decide the fate of the world by confining us to a virtual reality. If this is the plan to which the powers of this earth intend to make us yield, know that Jesus Christ, King and Lord of history, has promised that "the gates of Hell shall not prevail" (Mt 16:18).

Let us entrust government leaders and all those who rule over the fate of nations to Almighty God, that He may enlighten and guide them in this time of great crisis. May they remember that, just as the Lord will judge us Pastors for the flock which he has entrusted to us, so will He also judge government leaders for the peoples whom they have the duty to defend and govern.

With faith, let us beseech the Lord to protect the Church and the world. May the Blessed Virgin, Help of Christians, crush the head of the ancient Serpent and defeat the plans of the children of darkness.

8 May 2020
Our Lady of the Rosary of Pompei

24

Letter to Cloistered Religious Sister[1]

May 29, 2020

DEAR Sister,

Thank you very much for your letter, which I read attentively. I fully share your clear and realistic vision of the present situation of crisis that involves the Church and the world.

With a supernatural gaze, corroborated by Sacred Scripture and various messages of Our Lady, we can understand that in this moment we can now see with greater clarity the real dimension of the epochal clash between Good and Evil, between the sons of Light and the sons of Darkness. What leaves one truly scandalized is seeing how the top levels of the hierarchy are openly placing themselves at the service of the Prince of this world, adopting the demands made by the United Nations for the globalist agenda, Masonic brotherhood, Malthusian ecologism, immigrationism... What is being created is a single world religion without dogmas or morals, according to the wishes of Freemasonry... It is obvious that Bergoglio, along with those who are behind him and support him, aspires to preside over this infernal parody of the Church of Christ.

I am sure that you have also noticed, dear Sister, the insistence of so many prelates and of Catholic media on the presumed necessity of a New World Order: cardinals and bishops have spoken about it, as well as *La Civiltà Cattolica*, Vatican News, *Avvenire*, and *L'Osservatore Romano*, with the arrogance of those who are able to say things that were once unheard of [in Catholic circles] thanks to the

---

1. This letter first appeared at www.marcotosatti.com/2020/05/31/a-cloistered-sister-writes-to-vigano-the-two-letters. The website also contains the letters to which Viganò is responding.

protection they enjoy [from the leadership of the hierarchy]. But on closer look, the ability of the wicked to move and act, to conceal their intentions, is much less than first thought: they are so certain of having already reached their objective that they have openly revealed their intentions with arrogance and ostentation, laying aside the prudence and astuteness that formerly permitted them to remain hidden. Behold how openly the proponents of world government and the élites who want to impose their tyranny on the peoples may now be seen; behold how, along with them, a neo-paganism is also openly revealing itself as the religious arm of this tyranny, defined by some as green apostasy. We know who they are, what motivates their actions and what their goals are: behind them there is always the Prince of this world, against whom the Queen of Victories leads our battered militias, together with the far greater and terrible army of celestial hosts. But since we have already chosen what side we are on in the field of battle, we must not fear, because Our Lord has already conquered, while he offers us the precious opportunity to weave for ourselves an especially glorious crown in these apocalyptic days.

I believe that the essential point for effectively conducting a spiritual, doctrinal and moral battle against the enemies of the Church is the persuasion that the present crisis is the metastasis of the conciliar cancer: If we have not understood the causal relationship between Vatican II and its logical and necessary consequences over the course of the last sixty years, it will not be possible to steer the rudder of the Church back to the direction given it by her Divine Helmsman, the course that it maintained for two thousand years. For decades they catechized us with the hateful phrase "there is no going back" with regard to the liturgy, the Faith, moral teaching, penance, asceticism. Today we hear the same expressions slavishly repeated in the civil sphere, through which the attempt is made to indoctrinate the masses that "nothing will be as it was before." Modernism and COVID-19 are part of the same brand, and for anyone who has their gaze towards the transcendent it is not difficult to understand that the greatest fear of those who want us to believe that the race towards the abyss is both unavoidable and unstoppable is that we will not believe them; we will ignore them and unmask their conspiracy. This is our duty, today: to open the eyes of many people, both clergy and religious, who have not yet put together the overall picture, limiting themselves to looking at reality only in a partial and disjointed way. As soon as we have helped them to understand the mechanism, they will understand everything else.

It is possible to go back, dear Sister, it is possible to do so in such a way that the good that was fraudulently taken from us may be restored: but only in the coherence of doctrine, without compromises, without yielding, without opportunism. The Lord will deign to grant us a share in his victory, even if we are weak and without material means, only if we will abandon ourselves totally to him and to his Most Holy Mother.

I entrust myself to your prayers and to the prayers of your fellow Sisters, and I bless you and your entire community from my heart.

✠ Carlo Maria Viganò, Archbishop

25

Letter to Mothers: Against Globalist Dictatorship[1]

August 15, 2020

DEAR Sirs and Dearest Mothers,

I have received your kind email, in which you inform me of the initiative you have scheduled for this coming September 5 for the protection of the physical, moral, and spiritual health of your children. In responding to you, I address all the mothers of Italy.

The demonstration you are promoting intends to express the dissent of citizens and in particular of parents against the norms that the government, abusing its power, is preparing to issue in view of the new school year; norms that will have very grave repercussions on the health and psychosomatic equilibrium of students, as authoritative experts have rightly demonstrated.

First of all, the systematic effort to demolish the family, the foundation of society, must be denounced, with the multiplication of ferocious attacks not only against conjugal life, which Christ has elevated to a sacrament, but also against its natural essence, against the fact that marriage is by nature constituted between a man and a woman in an indissoluble bond of fidelity and reciprocal assistance. The presence of a father and a mother is fundamental in the upbringing of children, who need a male and female figure as a reference for their integral and harmonious development; nor can it be permitted that children, during the most delicate phase of their infancy and adolescence, be used to advance partisan ideological claims, with serious damage for their psychosomatic equilibrium,

1. Originally published at www.marcotosatti.com/2020/08/24/vigano-to-mothers-save-your-children-from-globalist-dictatorship.

by those who with their own rebellious behavior reject the very idea of nature. You can easily understand the impact of the destruction of the family on the civil consortium: today we have right before our eyes the results of decades of unfortunate policies that inevitably lead to the dissolution of society.

These policies, inspired by principles that are repugnant both to the law of nature inscribed in man by the Creator as well as to the positive law of God given in the Commandments, combine to permit children to be placed at the mercy of the whims of individuals, and the sacredness of life and conception to become objects of commerce, humiliating motherhood and the dignity of woman. Sons cannot be bred by mares for a fee, because they are the fruit of a love that Providence has ordained must always be an enduring love, even in the natural order.

Parents have the responsibility, as a primary and inalienable right, to educate their children: the State cannot arrogate this right, much less corrupt children and indoctrinate them in the perverse principles that are so widespread today. Do not forget, dear mothers, that this is the distinctive sign of totalitarian regimes, not of a civil and Christian nation. It is your duty to raise your voice so that these attempts to steal the education of your children may be denounced and rejected with force, because you will be able to do very little for them if your faith, ideas, and culture are judged incompatible with those of an impious and materialistic state. And it is not just a matter of imposing a vaccine on your children and teenagers, but also of corrupting their souls with perverse doctrines, with gender ideology, with the acceptance of vice and the practice of sinful behaviors. No law can ever legitimately make the affirmation of the truth a crime, because the authority of the law ultimately comes from God, who is himself the highest Truth. The heroic testimony of the martyrs and saints responded to the oppression of tyrants: may you too today be courageous witnesses of Christ against a world that would like to subject us to the unleashed forces of hell!

Another crucial aspect in this battle for the family is the defense of life from conception to natural death. The crime of abortion, which has claimed millions of innocent victims and which cries out for vengeance from heaven, is today considered as a normal health service, and just in recent days the Italian government has authorized the more widespread use of the abortion pill, encouraging an abominable crime and keeping silent about the terrible consequences on the psychological and physical health of the mother. If you think about how during the lockdown all care of the sick was suspended and yet abortions continued, you can understand what the priorities of those who govern us are: *the culture of death!* What progress can be invoked when society kills its own children, when motherhood is horribly violated in the name of a choice that cannot be free, since it involves the ending of an innocent life and violates one of God's Commandments? What prosperity can our country expect, what blessings from God can it hope for, if human sacrifices are being made in our clinics just as in the times of the most bloody barbarism?

The idea that children are the property of the state repulses every human person. In the Christian social order, the civil authority exercises its power to guarantee its citizens that the natural well-being is ordered towards the spiritual good. The common good pursued by the state in temporal things therefore has a well-defined object that cannot and must not be in conflict with the Law of God, the Supreme Legislator. Every time that the State infringes on this eternal and immutable Law, its authority is diminished, and its citizens ought to refuse to obey it. This certainly applies to the hateful law on abortion, but it should also be applied to other cases, in which the abuse of authority regards the imposition of vaccines the danger of which is unknown or the composition of which is ethically problematic. I am referring to the case in which a vaccine would contain fetal material coming from the bodies of aborted children.

But there are other disturbing aspects now envisaged, which regard not only the content of instruction but also the method of participation in the lessons: social distancing, the use of masks, and other forms of presumed prevention of contagion in classrooms and school environments cause serious damage to the mental and physical equilibrium of children and young people, compromising their ability to learn and the interpersonal relations between pupils and teachers, and reducing them to automatons that are not only ordered what to think but also how to move and even how to breathe. It seems that the very notion of common sense that ought to govern choices fraught with consequences in social life has been lost, and it seems that an inhumane world is being heralded in which parents have their children taken away from them if they test positive for an influenza virus, with mandatory health treatment protocols applied as in the most ferocious dictatorships.

It is also very perplexing to learn that the WHO has chosen Mario Monti as the President of the European Commission for Health and Development, who has distinguished himself by draconian measures imposed on Italy, among which, it must not be forgotten, is the drastic reduction of public appropriations for hospitals. These perplexities are confirmed by Monti's membership in supranational organisms like the Trilateral Commission and the Bilderberg Club,[2] whose aims are in clear contrast to the inalienable values protected by the Italian Constitution itself, which are binding on the Government. This mixing of private interests in public affairs, inspired by the dictates of Masonic and globalist thought, should be vigorously denounced by those who are representatives of the citizens, and by those who see their legitimate powers usurped by an elite that has never made a mystery of its true intentions.

We should not lose sight of a fundamental element: the pursuit of ideologically perverse goals is invariably accompanied by an interest of an economic nature, like a parallel track. It is easy to agree on the fact that there is no profit in the voluntary donation of umbilical cords, just as there is no profit in the donation of hyper-immune plasma for the treatment of COVID. Conversely, it is extremely profitable for abortion clinics to provide fetal tissue and for pharmaceutical companies to produce monoclonal antibodies or artificial plasma. Thus it is not surprising that, following a logic of mere profit, the most reasonable and ethically sustainable solutions are

---

2. The Bilderberg Club is a secretive meeting (by invitation only) of globalist leaders that occurs each year. All meetings are held in strict confidence, although the list of attendees is published. The meeting is understood to be a planning session for advancing the globalist New World Order in a coordinated manner among leaders.

the object of a deliberate campaign to discredit them: we have heard self-styled experts make themselves promoters of cures offered by companies in which they themselves—in a clear conflict of interest—hold shares or are well paid consultants.

Having said this, it is necessary to understand whether the solution of a vaccine is always and everywhere the best health response to a virus. In the case of COVID, for example, many exponents of the scientific community agree in affirming that it is more useful to develop a natural immunity rather than inoculate the depowered virus. But also in this case, as we know, herd immunity is attained without any costs, while vaccination campaigns involve enormous investments and guarantee equally large profits for those who patent and produce them. And it should also be verified—but in this the experts will certainly be able to speak with greater confidence—whether it is possible to produce a vaccine for a virus that does not yet seem to have been isolated according to the protocols of science-based medicine, and what potential consequences may come from using newly generated genetically modified vaccines.

The world health industry, led by the WHO, has become a true multinational corporation that has as its primary end the profit of shareholders (pharmaceutical companies and so-called philanthropic foundations), and its means of pursuing it is the transformation of citizens into chronically ill people. And it is obvious: the pharmaceutical companies want to make money by selling drugs and vaccines; if eliminating diseases and producing effective drugs leads to a reduction in the number of sick people and thus of profits, it will only be logical to expect that the drugs they make will be ineffective and that the vaccines they promote will be the instrument of spreading diseases rather than eradicating them. And this is precisely what is happening. How can we think that the search for cures and therapies is being promoted in a disinterested way if those who finance the search profit disproportionately from the persistence of pathologies?

It may seem difficult to persuade ourselves that those who ought to be protecting health instead wish to ensure the continuation of illnesses: such cynicism repulses—and rightly so—those who are strangers to the mentality that has been established in healthcare.

Letter to Mothers: Against Globalist Dictatorship

And yet this is what is happening right under our eyes, and it involves not only the emergence of COVID and vaccines—in particular anti-influenza vaccines, which were widely distributed in 2019 right in those areas where COVID has had the highest number of victims [in 2020]—but all treatments and therapies, as well as childbirth and care for the sick. Such cynicism, which is repugnant to the ethical code, sees in each of us a potential source of profit, while instead what should be seen in every patient is the face of the suffering Christ. We therefore appeal to the many, many Catholic doctors and all doctors of good will, asking you not to betray the Hippocratic oath and the very heart of your profession, which is mercy and compassion, love for those who suffer, and selfless service to the weakest among us, recalling the words of Our Lord: "As often as you did these things for the least of my brothers, you did it for me" (Mt 25:40).

The Catholic Church, especially in recent decades, has intervened authoritatively in this debate, thanks also to the Pontifical Academy for Life founded by John Paul II. Its members, up until a few years ago, gave medical-scientific directives that did not conflict with the inviolable moral principles of any Catholic person.

But just as in civil society we have witnessed a progressive loss of responsibility of individuals as well as those who govern in the various spheres of public life, including health care, so also in the "Church of Mercy" that was born in 2013 it is preferred to adapt the commitment of the Pontifical Dicasteries and the Academy for Life to a *liquid* vision—and I dare say a perverse vision because it denies the truth—which embraces the demands of environmentalism with connotations of Malthusianism. The fight against abortion, which opposes the reduction of births desired by the New World Order, is no longer the priority of many pastors. During the various pro-life demonstrations—such as those held in Rome in recent years—the silence and absence of the Holy See and the hierarchy has been shameful!

Obviously the moral principles which form the basis for norms to be adopted in the medical field remain perennially valid, nor could it be otherwise. The Church is the guardian of the teaching of Christ and she has no authority to modify or adapt it to her own

305

liking. We remain bewildered, however, as we witness the silence of Rome, which appears to be more concerned with promoting recycling—to the point of writing an encyclical about it—than with the lives of the unborn, the health of the weakest, and the assistance of the terminally ill. This is only one aspect of a much wider problem, a much greater crisis, which as I have said many times stems from the moment in which the deviant part of the Church, led by what was once the Society of Jesus, seized power and made her a slave to the mentality of the world.

When we consider the new orientation of the Pontifical Academy for Life (whose presidency has been entrusted to a person who is well-known for having shown the best of himself when he was bishop of Terni), we cannot expect any condemnation of those who use fetal tissue from voluntarily aborted children. Its present members hope for mass vaccination and the universal brotherhood of the New World Order, contradicting previous pronouncements of the same Pontifical Academy.[3] In recent days the Bishops' Conference of England and Wales[4] has entered this anomalous wave. On the one hand it recognizes that "The Church is opposed to the production of vaccines using tissue derived from aborted fetuses, and we acknowledge the distress many Catholics experience when faced with a choice of not vaccinating their child or seeming to be complicit in abortion," but it then affirms, in very grave contradiction with the stated unchanging principles of Catholic morality,[5] that "the Church teaches that the paramount importance of the health of a child and other vulnerable persons could permit parents to use a vaccine which was in the past developed using these diploid cell lines." This statement lacks any doctrinal authority and instead

---

3. VN: See Pontifical Academy for Life, *Note on the Nature of Vaccination*, July 31, 2017, www.academyforlife.va/content/pav/en/the-academy/activity-academy/note-vaccini.html.

4. VN: See Bishops' Conference of England and Wales, *The Catholic Position on Vaccination*, www.cbcew.org.uk/wp-content/uploads/sites/3/2020/03/catholic-position-on-vaccination-110820.pdf.

5. VN: See Pontifical Academy for Life, *Moral Reflections on Vaccines Prepared from Cells Derived from Human Fetuses*, June 5, 2005, www.immunize.org/talking-about-vaccines/vaticandocument.htm.

aligns itself with the dominant ideology promoted by the WHO, its principal sponsor Bill Gates, and pharmaceutical companies.

From a moral point of view, for every Catholic who intends to remain faithful to his or her Baptism, it is absolutely inadmissible to accept a vaccination that utilizes material coming from human fetuses in its process of production. This has also been restated authoritatively recently by the American Bishop Joseph E. Strickland in his April 27 Pastoral Letter[6] and in his August 1 tweet.[7]

We must therefore pray to the Lord, asking him to give Pastors a voice, in such a way as to create a united front that opposes the excessive power of the globalist elite which would like to subjugate us all. It should be recalled that while the pharmaceutical companies are proceeding on the plane of economic interests only, there are people operating on the ideological plane who, using the opportunity of the vaccine, would also like to implant devices for identifying people, and that these nanotechnologies—I am referring to project ID2020, "quantum dots" and other similar initiatives—are being patented by the same individuals who patented the virus as well as its vaccine. Furthermore, a cryptocurrency project has been patented to allow not only health identification but also personal and banking information to be monitored, in a delirium of omnipotence that up until yesterday could have been dismissed as the ranting of conspiracy theorists, but that today has already been initiated in several countries, including for example Sweden and Germany. We see the words of Saint John taking shape right before our eyes: "It forced all the people, small and great, rich and poor, free and slave, to be given a mark on the right hand and the forehead; so that no one could buy or sell without having the mark" (Rev 13:16–17).

---

6. VN: Bishop Joseph E. Strickland, *Pastoral Letter from Bishop Joseph E. Strickland on the Ethical Development of COVID-19 Vaccine*, April 23, 2020, https://stphilipinstitute.org/2020/04/27/pastoral-letter-from-bishop-joseph-e-strickland-on-the-ethical-development-of-covid-19-vaccine.

7. VN: Tweet of August 1, 2020: "I renew my call that we reject any vaccine that is developed using aborted children. Even if it originated decades ago, it still means a child's life was ended before it was born & then their body was used as spare parts. We will never end abortion if we do not END THIS EVIL!", https://twitter.com/bishopoftyler/status/1289613264125485057.

Given the gravity of the situation, we must also speak out with regard to these aspects: we cannot remain silent if the public authority would make vaccines obligatory that pose serious ethical and moral problems, or that more prosaically do not give any guarantee of obtaining the promised effects and that are limited to promising benefits that from a scientific point of view are absolutely questionable. May the pastors of the Church finally raise their voice to defend the flock entrusted to their care in this systematic attack against God and man!

Do not forget, dear Mothers, that *this is a spiritual battle*—even a war—in which powers that no one has ever elected and that do not have any authority other than that of force and the violent imposition of their own will seek to demolish all that evokes, even only remotely, the divine Paternity of God over His children, the Kingship of Christ over society and the Virginal Motherhood of Mary Most Holy. This is why they hate to mention the words "father" and "mother"; this is why they want an irreligious society that is rebellious against the Law of God; this is why they promote vice and detest virtue. This is also why they want to corrupt children and young people, securing hosts of obedient servants for the foreseeable future in which the name of God is being cancelled and the Redemptive Sacrifice of his Son on the Cross is blasphemed; a Cross that they want to banish because it reminds man that the purpose of his life is the glory of God, obedience to His Commandments and the exercise of Christian charity: not pleasure, self-exaltation, or the arrogant overpowering of the weak.

The innocence of children and their trusting recourse to Mary Most Holy, our Heavenly Mother, can truly save the world: for this reason the Enemy aims to corrupt them in order to distance them from the Lord and to sow the seed of evil and sin in them.

Dear mothers, never fail in your duty to protect your children not only in the material order but also, even more importantly, in the spiritual order. Cultivate in them the life of grace, with constant prayer, especially through the recitation of the Holy Rosary, with penance and fasting, with the practice of the corporal and spiritual works of mercy, assiduously and devotedly frequenting the sacraments and Holy Mass. Nourish them with the Bread of Angels, the true food of eternal life and our defense from the assaults of the Evil One. Tomorrow, they will be honest citizens, responsible parents, and protagonists of the restoration of the Christian society that the world would like to cancel. And please also pray, dear mothers, because prayer is a truly fearful weapon and an infallible *vaccine* against the perverse dictatorship that is about to be imposed on us.

I take this occasion to assure you of my prayer and to impart my Blessing to all of you: to you, dear mothers, and to your children, and to all those who are fighting to save our children and each one of us from this ferocious global tyranny that is striking our beloved Italy.

☩ Carlo Maria Viganò, Archbishop

26

First Open Letter to President Donald J. Trump

June 7, 2020

MR. President,

In recent months we have been witnessing the formation of two opposing sides that I would call biblical: the children of light and the children of darkness. The children of light constitute the most conspicuous part of humanity, while the children of darkness represent an absolute minority. And yet the former are the object of a sort of discrimination which places them in a situation of moral inferiority with respect to their adversaries, who often hold strategic positions in government, in politics, in the economy and in the media. In an apparently inexplicable way, the good are held hostage by the wicked and by those who help them either out of self-interest or fearfulness.

These two sides, which have a biblical nature, follow the clear separation between the offspring of the Woman and the offspring of the Serpent. On the one hand there are those who, although they have a thousand defects and weaknesses, are motivated by the desire to do good, to be honest, to raise a family, to engage in work, to give prosperity to their homeland, to help the needy, and, in obedience to the Law of God, to merit the Kingdom of Heaven. On the other hand, there are those who serve themselves, who do not hold any moral principles, who want to demolish the family and the nation, exploit workers to make themselves unduly wealthy, foment internal divisions and wars, and accumulate power and money: for them the fallacious illusion of temporal well-being will one day—if they do not repent—yield to the terrible fate that awaits them, far from God, in eternal damnation.

First Open Letter to President Donald J. Trump

In society, Mr. President, these two opposing realities coexist as eternal enemies, just as God and Satan are eternal enemies. And it appears that the children of darkness—whom we may easily identify with the deep state which you wisely oppose and which is fiercely waging war against you in these days—have decided to show their cards, so to speak, by now revealing their plans. They seem to be so certain of already having everything under control that they have laid aside that circumspection that until now had at least partially concealed their true intentions. The investigations already under way will reveal the true responsibility of those who managed the COVID emergency not only in the area of health care but also in politics, the economy, and the media. We will probably find that in this colossal operation of social engineering there are people who have decided the fate of humanity, arrogating to themselves the right to act against the will of citizens and their representatives in the governments of nations.

We will also discover that the riots in these days were provoked by those who, seeing that the virus is inevitably fading and that the social alarm of the pandemic is waning, necessarily have had to provoke civil disturbances, because they would be followed by repression which, although legitimate, could be condemned as an unjustified aggression against the population. The same thing is also happening in Europe, in perfect synchrony. It is quite clear that the use of street protests is instrumental to the purposes of those who would like to see someone elected in the upcoming presidential elections who embodies the goals of the deep state and who expresses those goals faithfully and with conviction. It will not be surprising if, in a few months, we learn once again that hidden behind these acts of vandalism and violence there are those who hope to profit from the dissolution of the social order so as to build a world without freedom: *Solve et Coagula*,[1] as the Masonic adage teaches.

Although it may seem disconcerting, the opposing alignments I

---

1. Latin for "dissolve and recompose." This was an aphorism of medieval alchemists who strove to manipulate nature and to turn one substance into another through dark arts.

311

have described are also found in religious circles. There are faithful Shepherds who care for the flock of Christ, but there are also mercenary infidels who seek to scatter the flock and hand the sheep over to be devoured by ravenous wolves. It is not surprising that these mercenaries are allies of the children of darkness and hate the children of light: just as there is a deep state, there is also a deep church that betrays its duties and forswears its proper commitments before God. Thus the Invisible Enemy, whom good rulers fight against in public affairs, is also fought against by good shepherds in the ecclesiastical sphere. It is a spiritual battle, which I spoke about in my recent Appeal which was published on May 8.

For the first time, the United States has in you a President who courageously defends the right to life, who is not ashamed to denounce the persecution of Christians throughout the world, who speaks of Jesus Christ and the right of citizens to freedom of worship. Your participation in the March for Life, and more recently your proclamation of the month of April as National Child Abuse Prevention Month, are actions that confirm which side you wish to fight on. And I dare to believe that both of us are on the same side in this battle, albeit with different weapons.

For this reason, I believe that the attack to which you were subjected after your visit to the National Shrine of Saint John Paul II[2] is part of the orchestrated media narrative which seeks not to fight racism and bring social order, but to aggravate dispositions; not to bring justice, but to legitimize violence and crime; not to serve the truth, but to favor one political faction. And it is disconcerting that there are bishops—such as those whom I recently denounced—who, by their words, prove that they are aligned on the opposing side. They are subservient to the deep state, to globalism, to aligned thought, to the New World Order which they invoke ever more frequently in the name of a universal brotherhood which has nothing Christian about it, but which evokes the Masonic ideals of those

2. On June 2, 2020, President Trump paid a visit to the John Paul II shrine in Washington, D.C., operated by the Knights of Columbus. Immediately following the visit, Wilton Gregory, the successor of Donald Wuerl and Theodore McCarrick, condemned the visit and the Knights of Columbus who permitted it.

who want to dominate the world by driving God out of the courts, out of schools, out of families, and perhaps even out of churches.

The American people are mature and have now understood how much the mainstream media does not want to spread the truth but seeks to silence and distort it, spreading the lie that is useful for the purposes of their masters. However, it is important that the good—who are the majority—wake up from their sluggishness and do not accept being deceived by a minority of dishonest people with unavowable purposes. It is necessary that the good, the children of light, come together and make their voices heard. What more effective way is there to do this, Mr. President, than by prayer, asking the Lord to protect you, the United States, and all of humanity from this enormous attack of the Enemy? Before the power of prayer, the deceptions of the children of darkness will collapse, their plots will be revealed, their betrayal will be shown, their frightening power will end in nothing, brought to light and exposed for what it is: an infernal deception.

Mr. President, my prayer is constantly turned to the beloved American nation, where I had the privilege and honor of being sent by Pope Benedict XVI as Apostolic Nuncio. In this dramatic and decisive hour for all of humanity, I am praying for you and also for all those who are at your side in the government of the United States. I trust that the American people are united with me and you in prayer to Almighty God.

United against the Invisible Enemy of all humanity, I bless you and the First Lady, the beloved American nation, and all men and women of good will.

✠ Carlo Maria Viganò, Archbishop

27

Letter Replying
to a Nun about Trump[1]

July 6, 2020

Noli æmulari in malignantibus, neque zelaveris facientes iniquitatem.
Ps 36:1 [Do not be provoked by evildoers; do not envy those who
do wrong.]

REVEREND Mother,

I have read the open letter that you sent to me last June 17, also on
behalf of your community, a letter that you wrote following the letter that I sent to the President of the United States. Since you
address yourself personally to me, I ask you to give me space on
your site to respond to you.

I remain bewildered by several expressions in your letter: not
only those regarding me personally, but also the showy misrepresentation of reality in accusing President Trump of being "the pro-
ponent of a policy that, in recent months, has shown itself to be
increasingly discriminatory and violent, both with regard to the
health emergency and these latest events of racism." In truth I do
not see how one can make him responsible for the events of racism,
which have arisen in a context in which the police and the local governments are in the hands of the Democratic Party, and which have
been proven by evidence that little by little is emerging to have been
orchestrated by the false flag financed by the globalist elites precisely in order to oppose the Republican party and the President

---

1. The original open letter by Sister Antonietta Potente and Viganò's reply first
appeared on July 10, 2020, at www.marcotosatti.com/2020/07/10/vigano-to-a-nun-
trump-is-not-a-racist-and-a-warmonger.

currently in office. At the international level, Trump's term of office is the only one for a long time in which the United States has not started any military conflicts, and in many cases peace treaties have been established and foreign military deployments have been withdrawn. The economy was in strong growth (until the COVID emergency), and thus also the protection of the rights of workers.

If then you maintain that establishing public order and demanding respect for the law is a discriminatory action, I fear that I have to remind you that civil authority has a moral duty to impose respect for the laws, and in order to do this it is permitted to use proportionate force: this doctrine is taught and wonderfully explained by Saint Thomas Aquinas, the patron of the Institute to which you belong. I do not believe that the President is "violent in words and also in actions," certainly no more that those who in their own political program favor and support the killing of millions of children right up until the moment before birth and even after birth: this violence, much more hateful since it rages the most against those who are the most defenseless, does not appear to me quite be in accord with your commitment as a religious sister.

You reprove me for using a "dualistic and discriminating language"—in fact, it is precisely that, and I think that it cannot be otherwise, when what is in question is the eternal battle between good and evil. The truth is always discriminatory when error places it into question. Light is also discriminatory, for it does not tolerate darkness or those who hide in it. Just as Our Lord, the stumbling stone, is discriminatory and divisive, who will gather the just to His right hand and drive out the wicked to His left. You are my friends, if you do what I command you, says the Lord (Jn 15:4). The condition for friendship with God is obedience to His Commandments and His Law, in the bond of charity. This too is discriminatory, because those who abuse their own freedom and do not conform themselves to the will of God will not be able to rejoice in the beatific vision, nor participate in His eternal glory. In the same way, the Sixth Commandment, which condemns sodomy as a sin that cries out for vengeance before the face of God, was given in a "homophobic and thus discriminatory mentality." Saint Paul discriminated, just as Christ discriminated, and so too in Eden the

Eternal Father discriminated, driving out our first parents who had disobeyed Him.

But if this discrimination made us through our own fault deserving of divine punishment, it also merited for us ever since the fall of our first parents the promise of a Redeemer born of the Virgin, of a new Adam and a new Eve. It was this "dualist" vision that led our fathers toward the Promised Land, in the abandonment of idolatry and the adoration of the One True God. The Martyrs too discriminated when they preferred to face torment and torture rather than burn incense to idols. The Doctors of the Church, including the Angelic Doctor, discriminated when they fought against heresies and preached true doctrine. Saint Dominic discriminated when he preached the Cross. You too, Reverend Mother, discriminate when you take positions against my words, against Trump, and against discrimination. You discriminate when you speak of "we women religious [*donne religiose*]" placing an accent on "women" that seems to want to claim a role that is not based on adhesion to the order willed by God nor to the admonition of the Apostle of the Gentiles.

You state: "We ask to work together so that the humble and not the rich may be exalted; we ask that the powerful and bullies who humiliate and destroy the hope of peoples may exist no longer." You recall, Reverend Mother, that the humble of whom the Gospel speaks are not necessarily those whom today's world exploits for cynical projects of social engineering, nor the many who are torn from their homeland in order to pander to the plans for destabilization that always enrich the usual people. And the rich are not always and necessarily evil: if Providence has granted them material goods, He asks them to become His cooperators in remembering the poor and needy. Nor are the powerful to be blamed, if their power is placed in service of the Good: it is those who abuse their power and the authority given to them who merit blame from the citizens and divine punishment.

I fear that your words find too much space for the thinking of the world, rather than a supernatural vision supported by sound doctrine and fed by solid piety. In substance, the absence of an exterior and visible sign of your religious vows appears to me to reveal implicitly your desire to hide your religious identity (perhaps in order not to offend others' sensibilities?), with the risk however of leaving yourself in an interior void that no ideology of this world will be able to fill. And yet it is precisely this that we ought to expect from a daughter of Saint Dominic and Saint Thomas: to ensure that the legitimate aspirations of the least ones find their own most authentic roots in Revelation, in the Christian social order, in the faithful application of the social doctrine of the Church. Because there is no charity where there is no truth: You teach me that they are both essential attributes of God, and it is not possible to love God if one does not also unconditionally welcome the integral truth that He has transmitted to us in the Holy Church, the one Ark of Salvation.

You write: "It should be clear, however, that we are on the side of the weakest and oppressed, certain that it is only to them that the wisdom that the rulers of this world did not know has been revealed (cf. 1 Cor 2:8)." I imagine that in that group of the weakest and oppressed you include the fathers and mothers of families who want to give a Christian education to their children; the many who are daily persecuted simply because they profess the Catholic faith; the millions of innocents that the modern Moloch sacrifices each day on the impure altar of abortion; the elderly whom economic interests and speculations condemn to abandonment or death because they are considered useless; the children ensnared in their most tender years by the infernal ideology of gender; the young people corrupted in their morality by LGBT thought; the elderly faithful of St. Louis who were assaulted a few days ago by a group of people who praise Black Lives Matter.

In conclusion, your open letter confirms what I have written many times: the alignments are being more clearly defined day by day, and this is certainly a tribute to the truth that permits many to understand what is really happening and which side each person intends to align with.

To you, Reverend Mother, and to your community I send my heartfelt blessing, entrusting myself to your prayers.

✠ Carlo Maria Viganò, Archbishop

28

Second Open Letter
to President Donald J. Trump

October 25, 2020

MR. President,

Allow me to address you at this hour in which the fate of the whole world is being threatened by a global conspiracy against God and humanity. I write to you as an archbishop, as a Successor of the Apostles, as the former Apostolic Nuncio to the United States of America. I am writing to you in the midst of the silence of both civil and religious authorities. May you accept these words of mine as the "voice of one crying out in the desert" (Jn 1:23).

As I said when I wrote my letter to you in June, this historical moment sees the forces of Evil aligned in a battle without quarter against the forces of Good; forces of Evil that appear powerful and organized as they oppose the children of Light, who are disoriented and disorganized, abandoned by their temporal and spiritual leaders.

Daily we sense the attacks multiplying of those who want to destroy the very basis of society: the natural family, respect for human life, love of country, freedom of education and business. We see heads of nations and religious leaders pandering to this suicide of Western culture and its Christian soul, while the fundamental rights of citizens and believers are denied in the name of a health emergency that is revealing itself more and more fully as instrumental to the establishment of an inhuman faceless tyranny.

A global plan called the Great Reset is underway. Its architect is a global élite that wants to subdue all of humanity, imposing coercive measures with which to drastically limit individual freedoms and those of entire populations. In several nations this plan has already been approved and financed; in others it is still in an early stage.

Second Open Letter to President Donald J. Trump

Behind the world leaders who are the accomplices and executors of this infernal project, there are unscrupulous characters who finance the World Economic Forum and Event 201, promoting their agenda.

The purpose of the Great Reset is the imposition of a health dictatorship aiming at the imposition of liberticidal measures, hidden behind tempting promises of ensuring a universal income and cancelling individual debt. The price of these concessions from the International Monetary Fund will be the renunciation of private property and adherence to a program of vaccination against COVID-19 and COVID-21 promoted by Bill Gates with the collaboration of the main pharmaceutical groups. Beyond the enormous economic interests that motivate the promoters of the Great Reset, the imposition of the vaccination will be accompanied by the requirement of a health passport and a digital ID, with the consequent contact tracing of the population of the entire world. Those who do not accept these measures will be confined in detention camps or placed under house arrest, and all their assets will be confiscated.

Mr. President, I imagine that you are already aware that in some countries the Great Reset will be activated between the end of this year and the first trimester of 2021. For this purpose, further lockdowns are planned, which will be officially justified by a supposed second and third wave of the pandemic. You are well aware of the means that have been deployed to sow panic and legitimize draconian limitations on individual liberties, artfully provoking a worldwide economic crisis. In the intentions of its architects, this crisis will serve to make the recourse of nations to the Great Reset irreversible, thereby giving the final blow to a world whose existence and very memory they want to completely cancel. But this world, Mr. President, includes people, affections, institutions, faith, culture, traditions, and ideals: people and values that do not act like automatons, who do not obey like machines, because they are endowed with a soul and a heart, because they are tied together by a spiritual bond that draws its strength from above, from that God that our adversaries want to challenge, just as Lucifer did at the beginning of time with his *non serviam*.[1]

---

1. Latin for "I will not serve," the battle cry of Lucifer (cf. Jer 2:20; Is 14:12–17).

Many people—as we well know—are annoyed by this reference to the clash between Good and Evil and the use of "apocalyptic" overtones, which according to them exasperates spirits and sharpens divisions. It is not surprising that the enemy is angered at being discovered just when he believes he has reached the citadel he seeks to conquer undisturbed. What is surprising, however, is that there is no one to sound the alarm. The reaction of the deep state to those who denounce its plan is broken and incoherent, but understandable. Just when the complicity of the mainstream media had succeeded in making the transition to the New World Order almost painless and unnoticed, all sorts of deceptions, scandals and crimes are coming to light.

Until a few months ago, it was easy to smear as "conspiracy theorists" those who denounced these terrible plans, which we now see being carried out down to the smallest detail. No one, up until last February, would ever have thought that, in all of our cities, citizens would be arrested simply for wanting to walk down the street, to breathe, to want to keep their business open, to want to go to church on Sunday. Yet now it is happening all over the world, even in picture-postcard Italy that many Americans consider to be a small enchanted country, with its ancient monuments, its churches, its charming cities, its characteristic villages. And while the politicians are barricaded inside their palaces promulgating decrees like Persian satraps, businesses are failing, shops are closing, and people are prevented from living, traveling, working, and praying. The disastrous psychological consequences of this operation are already being seen, beginning with the suicides of desperate entrepreneurs and of our children, segregated from friends and classmates, told to follow their classes while sitting at home alone in front of a computer.

In Sacred Scripture, Saint Paul speaks to us of "the one who opposes" the manifestation of the mystery of iniquity, the *kathèkon* (2 Thess 2:6–7). In the religious sphere, this obstacle to evil is the Church, and in particular the papacy; in the political sphere, it is those who impede the establishment of the New World Order.

As is now clear, the one who occupies the Chair of Peter has betrayed his role from the very beginning in order to defend and promote the globalist ideology, supporting the agenda of the deep church, who chose him from its ranks.

Mr. President, you have clearly stated that you want to defend the nation—One Nation under God, fundamental liberties, and non-negotiable values that are denied and fought against today. It is you, dear President, who are "the one who opposes" the deep state, the final assault of the children of darkness.

For this reason, it is necessary that all people of good will be persuaded of the epochal importance of the imminent election: not so much for the sake of this or that political program, but because of the general inspiration of your action that best embodies—in this particular historical context—that world, our world, which they want to cancel by means of the lockdown. Your adversary is also our adversary: it is the Enemy of the human race, He who is "a murderer from the beginning" (Jn 8:44).

Around you are gathered with faith and courage those who consider you the final garrison against the world dictatorship. The alternative is to vote for a person who is manipulated by the deep state, gravely compromised by scandals and corruption, who will do to the United States what Jorge Mario Bergoglio is doing to the Church, Prime Minister Conte to Italy, President Macron to France, Prime Minister Sanchez to Spain, and so on. The blackmailable nature of Joe Biden—just like that of the prelates of the Vatican's "magic circle"—will expose him to be used unscrupulously, allowing illegitimate powers to interfere in both domestic politics as well as international balances. It is obvious that those who manipulate him already have someone worse than him ready, with whom they will replace him as soon as the opportunity arises.

And yet, in the midst of this bleak picture, this apparently unstoppable advance of the "Invisible Enemy," an element of hope emerges. The adversary does not know how to love, and it does not understand that it is not enough to assure a universal income or to cancel mortgages in order to subjugate the masses and convince them to be branded like cattle. This people, which for too long has endured the abuses of a hateful and tyrannical power, is rediscovering that it has a soul; it is understanding that it is not willing to exchange its freedom for the homogenization and cancellation of its identity; it is beginning to understand the value of familial and social ties, of the bonds of faith and culture that unite honest people. This Great Reset is destined to fail because those who planned it do not understand that there are still people ready to take to the streets to defend their rights, to protect their loved ones, to give a future to their children and grandchildren. The leveling inhumanity of the globalist project will shatter miserably in the face of the firm and courageous opposition of the children of Light. The enemy has Satan on its side, He who only knows how to hate. But on our side, we have the Lord Almighty, the God of armies arrayed for battle, and the Most Holy Virgin, who will crush the head of the ancient Serpent. "If God is for us, who can be against us?" (Rom 8:31).

Mr. President, you are well aware that, in this crucial hour, the United States of America is considered the defending wall against which the war declared by the advocates of globalism has been unleashed. Place your trust in the Lord, strengthened by the words of the Apostle Paul: "I can do all things in Him who strengthens me" (Phil 4:13). To be an instrument of Divine Providence is a great responsibility, for which you will certainly receive all the graces of state that you need, since they are being fervently implored for you by the many people who support you with their prayers.

With this heavenly hope and the assurance of my prayer for you, for the First Lady, and for your collaborators, with all my heart I send you my blessing.

God bless the United States of America!

✠ Carlo Maria Viganò, Archbishop
Titular Archbishop of Ulpiana,
Former Apostolic Nuncio to
the United States of America

29

Interview with Francesco Boezi: Trump and Biden

October 1, 2020

ARCHBISHOP Viganò, why did you write a letter in favor of President Trump?

On August 14, 2011, Pope Benedict XVI let me know that it was his conviction that at that moment my providential position was the Nunciature in the United States of America. This is what he wrote to me: "I would like to tell you that I have reflected and prayed with reference to your condition after the recent events. The sad news of the passing away of His Excellency Archbishop Pietro Sambi has confirmed in me the conviction that your providential position at this moment is the Nunciature in the United States of America. On the other hand, I am certain that your knowledge of this great country will help you to undertake the demanding challenge of this work, which in many ways will prove decisive for the future of the universal Church."

My official assignment in that immense and beloved country has ended, but the challenge to which Pope Benedict referred to almost prophetically, and in which he chose to involve me, is still present more than ever; indeed, it has become ever more dramatic, taking on tremendous dimensions: the destiny of the world is being played out at this hour precisely on the American front.

Now that I am free from my official assignment, the inspiration confided to me by Pope Benedict permits me to address President Trump with the utmost freedom, pointing out his role in the national and international context and how decisive his mission is in the epochal confrontation that has been unfolding in recent months.

A Voice in the Wilderness

An epochal confrontation? Really?

It appears today that the Holy See is being assaulted by enemy forces. I speak as a bishop, as a Successor of the Apostles. The silence of the shepherds is deafening and upsetting. Some bishops even prefer to support the New World Order, aligning themselves with the positions of Bergoglio and Cardinal Parolin who, as a frequenter of the Bilderberg Club,[1] has slavishly submitted to its *diktats*, like so many politicians as well as the mainstream media.

I am persuaded that everything I denounced in my open letter to President Trump last June is still valid and can form an interpretive key to understanding the events that we are living through. It remains an invitation to have hope.

The Catholic Church in America, both in relation to the presidential elections and more generally, appears to be split. The pope says that dividing is a work of the devil, but the fracturing of the American episcopate is obvious. What is happening?

The split within the American episcopate is the result of an ideological action carried out since the 1960s especially within Catholic universities—and by the Jesuits in particular—in the formation of entire generations of young people. Progressive indoctrination (on the political front) and modernist indoctrination (on the religious front) have created an ideological support for 1968 which began with the Second Vatican Council, as Benedict XVI confirmed in his essay *Principles of Catholic Theology*: "Adherence to an anarchic and utopian Marxism [...] was supported on the front lines by many chaplains of universities and youth associations, who saw the blossoming of Christian hopes there. The dominant fact is found in the events of May 1968 in France. There were Dominicans and Jesuits on the barricades. The intercommunion that was held during an ecumenical Mass in support of the barricades was considered as a

1. See p.303, n.2. Secretary of State Parolin accepted an invitation to attend this globalist club in 2018. See Andrea Gagliarducci, "Analysis: Cardinal Parolin, Vatican secretary of state, at the elite Bilderberg meeting," *Catholic News Agency,* June 6, 2018, www.catholicnewsagency.com/news/analysis-cardinal-parolin-at-the-elite-bil derberg-meeting-55996.

kind of milestone in salvation history, a sort of revelation that inaugurated a new era of Christianity."

This split in the United States, which today has become even more obvious as the presidential elections approaches, is also widespread in Europe and Italy: the highest levels of the Church have desired to make a radical—and in my opinion unfortunate—choice, preferring to follow the mainstream thought of environmentalism, immigrationism, and the LGBT ideology, rather than courageously standing up against them and faithfully proclaiming the salvific truth announced by Our Lord. This choice took a great leap forward beginning in 2013 with the election of Jorge Mario Bergoglio, but it goes back to at least almost sixty years ago. It is significant that even then the Jesuits—and all of the Catholic intelligentsia of the Left—looked to Mao's China as a privileged interlocutor, almost a driving force behind the alleged social renewal, just as today *La Civiltà Cattolica* of Spadaro, S.J., looks to Xi Jinping's China. The Jesuits, who supported the guerillas in Latin America and who were on the French barricades in May of '68, today use social media to make similar claims, always with their eyes turned towards Beijing while carrying the same hatred towards America.

It is true that division is the work of the devil: Satan sows division between man and his Creator, between the soul and grace. The Lord, however, does not divide but separates: He creates a boundary between the City of God and the City of Satan, between those who serve the Lord and those who fight against Him. He himself will separate the just from the wicked on the Day of Judgment (Mt 25:31–46), after having placed himself "as a stumbling stone" (Rom 9:32–33). Separating light from darkness, good from evil, according to the teaching of the Lord, is necessary if we want to follow Christ and renounce Satan. But it is also necessary to separate when we choose who best protects the rights and faith of Catholics from those who only nominally proclaim themselves to be Catholic while in fact promoting laws that are clearly opposed to both divine and natural law. Just as the Shepherd who warns the flock about the attacks of the wolves is also divisive (Jn 10:1–18).

Accusing Trump of not being Christian solely because of the fact that he wants to protect national borders; evoking the specter of sovereignism as a disaster while human trafficking is allowed; remaining silent in the face of the persecution of Christians in China and elsewhere, or silent before the thousands of profanations of churches that have been happening for months all over the world: is not all this divisive?

Joe Biden is pro-abortion, but some American Catholic circles seem to overlook this aspect. Look, for example, at James Martin. What do you think?

Father James Martin, S.J., is the standard bearer of the LGBT ideology, and despite this—indeed, because of this—he was appointed by Bergoglio as Consultor of the Holy See's Secretariat for Communications. His work—which is truly "divisive" in the worst sense of the term—serves to strengthen a fifth column of the progressive agenda within the ecclesial body, so as to create an ideological and doctrinal split within the Church and to make people believe that the demands of progressivism, including the so-called *homoheresy*, come from the ground up. In reality we know well that the faithful are much less inclined to innovations than public opinion is led to believe, and that the desire to show that there is a supposed "will of the people" in order to legitimize choices incompatible with the perennial teaching of the Church is a ploy which has been used both at the ecclesial level (think of the liturgical reform, which nobody asked for) as well as at the civil level (for example, with gender ideology).

Permit me to recall the words of American Archbishop Fulton J. Sheen (1895–1979): "The refusal to take sides on great moral issues is itself a decision. It is a silent acquiescence to evil. The tragedy of our time is that those who still believe in honesty lack fire and conviction, while those who believe in dishonesty are full of passionate conviction." We learn to separate who is with Christ from who is against Him, since it is not possible to serve two masters.

You have spoken of the "deep church." Is it really possible that one exists? Who composes it?

The expression "deep church" gives a good idea of what is happening in a parallel way at the political and ecclesial level. The strategy is the same, just as the goals are the same, and, in the final analysis, the *mens* that is behind it. In this sense, the deep church is for the Church what the deep state is for the State: a foreign body that is illegal, subversive, and deprived of any sort of democratic legitimacy that uses the institution in which it is embedded to achieve goals that are diametrically opposed to the goals of the institution itself.

One example[2] is John Podesta, a "Catholic" liberal and Democrat, a former collaborator of Bill and Hillary Clinton,[3] who is tied to John Halpin's *Center for American Progress*. In an email of February 11, 2012, Sandy Newman wrote to Podesta asking him for directions on how to "plant seeds of a revolution" in the Church in matters of contraception, abortion, and gender equality. Podesta responded by confirming that in order to obtain this "springtime of the Church" (note the echo of the idea of the "conciliar springtime") the organizations *Catholics in Alliance for the Common Good* and *Catholics United* had been created. These ultraprogressive associations have been financed by George Soros, just as he has financed Jesuit foundations and Bergoglio's apostolic visit to the United States in 2015.[4]

We should also recall the conspiracy of the Saint Gallen Mafia, which sought to oust Benedict XVI, in concert with Obama and Clinton who saw Joseph Ratzinger as an obstacle to the spread of the globalist agenda.

As a Catholic and as a bishop, how do you judge what Trump has done?

I limit myself to observing what Trump has done during his term as President. He has defended the life of the unborn, cutting funding from the abortion multinational, Planned Parenthood, and just in recent days he has issued an executive order that requires immediate care for newborns who are not killed by abortion: up until now

---

2. VN: See https://formiche.net/2016/10/clinton-podesta-papa-francesco.

3. Most recently he was Hillary Clinton's campaign manager in the 2016 Presidential election. Many of his emails were released by WikiLeaks, one of which is quoted in the next sentence.

4. VN: See https://formiche.net/2016/10/clinton-podesta-papa-francesco.

they were allowed to die or they were exploited by harvesting their organs and selling them. Trump is fighting pedophilia and pedosatanism. He has not started any new war and he has drastically reduced the existing ones by obtaining peace agreements. He has restored God's right of citizenship, after Obama had even gone so far as to cancel Christmas and impose measures that were repugnant to the religious soul of Americans.

And I also observe the media war that has been waged by the press and the centers of power against the President: he has been demonized since 2016, despite the fact that he democratically obtained a majority of votes. It is well understood that the hatred against Trump—which is not dissimilar to what happens in Italy in the face of much softer members of the opposition—finds its real motivation in the awareness of his fundamental role in the battle against the deep state and all of its internal and external ramifications. His courageous denunciation of Communism—of which Antifa and BLM are the global versions while the Chinese dictatorship is the incubator—serves in some measure to remedy the silence of the Church, which despite the heartfelt appeals of the Blessed Virgin Mary at Fatima and La Salette has preferred not to renew its condemnation of this infernal ideology. And if Bishop Sanchez Sorondo can declare with impunity, against all the evidence, that "China is the best implementer of the social doctrine of the Church," we can rejoice over the words of the President of the United States and the no less courageous words of his Secretary of State Mike Pompeo.

It appears that Bergoglio will now not meet with the US Secretary of State [during Pompeo's trip to Italy].

We have now come to the point of paradox, indeed of the ridiculous. Certain attitudes seem more suited to the whims of an undisciplined schoolboy rather than prudence and diplomatic protocol. Pompeo denounced the violation of human rights in China and received a sharp response from Santa Marta: *And I won't play anymore.* These are unworthy behaviors which are beginning to cause feelings of undisguised shame even among members of Bergoglio's magic circle. Not only will he not receive the Secretary of State so as not to hear it said to him *ore rotundo* that the United States will not stand by watching idly as the Church hands itself over into the hands of a ferocious dictatorship, but he did not even respond to Cardinal Zen's request for an audience, confirming the specific intention of the Vatican to renew its submission to the Chinese Communist Party.

Did you organize a Rosary for Trump, and, if so, why?

I was urged by many people to launch this initiative,[5] and I did not hesitate to join it, becoming the promoter of this spiritual crusade. This is a war without quarter, in which Satan has been unchained and the gates of hell are trying in every way to prevail over the Church herself. Such a contradiction must be faced above all with prayer, with the invincible weapon of the Holy Rosary.

The involvement of Catholics in politics, under the guidance of their pastors, constitutes their concrete action as citizens who are members both of the Mystical Body of Christ as well as human society. Catholics are not "disassociated" people who believe that God is the Author and Lord of Life when they go to church, but then, at the ballot box or as elected officials, approve of the killing of innocent children.

This action of the natural order is accompanied—indeed it *must* be accompanied—by the awareness that human affairs, as well as social and political events, have a transcendent spiritual dimension, in which the intervention of Divine Providence is always the determining factor. For this reason, Catholics do not extract themselves from the world, they do not flee from the political arena, passively waiting for the Lord to intervene with bolts of lightning, but, on the contrary, they give meaning to their daily action, to their commitment in society, giving it a soul, a supernatural purpose.

Prayer, in this sense, calls down from the Lord of the world and

---

5. VN: See https://remnantnewspaper.com/web/index.php/articles/item/4965-remnant-league-of-the-sacred-heart-launches-rosary-crusade-new-prayer-by-archbishop-vigano-for-reelection-of-donald-trump.

history those graces and the special help which only He can give both to the actions of private citizens as well as to the work of those who govern. And if in the past even pagan kings were able to be instruments of the good in the hands of God, this can happen still today, at a moment in which the biblical battle between the children of darkness and the children of light has reached a crucial point.

What scenarios await the Catholics of the world if Trump should lose?

If Trump loses the presidential elections, the final *kathèkon* [withholder] will fail (2 Thess 2:6–7), that which prevents the "mystery of iniquity" from revealing itself, and the dictatorship of the New World Order, which has already won Bergoglio over to its cause, will have an ally in the new American President.

Joe Biden does not have his own identity: he is only the expression of a power that does not dare reveal itself for what it truly is and that is hiding itself behind a person who is totally incapable of holding the office of President of the United States, also because of his weakened mental capabilities; but it is precisely in his *weakness* for pending complaints, in his ability to be blackmailed for conflicts of interest, that Biden reveals himself as a marionette maneuvered by the elites, a puppet in the hands of people thirsting for power and ready to do anything to expand it.

We would find ourselves facing an Orwellian dictatorship desired by both the deep state and the deep church, in which the rights that today are considered fundamental and inalienable would be trampled with the complicity of mainstream media.

I want to emphasize that the universal religion desired by the United Nations and Freemasonry has active collaborators at the highest levels of the Catholic Church who usurp authority and adulterate the Magisterium. They are opposing the Mystical Body of Christ, which is mankind's only ark of salvation, with the mystical body of the Antichrist, according to the prophecy of the Venerable Archbishop Fulton Sheen. Ecumenism, Malthusian environmentalism, pansexualism, and immigrationism are the new dogmas of this universal religion, whose ministers are preparing the advent of the Antichrist prior to the final persecution and the definitive victory of

Our Lord. But just as the glorious Resurrection of the Savior was preceded by His Passion and Death, so too is the Church journeying towards her own Calvary; and just as the Sanhedrin thought that it would eliminate the Messiah by crucifying Him, so the infamous sect believes that the eclipse of the Church is a prelude to its end. A "tiny remnant" remains, made up of fervent Catholics, just as the Mother of God, Saint John, and Mary Magdalene remained at the foot of the Cross.

We know that the destiny of the world is not in the hands of men, and that the Lord has promised that He will not abandon His Church: "the gates of hell shall not prevail" (Mt 16:18). The words of Christ are the rock of our hope: "Behold, I am with you all days, until the end of the world" (Mt 28:20).

30

Interview with Scott Kesterson

October 28, 2020
Feast of the Apostles Simon and Jude

YOUR Excellency, you have become recently well known in the United
States for your powerful letter to President Donald J. Trump, published
on June 6, 2020, which we will discuss in more detail as we progress
through this interview. However, for many, especially non-Catholics,
your name is new. Can you provide a brief background of your accom-
plished history in the Church and where you are at today?

After my priestly ordination, on March 24, 1968, in the First Vespers
of the Annunciation, I was assigned for a few years to a pastoral work
in a parish. In 1973 I was called to the service of the Holy See, in its
diplomatic assignments: first in Iraq and Kuwait, then in the United
Kingdom. From 1978 to 1989 I have been serving at the Secretariat of
State; then sent to the Council of Europe in Strasbourg. Following
that, in 1992 I was ordained bishop by Pope John Paul II and sent as
Apostolic Nuncio to Nigeria. During this period abroad I was also
able to exercise intense pastoral ministry (pastoral visits, creation of
dioceses and ecclesiastical provinces, numerous priestly ordinations
and episcopal consecrations, opening of new seminaries).

Then in 1998 I was called back to the Secretariat of State where I
was the Delegate for Pontifical Representations, in charge of personnel both for the Roman Curia (the various departments of the
Holy See which assist the pope in his mission) and for the Apostolic
Nunciatures (Embassies) of the Holy See throughout the world.
Following that, in 2009 Pope Benedict XVI appointed me as the
General Secretary of the Governatorate of the Vatican City State,
with the task of supervising the various financial and civil adminis-
trations. I was removed from that position after just a year and a

half, for having worked in the consolidation of the financial administration and for having brought to light many cases of corruption: evidently my commitment created problems for someone.

So, on August 14, 2011, Pope Benedict XVI let me know that it was his conviction that at that moment my providential position was the Nunciature in the United States of America. This is what he wrote to me: "I would like to tell you that I have reflected and prayed with reference to your condition after the recent events. The sad news of the passing away of His Excellency Archbishop Pietro Sambi has confirmed in me the conviction that your providential position at this moment is the Nunciature in the United States of America. On the other hand, I am certain that your knowledge of this great country will help you to undertake the demanding challenge of this work, which in many ways will prove decisive for the future of the universal Church." I was therefore Apostolic Nuncio in your great and beloved country until May 2016.

Your Excellency, in your letter to President Donald J. Trump published on June 6, 2020, you state that "just as there is a deep state, there is also a deep church that betrays its duties and forswears its proper commitments before God." Can you explain to us what the deep church is?

The deep church is the ecclesiastical version of the deep state or rather its "Vatican branch" which depends on the deep state and closely collaborates with it. Imagine the same people, with the same vices, the same net of intrigue and blackmail, but who instead of wearing suits and ties wear Roman collars and often also pectoral crosses (well hidden inside their pockets) and the rings of episcopal consecration.

Our listeners are probably scandalized at the idea that people consecrated to the Lord and to the salvation of souls are in reality corrupt people, heretics and lustful men. But if you think about it, Our Lord warned us about them in the Gospel: "Woe to you, scribes and Pharisees, you hypocrites! You are like whitewashed tombs, which appear beautiful on the outside, but inside are full of dead men's bones and every kind of filth" (Mt 23:27).

What is horrifying, especially for those who believe, is that these people not only betray their mission, but they also profane the Mystical Body of Christ: they crucify the Lord once again when they celebrate the Mass, when they give scandal to the faithful, when they use the trust that people place in them to corrupt children and young people. By doing so they discredit the holiness of the Church, driving many souls away from her. The damage that they cause is immense, because their sins fall on the Bride of Christ, which is immaculate like the Virgin Mary.

You can imagine the souls of these unfortunate people: black souls, devoted to evil, to Satan—in the awareness that every one of their evil actions tears the flesh of Christ just as the torturers did during his scourging.

Where did the deep church originate and how deeply has it infiltrated the global network of the Catholic faith?

Let's just say that the deep church began to operate during Vatican II in the 1960s, and that it has progressively organized itself, above all when the conciliar revolution permitted members of the deep church to enter into Vatican Dicasteries, pontifical universities, seminaries, convents, monasteries, and dioceses—that is, right where they could do the most damage.

In this revolution, we ought to recognize that the deep church demonstrated a tremendous organization, a capacity for capillary infiltration, often due to the naivety of certain prelates or thanks to the complicity of others. Behind this activity, however, we see the mind of Satan, who being an angelic intelligence knows how to coordinate his servants in order to strike against the Church.

Today the deep church is in possession of practically the entire hierarchical structure of the Catholic Church, especially the highest levels. The scandals that we read about today in the media do not only involve priests but have come to involve bishops and cardinals. It is a bleak thing. But, if we think about it, it is not so absurd: someone who was a corrupt priest thirty or forty years ago and was not expelled by his superiors—perhaps because he was prudent and did not allow himself to be discovered—is still corrupt today, but in the meantime he has been promoted to the rank of bishop or cardinal. This is the case of archbishop Wilton Gregory, newly promoted cardinal!

Obviously, those who are corrupt are also able to be blackmailed. Think of Joe Biden: evidence is coming out that his son Hunter had photos of underage minors on his laptop. Do you think that, in addition to doing business with China, the Chinese have not blackmailed his father with those photos? And don't you believe that, if he became President of the United Sates, he would become even more vulnerable to blackmail? Now imagine: these blackmails can be done against dozens, hundreds of public officials who have something to hide—bribes, corruption, sexual scandals—and they end up subjecting the nation to the interests of those who blackmail them.

And has this also happened in the Church?

Certainly: the same thing has happened with the Church. The number of corrupt prelates has increased, because the deep church wanted there to be people who could be blackmailed and manipulated in the key posts of the Vatican, the Bishops' Conferences, etc. And thus the deep church promoted homosexuals, perverts, thieves, heretics—all people who had something to gain in terms of money, personal prestige, and visibility, but who in exchange had to obey their bosses' orders. "Promote this monsignor and put him in this important office," they tell him. And the bishop or cardinal does it, otherwise they will pull out the photo of him with the seminarian, the credit card statement with the charges for the escort, etc. The more obedient they are, the higher they rise in the hierarchy; and the higher they rise in the hierarchy, the more damage they cause and the more corrupt people they bring in.

How do the Shepherds who are faithful to the teaching of Our Lord react to this?

The good priests, the good bishops and cardinals, live through this situation with great suffering: they feel marginalized, and they really are, because if they are not blackmailable, if they love the Lord and are committed to the salvation of souls, then they are considered foreign bodies, even as adversaries to be eliminated because they denounce evil.

What does the deep church do?

The deep church demolishes the Church from within, just as the deep state destroys the State and its institutions from within, like a cancer. Think of the recent proposal of Joe Biden, who instead of promoting honest and incorrupt judges calls for the restructuring of the Supreme Court—just as the outstanding judge Amy Coney Barrett was about to be confirmed by the Senate. Speaking of candidate Joe Biden, it would be very appropriate to investigate his close ties, political and otherwise, with Mr. Theodore McCarrick, the well-known former cardinal and archbishop of Washington: in particular, their common interests in building close relations with the Chinese Communist Party and in order to prepare the secret agreement with the Holy See, which has just been renewed, in a criminal way, for two more years.

In order to destroy the Church, the deep church strikes her in her doctrine, morals, liturgy, and discipline—just as the deep state strikes against the State in its Constitution, laws, institutions, armed forces, schools and universities.

In order to destabilize and destroy the nation, the deep state has created and financed the Antifa and BLM movements. In the same way, the deep church uses members of the ecclesiastical hierarchy and gay-friendly theologians, protesters, and ultraprogressives to destroy the Church from within.

The deep church is the cancer of the Church, the fifth column which Satan uses to impede the salvation of souls. And not only this: it replaces the Church of Christ with the anti-church of Lucifer. And it lines itself up officially alongside the deep state just at the moment in which the State—which has, as its purpose, the common good of its citizens—is being replaced by an anti-state in the service of the New World Order.

A State that promotes abortion and even infanticide, euthanasia, gender theory, and LGBTQ ideology, simply wants to destroy itself from within, make itself sterile, erase the natural family, and corrupt children and young people. A population that is ignorant, without culture and traditions, composed of selfish people without any identity, of cowards without values, of people given over to vice without dignity, will never be willing to fight for their homeland, to sacrifice themselves in order to study, work, marry, and educate their children... And in this way, they will surrender to the enemy, or more simply they will accept being subjected, controlled, and spied on. The only thing they will want is to be allowed to have their cell phone and to be able to take selfies, with the illusion of having some sort of moral value only because they demonstrate with Greta Thunberg for ecology or with BLM against racism.

So, don't be surprised that in this battle conducted on two fronts—the deep state and the deep church—the ideas that you will hear are practically the same. They want to destroy us both as patriots and as Christians, because as both we are their sworn enemies. They want a world of slaves without identity, without values, without faith, without love, without passions... spineless larva, enslaved by cruel faceless masters who use us as obedient clients.

Your Excellency, in the same letter to President Donald J. Trump published on June 6, 2020, you reference the "Invisible Enemy, whom rulers fight against in public affairs" and "is also fought against by good shepherds in the ecclesiastical sphere." What is the Invisible Enemy? The term is used frequently these days, but for so many the idea is illusive.

Saint Paul says to us: "Our struggle is not against creatures made of flesh and blood but with the Principalities and Powers, against the rulers of this world of darkness, against the spirits of evil that dwell in the heavenly regions" (Eph 6:12). Here is the "invisible Enemy," which uses the deep state and the deep church to establish the New World Order, an openly anti-Christian tyranny that will prepare for the coming of the Antichrist of whom Scripture speaks.

Obviously, they call us fanatics, conspiracy theorists, nationalists, and sovereignists. But since when is it a fault to be coherent with one's own religion, love one's country, and have a sense of honor, authority, and order? As Catholics we also find ourselves in a similar situation: for sixty years those who want to remain faithful to the teaching of Christ and to the Magisterium of the Church have been called out as being outdated, the enemies of progress, integralists, and rigid. And if we do not approve the pagan cult of the Pacha-mama they call us "enemies of the pope." Just think if these things had happened at the time of Archbishop Fulton Sheen and Pius XII.

The enemy, in reality, is no longer invisible. The web of corruption, pedophilia, child pornography, ritual homicides, and Satanic worship unites all—and I repeat, *all*—of these servants of the global elite. Even those who pursue only economic interests, in the end, know that their bosses in one way or another are involved in criminal trafficking and are friends with people linked to the occult and witchcraft—think of Marina Abramovic,[1] for example—who in turn are celebrity endorsers of Bill Gates and the Rothschilds,[2] are invited to parties with the Clintons and John Podesta, with the Obamas, or to Epstein's Island.[3]

Your Excellency, you have become an outspoken critic of the corruption in the Church. You stated in your First Testimony dated August 22, 2018 that corruption had reached the very top of the Church's hierarchy. In that testimony, you stated, "Bishops and priests, abusing their authority, have committed horrendous crimes to the detriment of their faithful, minors, innocent victims, and young men eager to offer their lives to the Church, or by their silence have not prevented such crimes from continuing to be perpetrated." You go on to state, "We must tear down the conspiracy of silence with which bishops and priests have protected themselves at the expense of their faithful, a conspiracy of silence that in the eyes of the world risks making the Church look like a

---

1. A performance artist born in Yugoslavia in 1946. An email of hers appeared in the Podesta emails released by WikiLeaks in 2016 in which she invited Podesta's brother to a "spirit cooking" experience. Her defenders claimed that she was not a satanist but a spiritualist, but in the Catholic understanding these are the same thing.

2. One of England's wealthiest banking families, with ties to the Davos Great Reset.

3. An island owned by Jeffrey Epstein. It was alleged following Epstein's arrest by federal prosecutors that the island was used for pedophilia sex-trafficking. Epstein was reported to have committed suicide in prison. His associate Ghislaine Maxwell is still in prison undergoing her own criminal trial for her involvement in the crimes associated with Epstein Island.

sect, a conspiracy of silence not so dissimilar from the one that prevails in the mafia." Truth and transparency, Your Excellency, are what evil seeks to deny at any cost. How can this cult of silence be torn down? How can we restore the light to the darkness?

We are seeing it in civil life: the network of corruption of the deep state is coming to light, revealing complicity and crimes that no normal person would even conceive of. And the guilty, along with their accomplices in the press and institutions, try to hide them, to deny them, to ridicule those who denounce them. Their strategy is the same as that of the devil: hatred, lies, deception.

The same thing is happening in the Church, where the deep church is emerging with cases of pedophilia, the complicity of the "lavender mafia," the trafficking of money stolen from Vatican coffers to pay for the electoral campaign of Hillary Clinton or to bribe witnesses. In Australia it appears that money was sent from the Vatican to condemn Cardinal Pell, an innocent man accused of crimes against minors only in order to keep him away from Rome so that Cardinal Becciu, Archbishop Peña Parra, and others would not be discovered.

It seems that the Chinese Communist government is sending exorbitant sums to the Vatican in exchange for the silence and connivance of the Holy See. In the meantime, Christians are persecuted, good pastors are arrested or sent to reeducation camps, and the religious rights of the people are denied. But the deep church is not interested in defending the flock: they want power; they want money.

The real problem of bishops and priests who sin gravely against God and souls is that these crimes are not a painful exception to the norm, but almost a norm that has been tolerated for far too long in recent decades and that today has become an indispensable requirement for a career in the Vatican and in dioceses.

Your Excellency, corruption within the Church has sadly become more common than not. This has a devastating impact on trust and belief in those sharing and teaching God's word. In your letter sent to the Archdiocese of Washington DC dated June 3, 2020, you stated, "Unfortu-

nately, the Catholic Church is led by many false pastors. Over the past twenty years, your Diocese of Washington in particular, and now for the third time, has been and continues to be deeply afflicted and wounded by false shepherds whose way of life is full of lies, deceits, lust and corruption."

In that letter, I denounced the absurd attitude of the archbishop of Washington, Wilton Gregory, who had sharply criticized the visit of the President and First Lady to the National Shrine of Saint John Paul II, portraying it as a political stunt.

As a Nuncio, I can say that the Church has always been respectful and prudent, especially towards a sitting President. In this case the hatred of the deep church against Trump prevailed with an unworthy and unjustified attack. Why is it that these prelates never raise their voices when dealing with a Democrat? Why are they silent about the crime of abortion even to the point of infanticide, of which Joe Biden is a supporter and yet dares to call himself Catholic? I will say it to them: it is because they are corrupt, they are on the same side, they belong to the same world. And thus, they reciprocally defend each other; they help each other out; they cover up each other's wrongdoings.

Bergoglio, with a new move against Trump, has just promoted Gregory as a cardinal. Of course, Gregory supports the Dems' Agenda; just like Bergoglio, he is for Biden against Trump. Gregory is all for the poor, all for the migrants; just like Bergoglio he wants a poor church for the poor…

But I remember well… not only his luxurious car, a Lexus, but also how, in 2014, Archbishop Gregory was in hot water for buying a $2.2 million dollar mansion for his own use. What was even more troubling about this situation is where the money came from. A nephew of Margaret Mitchell, who authored the classic *Gone With the Wind*, left much of his estate to the archdiocese of Atlanta, asking that it be used for charitable purposes. Instead, the $15 million dollars was used by Gregory for purchasing property, leaving only about $3 million for Catholic charities. If it had not been for the intervention of the media that denounced the scandal, Gregory would have kept that villa.

Interview with Scott Kesterson

Your Excellency, how can the faithful know who the false shepherds are if their afflictions of lies, deceits, lust and corruption are not called out and these false shepherds are not identified by name?

The names that emerge are usually those that it is no longer possible to keep hidden from public opinion. We think, among others, of the McCarrick case: Bergoglio condemned him by authority with an administrative procedure, thus impeding the publication of the procedural acts and testimonies of the people involved, in order not to bring to light the complicity of the people truly responsible for this corruption. Who are the people who are responsible and their accomplices? The people that Bergoglio wanted, promoted and defended, despite the denunciations and dossiers of complaints against them. Pope Benedict XVI had imposed a retired life on McCarrick. And yet, Bergoglio sent him to China on his behalf to complete the agreement with the government, as if nothing had happened, as if the fact of being a pervert and a corrupter was not more than sufficient reason for keeping him away from the diplomatic affairs of the Holy See. Or rather: it was for this very reason that Bergoglio entrusted this mission to him!

I am not surprised: McCarrick was among those who supported the election of Bergoglio, both in 2005 after the death of John Paul II, although it did not succeed then, as well as in 2013 after the resignation of Benedict XVI. Thus Bergoglio was "indebted" to McCarrick, and it is obvious that he did not rage too much against him. I ask myself whether the former cardinal may not have also had elements of blackmail which he held over his own blackmailer...

What is the solution to this corruption?

Obviously, it is not enough to only punish the guilty, admitted and not granted that one really wants to punish them. What is needed is authentic personal conversion and a deep reform of ecclesiastical discipline.

The only way to restore credibility to the ministers of God is to bring souls back to Him, through a work of penance and conversion: we must cultivate the holiness of the clergy as an indispensable premise for the holiness of the people. It is a work that only the

341

Omnipotent Lord can accomplish, but that each one of us can ask of Him by means of prayer and sacrifice. And which the Authority of the Church must impose without exceptions, by cleaning up and expelling the unworthy from the temple.

I would like to add a reflection that is perhaps a bit banal but yet is true and verifiable. The good shepherds, the thousands of good bishops and priests around the world, do not need to say, "I am a good Shepherd," because they demonstrate it daily by their commitment. The Lord has told us that the sheep recognize His voice. Well, even today faithful Christians and honest people who fear God immediately know how to recognize, through that supernatural instinct that the Church calls the *sensus fidei*, who comes from God and who instead comes from Satan. Rather than having the "smell of the sheep," priests ought to have the sweet fragrance of Christ, the Anointed One, the Divine Shepherd.

Your Excellency, in your Appeal for the Church and the World, dated May 7, 2020, a prophetic statement within the text reads, "there are powers interested in creating panic among the world's population with the sole aim of permanently imposing unacceptable forms of restriction on freedoms, of controlling people and of tracking their movements. The imposition of these illiberal measures is a disturbing prelude to the realization of a world government beyond all control." Your Excellency, what would you say to people consumed with fear in these times? What would you say to assuage their fears, to give them strength and to help them find trust in our Lord Jesus Christ?

The purpose of Freemasonry is to create a world government with a universal syncretistic religion. But in order to establish this world government both national states as well as the Church must first be eliminated. And how can this be done? Fear is the most effective means to attain this end. Fear of a virus that the mainstream media present as if it was the gravest of plagues. So also the system boycotts the cures—in Italy the use of hydroxychloroquine has been banned by order of the World Health Organization—and sows the seeds of panic; it makes people believe that the intensive care wards are full of sick people, that thousands of people are dying, that the contagion is spreading death everywhere. This permits the deep state to impose the lockdown, limit citizens' liberties, use the army to control the population, close the churches and ban Masses. All with the consent of the hierarchy that is always obedient to its diktats, indeed the hierarchy is even zealous in anticipating the closures ahead of time and prohibiting priests from administering the sacraments.

And while citizens are besieged by this madness that imposes absurd laws and confinements, obliging social distancing and the use of masks even outdoors, the deep state and deep church are in agreement in making us be invaded by hordes of illegal immigrants who not only do not want to respect the religion, civilization, culture and laws of the countries that host them but even want to impose their own Islamic law and customs and almost always contribute to the increase of criminal behavior and violence. Then we discover that the organizations that oversee the reception of immigrants, which is a multimillion-dollar business, are evenly split between the Left and the Church. As always, the proclamations of Bergoglio and the Democrats hide economic interests that give them compensation for their support of aligned, mainstream thought.

In a climate of terror and economic crisis—provoked on purpose in order to aggravate the situation in various nations and to disturb the electoral process in the United States and prevent Trump's reelection—justification is given for the imposition of a totalitarian regime, the yielding of national sovereignty, and recourse to supernational organs that are miraculously supposed to guarantee health, social peace, and economic recovery.

But it is a deception: they have organized everything in order to arrive at this situation, taking orders from the Bill & Melinda Gates Foundation, from the GAVI "Vaccine Alliance" group, from pharmaceutical companies, in short from the deep state. Fear, I repeat, is the instrument with which they want to impose this infernal dictatorship, which is intended to prepare for the World Government.

To those who feel disoriented, to those who fear for the future of their family, their nations, and the entire world, I respond with the words of Our Lord: "Do not be afraid; I have conquered the world" (Jn 16:33).

343

No matter how they may unleash themselves, the powers of Hell will *never* prevail over the Church, and the trials we are facing, however painful and fraught with consequences, are waking people up, and opening the eyes of those who up until now have been unaware of what is happening in the political and ecclesial sphere.

Today, we can see it. Just think: if twenty years ago they would have told us that the world would grind to a halt with a pandemic and that they would try to force all of humanity to be subjected to an invasive control like the one Bill Gates wants with his nanochips, we would have said that these ideas were just "conspiracy theories." Today all of this is taking place, and we realize that the deep state had also told us shamelessly ahead of time, certain that we would not believe something so grave and disturbing.

So I ask you: when we read in Sacred Scripture about the end times, the great apostasy; when Saint Paul says to us: "Even if an angel should announce to you a Gospel other than the one that we preached to you, let him be anathema" (Gal 1:6–10); when the Blessed Mother in the apparition of La Salette (in France) warns us that "Rome will lose the Faith and will become the seat of the Antichrist," is this not what we are facing now? Why should we think that the end times are always far away? In the Book of Revelation, Saint John speaks thus about the end times: "No one could buy or sell if they did not bear the mark, that is the name of the beast or the number that corresponds to his name" (Rev 13:17). Doesn't it seem to you that the contact-tracing project—negotiated by Bill Gates with a member of Congress for 100 billion dollars in September 2019, six months before the pandemic—reminds us in a disturbing way of the "mark of the beast"? As does the "health passport" that some nations want to impose under the pretext of COVID-19, already being tested on certain flights from London to Newark.

How should we carry ourselves in this epochal situation?

We must not allow ourselves to become discouraged: despair is a diabolical temptation that makes us believe that salvation is impossible. The devil and his followers appear terrible, they go to great lengths to snatch as many souls as possible from God, but they know that they have already lost the war and that the Beast and his Prophet will be thrown alive "into the fiery pool burning with sulfur" (Rev 19:20). We have the Lord of hosts on our side fighting for us. We have the Immaculate Virgin, "terrible as an army set in battle array" (Song of Songs 6:10). We have Saint Michael, the Prince of the Heavenly Hosts and the Patron of the Church. And another important thing: we are not few in number! On the contrary! The deep state wants to make us believe that it is all-powerful and has many allies, but the sons of Light are far, far greater in number. They are—or rather *you* are, *we* are—perhaps not as visible, perhaps quieter and lacking the same organization; but we are many, and if we place all of our hopes in the Lord, He will help us, because His Heart will allow itself to be conquered by our prayer, by our penance, by the voice of so many good souls who call upon Him. A Father does not abandon His children, above all in the moment of the final confrontation.

Your Excellency, in your note sent to the National Catholic Prayer Breakfast on September 23, 2020, you state, "The presidential elections in November represent an epochal challenge, a biblical challenge, the outcome of which will be decisive not only for the United States of America but for the whole world." You go on to state that President Trump "is preparing to fight against the demonic forces of the deep state and against the New World Order." How must we as Christians fight this evil that is now settling in upon us? What would you say to Americans that are now preparing to make a decision at the polls that will literally define the future of the world?

The political situation in the United States on the eve of the presidential election is a mirror of what is happening on the global level: two sides are facing each other in an epochal battle between the children of Light and the children of Darkness. And in a battle, one must fight, not hope to get away by hiding. The Lord wants us to be courageous and loyal, and only in this way will we be worthy of wearing the spiritual armor that will protect us.

We must not be surprised that the darkness hates the Light: it would cease to be darkness if it allowed itself to be illuminated. "The

Light shines in the darkness, but the darkness did not welcome it"
(Jn 1:5). This darkness is in civil life and in political life, but also in
religious and ecclesial life. But we do not compartmentalize our lives:
our commitment as Christians must manifest itself in our behavior
as citizens as well as members of the faithful. And thus, we bear witness to our Faith with coherence, in every moment of our lives.

We are knights of Christ, who is our King. And if there are those
who would like to dethrone Him in society and even in the Church,
we ought to make Him reign in our hearts, our families, our civil
society, our workplaces, our schools, everywhere. One Nation under
God!

Your vote should be given to those who have demonstrated that
they want to protect life, the natural family, law and order, the prosperity of the nation, peace, and freedom all over the world. Not to
those who are in favor of abortion and infanticide, homosexual
unions, LGBTQ indoctrination, wild immigration, destruction of
religion, dissolution of our Christian civilization. With your vote,
you can truly change the fate of your homeland and of the world!
Our Lord is giving you the opportunity to be protagonists of this
change by placing a cross on the electoral ballot.

*Your Excellency, in your letter to President Donald J. Trump, published
on June 6, 2020, you state that "the investigations already under way
will reveal the true responsibility of those who managed the COVID
emergency not only in the area of health care but also in politics, the
economy, and the media. We will probably find that in this colossal
operation of social engineering there are people who have decided the
fate of humanity, arrogating to themselves the right to act against the
will of citizens and their representatives in the governments of
nations." Your Excellency, we know that COVID originated from
China. And while there are many facets of this tangled web of deceit, in
light of China's involvement, it is increasingly concerning to read that
the Vatican is now in the process of renewing the deal signed with the
Communist Party of China (CCP) that recognizes CCP-appointed
bishops. This sounds very much like an endorsement of social engineering through faith. What are your thoughts on this? Is this a step
towards a one world religion?*

Interview with Scott Kesterson

The Vatican's enslavement to the Chinese dictatorship is disconcerting. Cardinal Zen's courageous denunciations of this unfortunate policy confirm the betrayal of the Vatican with respect to the Chinese Catholics, bishops and priests, who despite the persecutions of the regime remained faithful to the Apostolic See.

China plays a leading role in the New World Order, and it is no coincidence that it is supported by corrupt and unscrupulous politicians who have drawn economic and power advantages from the Chinese Communist Party: think of the investigations that today involve the Biden family, for example.

The Holy See has made itself complicit in this world plan. In reality this behavior is consistent with the aims of the deep church, which acts as a servant of globalism and whose leaders aspire to play leading roles in the Masonic World Religion desired by the recent encyclical *Fratelli Tutti*.

Once again: let's open our eyes! They accuse us of being "conspiracy theorists," but whoever makes a plot is a "conspiracy theorist," not whoever denounces it! It would be like accusing those who call firefighters of being pyromaniac, and not those who set fire to a house.

Your Excellency, I always close the interviews with a prayer. Having you on the program today is an honor that is difficult to fully articulate in words. I would be deeply honored if you would lead this closing prayer today, for all Christians in the name of our Lord and Savior, Jesus Christ.

I would like to recite with you a very beautiful prayer, composed by Pope Leo XIII. In 1884, during the celebration of Mass, Leo XIII had a vision: Satan was asking the Lord for permission to persecute the world and the Church for one hundred years, in order to put good souls to the test. Following this vision, the pope wrote out, all at once, the exorcism against Satan and the apostate angels, and he ordered that at the end of Mass a prayer would be recited, which was then abolished after the Second Vatican Council.

Dear friends, let's pray together the Saint Michael the Archangel prayer, invoking from Heaven the powerful protection of God:

347

Sancte Michaël Archangele, defende nos in prœlio: contra nequitias et insidias diaboli, esto prœsidium. Imperet illi Deus, supplices deprecamur; tuque Princeps militiœ cœlestis, Satanam, aliosque spiritus malignos, qui ad perditionem animarum pervagantur in mundo, divina virtute in infernum detrude. Amen. (Saint Michael the Archangel, defend us in battle. Be our protection against the wickedness and snares of the devil. May God rebuke him, we humbly pray: and do thou, O Prince of the Heavenly Host, by the power of God, cast into hell Satan and all the evil spirits who prowl about the world seeking the ruin of souls. Amen.)

31

Letter to American Catholics and Americans of Good Will

Concerning the November 3 Election
November 4, 2020

DEAR Brothers and Sisters,

As devout Christians and faithful citizens of the United States of America, you have intense and heartfelt concern for the fate of your beloved country while the final results of the Presidential election are still uncertain.

News of electoral fraud is multiplying, despite the shameful attempts of the mainstream media to censor the truth of the facts in order to give their candidate the advantage. There are states in which the number of votes is greater than the number of voters; others in which the mail-in vote seems to be exclusively in favor of Joe Biden; others in which the counting of ballots has been suspended for no reason or where sensational tampering has been discovered: always and only against President Donald J. Trump, always and only in favor of Biden.

In truth, for months now we have been witnessing a continuous trickle of staggered news, of manipulated or censored information, of crimes that have been silenced or covered up in the face of striking evidence and irrefutable testimony. We have seen the deep state organize itself, well in advance, to carry out the most colossal electoral fraud in history, in order to ensure the defeat of the man who has strenuously opposed the establishment of the New World Order that is wanted by the children of darkness. In this battle, you have not failed, as is your sacred duty, to make your own contribution by taking the side of the Good. Others, enslaved by vices or blinded by infernal hatred against Our Lord, have taken the side of Evil.

349

Do not think that the children of darkness act with honesty, and do not be scandalized if they operate with deception. Do you perhaps believe that Satan's followers are honest, sincere, and loyal? The Lord has warned us against the Devil: "He was a murderer from the beginning and does not stand in truth, because there is no truth in him. When he tells a lie, he speaks in character, because he is a liar and the father of lies" (Jn 8:44).

In these hours, while the gates of Hell seem to prevail, allow me to address myself to you with an appeal, which I trust that you will respond to promptly and with generosity. I ask you to make an act of trust in God, an act of humility and filial devotion to the Lord of Armies. I ask that all of you pray the Holy Rosary, if possible in your families or with your dear ones, your friends, your brothers and sisters, your colleagues, your fellow soldiers. Pray with the abandonment of children who know how to have recourse to their Most Holy Mother to ask her to intercede before the throne of the Divine Majesty. Pray with a sincere soul, with a pure heart, in the certainty of being heard and answered. Ask her—she who is the Help of Christians, *Auxilium Christianorum*—to defeat the forces of the Enemy; ask her—she who is "terrible as an army set in battle array" (Song 6:10)—to grant the victory to the forces of Good and to inflict a humiliating defeat on the forces of Evil.

Have your children pray, using the holy words that you have taught them: those confident prayers will rise to God and will not remain unheard. Have the elderly and sick pray, so that they may offer their sufferings in union with the sufferings that Our Lord suffered on the Cross when he shed His Precious Blood for Our Redemption. Have young ladies and women pray, so that they turn to her who is the model of purity and motherhood. And you, men, must also pray: your courage, your honor and your boldness will be refreshed and strengthened. All of you, take up this spiritual weapon, before which Satan and his minions retreat furiously, because they fear the Most Holy Virgin, she who is almighty by grace, even more than Almighty God.

Do not allow yourselves to be discouraged by the deceptions of the Enemy, even more so in this terrible hour in which the impudence of lying and fraud dares to challenge Heaven. Our adversaries' hours are numbered if you will pray, if we will all pray with faith and with the true ardor of charity. May the Lord grant that one single devout and faithful voice rise from your homes, your churches, and your streets! This voice will not remain unheard, because it will be the voice of a people that cries out, in the moment when the storm rages most fiercely, "Save us, Lord, we are perishing!" (Mt 8:25).

The days that await us are a precious occasion for all of you, and for those who unite themselves spiritually to you from every part of the world. You have the honor and privilege of being able to participate in the victory of this spiritual battle, to wield the powerful weapon of the Holy Rosary as our fathers did at Lepanto to repel the enemy armies.

Pray with the certainty of Our Lord's promise: "Ask and it shall be given unto you, seek and you shall find, knock and the door shall be opened unto you" (Lk 11:9). The King of Kings, from whom you ask the salvation of your Nation, will reward your faith. Your testimony, remember this, will touch the heart of Our Lord, multiplying the heavenly graces which are, more than ever, indispensable in order to achieve victory.

May my appeal, which I address to you and to all people who recognize the Lordship of God, find you to be generous apostles and courageous witnesses of the spiritual rebirth of your beloved country, and with it the entire world. *Non prævalebunt.*

God bless and protect the United States of America!

One Nation under God.

☩ Carlo Maria Viganò, Archbishop
Former Apostolic Nuncio to the
United States of America

32

Message Read at
DC "Million MAGA March"

November 14, 2020

DEAR brothers and sisters,

Allow me to address this message to you, spiritually united with all of you in the legitimate request for truth and transparency, in the face of the election fraud that is coming to light.

Some would have us believe that the people have spoken out in favor of one candidate, and they were foolish enough to tell us this while the vote-counting was still in progress. They were so sure of victory that they did not accept any dissenting voices, and even went so far as to censor the very words of the current President of the United States.

It is true: the people have spoken, but not in favor of those who promote the killing of innocent lives in the womb; not in favor of those who impose deadly ideologies on our children; not in favor of those who obey an international elite who wish to establish a New World Order. The people have spoken out in favor of traditional values, in defense of life, in defense of the family, and in defense of national sovereignty. Values that have made America great and which form the basis of your country's freedom and peace, harmony and prosperity.

When the people do not obey media indoctrination, democracy no longer matters to the so-called Democrats: they have to resort to fraud, deception, and the manipulation of votes and consensus. But something has gone wrong: "The snare has been broken, and we have escaped" (Ps 123:7).

As Christians and honest citizens of this great and beloved Nation—which is proud to proclaim to be under God—we have a

352

duty to trust that justice and truth will triumph, also on this occasion. And they will triumph not only through the honesty and fairness of so many people, but also and above all through our prayer. As lawyers and magistrates investigate the abuses and crimes committed, let us turn to the Lord, the Supreme Judge, through the intercession of Mary Most Holy, our powerful Advocate. This is the "Supreme Court" to which we can and must appeal, that the will of God may be fulfilled, and truth may triumph over falsehood.

Prayer

O Lord Almighty God, Most Holy and Undivided Trinity, who in Thy love hast deigned to redeem sinful man through the Incarnation and Passion of Our Lord Jesus Christ: prostrate before Thee we invoke Thy powerful protection in this hour of great turmoil, when darkness seems to be spreading over our beloved Nation.

O Lord God of Hosts, drive back into hell the Enemy of mankind, who by Thy eternal decree is crushed by the foot of Our Mother and Queen, Mary Most Holy. Make vain the assaults of those who, blinded by vice and hatred of Thee, wish to subject our Nation and the whole world to the tyranny of sin and rebellion against Thy Most Holy Law. Grant wisdom and courage to those who are called to direct the fortunes of the United States of America, and to those who serve their country with fidelity and honor.

Lord, bless our President, our public officials, and our pastors. For those who exercise the power entrusted to them from above, obtain the graces necessary to carry out their duties with integrity and justice.

O Almighty God, who many times hast manifested the power of Thy right hand at the side of Christian armies, place Thyself at the head of this army of Thy children. Let the prayer we address to Thee through the intercession of Our Mediatrix, the Virgin Mary, rise up to Thee like incense, so that, resolved to observe Thy Commandments and to repent of our sins, we may attain the freedom and peace that Thou hast promised us: "Peace I leave you; My peace I give to you. Not as the world gives, do I

353

give to you. Let not your hearts be troubled, neither let them be afraid" (Jn 14:27).

Grant, O Lord God, peace to our people. Look not upon our unworthiness, but upon the merits of the Immaculate Virgin, the Queen and Patroness of the United States of America. May she present to the Throne of Thy Majesty our humble prayers, our holy intentions and our penances.

And just as in the time of the Maccabees, Thou didst raise up holy heroes and courageous witnesses of the Faith, so also today hear the prayer we raise to Thee, and scatter the proud in the conceit of their hearts, granting victory to those who serve under Thy holy banner. Amen.

God bless the United States of America.

God bless our President.

33

Jericho March Speech
Delivered to the DC March[1]

December 12, 2020

DEAR brothers and sisters,

I greet all of you on this day dedicated to prayer for our beloved Nation, the United States of America. Let's ask God to make truth and justice triumph! Let's ask Him to dispel the lies and deceptions of the children of darkness!

You have organized these marches in many cities in America, and named them after a biblical event: the siege of Jericho. Jericho was the first city that the people of Israel came to after they crossed the Jordan River and entered the Promised Land. The way that God commanded the Hebrew people to conquer Jericho shows us the wonderful ways of the Lord, which are so different from our ways! The Book of Joshua tells us that Jericho was walled up and completely closed—it appeared to be an impregnable fortress! It appeared that a long siege would be necessary to conquer it by hunger, or else that huge weapons of war would be needed to break down its walls. And yet the only thing God commanded was that the people walk around the city with the Ark of the Covenant, blowing the Jubilee Trumpets, as the soldiers and people followed in perfect silence, for seven days.

God did not want to make the city of Jericho fall immediately, in order to show mercy to its inhabitants and invite them to do penance. As Saint John Chrysostom says, "The Lord, who took six days to create the heavens and the earth, took seven days to destroy a sin-

---

1. Given by video conference.

ful city." The Jubilee Trumpets that sounded around the city were used by the Jews to announce pardon and forgiveness. God would not have made them sound without an ending that was full of goodness. In the same way, an ending that is full of goodness inspires our prayer today, for our country and for our President!

Even the little children walked with their mothers around the city: those little ones were the most chosen portion of all, because they embodied the innocence that overwhelmed wickedness. Thus, moral strength fought against brutal violence, faith fought against unbelief, obedience fought against arrogant rebellion, humility fought against pride, and faith in the Lord fought against the presumption of man. God revealed the superiority of the power of Good over the power of Evil through an astonishing intervention.

We too, in this hour of great tribulation for our Nation, are praying that truth will triumph over lies, justice over abuse and fraud, honesty over corruption, honor over infamy, faithfulness over betrayal, and that order will triumph over destruction.

We are the silent army of the children of Light, the humble ranks who overthrow evil by invoking God, the praying army that walks around the walls of lies and betrayal in order to bring them down.

We fight the battles of the Lord with faith and courage, carrying the Ark of the Covenant in our hearts, remaining faithful to the teachings of the Gospel of Our Lord! We do not need material strength to fight, because we have the Lord of Armies at our side! Nothing can resist the power of prayer. The walls of the deep state, behind which evil is barricaded, will come crashing down!

Jericho was also the place where Jesus Christ converted the tax collector Zaccheus. We pray for the conversion of public officials who have become complicit in public fraud and have betrayed their oath to serve our Nation.

Along the road that led from Jerusalem to Jericho, the Good Samaritan stopped to help and care for the traveler who was attacked by robbers. May his fraternal charity be an example for patriots who are called to serve our homeland that has been attacked and wounded by both internal and external enemies.

It was also in Jericho that the Lord healed Bartimaeus of his blindness. May the blind man's faith spur us on to conversion, so that we place our trust once again in God and that He may hear the cry of our prayer for our beloved Nation.

We are citizens of Heaven: this is the homeland that awaits us for eternity. On this earth we are also children of a homeland that gave us birth and in which we were raised and educated, a homeland we have served with dedication and courage. Be proud, as Christians and as patriots, to be able to give witness today to your faith in God and your love for the United States of America, for its Constitution, and for its President Donald J. Trump.

Let us pray...

O Lord, Almighty God, prostrate before Thee we invoke Thy powerful protection in this hour of great turmoil, when darkness seems to be spreading over our beloved Nation.

Make vain the assaults of those who, blinded by vice and hatred of Thee, wish to subject our Nation and the whole world to the tyranny of sin and rebellion. Grant wisdom and courage to those who are called to decide the fortunes of the United States of America, and to those who serve their country with fidelity and honor.

Lord, bless our President and our public officials. For those who exercise the power entrusted to them from above, obtain the graces necessary to carry out their duties with integrity and justice.

O Almighty God, who many times hast manifested the power of Thy right hand at the side of Christian armies, place Thyself at the head of this army of Thy children. Let the prayer we address to Thee through the intercession of Our Lady of Guadalupe, the Patroness of the Americas, rise up to Thee, so that we may attain the freedom and peace that Thou hast promised us.

And just as in the time of Joshua, Thou didst raise up holy heroes and courageous witnesses of the Faith, so also today hear the prayer we raise to Thee, and break down the walls of the City of darkness, granting victory to those who serve under Thy holy banner. Amen.

God bless our President.

God Bless the United States of America,

One Nation under God.

34

The Jesuits, the Church, and the Deep State[1]

"Corruptio optimi pessima."[2]
Saint Gregory the Great

SEEKING to find any coherence of the recent action of the Society of Jesus with the original intentions of Saint Ignatius of Loyola is an arduous if not impossible task, to the point that in hindsight one considers the reconstitution of the Order in 1814 after its suppression by Clement XIV in 1773 to have been ill-advised. It is not surprising that, in the process of dissolution and self-demolition to which the entire ecclesial body is subjected, the contribution of the Jesuits has been—and still remains—decisive. It is no coincidence that since 2013 even the highest throne has been occupied by a Jesuit, Jorge Mario Bergoglio, even though this is in violation of the Ignatian Rule that forbids members of the Society of Jesus to take up positions in the hierarchy.

In the international geopolitical context, the role of Italy may appear in some ways marginal, but in reality Italy is a testing-ground for the experiments of social engineering that the globalist agenda intends to extend to all governments over the span of the next ten years, both in the economic and political sphere as well as the religious one. It is therefore understandable why *La Civiltà Cattolica* and its omnipresent director Fr. Antonio Spadaro, S.J., have spent themselves in decomposed endorsements both of the Italian and global Left, including the Democratic Party in America and the

---

1. This article first appeared on September 26, 2020, at https://onepeterfive.com/corruption-of-the-best-is-the-worst-the-jesuits-the-church-the-deep-state.
2. Latin for "the corruption of the best is the worst."

The Jesuits, the Church, and the Deep State

Communist Party in China. On the other hand, the ideological closeness of the Society of Jesus to left-wing revolutionary movements dates back to the first symptoms of 1968, for which Vatican II laid the ideological foundations and which found their greatest expression in the theology of liberation, after having removed the condemnation of communism from the preparatory documents of the Council. It is significant that many of the protagonists of that unfortunate season in Latin America, after the indulgence and moderate sanctions imposed by the Holy See in recent decades, have been rehabilitated and promoted by an Argentine Jesuit.

Seeing Prodi and Gentiloni[3] together with Father Spadaro for the presentation of the essay *Nell'anima della Cina* [*In the Soul of China*] should not surprise anyone: they are the expression of that deplorable "adult Catholicism" that ignores the necessary consistency of Catholics in politics desired by John Paul II and Benedict XVI, but that holds together the heterogeneous bestiary of progressivism in the name of Malthusian environmentalism, the indiscriminate welcome of immigrants, gender theory, and the religious indifferentism sanctioned by the Abu Dhabi Declaration. The Assisi Conference— "Economy of Francesco"—and the coming Encyclical *Fratelli Tutti* confirm the anthropocentric imprint and the green shift of the Bergoglian church, which instead of the courageous and "politically incorrect" proclamation of the Gospel to all the nations has preferred the easiest environmentalist and immigrationist claims of the globalist agenda, which are dramatically risky for our Western civilization. And President Trump has understood this all too well.

Prodi and Gentiloni in Italy—and we would also add Premier Conte, given his origin and his education—have their counterparts on the American side in so-called Catholic personalities like Joe Biden, Nancy Pelosi, and Andrew Cuomo: all of them proudly support abortion and gender indoctrination, and all of them are proudly in favor of the Antifa and Black Lives Matter movements that are setting entire American cities on fire. An equitable and honest analysis of the international sponsors of these parties, these "spontaneous" movements and Catholic progressivism reveals a

---

3. Two former Italian Prime Ministers.

disturbing common thread running through all of these so-called philanthropists who manipulate the political and economic fortunes of the planet with enormous funding. In recent days it has been reported in the news that the Jesuits in America have received grants of nearly two million dollars (over four years) from George Soros, and it seems that the same agreement between the Holy See and the Chinese Communist regime has been financed by large annual donations from Beijing to the Vatican coffers that are in a disastrous state. The fact that the Church fell prostrate before the lockdown, suspending liturgical celebrations and closing churches all over the world, has led to considerable collateral economic damage, for which Chinese donations and the lucrative business of welcoming immigrants represent an obvious compensation.

The United States is witnessing the highest levels and centers of cultural influence of the American Catholic Church shamelessly siding in favor of the Democratic candidate and more generally in favor of the entire apparatus that has been consolidating in recent decades within the public administration. The deep state, Trump's sworn enemy, is joined by a deep church that spares no criticisms and accusations against the incumbent President while winking indecorously with Biden and BLM, slavishly following the narration imposed by the mainstream. It matters little that Trump is openly pro-life and defends the non-negotiable principles that the Democrats have renounced—the important thing is to transform the Catholic Church into the spiritual arm of the New World Order, so as to have an *imprimatur* from the highest moral authority in the world, something that was impossible with Benedict XVI.

Secretary of State Pompeo did well to censure the renewal of the secret agreement signed between Bergoglio and Xi Jinping![4] His lucid denunciation brings to light the aberrant Vatican attitude, the betrayal of the mission of the Church, the abandonment of the Chi-

4. This refers to the secret agreement signed in October 2018 that according to Vatican reports permits the Chinese Communist Party to select the bishops for the now Vatican-recognized schismatic Chinese Patriotic Association. This agreement was renewed in October 2020 and denounced by US Secretary of State Mike Pompeo. After denouncing the Vatican agreement, the Vatican retaliated by denying the

nese Catholic community out of sinister political calculation and the way it is in accord with aligned thought. Nor is the piqued reaction of the Jesuits and Catholic progressivism surprising, beginning with *Avvenire*.[5] If Bergoglio can affirm with impunity that "Trump is not Christian," evoking the ghosts of Nazism and populism, why would the US Secretary of State not have the right to express his opinion—with the more than legitimate objective of international security—about the connivance of the Holy See with the communist dictatorship that is more ferocious but also more powerful and influential than ever? Why does the Vatican, which is silent in the face of the Democratic party's support for abortion and the violation of the most basic human rights in China, consider the Trump Administration to have no right to interfere in an agreement that has obvious repercussions in the international political balance? It causes just as much astonishment to see that the *parrhesia* in political confrontation that is called for in words is contradicted in fact by those who see their wicked plans brought to light. And it is unclear why an agreement presented as absolutely transparent and devoid of any obscure points has been kept secret and cannot be read even by the well-deserving Chinese Cardinal, Joseph Zen.[6] On the other hand, if we consider that among the people who dealt with the drafting of the agreement between the Holy See and the Chinese Communist Party there was then-Cardinal McCarrick, who was sent by Bergoglio on his behalf,[7] we will also understand the reason that the acts of the canonical process that led to the pow-

---

US Secretary of State an audience with the pope. See Philip Pullella, "Pope denies audience with Pompeo; Vatican warns against playing politics over China," *Reuters*, September 30, 2020, www.reuters.com/article/us-usa-pompeo-vatican-china/pope-denies-audience-with-pompeo-vatican-warns-against-playing-politics-over-china-idUSKBN26L25G.

5. The daily newspaper of the Italian Episcopal Conference.

6. Cardinal Joseph Zen is the retired underground bishop of Hong Kong who has spoken out publicly against any capitulation to the Chinese Communist Party. Like Secretary of State Pompeo, Cardinal Zen was also denied an audience with the pope. See Rhoda Kwan, "Cardinal Zen returns to Hong Kong after failing to meet the Pope," *Hong Kong Free Press*, October 5, 2020, https://hongkongfp.com/2020/10/05/cardinal-zen-returns-to-hong-kong-after-failing-to-meet-the-pope.

7. VN: See www.catholicity.com/vigano/2020-07-22.html.

erful prelate being reduced to the lay state remain shrouded in secrecy: in both cases an operation of transparency and truth is urgent and necessary, because the honor and moral authority of the Catholic Church in the sight of the whole world is at stake.

September 22, 2020

35

Interview with Marco Tosatti: Democrat Catholics?[1]

September 14, 2020

YOUR Excellency, you served as Apostolic Nuncio in the United States from 2011–2016, and so you know this country very well. The Democratic candidate, Joe Biden, claims to be Catholic, but he is in favor of abortion until the ninth month and "same-sex marriage." Is it possible to be Catholic and, on an official level, that is, through political and publicly manifest choices, to oppose the teaching of the Church—not on secondary elements, but on vital issues?

The question you pose, dear Tosatti, requires a well-articulated response, but first and foremost it requires serious reflection and a clear recognition of who is responsible for creating the conditions that have led to the current situation.

It was September 22, 2015, the day of Pope Francis's arrival in Washington, D.C., on the occasion of his apostolic journey to the United States. During the dinner at the Nunciature, which was attended by several members of the papal entourage, I told Pope Francis: "I believe that in the history of the United States there has never been an Administration with so many Catholics at the top: Vice President Joe Biden, Secretary of State John Kerry, and House Speaker Nancy Pelosi. All three of them ostentatiously profess to be Catholic, pro-abortion and in favor of homosexual marriage and gender ideology, in defiance of Church teaching. How do you

---

1. Translation by Diane Montagna, originally published on www.marcotosatti.com/2020/09/14/vigano-interview-pro-abortion-catholics-they-betray-the-church.

363

explain this contradiction?" And I added: "A Jesuit, Father Robert Frederick Drinan, S.J., from Boston College, held the post of Democratic US Representative for the State of Massachusetts in Washington for ten years, from 1971 to 1981. Father Drinan was one of the most strenuous advocates and promoters of abortion!" Pope Francis did not react in the slightest, just as he did not react on June 23, 2013 when, answering one of his specific questions, I revealed to him who Cardinal McCarrick really was.

In 1967, two years after the close of the Second Vatican Council, another Jesuit, Father Vincent O'Keefe, S.J. (whom Bergoglio, as Provincial of the Society of Jesus, must have known, as O'Keefe was Vicar General under Father Pedro Arrupe) as President of Fordham University, together with then-Rector of the University of Notre Dame, Father Theodore M. Hesburgh, organized a meeting of all the presidents of the North American Catholic Universities in the United States, at Land O' Lakes in Wisconsin. During the meeting, they signed a document known as the Land O' Lakes Statement, which declared the independence of their Catholic universities and colleges from all authority and all bonds of fidelity to the Magisterium of the Church. This document—which I vigorously denounced in my report to Bergoglio and the competent Roman Dicasteries—had devastating consequences for the Church and civil society in the United States.

It is not surprising, then, that the formation of hundreds of thousands of young Catholics—some of whom later became political leaders—has led to this betrayal of the Gospel whose disastrous consequences we see today. It is also not surprising that Theodore McCarrick, then-president of the Catholic University of Puerto Rico, was among the signatories of that rebellious document.

Your analysis doesn't stop, then, at an observation of the current phenomenon, but goes back to its remote causes, behind which there is a mind that has a long-term plan.

What I wish to emphasize is the close connection between the rebellion of the ultraprogressive clergy—with the Jesuits in the lead—and the education of generations of Catholics, who were formed according to the modernist ideology, flowing into the Council, which served as a premise not only for the revolution of '68 in the political sphere, but also for the doctrinal and moral revolution in the ecclesial sphere. Without Vatican II, we would not have had the student revolution that radically changed life in the Western world, the vision of the family, the role of women, and the very concept of authority.

In short: the responsibility for the betrayal by these self-styled Catholic politicians rests entirely on the unfaithful clergy, secular and regular, enslaved to modernist ideology, and on the hierarchy, which neither knew how to, nor wanted to intervene with the necessary firmness to prevent this incalculable damage to the entire body of society. In this sense, the deep state and deep church have clearly acted in concert, with the aim of scientifically destabilizing both the civil and ecclesiastical order. Today we have the opportunity to understand the current situation, and it is once again the task of the Authorities to do everything possible to stop this race to the abyss: the Holy See and the United States Conference of Catholic Bishops (USCCB) have the duty to call to obedience both the rebel clerics, and the laity whom they continue to deceive and even publicly support.

Do you believe that an authoritative intervention by the bishops is necessary to call people back to adherence to non-negotiable principles?

When the Congregation for the Doctrine of the Faith issued very clear instructions on the exclusion from Holy Communion of Catholic politicians who do not follow the Church's teaching, it was McCarrick himself, together with Archbishop Wilton Gregory, then-president of the USCCB, who worked to prevent their implementation in the United States. Moral corruption and doctrinal deviation are intrinsically linked and, to effectively heal these wounds in the body of the Church, it is imperative to act on both fronts. If this dutiful intervention does not take place, the bishops and the leaders of the Church will answer to God for betraying their duty as pastors.

Why do you see a relationship between the Second Vatican Council and the 1968 student protests?

It is undeniable, even if only from a historical and sociological point of view, that there is a very close relationship between the conciliar revolution and 1968. The very protagonists of Vatican II admit it. Joseph Ratzinger stands out among them, writing: "Adherence to a utopian anarchistic Marxism [...] was supported on the front lines by university chaplains and student associations who saw in it the dawn of the realization of Christian hopes. The guiding light is to be found in the events of May 1968 in France. Dominicans and Jesuits were at the barricades. The intercommunion carried out at an ecumenical Mass at the barricades was considered a kind of landmark in salvation history, a kind of revelation that inaugurated a new era of Christianity."[2]

One of the *periti* at the Council, Fr. René Laurentin, wrote: "The demands of the May '68 movement largely coincided with the Council's grand ideas, particularly in the Council's Constitution on the Church and the World. To a certain extent, Vatican II was already a protest against the Curia by a group of bishops who were trying to create an institutionally prefabricated Council."[3]

And the Argentine theologian, Fr. Álvaro Calderón, affirmed: "If there is anything that immediately stands out to those who study the Second Vatican Council, it is the change, in a liberal sense, of the concept of authority. The pope stripped himself of his supreme authority in favour of the bishops (collegiality); the bishops stripped themselves of their authority in favour of theologians; theologians gave up their science in favour of listening to the faithful. And the voice of the faithful is nothing more than the fruit of propaganda."[4]

2. VN: Joseph Ratzinger, *Les principes de la théologie catholique* (Paris: Téqui, 1985), 433.

3. VN: René Laurentin, *Crisi della Chiesa e secondo Sinodo episcopale* (Brescia: Morcelliana, 1969), 16.

4. VN: Álvaro Calderón, *La lámpara bajo el celemín. Cuestión disputada sobre la autoridad doctrinal del magisterio eclesiástico desde el Concilio Vaticano II* (Buenos Aires: Ed. Rio Reconquista, 2009).

Interview with Marco Tosatti: Democrat Catholics?

This vision is also widely and proudly affirmed on the progressive front,[5] which saw the same demands of the conciliar revolution realized in 1968. Jacques Noyer, bishop emeritus of Amiens, recalls: "I am convinced that the spirit that inspired the preparation, celebration and implementation of the Second Vatican Council is a great opportunity for the Church and the world. It is the Gospel offered to the men of today. Deep down, May '68 was a spiritual movement, even a mystical one, consistent with the dream of the Council."[6]

Without a "green light" from the Church, the world would never have accepted or taken up the student movement's demands for rebellion. Beyond the Acts of the Council, it was precisely the *spirit* of Vatican II that marked the end of a hierarchically constituted society, and of the traditional values common to the Western world: until then, concepts such as authority, honor, respect for the elderly, a spirit of mortification and service, a sense of duty, the defense of the family and one's fatherland, were shared and, albeit in a weakened form compared to the past, still practiced.

Seeing the Catholic Church, a beacon of truth and civilization for nations, throw open its doors to the world and unhesitatingly discard her glorious heritage, going so far as to revolutionize the liturgy and water down morality, was an unequivocal signal to the masses, a sort of approval of the agenda that, at the time, didn't yet dare to reveal itself completely, even though all of its distinctive signs could be grasped. It destroyed the Church and society, compromised civil and religious authority, discredited marriage and the family, ridiculed patriotism and a sense of duty or labeled them as

5. VN: See "Il Maggio '68 e il Concilio Vaticano II," www.atfp.it/rivista-tfp/264-ottobre-2018/1494-il-maggio-68-e-il-concilio-vaticano-ii; see also "Il Sessantotto. Agostino Giovagnoli (storico): Profondo legame con il Concilio che ne ha anticipato alcuni tratti," www.agensir.it/italia/2018/04/26/il-sessantotto-agostino-giovagnoli-storico-profondo-legame-con-il-concilio-che-ne-ha-anticipato-alcuni-tratti; Marco Vergottini, "Il '68 e la sua ricaduta sul fronte ecclesiale," https://notedipastoralegiovanile.it/index.php?option=com_content&view=article&id=13936:il-68-e-la-sua-ricaduta-sul-fronte-ecclesiale&catid=353&Itemid=1074; and the interesting chronology published by Archivio 900: www.archivio900.it/it/documenti/doc.aspx?id=177.

6. VN: See www.atfp.it/rivista-tfp/264-ottobre-2018/1494-il-maggio-68-e-il-concilio-vaticano-ii.

fascism. All amid the silence of a complicit hierarchy! Those like me, who entered the seminary in the immediate postconciliar period, can testify that even the Roman Pontifical Seminaries were immediately conquered by this tremor of protest, emancipation and dissolution of all rules and discipline.

There can be no doubt about this. If this were not the case, the substantial funding that globalist organizations, such as Soros's Open Society, have allocated to the activities of the Society of Jesus, and presumably to other Catholic organizations, would be inexplicable.[7] All the premises that were laid down in a nutshell with Vatican II and the student revolution are now consistently proposed by Vatican leaders on the ecclesial front, and by government leaders on the globalist political front. Therefore, it should come as no surprise if the priorities of Bergoglio's political program coincide with Joe Biden's priorities. Migration, environmentalism, Malthusian ecologism, gender ideology, the dissolution of the family and globalism are common to the deep state and deep church agenda. Bergoglio's formal opposition to abortion and the LGBT indoctrination of children is disavowed in practice, both by the bishops' support for those who promote it politically, and for those who theorize about the use of birth control and the recognition of the rights of sodomites. The case of Father James Martin, S.J.[8] is emblematic, because it confirms an *idem sentire* between the exponents of globalism and the progressive Catholic intelligentsia. The mark that unites these movements is lying and deception, division and destruction, hatred for Tradition and Christian civilization. And ultimately, the theological aversion to Christ, typical of Lucifer and his followers.

Your Excellency, don't you think that this correspondence between the deep state and deep church is also confirmed in relations with China?

The Chinese communist dictatorship is courted by both the deep state and the deep church: Joe Biden is as subservient to the eco-

---

7. VN: See "Open Society di George Soros finanzia i Gesuiti," www.marcotosatti.com/2020/09/08/open-society-di-george-soros-finanzia-i-gesuiti.

8. A Jesuit priest who is well known for his support of the LGBTQ agenda; he was asked to offer an invocation at the 2020 Democratic National Convention.

nomic and political interests of Beijing as Jorge Mario Bergoglio. It doesn't matter if human rights are systematically violated in China, if Catholics faithful to the Catholic Church are persecuted, or if a hateful dictatorship massacres millions of innocent people by planning mass abortion: the interests of the globalist agenda prevail even over the evidence of the horrors carried out by the Chinese dictatorship.

I would add: the active support carried out by the Jesuits, since the time when McCarrick went to China to prepare the famous agreement that would later be ratified by the Vatican under the Bergoglio pontificate, is significant. The agreement aroused considerable perplexity even in the secular press. *The Times* recently published an article, entitled "The Pope is Beijing's unlikely admirer," in which Dominic Lawson denounced that "more and more nations have expressed their concern about the growing evidence of concentration camps and even genocide in the Chinese province of Xinjiang," and pointed out that "there has been silence from the one entity that has the whole of suffering humanity at the core of its mission. I refer to the Holy See." And he adds: "The failure to condemn the genocide is unforgivable."[9] Furthermore, during the Angelus last July 5, Francis's omission of the reference to the events in Hong Kong so as not to annoy Xi Jinping, after having circulated the text to the press,[10] caused a stir.

This subservience of the globalist movement and the Holy See to China is alarming, and is confirmed also by the meetings Father Spadaro, S.J. and other Jesuits had with representatives of the Communist Party during the lockdown, regarding the circulation of the Chinese edition of *La Civiltà Cattolica*.

Beyond the current situation, in which the Catholic candidates for the Democratic Party clearly do not hold to the Magisterium of the Church, what should a true Catholic politician be like?

9. VN: See www.thetimes.co.uk/article/the-pope-is-beijings-unlikely-admirer-knkvp2qv3.

10. VN: See www.lanuovabq.it/it/hong-kong-la-santa-sede-si-inchina-al-regime-cinese.

To be Catholic, one must not only be baptized, but must live in a manner consistent with the Faith he has received at the sacred font. Faith goes hand in hand with good works, as Sacred Scripture teaches us: without putting into practice our having become children of God through incorporation into the Mystical Body, our words are empty and our witness is incoherent, and indeed scandalous for the faithful and those who do not believe. Father James Martin, S.J. is therefore wrong to limit himself to the purely bureaucratic aspect; his words are refuted by those of the Savior: "You are my friends if you do what I command you" (Jn 15:14). Friendship with God—which consists in the soul being in the state of grace—depends on our obedience to Our Lord's orders. Not suggestions or advice: orders! Again, He says: "Not everyone who says to me: 'Lord, Lord,' will enter the Kingdom of heaven, but he who does the will of my Father who is in heaven" (Mt 7:21).

I would add that hell is not reserved for non-Catholics: among the eternal flames there are many baptized souls, even religious, priests and bishops, who have deserved damnation because of their rebellion against the will of the Lord. Self-styled adult Catholics and their preceptors ought to think carefully, before they hear the words of Christ resound: "I never knew you; depart from me, you evildoers" (Mt 7:23).

A Catholic who supports abortion or gender ideology denies not only the Magisterium, but also the natural law, which constitutes the moral basis common to all peoples, of all times and places. The seriousness of an inconsistency between belonging to the Church and being faithful to her teaching reflects the artificial dichotomy between doctrine and pastoral care, which has crept in since Vatican II, and reached its clearest formulation in *Amoris Lætitia*. Yet on closer inspection, the so-called "*laicità dello Stato*" [secular nature of the State] also poses serious problems, since it recognizes the right of civil society to deny the divine Kingship of Christ and to reject His Law, while at the same time asking the laity to give a testimony of faith in which the primacy of Catholic truth is lowered to the same level as error.

What is clear is that Catholics cannot vote for, much less the hierarchy approve, a "Catholic" politician who does not put the integrity of the Church's doctrine into practice. The self-styled Catholic Joe Biden, who supports partial-birth abortion, i.e., infanticide, and who even before Obama supported gender ideology and celebrated the "marriage" of two men, is not Catholic. Period.

Joe Biden has chosen Kamala Harris as his vice-presidential running mate. Harris defended Planned Parenthood, the world's largest abortion company, in California when it was accused of trading in aborted baby parts. What is the significance of this choice?

The culture of death that underlies today's prevailing anti-Christian ideology is consistent with itself: the murder of innocent creatures is one of the indispensable elements of those who want to erase not only Christianity, but humanity and creation, which manifests the work of the divine Creator.

As I have said many times, this process of dissolution is carried out on two levels: an ideological one, by those who deliberately want evil and want to implement their own hellish plan in forced stages; and an economic one, by those who support the ideology, not necessarily out of conviction, but for profit. Thus, the human sacrifices that have continued to be celebrated in abortion clinics, even during the COVID-19 emergency, have generated profits for Planned Parenthood and the entire chain of death that traffics in the organs of aborted babies. Let us not forget that the abortion lobby—like the LGBT movement—is one of the main financiers of left-wing election campaigns around the world. If companies ideologically oriented toward the culture of death lavishly fund certain political parties, it's not surprising that candidates from those parties support their sponsors with laws that favor them.

An American bishop, Thomas Tobin of Providence, Rhode Island, said that for the first time in a while, the Democrats don't have a Catholic on the ticket. Father James Martin, S.J. replied that Biden was baptized Catholic and therefore is one. What does this back and forth allow us to understand about the state of the Church in America?

I have already noted above that "Catholic candidates" are political candidates who not only call themselves Catholic, but who live in a manner consistent with the faith and morals taught by the Church. If being Catholic had no concrete impact, it wouldn't make any sense to vote for a candidate who doesn't in fact differ from the others. Father Martin, S.J.'s response is sophism, because he pretends not to see the divide between appearing and being Catholic, between exploiting the "designation" for an electoral advantage and being a true witness to the Gospel in private, civil and political life, and in institutions. What about Father James Martin, S.J.? He was baptized, confirmed, ordained a priest, and even made solemn vows of chastity and obedience; he is S.J.… he is LGBT. Someone else, one of the Twelve, betrayed Him. Let Father Martin, who is always impeccable in his clerical dress, look into the mirror of his soul, and see whom he resembles!

Your Excellency, why is the Church so interested in the dominant ideology, which is also clearly anti-Christian?

This is a problem we have been carrying around for seventy years. Since that time, Catholic clergy, and in particular the hierarchy, have suffered from a sense of inferiority that places them below their interlocutors in the world. They feel ontologically inferior. They consider Christ's teaching to be inadequate and clumsily try to adapt it to the secular mentality. They are afraid of appearing outdated, not in step with the times, even centuries late, as another illustrious Jesuit (R.I.P.) has said.

This terrible inferiority complex is the direct consequence of a dramatic loss of faith. Christ's saving message is irreconcilable with the seductions of the world; it is unworthy and illegitimate to adulterate the Magisterium in order to please the world, abusing a sacred authority which is aimed instead at preaching to "all nations, baptizing them in the name of the Father and the Son and the Holy Spirit, teaching them to observe all that I have commanded you" (Mt 28:19–20).

As long as Church leaders persist in not being the first to behave consistently with their own role and with Christ's teaching, it will be impossible to demand equal consistency from the laity, who look to them as an example. This is confirmed by the fact that there are self-styled "Catholic" politicians who today enjoy the support of self-styled "Catholic" clerics and bishops. It is also confirmed by the fact that those who defend life and the natural law, although they aren't Catholic, are accused of populism, compared to the dictators of the last century,[11] and told they are not Christian[12] or, as in the recent case of Father James Altman, accused by his bishop of being "divisive and causing scandal."[13]

What is the role of Planned Parenthood in American politics? Is it an instrument of freedom and the affirmation of rights, as the "progressives" say, or...

In the globalist society, Planned Parenthood mirrors and plays the opposite role of that played by charitable institutions and foundations that protect life in Christian nations. In Christian societies, children were welcomed with love, and even in situations of poverty and difficulty they were cared for, raised and educated to become good Christians and honest citizens, by putting the word of the Gospel into practice. In anti-Christian societies, Planned Parenthood is tasked with killing these innocents, putting into practice the culture of death inspired by the one who was a "murderer from the beginning" (Jn 8:44). Let us not forget that Planned Parenthood, together with the other multinational abortion companies, serves the Malthusian delirium of the globalist high command, which is planning a drastic decimation of the world population.

George Soros and others are trying to pressure Mark Zuckerberg into limiting the pro-life presence and activity on Facebook. The choice of

---

11. VN: "Papa: 'Populismo in Europa ricorda terribili degenerazioni passate,'" www.adnkronos.com/papa-populismo-in-europa-ricorda-terribili-degenerazioni-passate_e5QLdzXFmc6u0VbgaEkw8.

12. VN: "La conferenza stampa del Papa sul volo di ritorno dal Messico," www.toscanaoggi.it/Documenti/Papa-Francesco/La-conferenza-stampa-del-Papa-sul-volo-di-ritorno-dal-Messico.

13. VN: See https://quincy-network.s3.ca-central-1.amazonaws.com/wp-conten t/uploads/sites/10/2020/09/Statement-Father-James-Altman-090920.pdf, and ww w.lifesitenews.com/news/watch-priest-warns-us-voters-you-cannot-be-catholic-an d-be-a-democrat.

Joe Biden and Kamala Harris, and these maneuvers to limit those who defend life—what kind of global scenario do they lead to?

The Gospel spread throughout the world thanks to the preaching of the Apostles and the witness of the Martyrs and Confessors of the Faith. Likewise, the anti-gospel of the Synagogue of Satan is spreading because of the preaching of the children of darkness, the testimony of public figures, celebrities and entertainers, and self-styled philanthropists. In the end, what's left is always a division into two camps: on one side, the good, and on the other, the wicked, in the biblical war between good and evil. And if at one time our saints destroyed idols and pagan temples, leaving no room for devil worshippers, today it is inevitable that followers of groupthink will unite to desecrate and destroy churches, tear down crosses and statues of saints, and erase all memory of faith in Christ. In days gone by, forbidden books were censored in order to protect the simple ones, whose souls would be poisoned by them; today, what is good is censored, because evil does not tolerate it.

The global scenario that emerges is manifest before our eyes: until we understand that there can be no dialogue with evildoers (Mt 7:22), that there is no compatibility between the light of Christ and the darkness of Satan, we will not be able to win the battle, because we will not even have recognized that we are at war against the powers of hell. And in a war, there are necessarily two opposing sides: those who refuse to serve under the banner of Christ inevitably end up helping the servants of the Evil One.[14] This awareness is clear to our enemies, but it does not seem to be so clear to those who do not see the Christian life as a "battle."

Allow me to recall the words of President Trump at the end of the recent Republican National Convention: "Our opponents say that redemption for you can only come from giving power to them." This "redemption" consists in denying God's sovereign rights over

---

14. This sentence is reminiscent of one of the meditations in the Ignatian *Spiritual Exercises*, The Two Standards. It is not clear if Archbishop Viganò has made a retreat according to the traditional formula of St. Ignatius, but this image of choosing between the two banners seems indebted to it.

individuals, societies, nations, and replacing the gentle yoke of Christ with the odious tyranny of Satan. And it is, to all intents and purposes, a reversal of the Redemption—the redemption of the slave—which the Savior accomplished on the wood of the Cross. So let us not be fooled by the mellifluous words of those who usurp the biblical metaphor of the children of light and the children of darkness to establish the kingdom of Lucifer: the darkness and chaos we see in American cities are the fruit of the same ideology that approves of postnatal abortion and homosexual marriage, just as the backers of the BLM and Antifa movements are precisely the Democrats and the "philanthropic" foundations that furiously oppose Trump's reelection.[15]

Biden's mention, indeed, his ignominious usurpation of John Paul II's famous exhortation "Do not be afraid!" sounds like the Serpent's cunning trick to take of the fruit of the tree, rather than the courageous invitation that the Polish pope launched to a world far from Christ. And it is strange that the indignation of Archbishop Wilton Gregory, who was so ready to censure the presidential couple's visit to the Shrine of St. John Paul II, today doesn't also blast his opponent, Joe Biden, a perverted Catholic, who is using the image of the same pope, and of Bergoglio, to advance his electoral campaign.

Today, John Paul II's strong and authoritative words would make the Democrats and perhaps the bishops themselves tremble: "Do not be afraid to welcome Christ and accept his power. Help the pope and all those who wish to serve Christ and with Christ's power to serve the human person and the whole of mankind. Do not be afraid. Open wide the doors for Christ. To his saving power open the boundaries of States, economic and political systems, the vast fields of culture, civilization and development. Do not be afraid. Christ knows 'what is in man.' He alone knows it."[16]

---

15. VN: For some time the antifa.com domain redirected to Joe Biden's campaign site (joebiden.com); now [as of January 2021] it redirects to whitehouse.gov.

16. VN: Source: www.vaticannews.va/it/papa/news/2019-10/22-ottobre-1978-giovanni-paolo-ii-non-abbiate-paura.html; http://www.vatican.va/content/john-paul-ii/en/homilies/1978/documents/hf_jp-ii_hom_19781022_inizio-pontificato.html.

Today Christ's saving power is replaced by "the voice of creation which admonishes us to return to our rightful place in the created natural order." The redeeming Passion of Our Lord is replaced by the "groan of creation," and the scourges of divine Justice by the "wrath of Mother Earth," of the Pachamama.

President Trump stated: "Our opponents say that redemption for you can only come from giving power to them. But in this country, we don't turn to career politicians for salvation. In America, we don't turn to government to restore our souls. We put our faith in almighty God." I believe that this faith in God, which clearly must be matched by a consistency of Christian life and witness, will also confirm in the 2020 US presidential election that "the Lord's right hand has done mighty things" as Psalm 117 reminds us.

36

Letter on Election Fraud, Biden, COVID, and the USCCB

THE world in which we find ourselves living is, to use an expression from the Gospel, "*in se divisum*" [divided against itself] (Mt 12:25). This division, it seems to me, consists of a split between reality and fiction: objective reality on one side, and the fiction of the media on the other. This certainly applies to the pandemic, which has been used as a tool of social engineering that is instrumental to the Great Reset, but it applies even more to the surreal American political situation, in which the evidence of a colossal electoral fraud is being censored by the media, which now proclaims Joe Biden's victory as an accomplished fact.

The reality of COVID is blatantly in contrast with what the mainstream media wants us to believe, but this is not enough to dismantle the grotesque castle of falsehoods to which the majority of the population conforms with resignation. In a similar way, the reality of electoral fraud, of blatant violations of the rules and the systematic falsification of the results contrasts with the narrative given to us by the information giants, who say that Joe Biden is the new President of the United States, period. And so it *must be*: there are no alternatives, either to the supposed devastating fury of a seasonal flu that caused the same number of deaths as last year, or to the inevitability of the election of a candidate who is corrupt and subservient to the deep state. In fact, Biden has already promised to restore the lockdown.[1]

Reality no longer matters: it is absolutely irrelevant when it

---

1. VN: See https://www.infowars.com/posts/joe-biden-to-announce-covid-task -force-to-impose-mask-mandates-contact-tracing-on-americans.

stands between the conceived plan and its realization. COVID and Biden are two holograms, two artificial creations, ready to be adapted time and time again to contingent needs or respectively replaced when necessary with COVID-21 and Kamala Harris. The accusations of irresponsibility thrown at Trump supporters for holding rallies vanish as soon as Biden's supporters gather in the streets, as has already happened for BLM demonstrations. What is criminal for some people is permitted for others: without explanations, without logic, without rationality. The mere fact of being on the left, of voting for Biden, of putting on the mask is a pass to do anything, while simply being on the right, voting for Trump or questioning the effectiveness of masks is sufficient reason for condemnation and an execution that does not require any evidence or a trial: they are *ipso facto* labeled as fascists, sovereignists, populists, deniers—and those labeled with these social stigmas are supposed to simply silently withdraw.

We thus return to that division between good people and evil people that is ridiculed when it is used by one side—ours—and conversely held up as an incontestable postulate when used by our adversaries. We have seen this with the contemptuous comments responding to my words about the "children of Light" and the "children of darkness," as if my "apocalyptic tones" were the fruit of a ravingly mad mind and not the simple observation of reality. But by disdainfully rejecting this biblical division of humanity, they have actually confirmed it, restricting to themselves alone the right to give the stamp of social, political, and religious legitimacy.

They are the good ones, even if they support the killing of the innocent—and we are supposed to get over it. *They* are the ones supporting democracy, even if in order to win elections they must always resort to deception and fraud—even fraud that is blatantly evident. *They* are the defenders of freedom, even if they deprive us of it day after day. *They* are objective and honest, even if their corruption and their crimes are now obvious even to the blind. The dogma that they despise and deride in others is indisputable and incontrovertible when it is *they* who promote it.

But as I have said previously, they are forgetting a small detail, a particular that they cannot understand: the truth exists in itself; it exists regardless of whether there is someone who believes it, because the truth possesses in itself, ontologically, its own reason for validity. The truth cannot be denied, because it is an attribute of God; it is God Himself. And everything that is true participates in this primacy over lies. We can thus be theologically and philosophically certain that these deceptions' hours are numbered, because it will be enough to shine light on them to make them collapse. Light and darkness, precisely. So let us allow light to be shed on the deceptions of Biden and the Democrats, without taking even one step back: the fraud that they have plotted against President Trump and against America will not remain standing for long, nor will the worldwide fraud of COVID, the responsibility of the Chinese dictatorship, the complicity of the corrupt and traitors, and the enslavement of the deep church. *Tout se tient* [everything fits together].

In this panorama of systematically constructed lies, spread by the media with a disturbing impudence, the election of Joe Biden is not only desired, but is considered indispensable and therefore true and therefore definitive. Even though the vote counts are not completed; even though the vote verifications and recounts are only just beginning; even though the lawsuits alleging fraud have only just been filed. Biden must become President, because *they* have already decided it: the vote of the American people is valid *only* if it ratifies this narrative—otherwise, it is "reinterpreted," dismissed as plebiscite drift, populism, and fascism.

It is therefore not surprising that the Democrats have such coarse and violent enthusiasm for their candidate *in pectore*, nor that the media and the official commentators have such uncontainable satisfaction, nor that political leaders from around the world are expressing their support and sycophantic subjection to the deep state. We are watching a race to see who can arrive first, elbowing and sprawling to show off, so that they can be seen to have always believed in the crushing victory of the Democratic puppet.

But if we understand that the sycophancy of world heads of state and party secretaries is simply a part of the trite script of the global Left, we are frankly left quite disturbed by the declarations of the United States Conference of Catholic Bishops, immediately republished by Vatican News, which with disturbing cross-eyedness credits itself with having supported "the second Catholic President in the history of the United States," apparently forgetting the not-negligible detail that Biden is avidly pro-abortion,[2] a supporter of LGBT ideology and of anti-Catholic globalism. The archbishop of Los Angeles, José H. Gomez, profaning the memory of the *Cristeros* martyrs of his native country, says bluntly: "The American people have spoken."

The frauds that have been denounced and widely proven matter little: the annoying formality of the vote of the people, albeit adulterated in a thousand ways, must now be considered to be concluded in favor of the standard-bearer of aligned, mainstream thought. We have read, not without retching, the posts of James Martin, S.J., and all those courtiers who are pawing to get on Biden's chariot in order to share in his ephemeral triumph. Those who disagree, those who ask for clarity, those who have recourse to the law to see their rights protected do not have any legitimacy and must be silent, resign themselves, and disappear. Or rather: they must be "united" with the exultant choir, applaud and smile. Those who do not accept are threatening democracy and must be ostracized. As may be seen, there are still two sides, but this time they are legitimate and indisputable because it is *they* who impose them.

It is indicative that the US Conference of Catholic Bishops and Planned Parenthood are both expressing their satisfaction for the presumed electoral victory of the same person. This unanimity of consensus recalls the enthusiastic support of the Masonic Lodges on the occasion of the election of Jorge Mario Bergoglio, which was also not free from the shadow of fraud within the Conclave and was equally desired by the deep state, as we know clearly from the emails of John Podesta and the ties of Theodore McCarrick and his colleagues with the Democrats and with Biden himself. A very nice little group of cronies, no doubt about it.

With these words of the USCCB the *pactum sceleris* [plot to commit crime] between the deep state and the deep church is confirmed and sealed, the enslavement of the highest levels of the Catholic

2. VN: See https://catholicism.org/how-many-abortions-is-joe-biden-responsible-for.html.

hierarchy to the New World Order, denying the teaching of Christ and the doctrine of the Church. Taking note of this is the first, imperative step in order to understand the complexity of the present events and consider them in a supernatural, eschatological perspective. We know, indeed we firmly believe, that Christ, the one true Light of the world, has already conquered the darkness that obscures it.

American Catholics must multiply their prayers and beg the Lord for a special protection for the President of the United States. I ask priests, especially during these days, to recite the Exorcism against Satan and the apostate angels, and to celebrate the Votive Mass *Pro defensione ab hostibus*.[3] Let us confidently ask for the intervention of the Blessed Virgin Mary, to whose Immaculate Heart we consecrate the United States of America and the entire world.

November 8, 2020

---

3. A votive Mass may be offered by any priest on a day on which no other Mass is required to be offered due to its ranking. This particular votive Mass is "for defense against our enemies."

37

A Meditation on the "Great Reset" and the Liberty of Christians

O God, You are awesome from Your sanctuary;
the God of Israel gives strength and power to His people.
Psalm 68:35 [67:36, Vul.]

ON November 19, 2020, the founder of the World Economic Forum, Klaus Schwab, declared that "COVID is an opportunity for a global reset."

In reality, Schwab was slavishly repeating what Jacques Attali said in the French weekly *L'Express* on May 3, 2009 [so, 11 years ago]: "History teaches us that humanity evolves significantly only when it is really afraid: then it initially develops defense mechanisms; sometimes intolerable (scapegoats and totalitarianisms); sometimes useless (distractions); sometimes effective (therapies, which, if necessary, may depart from all previous moral principles). Then, once the crisis is over, fear transforms these mechanisms to make them compatible with individual freedom and inscribe them as policies of a healthy democracy."

Back then it was the swine flu which, according to the media, was expected to cause millions of deaths and for which nations bought millions of doses of vaccines never used, because they proved useless, from "Big Pharma." Useless for all—except for those who sold them, making huge profits.

One might wonder why a flu virus that according to recent WHO data has a mortality (0.13%) slightly higher than that of a normal seasonal flu syndrome (0.10%) could have led to the declaration of the pandemic and to a series of practically identical countermeasures in almost all European nations and the American continent.

The "Great Reset" and the Liberty of Christians

One might also wonder why COVID-19 *treatments* are generally discredited, minimized or prohibited, while the *vaccine* is considered the most effective solution.

And it needs to be explained how it is possible to create a vaccine, since—according to the statements of the US CDC (United States Centers for Disease Control and Prevention)—the virus has not yet been isolated.

What antigen may be used, if the virus SARS-CoV-2 cannot be isolated and replicated?

And what reliability can the virus tests have, since the tests are calibrated to detect only the generic "Coronavirus"?

And if on October 19 the Spallanzani Hospital in Rome announced the development of a test that distinguishes between normal flu and COVID-19, may we know what, so far, have patients who undergo the new test been found positive for?

Perhaps this lack of clarity is why some members of the Moderna and Pfizer boards of directors have sold part of their company shares.

So, let's go back to the questions that many posed to themselves months ago, and to the never-contradicted contents of my two Open Letters to President Trump: a world plan appears in its disconcerting reality. The architects of the plan, creating an unjustified social alarm about an alleged pandemic—that today we see is no more serious than a normal flu, as confirmed by official data from all over the world—have used it to create a tremendous global social and economic crisis and so to legitimize the drastic reduction of the basic rights of the population. It is what its authors themselves call the Great Reset: the global reset of the economy, of society and of masses of people.

In this project, the COVID virus plays a fundamental role, as an alibi that justifies—in the face of the "totem" of a science that has prostituted itself to the interests of an elite after having abdicated its mission to save human lives—the deprivation of freedom, the interference of governments in the private life of citizens, the establishment of a pseudo-health regime in which, against all objective scientific evidence, the number of diners, the distance between people, the possibility of buying, selling, breathing and even praying, is decided from above.

Someone, in the deafening silence of the Catholic hierarchy, has imposed the closure of churches or the limitation of religious celebrations, considering the House of God as a cinema or a museum, but at the same time declaring abortion clinics "essential services."

These are the paradoxes of a misguided power, managed by people corrupt in the soul and sold out to Satan, a power which, after obsessively repeating the mantras of "democracy" and "power belongs to the people" is now forced to impose a dictatorship on the people themselves, in the name of the achievement of objectives aimed at protecting the political and financial interests of the elite.

The rich are getting richer and richer, while the middle classes that constitute the social fabric and the very soul of nations are being cut down.

The French Revolution wiped out the Western aristocracy.

The Industrial Revolution obliterated the peasants and spread the proletarianization which led to the disaster of Socialism and Communism.

The Revolution of '68 demolished the family and the school.

This Great Reset, desired by the globalist elite, represents the final revolution with which to create a shapeless and anonymous mass of slaves connected to the internet, confined to the house, threatened by an endless series of pandemics designed by those who already have the miraculous vaccine ready.

Precisely in these days, with the harmony of a plan that seems orchestrated in every detail under a single leadership, the imposition of a vaccine is being theorized by many parties, even before the vaccine's actual effectiveness is fully known, and even before the vaccine's possible side-effects may be fully ascertained.

This obligation to receive a vaccine is projected by many to occur alongside the issuance of a "health passport," so that those who have such a passport may move without limitations, while those who refuse a vaccine would not be able to use means of transport, attend restaurants and visit public places, schools and offices.

That this represents an intolerable violation of the individual's freedoms does not seem to be a problem: lawmakers do not hesitate to sack parliaments to impose their tyrannical norms, knowing that their power exists as long as they obey the Great Reset agenda, endorsed by the international institutions such as the European Union and the UN.

Faced with such a massive and coordinated deployment of forces we remain astonished, bewildered by the impudence of those who are telling us, in essence, that we must silently accept the dictatorship of a faceless power group, because that is how the group has decided.

We are disconcerted by the enslavement of the world Left—and of the Democrats in the United States—to this agenda, which knows no limits, no restraints on its execution, to the point of organizing an electoral coup of such magnitude and gravity as to be horrifying.

The manual fraud of duplicate ballots, the votes of deceased people, citizens who discover they have voted a thousand times and employees who tamper with the results by obscuring the windows of the polling stations with cardboard panels, is accompanied by the use of a vote-counting apparatus which is proving not only to be open to fraudulent use, but even to have been designed at the software level to allow the shifting of votes from one candidate to another, based on a complex algorithm.

We discover that the people behind this macroscopic fraud are always the same, always of the same political party, always subservient to the same ideology. People corrupt in intellect and will, because they made themselves the slaves of a ruthless tyrant, after refusing to obey a good, just and merciful Lord.

Thus, as these have accepted the slavery of sin and rebellion against God, today they would like to drag the whole of humanity into an abyss of death and despair: it is the miserable revenge of Satan, who, not being able to defeat the One who cast him into hell, tries to drag with him as many souls as possible, in an attempt to frustrate the work of Redemption.

We, believers in Christ our only Lord, have no reason to fear, even against all human reason: we know that, reborn in Baptism, we are no longer servants but children of God, and that by preserving the friendship of our Lord with grace we can trust in Him, in His provident help, in His powerful protection.

Ultimately, this is true freedom: the freedom of the children of

God, who obey His law not out of fear but out of love, not out of compulsion but because in adhering to the divine will they will find their own perfect fulfillment and their complete realization.

For every soul is created for the greater glory of God, for eternal bliss as a reward of fidelity to the Savior.

Let not our hearts be troubled!

The maneuvers of those who work in darkness are coming to light, showing themselves in all their horror and revealing their perverse and infernal matrix.

Lies, deceptions, violence, death: this is the harsh reality of evil before which people of good will can only be horrified.

If Our Lord deigns to listen to the prayers of His children, this castle of lies and fraud will collapse miserably, and its architects will have to go back into hiding to escape the rigors of justice and the execration of peoples.

These are decisive hours: we continue to pray, to recite the Holy Rosary, to nourish ourselves with the Most Holy Eucharist, to do penance.

The choral voice that rises up to the throne of the divine Majesty will not remain unheard.

Let us not be discouraged, because it is in the moment of trial that the Lord gives us the opportunity to show our trust in Him and to see the greatness of His mercy.

"Whatsoever you ask in My Name, I will do, so that the Father may be glorified in the Son" (Jn 14:13). Our Lord told us clearly: anything.

We therefore ask the Father, in the Name of the Son our Lord and Redeemer, through the intercession of His most holy Mother our powerful mediatrix, to show His glory, to grant the exaltation of Holy Church, peace and prosperity to the Christian peoples, the conversion of sinners, the defeat of His enemies.

"God arises, and his enemies will be scattered, and those who hate him will flee before him" (Psalm 68[67]:1).

November 25, 2020
St. Catherine of Alexandria, Virgin and Martyr

38

"*Nolite timere*" [Do not fear]:
In Expectation of the Birth of
the Most Holy Redeemer

Sleep, O Celestial Child:
The nations do not know
Who has been born;
But the day will come
When they shall be
Your noble heritage;
You who sleep so humbly,
You who are hidden in dust:
They will know You as King.
—Manzoni, *Il Natale*

IN less than two weeks, by the grace of God, this year of Our Lord 2020, which has been marked by terrible events and great social upheavals, will draw to a close. Allow me to formulate a brief reflection with which to turn a supernatural gaze both towards the recent past as well as the immediate future.

The months that we leave behind represent one of the darkest moments in the history of humanity: for the first time ever, since the birth of the Savior, the Holy Keys have been used to close churches and restrict the celebration of the Mass and the sacraments, almost in anticipation of the abolition of the daily Sacrifice prophesied by Daniel, which will take place during the reign of the Antichrist. For the first time ever, at the Easter celebration of the Lord's Resurrection, many of us were forced to assist at Mass and Holy Week services through the internet, depriving us of Holy Communion. For the first time, we became aware, with pain and dismay, of being deserted by our bishops and parish priests, who were barricaded in their palaces and rectories out of fear of a seasonal flu that claimed about the same number of victims as in other years.

We have seen—so to speak—the generals and officers abandon their army, and in some cases they even joined the enemy ranks, imposing on the Church an unconditional surrender to the absurd reasons for the pseudo-pandemic. Never, down all the centuries, has so much faintheartedness, so much cowardice, so much desire to pander to our persecutors found such fertile ground in those who ought to be our guides and leaders. And what most scandalized many of us was the realization that this betrayal involved the highest levels of the hierarchy of the Church much more than the priests and the simple faithful. Precisely from the highest Throne, from which we should have expected a firm and authoritative intervention in defense of the rights of God, of the freedom of the Church and the salvation of souls, we have received instead invitations to obey unjust laws, illegitimate norms, and irrational orders. And in the words that the media promptly spread from Santa Marta, we recognized many, too many, nods to the insider language of the globalist élite—fraternity, universal income, new world order, build back better, great reset, nothing will be ever be the same again, resilience—all words of the new language, which testify to the *idem sentire* of those who speak them and those who listen to them.

It was a true act of intimidation, a thinly-veiled threat, with which our Pastors ratified the pandemic alarm, sowed terror among the simple, and abandoned the dying and the needy. In the height of a cynical legalism, it even reached the point of prohibiting priests from hearing Confessions and administering the Last Sacraments to those were abandoned in intensive care, depriving our beloved dead of religious burial, and denying the Blessed Sacrament to many souls.

And if on the religious side of things we saw ourselves treated as outsiders and barred access to our churches as by the Saracens of old—even as the implacable invasion of illegal immigrants continued to replenish the coffers of the self-styled humanitarian associations—on the civil and political side we discovered that our rulers had a vocation to tyranny: using a rhetoric now disproven by reality, they wanted to make us think of them as representatives of the

"*Nolite timere*" [Do not fear]

sovereign people. By heads of state and prime ministers, by regional governors and local mayors, the fullest rigors of the law were imposed on us as if we were rebellious subjects, suspects to be placed under surveillance even in the privacy of our own homes, criminals to be chased even in the solitude of the woods or along the seashore. We have seen people forcibly dragged by soldiers in anti-riot gear, elderly people fined while they were going to the pharmacy, shopkeepers forced to close their doors, and restaurants that first took costly measures in an effort to comply with the government's demands only to then to be ordered to be closed.

With bewilderment, we have heard scores of self-styled experts—most of whom are lacking any scientific authority whatsoever and largely in grave conflict of interest due to their ties to pharmaceutical companies and supranational organizations—pontificating on television programs and on the pages of newspapers about infections, vaccines, immunity, positive tests, the obligation to wear masks, the risks for the elderly, the contagiousness of the asymptomatic, and the danger of seeing one's family. They have thundered at us, using arcane words like "social distancing" and "gatherings," in an endless series of grotesque contradictions, absurd alarms, apocalyptic threats, social precepts and health ceremonies that have replaced religious rites. And as they have terrorized the population—all while being paid lavishly for their pronouncements made at every hour of the day—our rulers and politicians have flaunted their masks in front of all the television cameras, only to then take them off as soon as possible.

Forced to disguise ourselves as anonymous people without a face, they have imposed a muzzle on us that is absolutely useless for avoiding contagion and actually harmful to our health, but indispensable for their purposes of making us feel subjugated and forced to conform. They have prevented us from being cured with existing and effective treatments, promoting instead a vaccine that they now want to make obligatory even before knowing if it is effective, after only incomplete testing. And in order not to jeopardize the enormous profits of the pharmaceutical companies, they have granted immunity for the damage that their vaccines may cause to the population. The vaccine is free, they tell us, but it will actually be paid

389

for with taxpayers' money, even if its producers do not guarantee that it will protect from contagion.

In this scenario that is similar to the disastrous effects of a war, the economy of our countries lies prostrate, while online commerce companies, home delivery companies, and pornography producers are booming. The local shops close but the large shopping centers and supermarkets remain open: monuments to the consumerism in which everyone, even those with COVID, continue to fill their carts with foreign products, German cheeses, Moroccan oranges, Canadian flour, and cell phones and televisions made in China.

"The world is preparing for the Great Reset," they tell us obsessively. "Nothing will ever be the same again." We will have to get used to "living with the virus," subjected to a perpetual pandemic that feeds the pharmaceutical Moloch and legitimizes ever more hateful limitations of our fundamental liberties. Those who since childhood have catechized us to worship freedom, democracy, and popular sovereignty today govern us by depriving us of freedom in the name of health, imposing dictatorship, arrogating to themselves a power that no one has ever conferred on them, neither from above nor from below. And the temporal power that Freemasonry and the Liberals ferociously opposed in the Roman Pontiffs is today claimed by them in reverse, in an attempt to submit the Church of Christ to the power of the State with the approval and collaboration of the highest levels of the hierarchy.

Out of this whole humanly discouraging scenario, an unavoidable fact emerges: there is a chasm between those who hold authority and those who are subjected to it, between rulers and citizens, between the hierarchy and the faithful. It is an institutional *monstrum* in which both civil and religious power are almost entirely in the hands of unscrupulous people who have been appointed because of their absolute ineptitude and great vulnerability to blackmail. Their role is not to administer the institution but to demolish it, not to respect its laws but to violate them, not to protect its members but to disperse and distance them. In short, we find ourselves facing the perversion of authority, not due to chance or inexperience but pursued with determination and following a pre-established plan: a single script under a single direction.

"*Nolite timere*" [Do not fear]

We thus have rulers who persecute their citizens and treat them as enemies, while welcoming and financing the invasion of criminals and illegal immigrants; law enforcement officers and judges who arrest and fine those who violate social-distancing rules, even as they ostentatiously ignore criminals, rapists, assassins and treacherous politicians; teachers who do not transmit culture or the love of knowledge but instead indoctrinate students into gender and globalist ideology; doctors who refuse to treat the sick but impose a genetically-modified vaccine whose efficacy and potential side-effects are unknown; bishops and priests who deny the faithful the sacraments but who never miss an occasion for propagandizing their own unconditional adherence to the globalist agenda in the name of Masonic Brotherhood.

Those who oppose this overturning of every principle of civil life find themselves abandoned, alone, and without a leader who would unite them. Loneliness, in fact, allows our common enemies—as they have amply demonstrated themselves to be—to instill fear, despair, and the feeling of not being able to stand together to resist the assaults to which we have been subjected. Citizens are alone in the face of the abuse of civil power, the faithful are alone in the face of the arrogance of heretical prelates given over to vice, and those who wish to dissent, raise their voice, or protest within institutions are likewise alone.

Loneliness and fear increase when we give them ground to stand on, but they vanish if we think of how each one of us prompted the incarnation of the Second Person of the Most Blessed Trinity in the most pure womb of the Virgin Mary: *qui propter nos homines et propter nostram salutem descendit de cœlis.* And here we come to the Mysteries which we are preparing to contemplate in these coming days: the Immaculate Conception and the Lord's Holy Nativity. From these mysteries, dear friends, we can draw renewed hope with which to face the events that await us.

Above all, we must remember that none of us is ever truly alone: we have the Lord at our side. He always wants our good, and so he never fails to send us His help and His grace, if only we ask for it with faith. We have the Most Blessed Virgin at our side, our loving Mother and our secure refuge. We have near us the hosts of Angels and the multitude of Saints who from the glory of Heaven intercede for us before the Throne of the Divine Majesty.

The contemplation of this sublime community that is the Holy Church, the mystical Jerusalem that we are citizens of and living members, should persuade us that the last thing we ought to fear is being alone, and that there is no reason to be afraid, even if the devil rages to make us believe that there is. True loneliness is in Hell, where the damned souls do not have any hope: that is the loneliness we should truly fear, and before it we must beg for the grace of final perseverance, that is, to be able to merit the grace of a holy death from the mercy of God. A death for which we ought to always be prepared by keeping ourselves in a state of grace, in friendship with the Lord.

Of course, the trials that we are facing in this moment are tremendous, because they give us the feeling that evil is triumphing, that each of us is abandoned to ourselves, that the wicked have managed to get the better of the *pusillus grex* and of all humanity. But was not our Lord perhaps alone in Gethsemane, alone on the wood of the Cross, alone in the Tomb? And returning to the mystery of Christmas that is now fast approaching: were not the Blessed Mother and Saint Joseph perhaps alone when they found themselves forced to take refuge in a stable because *non erat locus illis in diversorio* [there was no room for them in the inn]? Imagine how the putative father of Jesus must have felt seeing his Most Holy Spouse ready to give birth in the cold of the night of Palestine; think of their worries during the Flight into Egypt, knowing that King Herod had unleashed his soldiers to kill the Infant Jesus. Even in these terrible situations, the solitude of the Holy Family was only apparent, while God arranged everything according to His plans. He sent an Angel to announce the birth of the Savior to the shepherds. He moved no less than a Star to call the Magi from the Orient to adore the Messiah. He sent choirs of His Angels to sing over the cave of Bethlehem. He warned Saint Joseph to flee in order to escape the massacre of Herod.

Also to us, in the solitude of the lockdown which many of us are forced to endure, in the abandonment of the hospital, in the silence of the deserted streets and the churches closed to worship, the Lord comes to bring his company. Also to us He sends His Angel to inspire us with holy purposes, his Most Holy Mother to console us, the Paraclete to give us comfort, *dulcis hospes animæ* [sweet guest of the soul].

We are not alone: we are never alone. And it is this, in the end, that the authors of the Great Reset fear most: that we become aware of this supernatural—but no less true—reality that makes the house of cards of their infernal deceptions collapse.

If we think of how we have at our side her who crushes the head of the Serpent, or the Archangel who has drawn his sword to drive Lucifer into the abyss; if we recall that our Guardian Angel, our Patron Saint, and our dear ones in Heaven and Purgatory are with us: what can we ever be afraid of? Do we want to believe that the God of armies drawn up for battle has any hesitation about defeating any servant of the eternally defeated one?

She who in the year 630 saved Constantinople from siege, terrorizing the Avars and Persians by appearing tremendous in the heavens; who in 1091 at Scicli in Sicily was invoked as Our Lady of the Militia and appeared on a shining cloud chasing away the Saracens; who in 1571 at Lepanto and again in 1683 at Vienna was invoked as Queen of Victories and granted victory to the Christian army against the Turks; who during the anti-Catholic persecution of Mexico protected the *Cristeros* and repelled the army of the Mason Elias Calles—she will not deny us her holy assistance; she will not leave us alone in the battle; she will not abandon those who have recourse to her with trusting prayer in the moment in which the conflict is decisive and the confrontation is nearing an end.

We have had the grace to understand what this world can become if we deny the Lordship of God and replace it with the tyranny of Satan. This is the world that is rebellious against Christ the King and Mary the Queen, in which each day thousands of innocent lives in the wombs of their mothers are sacrificed to Satan; this is the world in which vice and sin want to cancel every trace of good and virtue, every memory of the Christian religion, every law and vestige of our civilization, every trace of the order that the Creator has given to nature. A world in which churches burn, Crosses are knocked down, statues of the Virgin are decapitated: this hatred, this Satanic fury against Christ and the Mother of God is the mark of the Evil One and his servants. In the face of this total Revolution, this accursed New World Order that would prepare the way for the kingdom of the Antichrist, we cannot still believe that any brotherhood is possible if not under the Law of God, nor that it is possible to construct peace if not under the mantle of the Queen of Peace. *Pax Christi in regno Christi.*[1]

The Lord will give us the victory only when we bow down to Him as our King. And if we cannot yet proclaim Him as King of our Nations because of the impiety of those who govern us, we can nevertheless consecrate ourselves, our families, and our communities to Him. And to those who dare to challenge Heaven in the name of "Nothing will be the same again," we respond by invoking God with renewed fervor: "As it was in the beginning, is now and ever shall be, world without end."

Let us pray to the Immaculate Virgin, Tabernacle of the Most High, asking that in our meditation on the Holy Nativity of her Divine Son which now draws near, she may dispel our fear and solitude, gathering us together in adoration around the manger. In the poverty of the crib, in the silence of the cave of Bethlehem, the song of the Angels resounds; the one true Light of the world shines forth, adored by the shepherds and the Magi, and Creation itself bows down, adorning the vault of heaven with a shining Star. *Veni, Emmanuel: captivum solve Israël.* Come, O Emmanuel, free your imprisoned people.

December 13, 2020
Dominica Gaudete, III Adventus

---

1. "The peace of Christ in the reign of Christ"—the motto taken by Pope Pius XI, author of the encyclical *Quas Primas* on the kingship of Our Lord.

39

A Den of Thieves

Exsurgat Deus, et dissipentur inimici ejus:
et fugiant qui oderunt eum a facie ejus.
Psalm 67[1]

IN the past few days, the latest news is that Bergoglio is dedicating his time to making a television series called *Sharing the Wisdom of Time*,[2] produced by Netflix, a company which just published a post on Twitter[3] that summarizes its ideological point of reference: *Praise Satan*. It goes without saying that this multinational corporation is involved in the spread of immorality and vice, including the sexual exploitation of minors.

Similarly, in the past few days the Holy See has signed an agreement with the UN[4] to promote sustainability and gender equality, thereby giving its support to an organization that promotes abortion and contraception. On the very day dedicated to the Immaculate Conception—December 8, 2020—almost like a shameful insult against the Blessed Mother, a new partnership was officially instituted between the Vatican and the "Council for Inclusive Capital-

---

1. Latin for "Arise, O Lord, and let Thy enemies be scatted and let them that hate Thee flee from before Thy face."

2. VN: https://twitter.com/messainlatino/status/1339442807111561221/photo/1.

3. Archbishop Viganò provided here a link to a tweet that seems to have vanished, but his point can be established even more directly with https://twitter.com/sabrinanetflix/status/1338891577612234752, posted December 15, 2020. See, for background, Noel Murray, "Chilling Adventures of Sabrina finds a smart metaphor in Satanism," *The Verge*, October 30, 2018, https://www.theverge.com/2018/10/30/18043502/chilling-adventures-of-sabrina-review-netflix-river-dale-archie-comics-satan-satanist.

4. VN: See www.ncregister.com/blog/vatican-youth-symposium-2020-day1.

ism"[5] promoted by Lynn Forester de Rothschild, a close friend of Hillary Clinton and Jeffrey Epstein, after sending a message of praise to Klaus Schwab, the president of the World Economic Forum and theorist of the Great Reset. And in order not to give rise to misunderstandings, after numerous appeals to obey the authorities in the emergency of the psycho-pandemic, it appears that the COVID vaccine will be made obligatory for all the officials and staff of Vatican City, despite the fact that it has been produced with aborted fetal tissue and provides no guarantee of being either effective or harmless.

I believe it is now understood beyond all reasonable doubt that the leaders of the present Catholic hierarchy have placed themselves at the service of the globalist oligarchy and Freemasonry: the idolatrous cult of the Pachamama in the Vatican Basilica is now joined by a sacrilegious Nativity scene, whose symbology appears to allude to ancient Egyptian rites as well as aliens. Only a naive person or an accomplice can deny that in this whole chain of events there is a very clear ideological coherence and a lucid diabolical mind.

But as I have already pointed out, it would be misleading to limit oneself to an evaluation of events within the Church without framing them in the wider political and social context: there is only one direction being given in which both the main protagonists as well as the extras follow the same script. The purpose has now been declared: destroying Nations from within by means of the deep state and the Church of Christ by means of the deep church, in order to establish the kingdom of the Antichrist, with the help of the False Prophet.

The secret Sino-Vatican agreement, very strongly desired by Bergoglio and renewed a few weeks ago, fits perfectly into this disturbing picture, confirming the *pactum sceleris* which consigns Chinese

---

5. VN: See www.vatican.va/content/francesco/en/speeches/2019/november/doc uments/papa-francesco_20191111_consiglio-capitalismo-inclusivo.html; https://ww w.nytimes.com/2020/12/08/business/dealbook/pope-vatican-inclusive-capitalism. html; and https://www.maurizioblondet.it/lynn-forester-rothschild-e-la-nuova-papessa-della-chiesa-bergogliana-del-sacro-great-reset-viene-alla-luce-il-grande-piano-gnostico-finanziario-per-cui-bergoglio-e-stato-promosso.

Catholics to persecution, dissidents to reeducation, churches to demolition, Sacred Scripture to censorship and adulteration. It is no coincidence that this agreement, which the [preceding] popes always refused with disdain, was made possible thanks to the offices of the former Cardinal McCarrick and his accomplices, with the decisive help of the Jesuits: the actors, we know, are always the same. They are both corrupted and corruptors, both blackmailed and blackmailers, all united by their rebellion against doctrine and morals and indiscriminately subservient to anti-Catholic, indeed anti-Christian, powers.

Communist China constitutes the militant arm of the New World Order, both in the spread of a mutant virus created in a laboratory, as well as in the interference in the American Presidential elections and the enlistment of fifth columns in the service of the Beijing regime. It also promotes the apostasy of the leaders of the Church, preventing her from proclaiming the Gospel and placing herself as a defending wall against the attack of the élite. The fact that this brings economic advantages for the Vatican makes the Bergoglian sect's subservience to this infernal plan even more shameful, creating a significant counterpoint to the business of migrants, which is also part of the intentional dissolution of the society that once was Christian. It is disconcerting that such a scandalous betrayal of the mission of the Catholic Church does not merit firm and courageous condemnation from the Episcopate, which—in the face of evidence of an apostasy pursued with ever greater determination—does not dare to raise its voice out of fear or a false concept of prudence.

The words of Dr. Arthur Tane, Director of the Council on Middle East Relations,[6] may sound bold and strong, but they have the merit of highlighting without false fears the subversion carried out under this most ominous "pontificate." It is to be hoped that with the publication of Tane's letter to Cardinal Parolin there will be some who will finally open their eyes, before the plot of the conspirators is accomplished. In this regard, we agree with the commendable

---

6. A copy of this letter of Dr. Tane can be found at https://catholicfamily news.com/blog/2020/12/22/den-of-thieves-new-letter-of-archbishop-vigano.

denunciation made by Cardinal Burke[7] on the Feast of Our Lady of Guadalupe about the use of COVID for the purposes of the "Great Reset"—a denunciation that joins the one I made last May and have reiterated many times, as well as that of other Pastors who are faithful to the Word of God and solicitous towards their flock.

The letter of Arthur Tane to the Secretary of State closes with a citation from the Gospel that is more appropriate than ever: "Either the Church understands the significance of its mission, or it itself has become a temple of money changers. For in the words of Jesus: 'It is written that my house will be called a house of prayer, but you are making it a den of robbers' (Mt 21:12–13)."

As bishops, we cannot be silent: our silence would constitute an intolerable connivance and complicity with those mercenaries who, abusing a usurped power, deny Christ and consign souls to the Enemy of the human race.

---

7. VN: See "Cardinal Burke: Forces of the 'Great Reset' have used COVID to advance 'evil agenda,'" *Alpha News*, December 13, 2020, https://alphanewsmn.com/cardinal-burke-forces-of-the-great-reset-have-used-covid-to-advance-evil-agenda.

40

Interview with Steve Bannon

NOW that the Vatican has renewed its insidious secret agreement with China, a deal which you have repeatedly condemned as promoted by Bergoglio with the assistance of McCarrick, what can the "children of light" of the Great Awakening concretely do to undermine this unholy alliance with this brutal Communist regime?

The dictatorship of the Chinese Communist Party is allied to the global deep state, on the one hand so that together they can attain the goals that they have in common, on the other hand because the plans for the Great Reset are an opportunity to increase the economic power of China in the world, beginning with the invasion of national markets. At the same time that it pursues this project in its foreign policy, China is pursuing a domestic plan to restore the Maoist tyranny, which requires the cancellation of religions (primarily the Catholic religion), replacing them with a religion of the State which definitely has many elements in common with the universal religion desired by globalist ideology, whose spiritual leader is Bergoglio.

The complicity of Bergoglio's deep church in this infernal project has deprived Chinese Catholics of the indefectible defense that the papacy had always been for them. Up until the papacy of Benedict XVI, the papacy had not made any agreements with the Beijing dictatorship, and the Roman Pontiff retained the exclusive right to appoint bishops and govern dioceses. I recall that even at the time of the Bill Clinton administration during the 1990s, former Cardinal McCarrick was the point of contact between the deep church and the American deep state, carrying out political missions in China on behalf of the US administration. And the suspicions that the resignation of Benedict XVI involved China are quite strong and coherent with the picture that has been emerging in recent months.

Thus we find ourselves faced with an infamous betrayal of the mission of the Church of Christ, carried out by her highest leaders in open conflict with those members of the Chinese Catholic underground hierarchy who have remained faithful to Our Lord and to His Church. My affectionate thoughts and prayers are with them and with Cardinal Zen, an eminent confessor of the faith, whom Bergoglio recently shamefully refused to receive.

We believers must act on the spiritual level by fervent prayer, asking God to give special protection to the Church in China, and also by continually denouncing the aberrations carried out by the Chinese regime. This action must be accompanied by a work of raising awareness within governments and international institutions that have not been compromised by the Chinese communist dictatorship, so that the violations of human rights and the attacks on the freedom of the Catholic Church in China may be denounced and punished with sanctions and strong diplomatic pressure. And this is the line that President Trump is pursuing with decisive courage. Beijing's complicity with political and religious elements that are involved in murky operations of speculation and corruption must likewise be exposed. These profit-driven dealings constitute a very grave act of treason by politicians and public officials against their nation and also a grave betrayal of the Church by the men who lead her. I also think that in some cases this betrayal is not only carried out by individuals but also by the institutions themselves, as in the case of the European Union, which is currently finalizing a commercial agreement with China despite its systematic violation of human rights and its violent repression of dissent.

It would be an irreparable disaster if Joe Biden, who is heavily suspected of being complicit with the Chinese dictatorship, would be designated as President of the United States.

You have been very confident that God desires a Trump victory in order to defeat the forces of evil inherent in the globalists' Great Reset. What would you say to convince the naysayers who are ambivalent to the idea that this is a momentous battle between the children of light and the children of darkness?

Interview with Steve Bannon

I simply consider who Trump's adversary is and his numerous ties to China, the deep state, and the advocates of globalist ideology. I think of his intention to condemn us all to wear masks, as he has candidly admitted. I think of the fact that, incontestably, he is only a puppet in the hands of the elite, who are ready to remove him as soon they decide to replace him with Kamala Harris.

Beyond the political alignments, we must further understand that—above all in a complex situation like the present one—it is essential that the victory of the one who is elected President must be guaranteed in its absolute legal legitimacy, avoiding any suspicion of fraud and taking note of the overwhelming evidence of irregularities that has emerged in several states. A President who is simply proclaimed as such by the mainstream media affiliated with the deep state would be deprived of all legitimacy and would expose the nation to dangerous foreign interference, as has already been shown to have happened in the current election.

You seem to suggest that the Trump Administration could be instrumental in helping to return the Church to a pre-Francis Catholicism. How does the Trump Administration accomplish that, and how can American Catholics work to save the world from this globalist 'reset'?

Bergoglio's subservience to the globalist agenda is obvious, as well as his active support for the election of Joe Biden. In the same way, Bergoglio's hostility to Trump and his repeated attacks against the President are evident. It is clear that Bergoglio considers Trump as his principal adversary, the obstacle that needs to be removed, so that the Great Reset can be put in motion.

Thus on the one hand we have the Trump administration and the traditional values that it holds in common with Catholics; on the other hand we have the deep state of the self-styled Catholic Joe Biden, who is subservient to the globalist ideology and its perverse, antihuman, antichristic, infernal agenda.

In order to put an end to the deep church and restore the Catholic Church, the extent of the involvement of the leaders of the Church with the Masonic-globalist project will have to be revealed: the nature of the corruption and crimes that these men have carried out, thereby making themselves vulnerable to blackmail, just as happens in a similar way in the political field to members of the deep state, beginning with Biden himself. Thus it is to be hoped that any proof of such crimes that is in the possession of the Secret Services would be brought to light, especially in relation to the true motives that led to the resignation of Benedict XVI and the conspiracies underlying the election of Bergoglio, thereby permitting the expulsion of the mercenaries who have seized control of the Church.

American Catholics still have time to denounce this global subversion and stop the establishment of the New Order: let them think about what sort of future they want for the coming generations, and of the destruction of society. Let them think about the responsibility that they have before God, their children, and their nation: as Catholics, as fathers and mothers of their families, and as patriots.

Against all odds, average Americans are fighting to expose the massive and coordinated theft of our election: what advice would you give to our recalcitrant politicians about what is at stake for our nation and the world if we submit to this theft?

The truth can be denied by the majority for a certain amount of time, or by some people forever, but it can never be hidden from everyone forever. This is the lesson of history, which has inexorably revealed the great crimes of the past and those who perpetrated them.

Thus I invite politicians, beyond their political loyalties, to become champions of the truth, to defend it as an indispensable treasure which alone can guarantee the credibility of institutions and the authority of the people's representatives, in accord with the mandate they have received, the oath they have sworn to serve their country, and their moral responsibility before God. Each one of us has a role that Providence has entrusted to us, and which it would be culpable to shrink from. If the United States misses this opportunity, *now*, it will be wiped out from history. If it allows the idea to spread among the masses that the electoral choice of the citizens— the first expression of democracy—can be manipulated and thwarted, it will be complicit in the fraud, and will certainly deserve

402

the execration of the entire world, which looks to America as a nation which has fought for and defended its freedom.

In your letter to the President on October 25, the Solemnity of Christ the King, you spoke of the efforts of the deep state as "the final assault of the children of darkness." There is a concerted effort by the globalists and their media partners to conceal and obscure the true tyrannical agenda implicit in the Great Reset, by calling it a wild conspiracy theory. What would you say to the skeptics who blissfully ignore the signs and plan to submit humanity to the domination of the global elites?

The plan of the Great Reset makes use of the mainstream media as an indispensable ally: the media corporations are almost all actively part of the deep state and know that the power that will be guaranteed to them in the future depends exclusively on their slavish adherence to its agenda.

Labeling those who denounce the existence of a conspiracy as "conspiracy theorists" confirms, if anything, that this conspiracy exists, and that its authors are very upset at having been found out and reported to public opinion. And yet they themselves have said it: *Nothing will be the same again.* And also: *Build Back Better,* in an effort to make us believe that the radical changes they want to impose have been made necessary by a pandemic, by climate change, and by technological progress.

Years ago, those who spoke of the New World Order were called conspiracy theorists. Today, all of the world's leaders, including Bergoglio, speak with impunity about the New World Order, describing it exactly in the terms that were identified by the so-called conspiracy theorists. It is enough to read the globalists' declarations to understand that the conspiracy exists and that they pride themselves on being its architects, to the point of admitting the need for a pandemic in order to reach their objectives of social engineering.

To the skeptics I ask: if the models that are proposed to us *today* are so terrible, what will our children be able to expect when the elite will have succeeded in taking total control over the nations? Families without father and mother, polyamory, sodomy, children who can change their sex, the cancellation of religion and the imposition of an infernal cult, abortion and euthanasia, the abolition of private property, a health dictatorship, a perpetual pandemic. Is this the world that we want, that you want for yourselves, your children, and your family and friends?

We must all become aware of how much the proponents of the New World Order and the Great Reset hate the inalienable values of our Greco-Christian civilization, such as religion, the family, respect for life and the inviolable rights of the human person, and national sovereignty.

You have repeatedly warned that the deep state and the deep church have colluded to plot in various ways to overthrow Benedict as well as President Trump. Besides Theodore McCarrick, who else is behind this infernal alliance, and how do Catholics undermine and expose it?

It is apparent that McCarrick acted on behalf of the deep state and the deep church, but he certainly did not do it alone. All of his activity suggests a very efficient organizational structure composed of people whom McCarrick had promoted and covered by other accomplices.

The events that led to the resignation of Benedict XVI still need to be clarified, but one of the members of the deep church, the deceased Cardinal Danneels, admitted that he was a part of the so-called Saint Gallen Mafia, which essentially worked to bring about the "springtime of the Church" which John Podesta, Hillary Clinton's chief of staff, wrote about in his emails published by Wiki-Leaks.

Thus there is a group of conspirators who have worked and still work in the heart of the Church for the interests of the elite. Most of them are identifiable, but the most dangerous are those who do not expose themselves, those whom the newspaper never mentions. They will not hesitate to force Bergoglio to resign also, just like Ratzinger, if he does not obey their orders. They would like to transform the Vatican into a retirement home for popes *emeriti*, demolishing the papacy and securing power: exactly the same as what happens in the deep state, where, as I have already said, Biden is the equivalent of Bergoglio.

Interview with Steve Bannon

In order to bring down the deep state and the deep church, three things are essential:

1. First of all, becoming aware of what globalism's plan is, and to what extent it is instrumental to the establishment of the kingdom of the Antichrist, since it shares its principles, means, and ends;

2. secondly, firmly denouncing this infernal plan and asking the Shepherds of the Church—and also the laity—to defend her, breaking their complicit silence: God will demand of them an account for their desertion;

3. finally, it is necessary to pray, asking the Lord to grant each one of us the strength to resist—*resistite fortes in fide*, Saint Peter warns us (1 Pet 5:9)—against the ideological tyranny that is daily imposed on us not only by the media but also by the cardinals and bishops who are under Bergoglio's thumb.

If we can prove ourselves strong in facing this trial; if we know how to hold ourselves anchored to the rock of the Church without allowing ourselves to be seduced by "false christs and false prophets" (Mt 24:24), the Lord will permit us to see—at least for now—the defeat of the assault of the children of darkness against God and men. If out of fear or complicity we follow the prince of this world, denying our baptismal promises, we will be condemned with him to inexorable defeat and eternal damnation. I tremble for those who do not realize the responsibility that they have before God for the souls that He has entrusted to them. But to those who fight courageously to defend the rights of God, the nation, and the family, the Lord assures his protection. He has placed His Most Holy Mother at our side, the Queen of Victories and the Help of Christians. We invoke her faithfully during these difficult days, confidently certain of her intervention.

January 1, 2021
Die Octavæ Nativitatis Domini

EPILOGUE

42

Meditation for *LifeSiteNews*[1]

THE ultimate solution to the epochal battle being waged in Church and State to which Archbishop Viganò directs us is spiritual. We need the true Mass and sacraments and we must embrace a sincere and humble prayer life. The final step in the three-part battle plan he provided in the Steve Bannon War Room interview is prayer. Even those fighting for the children of light, be they the Society of St. Pius X or Donald Trump, are merely instruments God has chosen in His Divine Providence. The Victory will be won by Christ the King. Although we need to do what is within our sphere of influence (seek out the traditional Mass and sacraments or support politicians fighting for the natural law), we must accompany this practical action with prayer. Archbishop Viganò told Francesco Boezi in his interview: "This is a war without quarter, in which Satan has been unchained and the gates of hell are trying in every way to prevail over the Church herself. Such a contradiction must be faced above all with prayer, with the invincible weapon of the Holy Rosary." Almost all interventions of Archbishop Viganò end with an exhortation to turn to prayer and particularly prayer to Our Lady. In this epilogue we include an important meditation that Archbishop Viganò gave to the staff of LifeSiteNews, another instrument used by God to fight to defend the Church's teaching on life. We also include the prayer composed by the archbishop especially for our country and our president. Let us all continue to recite this prayer for our country and commit ourselves to the reign of Christ the King.

1. Originally published as "Abp. Viganò: Christ the King has been 'dethroned' not only 'from society but also from the Church,'" *LifeSiteNews*, August 12, 2020, www.lifesitenews.com/blogs/ap-vigano-christ-the-king-has-been-dethroned-not-only-from-society-but-also-from-the-church.

A Voice in the Wilderness

TE ADORET ORBIS SUBDITUS[2]

O ter beata civitas cui rite Christus imperat, quæ jussa pergit exsequi edicta mundo cælitus! Thrice happy city, basking fair beneath His royal sway, where at the mandates from His throne all hearts with joy obey!

> Jesus took Peter, James, and his brother John and led them up a high mountain by themselves. And he was transfigured before them; his face shone like the sun and his clothes became white as light. And behold, Moses and Elijah appeared to them, conversing with him. Then Peter said to Jesus in reply, "Lord, it is good that we are here. If you wish, I will make three tents here, one for you, one for Moses, and one for Elijah." While he was still speaking, behold, a bright cloud cast a shadow over them, then from the cloud came a voice that said: "This is my beloved Son, with whom I am well-pleased; listen to him." When the disciples heard this, they fell prostrate and were very much afraid. But Jesus came and touched them, saying: "Rise, and do not be afraid." And when the disciples raised their eyes, they saw no one else but Jesus alone. As they were coming down the mountain, Jesus charged them, "Do not tell the vision to anyone until the Son of man has been raised from the dead" (Mt 17:1–9).

Permit me, dear friends, to share with you some reflections on the Kingship of Our Lord Jesus Christ, manifested in the Transfiguration that we celebrate today, after other significant episodes of the earthly life of the Lord: from the Angels over the Cave of Bethlehem to the Adoration of the Magi to His Baptism in the Jordan River.

I have chosen this theme because I believe that in a certain way the focal point of our and your commitment as Catholics may be summarized in it; not only in private and family life but also and above all in social and political life.

First of all, let us revive our faith in the Universal Kingship of Our Divine Savior.

2. Translation: Let the world, subdued [under the yoke of Christ], adore Thee!

He is truly the Universal King, that is, he possesses absolute Sovereignty over all creation, over the human race, over all people, even over those who are outside his fold, the Holy, Catholic, Apostolic, Roman Church.

Each person is truly a creature of God. Every person owes his entire being to Him, both in his nature as a whole and in each of the individual parts that compose it: body, soul, faculties, intelligence, will, and senses. The actions of these faculties, as well as the actions of all the organs of the body, are gifts of God, whose dominion extends to all of His goods as fruits of His ineffable liberality. The simple consideration of the fact that no one chooses or can choose the family to which he belongs on earth is sufficient to convince us of this fundamental truth of our existence.

From this it follows that Our Lord God is the Sovereign of all men, both considered individually and also united in social groups, since the fact that they form various communities does not mean that they lose their condition as creatures. In fact, the very existence of civil society obeys the designs of God, who made human nature to be social. Thus all people, all nations, from the most primitive to the most civilized, from the very smallest to the superpowers, are all subjected to the Divine Sovereignty and, in and of themselves, have the obligation to recognize this sweet celestial Dominion.

The Kingship of Jesus Christ

As the Sacred Scriptures frequently attest, God has conferred this Sovereignty on his Only-Begotten Son.

Saint Paul affirms, in a general way, that God made his Son "heir of all things" (Heb 1:2). Saint John, for his part, confirms the thought of the Apostle of the Gentiles in many passages of his Gospel: for example, when he recalls that "the Father does not judge anyone, but He has given all judgment to His Son" (Jn 5:22). The prerogative of administering justice belongs, in fact, to the king, and whoever possesses it does so because he is invested with sovereign power.

This Universal Kingship that the Son has inherited from his Father should not be understood only as the eternal inheritance through which, in his Divine Nature, He has received all of the

411

attributes that make him equal and consubstantial to the First Person of the Most Holy Trinity, in the unity of the Divine Essence.

This Kingship is also attributed in a special way to Jesus Christ inasmuch as he is truly man, the Mediator between heaven and earth. In fact, the mission of the Word Incarnate is precisely the establishment on earth of the Kingdom of God. We observe that the expressions of Sacred Scripture relative to the Kingship of Jesus Christ refer, without a shadow of a doubt, to his condition as man.

He is presented to the world as the son of King David, for whom he comes to inherit the Throne of his father, extended to the ends of the earth and made eternal, without a count of years. Thus it was that the Archangel Gabriel announced the dignity of the Son of Mary: "You shall bear a son, and you shall name Him Jesus. He will be great and will be called Son of the Most High. The Lord God will give him the throne of David, his father, and he will rule over the house of Jacob forever and his kingdom shall have no end" (Lk 1:31–33). And, furthermore, the Magi who came from the East to adore him seek him as a King: "Where is the newborn King of the Jews?" they ask Herod, on their arrival in Jerusalem (Mt 2:2). The mission that the Eternal Father entrusts to the Son in the mystery of the Incarnation is to establish a Kingdom on earth, the Kingdom of Heaven. Through the establishment of this Kingdom, the ineffable charity with which God has loved men from all eternity, mercifully drawing them to Himself, becomes concrete: "*Dilexi te, ideo attraxi te, miserans.*" "I have loved thee with an everlasting love, therefore with loving kindness have I drawn thee" (Jer 31:3).

Jesus consecrates his public life to the proclamation and establishment of his Kingdom, at times referred to as the *Kingdom of God* and at others as the *Kingdom of Heaven*. Following the Eastern practice, Our Lord makes use of fascinating parables in order to inculcate the idea and the nature of this Kingdom that he has come to establish. His miracles aim to convince the people that his Kingdom has already come; it is found in the midst of the people. "*Si in digito Dei ejicio dæmonia, profecto pervenit in vos regnum Dei*"—"If it is by the finger of God that I cast out demons, then the Kingdom of God is upon you" (Lk 11:20).

The constitution of his Kingdom so absorbed his mission that the apostasy of his enemies took advantage of this idea to justify the accusation raised against him before Pilate's tribunal: "*Si hunc dimittis, non es amicus Cæsaris*"—"If you release him, you are not a friend of Caesar." They cried out to Pontius Pilate: "Everyone who makes himself king opposes Caesar" (Jn 19:12). Validating the opinion of his enemies, Jesus Christ confirms to the Roman governor that He is truly a King: "You say: I am a king" (Jn 18:37).

A King in a True Sense

It is not possible to question the regal character of the work of Jesus Christ. He is King.

Our faith, however, requires that we understand well the scope and meaning of the Royalty of the Divine Redeemer. Pius XI immediately excludes the metaphorical sense by which we call "king" and "kingly" whatever is excellent in a human way of being or acting. No: Jesus Christ is not king in this metaphorical sense. He is King in the proper sense of the word. In Sacred Scripture, Jesus appears exercising royal prerogatives of sovereign government, dictating laws and ordering punishments against transgressors. In the famous Sermon on the Mount, we may say that the Savior promulgated the Law of his Kingdom. As a true Sovereign, He requires obedience to His laws under pain of nothing less than eternal condemnation. And also in the scene of the Judgment, which announces the end of the world, when the Son of God will come to administer His judgment to the living and the dead: "The Son of Man will come in his glory ... and He will separate them one from another, as a shepherd separates the sheep from the goats.... Then the King will say to those on his right: 'Come, you who are blessed by my Father....' Then He will say to those on his left: 'Depart from me, you accursed, into the everlasting fire....' And these will go off to eternal punishment, but the righteous to eternal life" (Mt 25:31ff.). A sentence that is both sweet and terrible. Sweet for the good, because of the unparalleled excellence of the prize that awaits them; terrible and frightening for the wicked, because of the terrifying judgment to which they are condemned for eternity.

A consideration of this sort is sufficient in order to realize how it is of the highest importance for people to identify rightly where the

Kingdom of Jesus Christ is here on earth, because belonging or not belonging to it decides our eternal destiny. We have said "here on earth" since man merits the reward or punishment for the afterlife in this world. On earth, therefore, men ought to enter and become part of this ineffable Kingdom of God, which is both temporal and eternal, because it is formed in this world and flowers forth fully in heaven.

The Present Situation

The fury of the Enemy, who hates the human race, is unleashed primarily against the doctrine of the Kingship of Christ, because that Kingship is united in the Person of Our Lord, True God and True Man. The secularism of the nineteenth century, fueled by Freemasonry, has succeeded in reorganizing itself into an even more perverse ideology, since it has extended the denial of the royal rights of the Redeemer not only to civil society but also to the Body of the Church.

This attack was consummated with the renunciation by the papacy of the very concept of this vicarious Kingship of the Roman Pontiff, thereby bringing into the very heart of the Church the demands for democracy and parliamentarianism which had already been used to undermine nations and the authority of rulers. The Second Vatican Council greatly weakened the papal monarchy as a consequence of the implicit denial of the Divine Kingship of the Eternal High Priest, and by doing so inflicted a masterful blow against the institution which until then had stood as a wall of defense against the secularization of Christian society. The sovereignty of the Vicar was diminished, and this was progressively followed by the denial of the sovereign rights of Christ over His Mystical Body. And when Paul VI deposed the triple royal diadem with an ostentatious gesture, as if he was renouncing the sacred vicarious Monarchy, he also removed the Crown from Our Lord, confining His Kingship to a merely eschatological sphere. The proof of this is the significant changes made to the liturgy of the Feast of Christ the King and its transfer to the end of the liturgical year.

The purpose of the Feast, namely the celebration of the social Kingship of Christ, also illuminates its place in the calendar. In the traditional liturgy it was assigned to the last Sunday of October, so that the Feast of All Saints, who reign by participation, would be preceded by the Feast of Christ, who reigns by his own right. With the liturgical reform approved by Paul VI in 1969, the Feast of Christ the King was moved to the last Sunday of the Liturgical Year, erasing the social dimension of the Kingship of Christ and relegating him to the merely spiritual and eschatological dimension.

Did all these Council Fathers, who voted for *Dignitatis Humanæ* and proclaimed religious freedom with Paul VI, realize that they in fact ousted Our Lord Jesus Christ, stripping him of the Crown of his social Kingship? Did they understand that they had very concretely dethroned Our Lord Jesus Christ from the throne of his divine Kingship over us and over the whole world? Did they understand that, making themselves the spokesmen of apostate nations, they made these execrable blasphemies ascend towards His Throne: "We do not want this man to be our king" (Lk 19:14); "We have no king but Caesar" (Jn 19:15)? But He, faced with that confused rumor of senseless men, withdrew his Spirit from them.

For those who are not blinded by bias, it is impossible not to see the perverse intention to *downsize* the Feast instituted by Pius XI and the doctrine expressed by it. Having dethroned Christ not only from society but also from the Church was the greatest crime with which the hierarchy could have been stained, failing in its role as the custodian of the Savior's teaching. As an inevitable consequence of this betrayal, the Authority conferred by Our Lord on the Prince of the Apostles has substantially disappeared. We have had confirmation of this ever since the edict of Vatican II, when the infallible authority of the Roman Pontiff was deliberately excluded in favor of a *pastorality* that created the conditions for equivocal formulations that are strongly suspected of heresy if not bluntly heretical. We therefore find ourselves not only besieged in the civil sphere, in which for centuries dark forces have refused the gentle yoke of Christ and imposed the hateful tyranny of apostasy and sin on the nations; but also in the religious sphere, in which the Authority demolishes itself and denies that the Divine King should also reign over the Church, her Pastors and her faithful. Also in this case, the sweet yoke of Christ is replaced by the hateful tyranny of the innovators, who with an authoritarianism not dissimilar to that of their secular counterparts impose a new doctrine, a new morality, and a new liturgy in which the only mention of the Kingship of Our Lord is considered as an awkward legacy from another religion, another Church. As Saint Paul said: "God is sending them a deceiving power so that they may believe the lie" (2 Thess 2:11).

It is therefore not surprising to see that, just as in the secular world judges subvert justice by condemning the innocent and acquitting the guilty, rulers abuse their power and tyrannize citizens, doctors violate the Hippocratic oath by making themselves accomplices of those who want to spread disease and transform the sick into chronic patients, and teachers do not teach love of knowledge but cultivate ignorance in and ideological manipulation of their students, so also in the heart of the Bride of Christ there are cardinals, bishops, and clergy who give scandal to the faithful by their reprehensible moral conduct, spreading heresy from the pulpits, favoring idolatry by celebrating the Pachamama and the worship of Mother Earth in the name of an ecologism of a clearly Masonic matrix that is perfectly in accord with the plan of dissolution intended by globalism. "This is your hour, the hour of darkness" (Lk 22:53). The *kathèkon* would seem to have disappeared, if we did not have the certainty of the promises of Our Savior, Lord of the world, of history, and of the Church herself.

Conclusion

And yet, while they destroy, we have the joy and honor of rebuilding. And there is a still greater happiness: a new generation of laity and priests are participating with zeal in this work of reconstruction of the Church for the salvation of souls, and they do so well aware of their own weaknesses and miseries, but also allowing themselves to be used by God as docile instruments in his hands: helpful hands, strong hands, the hands of the Almighty. Our fragility highlights the fact that this is the Lord's work even more, especially where this human fragility is accompanied by humility.

This humility ought to lead us to *instaurare omnia in Christo*, beginning from the heart of the Faith, which is the official prayer of the Church. Let us return to the liturgy in which Our Lord is recognized in his absolute Primacy, to the worship that the innovators adulterated precisely out of hatred for the Divine Majesty in order to proudly exalt the creature by humiliating the Creator, claiming the right to rebel against the King in a delusion of omnipotence, uttering their own *non serviam* against the adoration that is owed to the Lord.

Our life is a war: Sacred Scripture reminds us of this. But it is a war in which *"sub Christi Regis vexillis militare gloriamur"*[3] and in which we have at our disposal very powerful spiritual weapons, a deployment of angelic forces before which no earthly or infernal stronghold has any power.

If Our Lord is King by hereditary right (since he is of royal lineage), by divine right (in virtue of the hypostatic union), and by right of conquest (having redeemed us by his Sacrifice on the Cross), we must not forget that, in the plans of Divine Providence, this Divine Sovereign has at his side as Our Lady and Queen, His own August Mother, Mary Most Holy. There can be no Kingship of Christ without the sweet and maternal Queenship of Mary, whom Saint Louis Marie Grignion de Montfort reminds us is our Mediatrix before her Son's Majestic Throne, where she stands as a Queen interceding before the King.

The premise of the triumph of the Divine King in society and in nations is that He already reigns in our hearts, our souls, and our families. May Christ also reign in us, and His Most Holy Mother along with him. *Adveniat regnum tuum: adveniat per Mariam.*

Marana tha, Veni Domine Iesu! Oh come Lord Jesus!

August 12, 2020

---

3. From the Postcommunion of the traditional Mass of Christ the King. The full prayer reads: "Having received the food of immortality, we beseech Thee, O Lord, that we who glory in our military service under the banners of Christ the King, may be able to reign with Him forever on His heavenly throne. Who with Thee liveth and reigneth. . . ."

Prayer for the
United States of America

Almighty and Eternal God, King of Kings and Lord of Lords: graciously turn your gaze to us who invoke you with confidence.

Bless us, citizens of the United States of America; grant peace and prosperity to our nation; illuminate those who govern us so that they may commit themselves to the common good, in respect for your holy law.

Protect those who, defending the inviolable principles of the natural law and your commandments, must face the repeated assaults of the enemy of the human race.

Keep in the hearts of your children courage for the truth, love for virtue and perseverance in the midst of trials.

Make our families grow in the example that our Lord has given us, together with his Most Holy Mother and Saint Joseph in the home of Nazareth; give to our fathers and mothers the gift of strength, to educate wisely the children with which you have blessed them.

Give courage to those who, in spiritual combat, fight the good fight as soldiers of Christ against the furious forces of the children of darkness.

Keep each one of us, O Lord, in your Most Sacred Heart, and above all he whom your providence has placed at the head of our nation.

Bless the President of the United States of America, so that aware of his responsibility and his duties, he may be a knight of justice, a defender of the oppressed, a firm bulwark against your enemies, and a proud supporter of the children of light.

Place the United States of America and the whole world under the mantle of the Queen of Victories, our unconquered leader in battle, the Immaculate Conception. It is thanks to her, and through your mercy, that the hymn of praise rises to you, O Lord, from the children whom you have redeemed in the Most Precious Blood of our Lord Jesus Christ.

Amen.

Index of Proper Names

Index of Proper Names

Index of Proper Names

Index of Proper Names

ARCHBISHOP CARLO MARIA VIGANÒ was born on January 16, 1941 in Varese, Italy. He was ordained a priest on March 24, 1968 and incardinated in the Diocese of Pavia (Italy). He has a doctorate in both canon and civil law (*utroque iure*). His Excellency started his service in the Diplomatic Corps of the Holy See as Attaché in 1973 in Iraq and Kuwait. In 1976 he was transferred to the Apostolic Nunciature in Great Britain, and from 1978 until 1989 worked at the Secretariat of State of Vatican City. On April 4, 1989 he was nominated Special Envoy with the functions of Permanent Observer to the European Council in Strasbourg. He was consecrated an archbishop on April 26, 1992 and made Titular Archbishop of Ulpiana. He was nominated Apostolic Pro-Nuncio in Nigeria, on April 3, 1992. On April 4, 1998 he was nominated Delegate for the Pontifical Representations. Archbishop Viganò served as Secretary General of the Governorate of the Vatican City State from July 16, 2009 until September 3, 2011. On October 19, 2011 Pope Benedict XVI appointed him Apostolic Nuncio to the United States, a post he held until his retirement in April of 2016. He speaks Italian, French, Spanish, and English.

BRIAN M. McCALL holds the Orpha and Maurice Merrill Chair in Law at the University of Oklahoma College of Law. With degrees from Yale, University of Pennsylvania, and Kings College University of London, he is the author of five other books—*Contracts: Modern Pacts* (Kindle, 2019); *The Architecture of Law* (Notre Dame University Press, 2018); *La Corporación como Sociedad Imperfecta* (Marcial Pons, 2015); *To Build the City of God: Living as Catholics in a Secular Age* (Angelico Press, 2014); and *The Church and the Usurers: Unprofitable Lending for the Modern Economy* (Sapientia Press of Ave Maria University, 2013)—and dozens of articles. He has served as Editor-in-Chief of *Catholic Family News* since 2018. He and his wife, Marie Elaina, have six children.

Made in the USA
Coppell, TX
09 June 2021